Edgar Saltus, Alfred Rambaud

Russia

Vol. 2

Edgar Saltus, Alfred Rambaud

Russia
Vol. 2

ISBN/EAN: 9783337297138

Printed in Europe, USA, Canada, Australia, Japan

Cover: Foto ©ninafisch / pixelio.de

More available books at **www.hansebooks.com**

RUSSIA

BY

ALFRED RAMBAUD

TRANSLATED BY LEONORA B. LANG

IN TWO VOLUMES

WITH A SUPPLEMENTARY CHAPTER OF RECENT EVENTS
By EDGAR SALTUS

ILLUSTRATED

VOL. II

NEW YORK
PETER FENELON COLLIER
MDCCCXCVIII

CONTENTS, VOL. II.

PETER THE GREAT.

CHAPTER I.
PETER THE GREAT: STRUGGLE WITH CHARLES XII. (1700–1709).
Narva (1700): conquest of the Baltic provinces — Charles XII. invades Russia: Pultowa (1709), - - - - 9–21

CHAPTER II.
PETER THE GREAT: THE REFORMS.
General character of the reforms: the instruments of Peter the Great — Social reforms: the *tchin*; emancipation of women — Administrative, military, and ecclesiastical reforms — Economic reforms: manufactures — Utilitarian character of the plans of education — Foundation of St. Petersburg (1703), - - - 22–40

CHAPTER III.
PETER THE GREAT: LAST YEARS (1709–1725).
War with Turkey: Treaty of the Pruth (1711) — Journey to Paris (1717) — Peace of Nystad (1721) — Conquests on the Caspian — Family affairs: Eudoxia; trial of Alexis (1718); Catherine, - 41–52

THE EMPRESSES OF THE 18TH CENTURY.

CHAPTER IV.
THE WIDOW AND GRANDSON OF PETER THE GREAT: CATHERINE I. (1725–1727) AND PETER II. (1727–1730).
The work of Peter the Great continued by Catherine — Menchikof and the Dolgorouki — Maurice de Saxe in Courland, - 53–57

CHAPTER V.
THE TWO ANNES: REIGN OF ANNE IVANOVNA, AND REGENCY OF ANNE LEOPOLDOVNA (1730–1741).
Attempt at an aristocratic constitution (1730): the "Bironovchtchina" — Succession of Poland (1733–1735) and war with Turkey (1735–1739) — Ivan VI. — Regency of Biren and Anne — Revolution of 1741, - - - - - - - 58–70

CONTENTS.

CHAPTER VI.
ELIZABETH PETROVNA (1741-1762).
Reaction against the Germans : war with Sweden (1741-1743) — Succession of Austria : war against Frederic II. (1756-1762) — Reforms under Elizabeth ; French influence,   -   -   -   71-80

CHAPTER VII.
PETER III. AND THE REVOLUTION OF 1762.
Government of Peter III. and the alliance with Frederic II. — Revolution of 1762 : Catherine II.,   -   -   -   -   81-86

CHAPTER VIII.
CATHERINE II. : EARLY YEARS (1762-1780).
End of the Seven Years' War : intervention in Poland — First Turkish war : first partition of Poland (1772) : Swedish Revolution of 1772 — Plague at Moscow — Pougatchef,   -   -   87-99

CHAPTER IX.
CATHERINE II. : GOVERNMENT AND REFORMS.
The helpers of Catherine II. : the great legislative commission (1766-1768) — Administration and justice : colonization — Public instruction — Letters and arts — The French Philosophers,   100-110

CHAPTER X.
CATHERINE II. : LAST YEARS (1779-1796).
Franco-Russian mediation at Teschen (1779) — Armed neutrality (1780) — Annexation of the Crimea (1783) — Second war with Turkey (1787-1792) and war with Sweden (1788-1790) — Second partition of Poland : Diet of Grodno — Third partition : Kosciuszko — Catherine II. and the French Revolution—War with Persia, 111-127

THE FOUR EMPERORS.

CHAPTER XI.
PAUL I. (17TH NOVEMBER, 1796-24TH MARCH, 1801).
Peace policy : accession to the second Coalition — Campaigns of the Ionian Islands, Italy, Switzerland, Holland, and Naples — Alliance with Bonaparte : the League of Neutrals, and the great scheme against India,   -   -   -   -   -   128-141

CHAPTER XII.

ALEXANDER I. : FOREIGN AFFAIRS (1801-1825).

First war with Napoleon : Austerlitz, Eylau, Friedland, and **Treaty of Tilsit** — Interview at Erfürt : wars with England, Sweden, Austria, Turkey, and Persia — Grand Duchy of Warsaw : causes of the second war with Napoleon — The " Patriotic War :" battle of Borodino ; burning of Moscow : destruction of the Grand Army — Campaigns of Germany and France : treaties of Vienna and Paris — Kingdom of Poland : congresses at Aix-la-Chapelle, Carlsbad, Laybach, and Verona, - - - - 142-209

CHAPTER XIII.

ALEXANDER I. : INTERNAL AFFAIRS.

Early years : the triumvirate ; liberal measures ; the ministers ; public instruction — Speranski ; Council of the Empire ; projected civil code ; ideas of social reform — Araktchéef : political and university reaction ; military colonies — Secret Societies : Poland — Literary and scientific movement, - - - 210-225

CHAPTER XIV.

NICHOLAS I. (1825-1855).

The December insurrection — Administration and reforms — Public education and literature — War with Persia (1826-1828) — First Turkish war : liberation of Greece (1826-1829) — The Russians and English in Asia — Polish insurrection (1831) — Hostility against France : the Eastern question : Revolution of 1848 : intervention in Hungary — Second Turkish war : the allies in the Crimea — Awakening of Russian opinion, - - - 226-254

CHAPTER XV.

ALEXANDER II. (1855—1877).

End of the Crimean war : Treaty of Paris — The Act of the 19th of February, 1861 : judicial reforms : local self-government — The Polish insurrection — Intellectual movement : industrial progress ; military law — Conquests in Asia — European policy,   255-285

OBSERVATIONS, - - . - - - - 286
BIBLIOGRAPHICAL NOTES, - - - - - - 288
TABLE OF MEASURES, WEIGHTS, &c., - - - - 293

LIST OF ILLUSTRATIONS

RUSSIA

VOL. II

Frontispiece—Catherine II, Empress of Russia
The Kremlin, Imperial Palace .
Astrakhan in Russia .
Nicholas I .

HISTORY OF RUSSIA.

HISTORY OF RUSSIA.

CHAPTER I.

PETER THE GREAT : STRUGGLE WITH CHARLES XII. (1700-1709).

Narva (1700) : conquest of the Baltic provinces—Charles XII. invades Russia: Pultowa (1709).

NARVA (1700): CONQUEST OF THE BALTIC PROVINCES.

PETER I. had navigated the White Sea, and conquered a port on the Sea of Azof ; but by the Baltic alone could he secure rapid and regular communication with the nations of the West. It was only by taking up a position on the Baltic that Russia could cease to be an Oriental State, and could form part of Europe. The Baltic at that time belonged to Sweden, whose possessions on the coasts—Finland, Carelia, Ingria, Esthonia, Livonia, and Pomerania—made it a Swedish Mediterranean. Stockholm was situated in the centre of the monarchy of the Vasas, instead of lying, as it does at present, on its maritime frontier. To "open a window" into the West, it was necessary to break in some point the chain of Swedish possessions. The opportunity seemed favorable. The struggle still continued in Sweden between the aristocracy and the crown; the last king, Charles XI., had in 1680 rendered his authority absolute, and ordered the nobles to restore to the throne all the crown lands alienated since 1609. This edict of resumption, scarcely mitigated by a promise of indemnity, ruined the aristocracy. In Livonia especially, the German nobility, descendants of the old Order, protested strongly. They sent a deputation to the king, Charles XI., with John Reinhold Patkul at its head. He was a proud, energetic, vindictive, and intelligent man, whose free speech displeased the king; and as his colleagues supported him in all his acts, he and they were arrested, carried before a court-martial, and condemned to death. Patkul managed to escape, and burning with rage he sought on all sides enemies of Charles XI. and his young son Charles XII. It was he who proposed to Augustus of Saxony, king of Poland, a scheme by which Sweden was to be attacked simultaneously by all her neighbors. Poland was to take from her Livonia and Esthonia, Russia was to conquer Ingria and Carelia, Denmark was to invade Holstein, which belonged to a brother-in-law of Charles XII. Peter accepted the overtures of the King of Poland : he desired nothing better than to carry out the designs of Ivan the Terrible and of his father Alexis. The youth of the new King of Sweden, and his reputed incapacity, led Peter to expect rapid success. Peter I. acceded to the coalition by virtue of the Treaty of Preobrajenskoé. In the manifesto by which he declared war, he took pains to recall his grievances, puerile though they were, against the governor of Riga.

When Peter appeared under the walls of Narva, Patkul at first rejoiced, but speedily became uneasy; he had not intended that Narva should be attacked by the Russians, but advised Augustus not to raise the question. The coalition was almost immediately smitten by two unexpected blows. The King of Denmark, threatened in Copenhagen, had been forced to sign the Treaty of Traventhal, and at the approach of the Swedes the King of Poland had been forced to raise the siege of Riga. Without waiting to pursue the Poles, Charles turned against the Russians.

A desire to please the victors has caused the numerical disproportion between the two armies to be exaggerated. Voltaire himself was forced to rectify, in his ' History of Peter the Great,' the numbers that he had given in the ' History of Charles XII.' The latter had hardly 8430 men; the Russians amounted to 63,500 men, of whom only 40,000 took part in the action. The army was composed of regular troops, beside *streltsi*, Cossacks, *dieti-boyarskié*, and men raised in haste. In the absence of the Tzar, who had quitted the camp on the previous evening to hasten the arrival of the reinforcements, it was placed under the command of an old general of the Emperor of Germany the Duc de Croï, whom the troops suspected from the fact of his being a stranger. In the siege of Narva, they had at their backs the Narova, or river of Narva, and occupied a fortified line of seven versts (4 miles), the whole extent of which it was impossible to defend. In some places there was only a single line of soldiers, placed about six feet from one another. In front, about the centre, they had erected a great battery; before the entrenchments, on the route to Revel, were outposts to the number of 4000 men.

On the 30th (19th) of November, 1700, the battle began by a cannonade that lasted till two in the afternoon. At that time the Swedes reached the foot of the entrenchments under cover of a snow-storm, which prevented the Russians from seeing twenty paces in front. In an instant the Swedes had crossed the fosse and the parapet, and the Russian camp was seized with panic. "The Germans have betrayed us," cried the soldiers, and began to stab the foreign officers. The Duc de Croï and his staff saw no refuge from their own soldiers except in flight to the Swedish camp. Cheremetief, who commanded the cavalry, hurried to the river Narova, and succeeded in crossing it, though more than a thousand men were lost in the passage. One body alone defended itself with the energy of despair: the Preobrajenski and the Semenvoski, favorite regiments of Peter the Great, which had been organized after the European fashion, entrenched themselves in haste behind a barrier formed of artillery wagons, and repulsed all the attacks of the Swedes, directed by the king in person. In spite of this gallant defence, the Russian army was cut in two by the capture of the great central battery. Night came on and increased the disorder. The right wing. commanded by Dolgorouki, Golovine. Boutourline, and Alexander, Tzarévitch of Imeritia, entered into negotiations with the king; the generals signed a capitulation which insured them a free retreat with arms, standards, and baggage, but they had to abandon all their artillery, except six pieces of cannon. The Preobrajenski and Semenovski guards left their fortress of wagons and retired in good order, and to hasten their retreat the Swedes themselves built them a bridge over the Narova. The left wing, which had suffered more severely, was obliged to sign a more rigorous capitulation: it was allowed to retire, but had to lay down its arms. Charles XII. then allowed the Russian army to cross the river, neither from generosity nor disdain, as has sometimes been said, but from prudence. Wrede, the Swedish general, writes: "If the Russian general Weide, who had 6000 men under arms, had had the courage to attack us, we should have been lost; we were completely exhausted, having had neither rest nor food for many days, and our soldiers were so intoxicated with the wine that they found in the Russian camp that it would have been impossible to restore order." The King of Sweden, by slightly straining the terms of capitulation, retained as prisoners Croï and the officers who had taken refuge in his camp. Many remained for twenty years in Sweden. Besides the prisoners, the Russians had lost 6000 men, the Swedes nearly 2000 men.

There are salutary defeats and fatal victories. Charles was overwhelmed by flatteries from the whole of Europe. Medals were struck in his honor with the inscriptions, "*Superant operata fidem*," or again, "*Tres uno contudit ictu.*" The young king could not entirely shake off the intoxication of his success. "He dreams of nothing but war," writes his general Stenbock; "he no longer listens to advice; he behaves as one who thinks that God directly inspires him for what he has to do." He despised enemies so easily conquered, and, counting the Russian army for nothing, made great preparations for the downfall of the harmless King of Poland. During five years he did nothing but plot for his dethronement, meddling in the intrigues of the Polish diets, and trying to crush the partisans of Augustus, as if the elevation and support of Stanislas Leszczinski had been really of vital importance to Sweden in the same way as the possession of its maritime provinces. Peter understood how much it was for his advantage that his rival should be thus occupied; he aided Augustus of Saxony with troops and money, to keep his own hands free in the regions of the Baltic. It was enough for him to know that the impetuous King of Sweden was for some time entangled among the marshes and intrigues of Poland.

Peter had taken courage after Narva. Nothing was really lost, since the greater part of his army remained intact; he had only to turn to profit this rude lesson in the military art. He increased the fortifications of Pskof, Novgorod, and the frontier towns; every one was set to work. He frightened, by terrible examples, robbers of treasure and dishonest officials. With the church bells he cast three hundred cannon; he created ten new regiments, each consisting of a thousand dragoons. He sent 250 children to the military schools.

The year after the defeat at Narva, Cheremetief attacked the Swedish general Slipenbach near Ehresfer in Livonia. The Russians were the more numerous, but it was an advance to conquer the Swedes, even at odds of three to one. Out of 7000 men Slipenbach lost 3500, and only 350 prisoners were taken— a fact which proves the fierceness of the fighting. This "eldest of Russian victories" was celebrated at Moscow by a triumph in which the arms, guns, and banners of the vanquished filed past. Cheremetief was created field-marshal, and Peter exclaimed. "Glory be to God! one day we shall be able to beat the Swedes" (1701). The same year seven Swedish vessels were repulsed by the fleet of the Tzar. In 1702 Cheremetief again defeated

Slipenbach at Hümmelsdorff, took from him all his artillery, and killed 6000 out of his 8000 men.

The ultimate aim of Peter was the possession of the Neva, which had belonged to the early Russian princes, and where Saint Alexander Nevski had won his glorious surname by victories over Swedish enemies. He took Noteburg, the ancient Orécheck (*the nut*) of the Novgorodians, which commanded the Neva where it leaves Lake Ladoga, and called it Schlüsselburg (fortress of the key), because the post would make him master of the river. Near the mouth of the Neva the Swedes held the small fort of Nienschantz; he captured and destroyed it, and in a neighboring island he founded the citadel round which his future capital was to cluster; the islet of Cronslott became Cronstadt, which was to close against the Scandinavians the entrance on the side of the sea. The Neva was his. The same year (1703) he seized two Swedish vessels in its waters—" an unheard-of success," he wrote to Moscow. Then Koperie, Iam, and Dorpat (once a vassal city of Novgorod) fell into his hands, and he revenged himself for his defeat at Narva by capturing that town (1704), and by protecting the citizens from his own soldiers, who were drunk with blood. During this time Livonia and Esthonia, provinces inherited by Charles XII., were given up to frightful devastation, worse than that of the Palatinate by Louis XIV. The days of Ivan the Terrible seemed to have returned, The Russians signalized the reconquest of their ancient territory by atrocities. Volmar, Marienburg, Wenden, and Wesen were pillaged; Cheremetief only spared Riga, Pernau, and Revel (or Kobyvan, as it was called by the Tchouds). The Letto-Finnish country was made a desert; the Cossacks, Kalmucks, Bachkirs, and Tatars did not know what to do with their prisoners. The Zaporogues alone carried 4000 captives—men, women, and children—back to the Lower Dnieper. Neither the capture of the fortresses, the burning of the towns, nor the extermination of the people, could distract Charles XII. from the attempt to ruin Augustus.

In 1705 the Tzar felt it was necessary to keep an eye on the actions of the Swede in Poland, and not to allow his ally Augustus to be entirely crushed. It was enough to have taken from him his share of the booty, Esthonia and Livonia. The Russians crossed the Dwina, occupied Courland and Wilna, and concentrated themselves in an entrenched camp at Grodno. Peter, like Ivan the Terrible, had not only to struggle with his external enemies; the internal factions had not yet been subdued. At the moment that he was preparing to give battle to **the Swedes**, the revolt of Astrakhan obliged him to send to the

Lower Volga a portion of his troops under Cheremetief, one of his best generals. It was time Cheremetief arrived, for already the *streltsi* of Astrakhan had appealed for help to the Cossacks. The Russian army in Lithuania found itself for an instant in great straits: Schulenburg, the general of Augustus, had been defeated at Frauenstadt (1706), and been forced to fall back on Saxony Thanks to the skilful dispositions of Peter, the Russian army succeeded in retreating without opposition to Kief. About the year 1706 Menchikof inflicted on the Swedish general Mardefelt, with nearly equal numbers, a bloody defeat near Kalisch.

CHARLES XII. INVADES RUSSIA: PULTOWA (1709).

Charles XII. had pursued the army of the King of Poland into Saxony; to punish his new enterprise against Stanislas Leszczinski and his entrance into Warsaw, he crushed the Electoral States by his extortions and requisitions; he traversed Silesia without deigning to ask leave of the Emperor Joseph, despising the protestations of the diet of Ratisbon; he received the complaints of the Protestants of this province who were persecuted by Austria, and appeared before the malcontents of Hungary as the great redresser of wrongs. This happened at the most critical moment in the war of the Spanish Succession. France, defeated at Hochstadt, Ramilies, and Turin, turned her eyes towards victorious Sweden. England, Holland, Austria, Brandenburg, Hanover, all the powers concerned in the attack on the French frontiers, trembled lest the Swedish army should assail the coalition in the rear. Had not Sweden been the ally of France since the time of Gustavus Adolphus and of Oxenstiern? Had she not been the companion of her days of glory? Did she not owe France her great position in Germany? Had she not to fear lest she might suffer from the defeat of France? Was not Charles XII. at this moment receiving subsidies from the Grand Monarque? Was his help not entreated by the French envoys? The fate of the world seemed to lie in the hands of the young victor. If he turned to the West, if he revenged his own grievances and those of Protestantism against Austria, France was saved, and Sweden, whom fearful things awaited on the plains of Russia, was saved also. There was a pause of anxious and solemn expectation, all the greater because the proud and silent monarch had allowed no hint of his projects to escape him. The situation appeared so grave that in April 1707 Marlborough resolved to seek him in his camp. Few words were exchanged between these two great captains, whose characters were so different, but the clever Englishman was able to guess Charles's hatred and jealousy of France; he saw that his eyes glittered at the mention of the Tzar; he remarked spread out on the table a map of Russia. Marlborough retired full of hope. Those who feared Charles agreed to whatever he proposed to them; Augustus accepted the humiliating treaty of Altranstadt; he delivered up Patkul, whom the Tzar had accredited to him as ambassador, and whom, in spite of his inviolable position, the son of Charles XI. broke on the wheel. The Emperor relinquished a hundred churches to the Protestants of Silesia, dismissed a chamberlain of whom the King had reason to complain, surrendered 1500 Russian refugees, and recalled 400 German officers who had taken service with the Tzar. The Elector of Brandenburg signed a perpetual peace. Charles XII. might now break up his camp at Leipzig; he saw only one enemy, the Tzar of Russia.

The adversary of Peter the Great was an admirable knight-errant rather than a sovereign. The absolute power of which he became possessed at an early age left without counterpoise his fiery temper and obstinate character—his "iron head," as the Turks said at Bender. Voltaire observes that he carried all his virtues to such an excess that they became as dangerous as the opposite vices. His dominant virtue and vice was a passion for glory. Glory, and glory alone, was to him the end of war. He does not appear to have understood that it was possible to acquire it by practising the arts of peace. Up to the moment when the news of the coalition formed against him revealed to him his military vocation, he seemed the most insignificant of all the European princes. His conduct appeared to be regulated, not by the political principles current in the eighteenth century, but by some strange and archaic point of honor. He only knew Alexander the Great as the romantic hero of Quintus Curtius, and this phantom he took for his ideal. He was nourished on the old Scandinavian sagas, and we may truly say that the soul and spirit of the old vikings revived in him: he had their wonderful deeds forever before his eyes, and the versified maxims of the Scalds forever present to his memory. Charles XII. was a hero of the Edda set down by mistake in a matter-of-fact century. A Russian historian, M. Guerrier, calls him "The last of the Varangians"; he was the last of those Scandinavian adventurers who had marched over the Russian plains from Novgorod to Kief, but to whom henceforth the road to the south remained forever shut. Pitiless to others as well as to himself, we find him undergoing useless dangers and fatigues, seeking adventures like a sea-king who had only his head to risk; considering a war as a single combat between two champions, which could only end, if not with the death, at least with the dethronement, of the vanquished; fighting not to gain crowns, but to distribute them; giving largesses to his soldiers as if he had always the treasures of pillage, the "red gold of Fafnir's heath," at his disposal; despising all the luxuries of life, like the Northmen who boasted of never having slept beneath a roof: flying from women, "whose silken hairs," say the sagas, "are nets of perfidy"; regarding a backward movement as dishonor, and considering prudent advice an evidence of weakness; ready to face water, as in the marshes of Lithuania; or fire, as in the conflagration of Bender. He had his own guard of *drabans*, as the *konungs* of fabulous times had their *droujina*, as Alexander had his *hetairoi*. His companioos also are heroes of sagas, and legend has gilded their exploits. It is related in Sweden that Hinstersfelt carried off the enemy's guns on his shoulders, and that, passing through a vaulted gateway, from which hung a ring, he put his little finger through it and pulled himself up by it, and with him the horse which he pressed between his knees. "When I have nine of my drabans with me," said Charles, "nothing can hinder me from going where I will." He was thus impelled to seek adventures in distant lands, and, like the warriors of old, to "win the world by the force of his arm." He sent officers even into Asia and Egypt to reconnoitre and to collect information.

The poet Pouchkine puts into the mouth of the disappointed Mazeppa the following remark:—" I have been mistaken about this Charles: no doubt he is a bold and audacious youth; he can gain two, or even three battles; he can fall suddenly on the enemy, eat his breakfast, reply to a bomb with a burst of laughter; like any sharpshooter, he can glide by night into the camp of the foe, overthrow some Cossack as he has done to-day, give blow for blow, and wound for wound: but he is not of a stature to cope with the giant; he wishes to make Fortune manœuvre like a regiment at the sound of the drum. He is blind, obstinate, impatient; he is thoughtless and presumptuous; he believes in God knows what star. He measures by his past success the new forces of his enemy. He must be taught better. I am ashamed in my old age to have allowed myself to be seduced by a military wanderer,—to have been dazzled, like a young girl, by the courage and the luck of an adventurer."

The two adversaries were to meet at last. Charles quitted Saxony with 43,000 men, enriched with the spoils of the country; he left behind 10,000 to support Stanislas on the throne, and marched towards the Niemen. He was the first to enter Grodno with 600 men, and only the prodigies of valor which he performed prevented his being captured by the Russian rear-guard (1708). The Tzar, in pursuance of a system which was to be followed in 1812, fell back on Russia, laying waste Lithuania as he went. The Swedish name was still a universal terror. Besides the 33,000 men who followed Charles, Lewenhaupt was to bring up 18,000 from Poland. No Russian force seemed fit to cope with the most experienced army in Europe. The internal affairs of Russia also troubled Peter; it was at this decisive moment that the revolt of Boulavine, in the camp of the Don, occurred, and the first agitation among the Cossacks of the Dnieper. Before risking the safety of his empire, within which terrible disorders were still fermenting, before exposing his new creations to the horrors of an invasion, Peter tried to negotiate with his enemy; he offered to be content with a single port on the Baltic. I will treat with the Tzar in Moscow," said Charles.

From the Niemen, across the forest of Minsk, where the Swedes were obliged to cut a passage with their axes, Charles XII. reached the Berezina, which he crossed at the head of a body of 3000 men. At Hollosin he came up with 20,000 Russians; whose steadiness should have given him pause, for they only yielded at the seventh charge of the king. He reached the Dnieper at Mohilef, and even got as far as Mstislaf. At Dobroë, south of Smolensk, he attacked a body of 10,000 Russians and 6000 Kalmucks. This time he had a horse killed under him, two aides-de-camp killed at his side, and, finding himself alone with five men, slew twelve foes with his own hand, and only escaped by a miracle. Russia, however, was not going to allow herself to be conquered so easily. He then found himself on the road to Moscow, which Napoleon was afterwards to take, 300 miles from the Russian capital. It was already the end of September; winter approached, and showed signs of being severe; provisions were scarce, and Charles was advised to retreat from Mstislaf to Mohilef, and there await Lewenhaupt, who would bring up 18,000 men and plenty of food. Charles, however, allowed himself to be tempted by the offers of Mazeppa, who promised him a reinforcement of 30,000 Cossacks, and by the hopes of abundance in the fertile plains of the south. Besides, as he confessed to Gyllenkruk, who was horrified by this confidence, "he had no plan." So he turned towards the Ukraine. Then the Tzar and his generals hung like wolves on the flank of Lewenhaupt, who found himself isolated and without support on the plains of the

Dnieper. At Lesna, on the banks of the Soja, they fought a battle which raged for three days, and where, this time, the numbers were equal. The Swedish general lost 12,000 out of his 18,000 men, and was forced to spike his cannon and burn a thousand wagon-loads of provisions, besides the 6000 captured by the Russians. All the convoy, which was the only hope of the royal army, was destroyed. Lewenhaupt only brought to Charles what remained from the disaster.

By this time winter had come, the terrible winter of 1709. In the forced marches which the King of Sweden had the imprudence to impose on his army, the men, who lacked winter clothing, and the starving horses perished by thousands; the guns were thrown into the river for want of beasts to transport them. The very crows fell dead from the cold, and the doctors were employed in amputating frost-bitten hands and feet. Charles continued his march, ascertained the distance which separated him from Asia, and consoled his half-naked soldiers with the assurance that he would conduct them so far that they could only receive news of Sweden three times a year. A soldier showed him the horrible mouldy bread on which the army was fed. Charles took it, tasted it, and observed quietly, "It is not good, but it may be eaten."

The arrival of spring did not put an end to the sufferings of the army. Prince Menchikof sacked Batourine, the capital of the fugitive hetman, and razed the *sétcha* of the Zaporogues (May 1709). Charles reached the walls of Pultowa, and halted there, to wait for the Turks and the Poles of Leszczinski, who were never to arrive. While awaiting them he determined to attack Pultowa, "for a diversion." It was in vain that the uselessness of the enterprise and the impossibility of success were represented to him. What was the good of wasting powder and the munitions of war, which had now become rare in the camp? "Yes," replied the Iron-head to Gyllenkruk, "we are obliged to do extraordinary things to gain honor and glory;" and to Piper, "An angel would have to descend from heaven with orders for me to go before I stirred from this place." When had his favorite heroes of the Eddas ever been seen to retreat? He made Gutman, his servant, recite the saga of Rolf Ericsen, who "vanquished the Russian sorcerer in the isle of Retusari, and conquered all Russia and Denmark, so that his name is honored and glorified throughout the North." Menchikof then came up and showed that he had profited by the lessons of the Swedes by making a feint, which enabled him to throw some troops into Pultowa.

The Tzar arrived (4th—15th June, 1709) with 60,000 men,

whom he covered by an entrenchment raised during a single night. Charles's army was now reduced to 29,000 men, who lacked everything, suffered as much from the extreme heat as they had formerly done from the extreme cold, and were exhausted by suffering and privations. He had only four field-pieces against the seventy-two guns of the Tzar. In one of his nightly sallies, when he was trying to harass the enemy's vanguard, Charles received a wound in his heel which necessitated a cruel operation, and on the day of the famous battle (27th June—8th July, 1709) he had to be carried in a litter. The generals on whom the responsibility of command fell could not agree ; he himself thwarted the dispositions of Rehnskold, who was nominated general-in-chief.

Peter had confided the centre to Cheremetief, the right to Renne, the left to Menchikof, and the artillery to Bruce. He then harangued his troops. " The moment is come," he said ; " the fate of our country is to be decided. You must not think ' it is for Peter we fight ' ; no, it is for the empire confided to Peter, it is for the country, it is for our orthodox faith, for the Church of God. As for Peter, know that he is ready to sacrifice his life for a prosperous and glorious future for Russia."

The Swedes took the offensive. " All those who have served in the Swedish army," says Voltaire, " know that it was impossible to resist their first shock." They saw in victory an end of their sufferings, and fought like the wild Bersarkers of the legends. They charged with fury the cavalry placed at the right of the Russians, wounded Renne, who had to yield his command to Bauer, and took two redoubts. Peter, in trying to rally his cavalry, received a ball in his hat. Menchikof had three horses killed under him.

Unluckily for Charles, the corps of Kreutz, which ought to have made a *détour* and fallen on the enemy's flank, was lost, and never appeared. The superior artillery of the Russians arrested the charge of the Swedes. Menchikof marched boldly on their rear, and thus separated the body of the army from the camp under Pultowa, which he finally reached. The Russian fire on the front of the Swedes was so violent that the horses harnessed to Charles's litter were killed ; his drabans then took it in turns to carry him, but twenty-one out of the twenty-four were left where they fell. The Russian cavalry rallied, and the Russian infantry which was now put in motion broke the Swedish line. Attacked in front by Peter, and in the rear by Menchikof, the Swedes were speedily thrown into disorder. They fled, and Charles was placed on horseback by his guards, and obliged to go with the stream. He hardly escaped being taken.

Accompanied by Mazeppa and by the Pole Poniatowski, he arrived after two days' flight at the banks of the celebrated Borysthenes, which in the tenth century so many Scandinavian fleets had sailed down. He crossed the Dnieper in a little boat with Mazeppa, and continued his route to Otchakof. It was thus that " the last of the Varangians and the last of the free Cossacks entered the land of the Sultan as fugitives." The Swedes had lost about 10,000 men—3000 were taken on the field of battle; the bulk of the army, which had continued, under Lewenhaupt, its march to the Dnieper, had to pause on its banks. Menchikof, sent there hastily by the Tzar, obliged 16,000 more Swedes to lay down their arms (Capitulation of Perevolotchna). Of the magnificent army which at Leipzig had made all Europe tremble, not a battalion escaped.

The evening after the battle the Tzar received in his tent those Swedish generals whose names had been cited among the first captains of the age. He treated these glorious prisoners courteously and drank to the health of "his masters in the art of war." He accepted the grades of general and vice-admiral, the Russian churches resounded with songs of triumph, the Tzar was exalted in eloquent sermons, and Kourbatof wrote to him, " Rejoice, because obedient to the Word of God thou hast exposed thy life for thy servants; rejoice, because thou hast forged thine army by thy courage, as men heat gold in a furnace; rejoice, because thou mayest hope for the realization of thy dearest wish—the domination of the sea of the Varangians." Peter after Pultowa, like Charles after Narva, tasted in his turn the sweets of glory. But the success of Pultowa differed from the success of Narva. Narva had been only a victory; Pultowa marks a new era in universal history. Sweden, which under Gustavus Adolphus, and again under Charles XI., had played in Europe the part of a great Power, which had even obtained an importance out of all proportion with her actual resources, was suddenly relegated to the third rank among States. The place she had left vacant in the North was taken by a nation which had at its disposal far larger resources, besides a greater power of expansion. The shores of the Baltic were to pass into its hands. Already Russia declared herself, not only a Power of the North, but a Power of Europe. Muscovy, which, had been formerly held in check by little Sweden, by anarchic Poland, by decrepit Turkey, or even by the Khan of the Tatars, was destined to become formidable to France, to England, and to the house of Austria. With Russia, the Slav race, so long humiliated, made a triumphal entry into the stage of the world. Finally, Pultowa was not only a victory, it was the proof of the regeneration of Russia; it justified the Tzar, his foreign auxiliaries, his regular army; it left his hands free to reform, gave to the empire a new capital, and promised to Europe a new civilized people. "Now," he wrote to Apraxine from the field of battle, "the first stone for the foundation of St. Petersburg is laid, by the help of God."

CHAPTER II.

PETER THE GREAT: THE REFORMS.

General character of the reforms; the instruments of Peter the Great—Social reforms: the *tchin*; emancipation of women—Administrative, military, and ecclesiastical reforms—Economic reforms; manufactures—Utilitarian character of the plans of education—Foundation of St. Petersburg (1703).

GENERAL CHARACTER OF THE REFORMS: THE **COLLABORATORS** OF PETER THE GREAT.

1. THE way for the reforms of Peter the Great had been made smooth by those of Alexis, and by all the movement of the 17th century. Under the Ivans, under Boris, under the early Romanofs, Russia had been gradually thrown open to strangers. It by no means followed that the whole country was disposed to follow Peter the Great in his innovations. Opposed to him were those who had refused to accept the reforms of Nicon, and many who, while accepting them, had no idea of going further. The *raskols*, and certain members of the State Church, were his enemies; the Russian people were more averse to innovation than any in Europe. "Novelty brings calamity," says a proverb; the nobles were also hostile to everything that could contribute to autocratic centralization.

Peter the Great found, then, a steady resistance among the majority of the nation; to conquer it, where persuasion and his own example did not suffice, he employed the energy of his semi-barbarous character, and the terrible resources of absolute power. By main force he dragged the nation in the path of progress; at every page of his reforming edicts we find the knout and the penalty of death.

2. These innovations effected by the prince were not intended to prejudice his own authority; nay, they had, we may say, for their sole end the transformation of a patriarchal into a modern despotism. The force of the government was to be increased without any essential change in its character. The Tzar remained as much an autocrat as Ivan the Terrible, but his au-

thority was to be exercised by means of more perfect instruments, and by agents subjected to the disciplines and rules of the West.

3. The mass of the people still remained serfs and attached to the soil,—twenty millions of human beings were the property of the territorial oligarchy; but, notwithstanding, the Russian nation was to be furnished with the instruments necessary to enter into regular communications with the free people of Europe. Russia was to seem a state centralized and civilized like the France of Louis XIV., yet the patriarchal and Asiatic principle, which, confounding paternal and territorial authority with political rule, presided over the relations of the father with his children, of the Tzar with his subjects, of the proprietor with his slaves, of the superior with his inferiors, was still unimpaired. On a social organization, which seemed to date from the 11th century, were to rise diplomacy, a regular army, a bureaucratic hierarchy, schools and academies, and the trade and manufactures of a luxurious civilization.

4. A fourth characteristic of the reforms of Peter the Great was that, in order completely to transport European civilization into Russia, he was obliged to borrow everything from strangers, without always having the time to choose the institutions best suited to his purpose. What was meant by civilization was then, and is still, the civilization of the West; therefore Peter surrounded himself with Dutchmen, Englishmen, Scotchmen, Swiss, and Germans. For the same reason he imported in the mass manufactures, trades, and artisans; had Western books translated, and sprinkled his administrative terminology with words borrowed from Sweden or Germany. That he might introduce Western ideas, he made himself a Dutchman and a German, forbade his subjects to wear the long garments peculiar to Asia, and wished them to adopt the short trousers, the cocked hat, and buckled shoes of Europe.

5. There was nothing servile, however, in this imitation; it was the method of a man of genius, who wished to outstrip time and hasten reforms by a hundred years. He intended that the Russians should be the pupils and not the subjects of the Germans; and as under his German dress he remained a Russian patriot, he reserved the first posts in the army and State for the natives. No doubt we may cite among his fellow-workers his admiral, the Genevese Lefort; the Scotch Gordon, created general; Bruce, a Scotchman born in Westphalia, who organized the artillery, directed the diplomacy, and after the publication of the almanack passed with the people for a sorcerer and a magician. Ostermann, son of a pastor in the county of La

Marck, was a skilful negotiator, of whom Peter saïd that he never committed faults in diplomacy; Münich, a good engineer, who later became field-marshal, and meantime constructed for Peter the canal of the Ladoga, was a native of the county of Oldenburg. But among the chosen companions of Peter the Great, in the nest of "Peter's eaglets," as Pouchkine calls them, we find many Russians, and in the highest post among these men Menchikof, a "new man," who rose from nothing to become prince, field-marshal, admiral, and conqueror, but whose probity did not stand as high as his talents. Another was Boris Cheremetief, a great noble, whose name and exploits are still preserved in the songs of the people, who travelled in the West before Peter, and came back to Russia in German clothes, a man as honest as he was brave, first in date of the Russian marshals. There were also Dmitri Mikhaïlovitch, head of the princely family of Galitsyne, who devoted himself to the reformer, though detesting "new men"; his brother Michael Galitsyne, who when he became field-marshal continued to show to his elder brother an old-fashioned deference, and refused to sit at the same table with him; Jacob Dolgorouki, who could brave the wrath of Peter and force him to hear the truth; Golovine, high admiral and diplomatist; Apraxine, admiral, conqueror on the Swedish seas; the diplomatist Golvokine, grand chancellor; Chafirof, vice-chancellor of the empire; Gregory and Vassili Dolgorouki; Andrew Matvéef; the Kourakines, ambassadors, father and son, to the courts of the West. Not to be forgotten are the intelligent and quick-tempered Jagoujinski, afterwards procurator-general of the senate; Tolstoï, an accomplice of Sophia, pardoned on account of his high intelligence, an excellent negotiator and administrator of justice; Romodanovski, the cruel director of the State inquisition; Kourbatof, the financier of the new *régime,* besides three Little Russians, three ecclesiastics, three brilliant pupils of the Academy of Kief, —Saint Dmitri of Rostof, Stephen Javorski, and Feofane Prokopovitch, to whom we must add the bishop Feofilakt Lopatinski. Such were the Russian men of the *vrémia* of Peter the Great.

SOCIAL REFORMS: THE "TCHIN;" EMANCIPATION OF WOMEN.

The most numerous class in Russia was that on which the reform made the State press with a ily increasing weight, and which paid by the sweat of its brow for the expenses of regeneration—the rural population. It was subdivided into *odnovortsi,* peasants with a free or even noble origin; into farmers on the *métayer* system (*polavinki*), who cultivated the land of the nobles and handed over to them half the products, but who had retained their personal liberty; into *peasants* of the crown, of the monasteries and of proprietors, all attached to the soil. The edicts of Peter confounded all these classes, and subjected all the cultivators to a capitation tax and a fixed residence: this was equivalent to serfage. The reasons which had caused Godounof to legalize their attachment to the soil still subsisted in all their original force, and were likely to cause severe legislation. The tax on the *fires* became the tax upon *heads*, and the proprietors, by a considerable augmentation of their seignorial authority, were intrusted with its collection. Peter the Great merely promulgated an edict which sought to regulate the sale of slaves. " If the sale cannot be abolished completely, slaves must be sold by families without separating husbands from wives, parents from children, and no longer like head of cattle, a thing unheard of in the whole world." This act, at least in its philanthropic clauses, never received any sanction. Anne Ivanovna later legalized this shameful abuse by collecting her dues on the sale of slaves.

The inhabitants of the towns were divided into three categories. To the first belonged bankers, manufacturers, rich traders, physicians, chemists, capitalists, merchants, jewellers, workers in metal, and artists; to the second, small traders and masters of crafts; to the third, the lowest class of journeymen and artisans. The first two of these divisions took the German name of " first and second guilds," and were invested with certain privileges.

Foreigners obtained the right of freely engaging in trade or commerce, of acquiring real property, of intermarrying with Russians, of entering the service of the State, of practising their respective modes of worship, and of leaving the empire at will, on condition of giving up the tenth of their goods.

The Russian nobility assumed the character of a *nobility based on service*. The two ideas of nobility and the service of the Tzar became correlative. Every noble was obliged to serve, and whoever, Russian or foreigner, entered the service of the State became a gentleman. Peter the Great was as inexorable as Louvois in exacting service from the aristocracy: every *dvorianine* was at the disposal of the government till his death. Thus was the distinction finally effaced between the two kinds of lands possessed by the nobles, the *pomiestia*, or fiefs, and the *votchiny* or allods; both were henceforward only held as fiefs of the Tzar, on condition of military service. Up to this time the civil, military, naval, and ecclesiastical hierarchies had no common standard. Peter established in each hierarchy corresponding grades, confounded hereditary nobility and the nobility of service, and distributed the officers of the State among the fourteen degrees of the Tchin. These extended, in the civil order, from the registrar of the college to the chancellor of the empire; in the military order, from the cornet or ensign to the field-marshal; in the fleet, from the standard-bearer to the high admiral; in the court, from the *tafeldecker* to the grand chamberlain; in the Church, from the deacon to the metropolitan.

Peter borrowed from German legislation a settlement wholly antipathetic to the Russian laws, which insisted on equality in the division of property. He introduced the custom ("Majorat") by which the property passed to the heir with the title. In virtue of this new law, the land of a noble belonged exclusively to the eldest, or to one of the sons nominated heir by his father. Peter saw in this practice, which was to survive him but a short time, the following advantages: the noble families could no longer ruin and impoverish themselves by repeated partitions of the property; the peasants would be happier under the rule of one rich proprietor than under that of his needy co-heirs; the younger branches, no longer reckoning on the paternal estate, would be obliged to seek their livelihood in commerce or in the service of the State, "idleness being the mother of all the vices." The younger members of the nobility were besides only to be admitted into the service under certain conditions of elementary or special instruction, and technical preparation. Even marriage was forbidden to an uneducated gentleman. The foundation of the orders of Saint Andrew and Saint Catherine finished the destruction of the barrier of caste.

The seclusion of women was an Asiatic custom with which Peter waged fierce war. He would abolish the *terem* locked "with twenty-seven bolts," the *fata* over the face, and litters with closed curtains. Six weeks before every marriage the betrothal was to take place, and from that moment the bridal pair might freely see each other, and might even break off the engagement if they were not satisfied on further acquaintance. Fathers and guardians had to swear that they would not marry young people against their will; and masters, that they would not force the consent of their slaves. Midwives were forbidden to put to death misshapen infants. Peter the Great took wives and daughters from their domestic cloisters, and brought them into the life of European *salons*. He instituted assemblies, free meetings which might take place in any house, where men and women appeared in European dress, where they partook together of refreshments, danced Polish or German dances, and where French or Swedish prisoners served as teachers of manners. The assemblies of Peter the Great were at first only a parody of those of Versailles. Bergholtz complains that men allowed themselves to smoke in the presence of the ladies; that the ladies sat apart, embarrassed, dressed up, silently watching each other; that the drunken nobles were often carried away by their drunken lackeys. Did not Peter himself institute as a punishment for any breach of good behavior the emptying of the "great eagle," a huge goblet filled with brandy? To amuse the new society and give life to his capital, he invented masquerades, cavalcades of disguised lords and ladies, the feast of fools, the Great Conclave, presided over by the "Prince-pope" surrounded by "Cardinals" dead drunk. He forbade the use of servile diminutives and prostrations before the Tzar, and by blows with his cane he taught his nobility to feel themselves free men and Europeans.

ADMINISTRATIVE, MILITARY, AND ECCLESIASTICAL REFORMS.

The ancient *douma* of the boyards was replaced by the "directing senate," composed of nine members, which at first never acted save in the absence of the prince. The number was afterwards increased, and it became permanently both the great council of government, high committee of finance, and supreme court of justice. Peter commanded the Senate to be obeyed like himself, but on all important questions the Senate made its report to the Tzar. He appointed, in connection with this body, a procurator-general, charged with superintending the execution of the laws. Peter often reproached the new senators with conducting affairs "after the old fashion," with dragging out deliberations, and taking bribes. He had to make a new rule, in virtue of which senators were forbidden, under different penalties, to cry out, to beat each other, or to call each other thieves.

Peter suppressed the ancient Muscovite *prikazes*. He created instead, by the advice of Leibnitz, and after the German model, "colleges" of government similar to those by which the regent Orleans replaced the ministers of Louis XIV. There were ten of these colleges: those of foreign affairs, war, admiralty, treasury, revenue, justice, property of the nobles, manufactures, mines, and commerce. A collection of Swedish edicts was translated for their use. As they had few capable men, strangers were employed, in the proportion of one for each college, and often they were obliged to resort to interpreters to enable them to understand each other. Captive Swedish officers and dragoons might be seen administering the empire. **Peter sent for Slavs from Bohemia, Silesia, and Moravia**, as being quicker at learning the Russian language. He despatched forty young men to Königsberg to study the elements of administration and finance. This autocrat permitted his colleges to elect their presidents. In 1722 the office of president of the college of justice being vacant, he assembled at the palace the senators, generals, officers, and a hundred members of the nobility, and after having taken their oaths made them proceed to the election in his presence.

Before Peter the Great the provincial governments were in hopeless confusion. The governors of provinces and the voïevodes directed at once war, finance, justice, and superintendence of buildings. Peter divided the empire into twelve governments, subdivided into forty-three provinces; the former were administered by governors and vice-governors, the latter by voïevodes. These representatives of the sovereign were assisted by a council, or *landrath*, elected by the nobles. The towns received an autonomous and municipal government; the citizens elected *burgomasters*, and these a president or mayor. The burgomasters and the mayor formed the *rathhaus* or corporation of the city. In special cases the citizens of the first and second *guilds* were summoned to the council. All the magistrates of Russia were subject to a chief magistrate, chosen from the municipal council of St. Petersburg, of which one-half was composed of foreigners. The chief magistrate watched over the prosperity of commerce and manufactures, sanctioned the sentences of death pronounced by the corporations of the province, decided disputes between the *rathhaus* and the citizens, confirmed the municipal elections, and sent in reports to the Senate. He was nominated by the Tzar. The towns had their *landmiliz*. The patriarchal and socialist constitution of the rural communes was not touched.

Ignorance, inexperience, and corruption were the vices of the new administration. The functionaries had always present to their minds the advice of the ancient Tzars—" Look to thy office, and indemnify thyself." Peter attacked with fury this deeply-rooted abuse, practised by the chief personages of the empire, headed by Menchikof. The exactions of the governor provoked a revolt at Astrakhan. Another governor of the same city was condemned by Peter to be torn by pigs, Gagarine, governor of Siberia, and Lapoukhine, of Revel, were decapitated. Chafirof was pardoned on the scaffold. Nesterof, after having made the denunciation of thieves a profession, was himself broken on the wheel as a thief. One day

Peter made one of his nobles show him the accounts of his expenditure, and proved to him that he himself robbed the State, and was robbed in turn by his steward. The Tzar beat him with his own hand, and said to him, "Now go and find your steward, and settle accounts with him." It is said that Menchikof himself was not safe against the imperial correction. The recruits were the chief sufferers from their extortions. These unhappy men, who were torn from their native villages and chained like galley-slaves, were thrown into prison on arriving at their halting-place, were fed upon mushrooms which their captains made them graze on in the forests, and naturally died by hundreds before reaching their regiments. Peter was obliged to invite his subjects to denounce the thieves by promising to give the accusers the *tchin* and the fortune of the accused.

The code of Alexis Mikhaïlovitch was no longer suitable to the Russia of Peter the Great. The latter wished to adopt the Swedish code, and to modify what was inapplicable in it to the Russians by means of ancient Muscovite laws, or new legislation. This project could not be realized. In criminal cases he still employed torture, though with mitigations. He replaced the old *pravege* by labor in the public works. He introduced a written procedure in the tribunals, which had all the faults of an inquisitorial procedure. Justice was administered in various districts, now by tribunals properly so called, now by the voïevodes, the *landrichter*, or by the magistrates of the towns. At Petersburg sat the supreme court, consisting of delegates from the Senate.

The Petersburg police was controlled by the *general politzmeister*, that of Moscow by the *ober-politz-meister*. In the large towns there was an inspector of police for every ten houses; all the citizens over twenty years of age had to enter the service of the watch. The governors, voïevodes, commissioners of the country, and all who held authority were responsible for the public safety. The Russia of that date needed strict superintendence. Moscow, whose streets were common sewers, began to be paved with wood. Servants, under penalty of fines, stripes, or the knout, were enjoined to keep the house-front clean. Beggars multiplied; well-to-do citizens were not ashamed to ask for alms, or to send their children to beg in the streets; they were in future to be arrested and taken before the police. People who pretended to be in the public service and were furnished with false credentials, and imposed on the credulity of the peasants, were sought out and punished. Hospitals were established for the sick, workhouses for vagabonds, mad people were housed together, coiners and forgers were rigorously proceeded against.

Most difficult of all to deal with were the brigands. Brigandage was habitual in Russia, and was favored by the vast and vacant wilds, the deep forests, the passive temper of the peasants, who did not dare to arm for the defence of one of their members, and would allow him to be despoiled and tortured in presence of the whole village by a few bandits. The brigands formed themselves into great troops, armed and disciplined in the European manner, furnished with cavalry and artillery; they pillaged the Crown taverns, burned the villages, invaded the dwellings of the nobles, and took the small towns by assault. Their recruits were Cossacks, fugitive peasants, soldiers who had deserted, unfrocked priests; gentlemen and even noble ladies were seen riding at their head, thus augmenting their revenues by robbery. Battles had to be fought before security could be restored.

The open or sullen opposition his reforms met with caused Peter to create a State inquisition. This opposition came to light on all occasions. The ladies of honor, who wore the European costume when the Tzar was present, threw it off with contempt when he went away. Insulting placards were affixed to the walls. Even in the bosom of his own family the Tzar met with hostility. He instituted the bureau of reformation (*Préobrajenskoé prikaz*), or *secret court of police*, which has left a terrible memory. To ruin his enemy a man had only to raise the cry of *slovo i diélo* (word and deed), immediately the accuser and accused were arrested and conducted to the "hall of the question," which the latter seldom left unconvicted.

In the matter of finance Peter replaced the tax on fires, which gave rise to perpetual disputes, by a poll-tax. Ecclesiastics, nobles, broken soldiers, the inhabitants of the Baltic provinces, Bachkirs, and Lapps were alone exempted from it. Even free peasants were liable. Kourbatof introduced the tax of the *eagle paper* (*gerbovaïa boumagha*), or stamped paper. But in the midst of the terrible necessities of war Peter had recourse to other expedients. The officials were often deprived of part of their pay. The raskolniks were doubly taxed. Those who wore beards had to pay from 30 to 100 roubles, according to their fortune. The peasants were taxed two *deniers* for their beards when they entered the towns. Baths, mills, huts, and bees were taxed.

One day Peter ordered all oak coffins at the makers' to be seized and sold for his profit. The crown had for a long while absorbed the commerce of soda, potash, and of tar, which were the produce of the forests of the north. The revenues of the State, in fifteen years alone, from 1710 to 1725, rose from three to ten million roubles.

After the dissolution of the *streltsi*, the regular army was composed of infantry and dragoons, dressed in European uniforms, and raised to 210,000 men. The peasantry were subjected to a system of conscription, which was to be for long a source of despotism and tyranny. At this period was formed a whole popular literature of "lamentations of recruits." The irregular troops of the Cossacks and the tribes of the east furnished endless numbers of soldiers. A maritime conscription was established along the banks of the lakes, rivers, and the sea. Soon the Russian fleet numbered 48 ships of the line, 800 boats of a lower class, and 28,000 sailors.

On the death of the patriarch Adrian, who had little sympathy with the reforms (1700), Peter conferred on Stephen Javorski the title of "Superintendent of the Patriarchal Throne." Peter had resolved to abolish this institution of Godounof, and to give to the Church herself the collegiate organization with which he was at that time so fascinated. The preamble of the edict instituting the Holy Synod, which was compiled by Feofane Prokopovitch, is very curious: "The collegiate organization will not cause the country to fear the troubles and seditions that may arise when only one man finds himself at the head of the Church. The simple people are not quick to seize the distinction between the spiritual and imperial power; struck with the virtue and the splendor of the supreme pastor of the Church, they imagine that he is a second sovereign, equal and even superior in power to the autocrat. If a dispute takes place between the Patriarch and the Tzar, they are disposed to take the side of the former, believing that they thus embrace the cause of God." This mistrust of the spiritual power is again found in the Oukaze, where bishops are recommended to avoid pride and show, never to allow themselves to be supported under the arm in walking, unless they are ill, and to permit no prostrations before them. In the same manner as Peter had suppressed the hetmanate and established the College of Little Russia, he suppressed the patriarchate, and founded the Holy Synod. He wished to be sole emperor in Moscow, as in the Ukraine.

The Holy Synod was composed of a certain number of bishops, among whom a procurator-general, often a soldier, represented the Tzar. The Holy Synod was to be the instrument of reform in the Church. Each bishop was ordered to keep a school in his palace; the sons of the popes who refused to be educated were to be taken as soldiers. The grave question of monasteries was re-opened, but Peter did not yet dare to undertake the liquidation of their property. As Russia needed to be peopled, no Russian was allowed to become a monk till he was thirty. No servant of the State might enter a cloister without leave. As the monks showed themselves more and more hostile to reform, they were forbidden to shut themselves up to write, or to have ink or pens in their cells. They were, however, compelled to work at some trade. Hospitals and schools were given into their charge, and also broken-down soldiers, who found in the monastery an honorable asylum. The bishops, on the contrary, were encouraged by Peter to write. Stephen Javorski published his book called 'The Signs of the Antichrist,' to refute Talitski, who had seen in the reforms of Peter the omens of the end of the world. As Voltaire relates, Talitski was put to death, and Javorski rewarded. 'The Stone of the Faith,' another of his works, was directed against Protestantism, while Saint Dmitri of Rostof wrote his 'Researches on the Raskolnik Church of Brynsk'

Assailed at once by the religions of the West and by the raskol sects, the orthodox Church was forced to defend herself. The raskols were about this time divided into communities with priests and communities without priests (*bezpopovchtchina*). The most fanatical raskolniks fled into the deep forests, and there founded hermitages and even centres of population, which escaped for a long while the knowledge of government. Tracked and driven to extremity, certain enthusiasts burned themselves in a sort of *auto da fé*. Many of these shepherds of the desert, like Daniel Vikoulof and the brothers Denissof, made themselves famous by polemical works. Peter wished to relax the systems of preceding *régimes*, and protected all peaceable subjects who did not interfere with politics. Passing though the deserts of the Vyga, he found there a colony of industrious raskolniks, ordered them to be left in peace, and begged them to pray for him. "God," he said, "has given the Tzar power over the nations, but Christ alone has power over the consciences of men." He contented himself with doubling the taxes, and imposing a peculiar dress on the raskolniks of Moscow. Being however, a true believer, he regarded the faith of the raskol as an error, and did not wish it to spread. Penalties were enforced against its propagators, and precautions taken with regard to their listeners. The proper attendance every Sunday at church and an Easter Communion became a matter of obligation.

He followed the same policy with regard to Western religions, allowed foreigners to have their churches in St. Petersburg, and himself attended the French church, where his chair is still preserved. The Nevski Prospect, bordered with dissenting churches, was the "prospect of tolerance." He protected the Capuchins established at Astrakhan, and even tried to live on good terms with the Jesuits; but as they continued to work at their propaganda, they were banished in 1689, then recalled, then again definitely expelled in 1710. " He endured the Capuchins," says Voltaire, " as being monks of no consequence, but regarded the Jesuits as dangerous political enemies." The friend of the Dutch and the English persecuted the foreign Protestants who insulted the orthodox faith by word or deed. A Russian woman, Nastasia Zima, having spread the principles of Luther, was conducted, with her husband and six other neophytes, before the terrible secret chamber, and was cruelly tortured.

ECONOMIC REFORMS: MANUFACTURES.

Peter the Great had toiled so hard to establish himself on the Baltic because he felt that the White Sea, frozen over for so many months in the year, was insufficient to secure to Russia uninterrupted communication with the West. When St. Petersburg was founded, he wished to suppress Arkhangel for the benefit of the new port, and forbade the merchants to carry their merchandise down the Dwina. This project met with the most lively opposition. Apraxine assured him that such a measure would be the ruin of Russian commerce. The Dutch traders and the Hanseatic towns represented that the money they had spent in establishing themselves at Arkhangel would be lost, that it would be necessary to build vessels for the Baltic on an entirely different model, that they were obliged to pay Sound dues, and that in case of a war the smallest merchant ships would there need a convoy. The Russians who were accustomed to go to Arkhangel showed great repugnance to the journey to St. Petersburg, across a wide space without forage, and where they would find no inns such as had been established for centuries on the route to the White Sea. It was necessary to make a complete revolution in the habits of Russian commerce, in the distribution of the centres of industry and of the depôts. The conductors of the caravan, in despair at the length of the voyage, often deserted, abandoning tre wagons, or pillaging the merchandise. Peter the Great yielded, leaving time to justify his preference for the new city. He authorized trade both by way of Arkhangel and St. Petersburg, contenting himself with raising by a fourth the tariff of customs of the former town. Above all, he resolved to connect the city of the Neva with the great river artery of Russia, the Volga. To this end he created the canal of the Ladoga, projected a communication of the White Sea with the Gulf of Finland, and hoped to unite the Black Sea with the Caspian by means of a canal between the Don and the Volga.

Peter negotiated treaties of commerce with many European States, stirred up the national agriculture, whose progress had been hindered by the slavery of the people, promulgated an edict which forced them to reap with scythes, instead of the old hooks, encouraged the cultivation of the vine and the mulberry in the regions of the south-east, ordered tobacco to be planted, introduced new kinds of cattle into the central provinces (such as that of Kholmogory), stimulated sheep-farming, which was necessary for wool factories, sent for Silesian shepherds, and made the Russians go to learn their trade in Silesia, and created besides the imperial stud. He took measures to preserve the forests, and sought for beds of combustible minerals. To counteract the indolence of such nobles as might have mines upon their lands, he declared that, in the case of their remaining unworked, strangers should have leave to work them, paying only a small premium to the proprietor. He decreed stripes and the penalty of death against any one who should dare to interfere with the mining labors and researches. Under him began the fortunes of the Demidofs, the great metallurgists, as in the reign of Ivan IV. the fortunes of the Strogonofs. He founded and encouraged his courtiers to found manufactures of chemical productions; of cloth, from the managers of which he purchased the materials which he wanted for the uniforms of the army; of sail-cloth, for which the navy would furnish a ready market. The French were specially skilled in making use of the Russian wool. The Russians owe them the first manufactories of tapestries; a Frenchman named Manvriou opened a stocking manufactory at Moscow. The Englishman Humphrey introduced an improvement in the fabrication of Russian leather; the Tzar required every town to send a certain number of shoemakers to take lessons in their art at Moscow, threatening them, if they continued to work in their old way, with confiscation and the galleys. The admiral Apraxine manufactured silk brocades. A mougik invented a lacquer superior to anything in Europe, except that of Venice. Thanks to the versatility of the national genius, economic progress would have immensely developed if the Tzar had been able to secure the Russian merchants against the cupidity of the great and the exactions of the officials, a danger already noted by Fletcher in the sixteenth century. Notwithstanding this drawback, **more than two hundred mills were opened in this reign.**

UTILITARIAN CHARACTER OF THE ESTABLISHMENTS FOR INSTRUCTION.

Peter the Great took great pains with the education of his people. He felt that the surest means of obtaining those who would help him and would continue his work was gradually to initiate the nation into his new ideas, and little by little to reconcile them to reform. He especially insisted on the education of the sons of nobles and priests, for the means of instructing the mass of the people had long been wanting. A certain number of elementary schools were, however, founded in all the provinces, and the pupils of the mathematical schools of St. Petersburg were sent there as masters. These schools of Peter's had all a practical character and a present utility. Classical studies were neglected, and he did not trouble himself to create supplementary establishments to the Greco-Latin academy at Moscow. In his fierce struggle with the forces of the past he hastened to throw Russia open to his natural auxiliaries, the ideas and sciences of the West. The schools he multiplied were special schools—a naval academy, a school of engineers, a school of book-keeping. The literature he encouraged was a literature of translation, which enabled a huge mass of European ideas to be introduced in the lump; or else a polemic literature, to plead the cause of reform before the opinion of Russians and foreigners. It was for this reason he had an enormous number of technical books translated, employing for the purpose the professors of the Greco-Latin academy, the brothers Likhoudi, who had retired to Novgorod, and even the members of the synod. They worked at Moscow, and many books were translated abroad, some at first into Tcheque, so that the Muscovites might more easily reproduce them in their own tongue. History, geography, jurisprudence, political economy, navigation, military sciences, agriculture, and languages, were soon represented in Russia by numerous books, translations from Western languages. Peter himself gave his brigade of writers advice which shows his practical sense, and even his instinctive literary taste. "You must," he said to Zotof, "beware of translating word for word without knowing the complete meaning of the text. You must read with care, become penetrated with the sense of your author, must be able to think his thoughts in Russian, and only after that try to reproduce them." He also recommended them to refrain from long dissertations and useless digressions, "with which the Germans fill their books to make them appear thicker, and which only serve to waste time and to disgust the reader." On the other hand, he forbade the suppression of some passages in Puffendorf, where Russian barbarism is denounced. His subjects must learn to blush for their rudeness before they could cure themselves of it. He caused books to be printed in Holland, in which he attempted to teach the Europeans what Russia was, and to appreciate her reforms; whilst he published others in Russia to make his subjects acquainted with Europe. He had recourse to Saint Dmitri, Feofane, and Feofilakt, who by their polemical writings combated superstitions and sects hostile to the State. Other writers turned into ridicule on the stage, in what were called operettas, all the enemies of reform, fanatical raskolniks, the deacon who wept because his son was torn from him and sent to school, the *employés* who fished in troubled waters, the partisans of the ancient customs, who regretted the "good old times," when German garments were unknown, and men wore long beards. Natalia, Peter's sister, associated herself in his work, by composing Russian plays. The merchant Passochkof wrote his book on 'Poverty and Riches,' a sort of *domostroï*, where all the changes in manners since the time of the priest Silvester can be followed. Passochkof dared to lift his voice in favor of the oppressed peasant, to demand the establishment of a tribunal before which all Russian subjects should be equal, a regular organization of justice and administration, which should protect the people against those who rob in public (brigands and thieves) and those who steal in secret (*employés* and officials). He expected everything of Peter. " Unhappily," he says," our great monarch is almost alone, with ten others, in pulling upwards, while millions of individuals pull downwards. How then can we hope for a good result ? "

Peter needed means of rapid publication. Now Russian printing had made little progress since the 16th century; it had tried specially to imitate the ancient Slavonic manuscripts, and its method was extremely slow. Peter abandoned the Slavonic alphabet, no longer in use except for the Church books; he was the creator of the Russian alphabet properly so called, the civil alphabet. He improved the machines and the types, imported Dutch printers, and made printing an instrument of a powerful and rapid propaganda. In his reign there were two printing presses instead of one at Moscow, four at St. Petersburg, and others at Tchernigof, Novgorod the Great, and Novgorod-Severoki. He founded the Gazette of St. Petersburg, the first public newspaper in Russia.

A prince who had studied medicine and surgery in the West, who sometimes practised on his courtiers, took out a tooth or lanced an abscess, could not neglect an art so necessary to his vast empire, where the mortality of infants was a bar to the increase of population. He entrusted to Doctor Bidloo the management of the hospitals, and the instruction of fifty young men. In 1718 he put forth an edict enjoining the collection of valuable minerals, of extraordinary bones that might be found in the fields, of antique inscriptions on stone or metal, or any monstrosities of birth occurring among men or animals. "There are certain to be some of these births," says the ordinance, "but ignorant people make mysteries of them, believing that the birth of these monsters is due to some diabolic influence. This is impossible, for it is God and not the devil who is the creator of all things." Peter had a taste for geography: in 1719 he fitted out an expedition to Kamscnatka, to solve the question asked by Leibnitz, Is Asia united to America? In 1720 he opened a school of cartography. The science of history also has deep obligations to him: in 1722 he ordered a collection to be made, in the archives of the monasteries, of the chronicles and letters of the Tzars, and had copies taken of them. Polykarpof wrote a History of Russia from the 16th century, for which the Tzar gave him a reward of 200 roubles. Finally, in 1724, Peter the Great, already correspondent of the Academy of Sciences in Paris, founded that of St. Petersburg, and assigned it a revenue of 25,000 roubles on the revenues of the customs of Narva, Dorpat, and Pernau, desiring it above all to devote itself to translations, and to teach its pupils practical sciences and languages. The utilitarian character of Peter's creations is found even in his Academy. As it was not possible at that time to count on the Russians to form a learned body, the first academicians were necessarily foreigners. Germany furnished Wolff and Hermann; France, Bernouilli and De l'Isle. Thus a country which as yet had neither secondary schools nor universities was given an academy.

FOUNDATION OF ST. PETERSBURG (1703).

St. Petersburg had just been founded. Its situation, as Goethe remarks, "recalls that of Amsterdam, or of Venice, the Italian Amsterdam." The wide and majestic Neva, which issues from the great lakes of the north, there divides into four arms, the great and little Neva, and the great and little Nevka. If we add to these her numerous affluents, the Fontanka, the Okhta, and the two Tchernaïas, we shall at present find about fourteen watercourses, a lake, eight canals, and nineteen islands.

It is the aquatic city *par excellence*, and is exposed to terrible inundations when the prodigious reservoirs of the Ladoga and Onega overflow. No building is ever made there without first strengthening the foundation by driving in innumerable piles of wood. When Peter the Great first cast his eyes over the country, after the capture of Nienschantz, there were only dark forests, vast marshes, dreary wastes, where, according to the poet, "a Tchoud fisherman, a sorrowful son of his stepmother Nature, might occasionally be seen alone on the marshy shore, casting his worn-out line into these nameless waters." The Finnish names then borne by the islands, on which palaces were afterwards to rise, are very significant; there were the Isle of Brushwood, the Isle of Birches, the Isle of Goats, the Isle of Hares, the Isle of Buffaloes, Isle Michael (a name for the bear), and the Wild Isle. In Eniçary, or "the Isle of Hares," Peter built in 1703 the new fortress (Saint Peter and Saint Paul). There he assembled regular soldiers, Cossacks, Tatars, Kalmucks, Ingrian or Carelian natives, and peasants of the interior, in all more than 40,000 men. No tools were provided for their first labors; the mougik dug the soil with sticks or his nails, and carried the earth in his caftan. He had to sleep in the open air among the marshes; he often lacked food, and the workmen died by thousands. Afterwards the service was made more regular. Peter installed himself in the celebrated little wooden house on the right bank, watching the building, sometimes piloting with his own hand the first Dutch ships which ventured into these waters, sometimes giving chase to Swedish vessels, which came to insult the infant capital. On the Isle of Buffaloes, on the northern bank of the Neva, afterwards the Vassili-Ostrof, numerous edifices rose; the southern bank, which became the real site of the town, was at that time neglected. It only contained the Admiralty, to which Anne Ivanovna added a spire; the church of Saint Isaac, then built of wood, now of marble and bronze; that of Saint Alexander Nevski, where Peter the Great deposited the remains of the first conqueror of the Swedes; the house of Apraxine, where Elizabeth built the Winter Palace, the already splendid *hôtels* of the Millionaïa, and where the Nevski Prospect, the most magnificent boulevard in Europe, was to run. The city was built by dint of edicts. Finns, Esthonians, Tatars, Kalmucks, Swedish prisoners, and merchants of Novgorod were transplanted thither; and in 1707 they were aided by 30,000 day laborers from the country, To attract all the masons of the empire, it was forbidden on pain of exile and confiscation to construct stone houses anywhere but at St. Petersburg. Every proprietor owning five hundred peasants was obliged to raise a stone house of two stories; those who were poor clubbed together to build one among themselves. Every boat that wanted to enter had to bring a certain number of white stones, for stone was lacking in these wastes. Forage was also wanting, and to save forage Peter proscribed the use of carriages, and encouraged navigation by the river and canals; every inhabitant must have his boat, the court could only be approached by water.

In 1706 Peter wrote to Menchikof that all was going on wonderfully, and that "he seemed here in paradise." He decorated the church of the fortress with carvings in ivory, the work of his own hands; hung it with flags conquered from the Swedes; consecrated there his little boat, "ancestor of the Russian fleet"; and, breaking through the tradition which insisted on the princes being buried at Saint Michael at Moscow, chose out at Saint Peter and Saint Paul his own tomb and that of his successors. "Before the new capital," says Pouchkine, "Moscow bowed her head, as an imperial widow bows before a young Tzarina."

St. Petersburg had another enemy besides the Swedes—the inundations. The soil was not yet raised by the incessant heaping up of materials; the granite quays did not yet confine the formidable river. In 1705 nearly the whole town was flooded; in 1721 all the streets were navigable, and Peter was nearly drowned in the Nevski Prospect. The enemies of reform, exasperated by the desertion of Moscow, rejoiced over these disasters, and predicted that this German town, built by foreign hands and soiled by the presence of heretic temples, would disappear beneath the floods. One day the place of this cursed city should be sought in vain. Even at the end of the reign of Peter, it was the general opinion that after his death the court and the nobility would return to Moscow, and that the city and the fleet created by the Tzar would be abandoned. They were mistaken; the town that he had flung like a forlorn hope on the newly-conquered soil remained the seat of the empire. Russia is almost the only State that has built her capital on her very frontiers. St. Petersburg was not only to be the "window" open to the West, but it was to be also the centre of the Russian regeneration. More freely, more completely than at Moscow the Holy, where everything recalled the traditions and recollections of the past, Peter could enthrone at St. Petersburg the sentiments of toleration for the Protestant and Catholic religions, and sympathy for strangers, who were always detested at Moscow. He could more easily persuade the nobles to adopt **German** fashions, to speak Western languages, to cultivate sciences and useful arts, to discard with the national caftan the old Russian prejudices. At Moscow, the City of the Tzars, foreigners were confined in the German *slobode;* at St. Petersburg, the City of the Emperors, the Russian and the stranger would meet and mingle.

CHAPTER III.

PETER THE GREAT: LAST YEARS (1709-1725).

War with Turkey: treaty of the Pruth (1711)—Journey to Paris (1717)—Peace of Nystad (1721)—Conquests on the Caspian—Family affairs; Eudoxia; trial of Alexis (1718); Catherine.

WAR WITH TURKEY: TREATY OF THE PRUTH (1711).

CHARLES XII., who had allowed himself to be detained in Poland during the five years that followed Narva, was to languish at Bender during five other years that followed Pultowa (1709-13). Peter turned this new delay to advantage with as much energy as the former. Charles's Polish king Leszczinski was obliged to retire into Pomerania, and Augustus of Saxony reentered Warsaw. In the north Peter completed the conquest of Livonia and Esthonia, took a slice out of Finland, thus widening the opening he was trying to secure on the Baltic, and captured Riga, Dünamunde, Pernau, Revel, Viborg, and Kixholm (1710). He could not conquer Courland, a subject state of Poland, but he paved the way for its union with Russia by marrying the Duke to Anne Ivanovna, daughter of his brother Ivan.

The agents of Sweden and of Stanislas, Désaleurs, ambassador of France, and the Khan of the Tatars, all urged the Divan to go to war. Achmet III. longed to recapture Azof. Peter learned that his ambassador had been confined in the Seven Towers, and that Baltagi-Mahomet was assembling an immense army in the plains of Adrianople. The Tzar received this declaration of war almost with joy; the whole of Russia trembled with gladness at the thought of treading in the steps of her ancient princes, of marching to the "Sovereign City" (Tzargrad), of freeing the Christians of the East, of exterminating the old enemies of the Slav race, and of eclipsing the glory of Ivan the Terrible. The Eastern world was shaken to its depths: Kantemir, Hospodar of Moldavia, Brancovane, Hospodar of Wallachia, Servians, Montenegrins, and Greeks, all ardently desired a liberator. Carried away by his enthusiasm, Peter committed, in 1711, the same fault as Charles XII. in 1709. He counted on the doubtful help that he might find in these barbarous and thinly-peopled countries, and did not wait for the more effective contingent of 30,000 men promised him by Augustus. He crossed the Dniester, found Moldavia almost destitute of inhabitants, devastated by locusts, without a commissariat, while the Hospodars were undecided and powerless as Mazeppa. Kantemir, deserted by most of his boyards, appeared near'y alone in the Russian camp. Brancovane, Hospodar of Wallachia, declared for the Sultan. Peter found himself on the banks of the Pruth, with 38,000 weary and starving soldiers, surrounded by 200,000 Turks or Tatars. The bravery displayed by this handful of men in a fight in which 7000 Janissaries perished, made the Grand Vizier pause and reflect. He heard that Renne, Peter's l utenant, had taken Braïlof and menaced the bridges thrown across the Danube.

Notwithstanding this success, the greatest consternation re gned in the Russian camp, which was encu b ied with wounded men and women. It was Catherine, the future empress, who r vived their ourage. She collected all the money and jewels that could b ound in the camp as a present for the Grand Vizier, and e.su ded the Tzar t end envoys to the Turkish entrenchments. These envoys had orders to make any sacrifice demanded by the Turk to restore Azof, Livonia, even Esthonia and Carelia, but to hold fast Ingri, the loss f which would involve that of the new capital, and rather sacrifice even Pskof. Peter was ready to yield n the Polish question. If the Turks demanded that they shoul ' surrender at discretion, the Russians "were prepared to force a passage, and to fight to the last man." The Vizier's demands were smaller than were anticipated: he contented himse f with the restitution of Azof, the destruction of the fortresses erected on the Turkish territory, and the promise that Charles XII. should be left in peace when he returned to his own kingdom. Such was the celebrated Treaty of the Pruth or Falksen, wh ch caused un versal jo in the Russian army, but which always left a trace of sadness in Peter the Great. To have come as deliverer of the Christian world and to be forced to capitulate, to surrender Azof, h's first conquest, to annihilate his fleet on the Black Sea, which had cost him so many efforts! He took his revenge on another side!

JOURNEY TO PAR (.717)—PEACE OF NYSTAD (1721)—CONQUE TS ON THE CASPIAN.

In 17·2 and 1713, whil ance was passing through a supreme crisis in the war of the Spanis Succession, the Russians, with their Danish and Saxon allies, were expelling the Swedes from Pomerania. In May 1713 a fleet of 200 Russian ships, commanded by Apraxine, with Peter for vice-admiral, left the Neva, took Helsingfors, capital of Finland, and Abo, the library of which was sent to St. Petersburg, and disembarked troops who defeated the Swedes at Tammersfors. The following year the Russians again defeated the enemy's fleet at Hankül, and occupied the isles of Aland. Even Stockholm was threatened, the Russians not being more than fifteen miles from the Swedish capital. The capture of Nyslott completed the conquest of Finland, and Charles XII., who hastened from Bender, could save neither Stralsund nor Wismar. After long hesitation, the King of Prussia had joined his enemies, and the last Swedish fortresses in Pomerania had fallen. The Elector of Hanover, King of England, also turned against him, and took Werden, a possession of Charles on the Weser. With Sweden deprived of her provinces in the German empire, the results of the Treaty of Westphalia were imperilled. The war in the North, formerly localized in the Eastern Baltic, became a European war, and threatened the equilibrium of the Continent. Russian armies, for the first time, poured into Northern Germany. Peter, who had married one of his nieces to the Duke of Courland, found a husband for the other, Catherine Ivanovna, in the Duke of Mecklenburg, and lent his support to help this prince to reduce his nobility to obedience. North Germany seemed ready to fall under the Muscovite yoke, as in the seventeenth century she had passed under the Swedish rule. The allies of the Tzar began to fear his ambition. The Mecklenburg nobles took their revenge by everywhere stirring up enemies against him. Bernsdorff induced George of Hanover to break off his alliance with the Tzar, and two other Mecklenburgers obtained the promise of the King of Denmark to close the gates of Wismar on Peter. Peter felt that he also must find support, and, as the question had now become European, must seek European allies. It was at this juncture that Baron Görtz undertook to reconcile him with Charles XII., whose courage was to be used to overthrow the King of England, and to replace the Stuart dynasty on the throne. Peter wished, moreover, to enter into relations with France. In 1711 he had sent Gregory Volkof to Louis XIV., to ask his mediation, but the Grand Monarque thought himself too deeply involved with Sweden, though Charles had but scantily fulfilled his own obligations. After the death of Louis XIV. the Duke of Orleans became Regent. Peter decided to visit Versailles, and Zotof, his agent at the Court of France, assured him of the good-will of the Duke. The Tzar had therefore grounds to hope for the conclusion of a close alliance with a powerful kingdom, and perhaps to look forward to the marriage of his daughter Elizabeth with the young King Louis XV. The circumstances under which Peter made his second journey to the West were all unlike those of his former tour. He was no longer the young prince, only half civilized, master of a nearly unknown State in Eastern Europe, but the conqueror of Pultowa and of Hankül, the master of the Baltic and Northern Germany, the reformer of a numerous people, the founder of a new capital and a new empire, the head of a great European nation.

"This monarch," says Saint Simon, " astonished Paris by his extreme curiosity on all points of government, commerce, education, and police,—a curiosity which disdained nothing, but probed everything. All his conduct displayed the breadth of his views and the acuteness of his reasoning. His manner was at once the most dignified, the proudest, the most sustained, and at the same time the least embarrassing. He had the sort of familiarity that springs from boundless liberty, but he was not exempt from a trace of the old-world rudeness of his country, which made him abrupt and even uncourteous, and with nothing certain about his wishes but the fact that not one of them was to be contradicted. His habits at meals were rough; the revelry that followed was even more barbaric. He seldom tried to hide in his establishment the freedom and the self-will of a king. The wish to be at his ease, dislike of being made a spectacle, the habit of liberty for which he was accountable to none, made him prefer hired carriages, even *fiacres*. He would jump into the first empty carriage he met with, without caring to whom it belonged, and have himself driven about the town or beyond the walls. He was a very tall man, well made, though rather thin, his face somewhat round, with a wide forehead, beautiful eyebrows, a short nose, thick at the end; his lips were rather thick, his skin brown and ruddy. He had splendid eyes, large, black, piercing, and well opened; his expression was dignified and gracious when he liked, but often wild and stern, and his eyes, and indeed his whole face, were distorted by an occasional twitch that was very unpleasant. It lasted only a moment, and gave him a wandering and terrible look, then he was himself again. His air expressed intellect, thoughtfulness, and greatness, and had a certain grace about it. He wore a linen collar, a round peruke, brown and unpowdered, which did not reach his shoulders; a brown *juste-au-corps*, with gold buttons, a vest, breeches, stockings, and neither gloves nor cuffs; the star of his order on his coat, and the ribbon underneath it; his coat was often unbuttoned, his hat lay on the table and never on his head, even out of doors. In this simplicity, however shabby might be his carriage or scanty his suit, his natural air of greatness could not be mistaken."

Peter visited both the Regent and the King, took Louis XV. in his arms, to the great consternation of the courtiers, and wrote to his wife Catherine: "The little king is scarcely taller than our dwarf Loaki; his face and figure are distinguished and he is tolerably intelligent for his age." The Tzar, despised all that was merely fashionable and unproductive luxury, and occupied himself entirely with government, commerce, science, and military affairs. He neglected to call on the princes of the blood, but entered the shops of coach-builders and goldsmiths. He tasted the soup of the Invalides, drank their health, struck them on the shoulder, and treated them as comrades. The Gobelins, the Observatory, the King's garden, the collection of plans in relief of fortified places, the works of the Pont Tournant, and the machine at Marly, captivated his attention. A medal was struck for him at the Mint with his own effigy and the motto "*Vires acquirit eundo*." He was present at a meeting of the Academy of Sciences, which elected him a member, and corrected with his own hand a map of his dominions which was shown to him. He embraced a bust of Richelieu at the Sorbonne, and wished to see Madame de Maintenon as a relic of the great reign.

Things did not run quite as smoothly as he wished in the matter which had chiefly brought him to France. He sought an ally against George I.; but the English alliance was then the corner-stone of the French foreign policy. "The Tzar," says Saint Simon, "had an intense desire to unite himself with France. Nothing could have been better for our commerce, or for our position with regard to Germany, the North, and the whole of Europe. Peter held England in check by her fears for her commerce, and King George by his fears for his German territories. He made Holland treat him with respect, and kept the Emperor in great order. . . . No one can deny that he made a grand figure both in Europe and Asia, and that France would have gained enormously by an alliance with him. . . . We repented long ago of our fatal infatuation for England, and our silly contempt for Russia."

Notwithstanding the mad confidence of the Regent in the Abbé Dubois, the plenipotentiaries of Peter the Great concluded at Amsterdam, after the return of the Tzar to his dominions, a treaty of commerce with France (1717). The two Powers, now joined by Prussia, declared that they specially united to guarantee the Treaty of Utrecht, and the eventual peace of the

North; they laid down the basis of a defensive alliance, the ways and means hereafter to be considered. Peter afterwards found himself slightly compromised in the plans of Görtz and Alberoni, which caused a coolness between them. A regular communication between the two countries was, however, inaugurated. First Kourakine and then Dolgorouki were nominated ambassadors at Paris, while Campredon represented France at St Petersburg. More than once negotiations were set on foot for Elizabeth's marriage, sometimes with Louis XV., sometimes with the Duke of Bourbon, or some other French prince. France lent her good offices to Russia, in the matter of peace with Sweden.

Görtz was on the point of reconciling Peter with Charles, and a congress had already opened in the isles of Aland, between Bruce and Ostermann on the one hand and Görtz and Gyllenburg on the other, when the King of Sweden was killed in Norway (1718). An aristocratic reaction broke out at Stockholm: Charles Frederic of Holstein-Gottorp, nephew of Charles XII., was excluded from the throne, and the crown was offered to the youngest sister of the late king, Ulrica-Eleonora, wife of Frederic of Hesse-Cassel, who was regarded as more pliable. An aristocratic constitution was established which deprived the crown of nearly all its prerogatives, and left Sweden a prey to fifty-three years of anarchy and insignificance. Authority passed into the hands of a diet composed of the deputies of the four orders (nobles, clergy, citizens, and peasants), but in which the nobles had a decided majority. Görtz was recalled to Stockholm and condemned to death, and his policy was abandoned. The Diet revived, on the contrary, the alliance with Hanover, and resolved to continue the war with Russia, with the probable support of the English fleet. Peter accepted the challenge, and waged with his enemies a war of extermination. In 1719 his army landed on the shores of Sweden itself, and burned two towns and a hundred and twenty-nine villages. Apraxine extended his ravages to within seven miles of Stockholm. In 1720 the devastation recommenced, in the very presence of the English fleet, which did not dare to pursue the Russians into the recesses of the Swedish coast. In 1721 the Diet decided to treat. Peter kept Livonia, Esthonia, Ingria, part of Finland, and Carelia. Such was the Peace of Nystad, which avenged Ivan the Terrible and Alexis Mikhaïlovitch.

When the Tzar felt the weight of this twenty-two years' war lifted from his shoulders, he returned to St. Petersburg to announce the happy news of peace to his people, and, mounted on a platform, he drank to the health of his subjects. A whole week was given up to fêtes and masquerades. Peter, in his joy, burned 12,000 roubles' worth of powder, put on a fancy dress, danced on the table, and "sang songs." The Senate united with the Holy Synod in a great council, decreed to the Tzar the title of "Great, Father of his Country, and of Emperor of all the Russias." It was thus that the son of Alexis became, according to the popular songs, "the first emperor of the country." Feofane Prokopovitch preached one of his most beautiful sermons on this occasion.

Peter's great desire was to make Russia the centre of communication between Asia and Europe. He had conquered the shores of the Baltic, but it was necessary that he should find an equivalent for Azof and throw open at least one of the seas of the East. Persia, mistress of the Caspian, was then a prey to anarchy under a weak prince, who was attacked by rebels on all sides. Russian merchants had been robbed, and Peter took advantage of this pretext for war to seize Derbend, and himself commanded the expedition which descended the Volga, from Nijni to Astrakhan (1722). The operations still continued after his departure: the Russians took Bakou, interfered in the internal affairs of Persia, promised help to the Shah against his enemies, and occupied Daghestan, Ghilan, and Mazanderan, with Recht and Asterabad.

FAMILY AFFAIRS : EUDOXIA ; TRIAL OF ALEXIS (1718) ; CATHERINE.

The last years of Peter the Great were saddened by terrible domestic tragedies. He had been married, at the age of seventeen, to Eudoxia Lapoukhine, the daughter of a very conservative family. As she shared the views of her relations, Peter soon began to hate her. After the capture of Azof he signified that he did not wish on his return to find her at the palace, and she was obliged to retire to the Pokrovski monastery at Souzdal. Soon afterwards he obtained a divorce, in order to marry Catherine. Banished and divorced, Eudoxia still retained her power. In the eyes of the people, and of a large part of the clergy, she remained the Tzar's only lawful wife; she was the mother of the Tzarévitch Alexis, over whose mind and character she had, during the frequent absences of the Tzar, exercised the most fatal influence. After the dismissal of Eudoxia, Peter paid more attention to the education of his heir, and gave him foreign masters. It was too late: Alexis was already a young man. Narrow-minded, indolent, lazy, feeble, and obstinate, the son of the reformer was a pure Lapoukhine. Whilst Peter was exposing himself on battle-fields in Finland, Lithuania, and the Ukraine, Alexis was surrounded by monks, devotees, and visionaries; the way to his heart lay in the abuse of the reforms and the new laws. Against his own wishes he was forced to marry Charlotte of Brunswick at Torgau, but consoled himself with the idea that he would one day have the heads of the authors of the marriage. When his confidant tried to make him fear that he would only alienate the nobles, "I spit upon them," he replied· "the people are on my side. When my father dies, I shall have only to say a word in the ear of the archbishops, who will tell their priests, who will whisper it to their parishioners, and I shall be made Tzar, even were it in spite of myself." During his travels in Germany he would learn nothing, he wounded his hand that he might not be obliged to draw, and alleged his feeble health as an excuse for living in idleness. Peter tried to bring him to reason. " Disquiet for the future destroys the joy caused by my present successes. I see that you despise all that can make you worthy to reign after me. What you term incapacity I call rebellion, for you cannot excuse yourself on the ground of the feebleness of your mind and the weakness of your health. We have only struggled from obscurity through the toils of war, which has taught other nations to know and respect us, and yet you will not even hear of military exercises. If you do not alter your conduct, know that I shall deprive you of my succession. I have not spared, and I shall not spare, my own life for my country and my people: do you think that I shall spare yours? I would rather have a stranger, who was worthy, for my heir, than a good-for-nothing member of my own family." Alexis still persisted that he had neither health nor memory, and would prefer becoming a monk. His confidant, Kikine, advised him to dissemble, and to allow himself to be shut up in a convent : " You can come out of it," he said; " they do not nail the *khlobouque* on your head." During his father's travels in the West, the Tzarévitch fled to Germany with his mistress, the serf Euphrosyne. He went to the court of Vienna, which promised to provide him with a secret and secure asylum. It was in this manner that he was successively confined in the castle of Ehrenberg, in the Tyrol, and of Sant' Elmo, near Naples. His father's agents, who had instantly started in pursuit, ended by tracing him, and Tolstoï obtained an interview with Alexis, who was assured of pardon, and persuaded to return to Moscow. The Tzar immediately assembled the three orders at the Kremlin, arraigned the prisoner before it, and obliged him to sign a formal renunciation of the crown. Alexis had also to denounce his accomplices, and in the course of the interrogation some terrible disclosures were made to Peter. His son was the centre of a permanent conspiracy against his reforms, the hope of all who after his death would seek to destroy his work. If Alexis had consented to enter the cloister, it was in the expectation of one day leaving it, his renunciation of the throne could not have been sincere: he did not belong to himself, he belonged to the enemies of his father, who would understand how to absolve him from his vows. Peter learnt, among other things, that Alexis had solicited at Vienna the armed protection of the Emperor, that he had intrigued with Sweden, and that, on the occasion of a sedition in the Russian army of Mecklenburg, he entered into relations with the leaders, and only awaited a letter to hasten to the camp. He had longed for the death of his father, and his confessor, Varlaam, had said, " We all desire it." The threads of the plot between the palace of the Tzarévitch and the convent of the divorced Tzarina were soon grasped. Eudoxia was treated, not as a nun, but as a Tzarina; she had her court of malcontents, wore a secular costume, was mentioned in the prayers like a sovereign. Dositheus, Archbishop of Rostof, had predicted to her the approaching death of the Tzar, and to hasten it the Archimandrite Peter made hundreds of prostrations before the holy images. A certain Glebof, who had established a correspondence in cypher with the Tzarina, avowed he was her lover, and that he was to marry her after the death of the Tzar. Her relations, her brother Abraham Lapoukhine, among others, were concerned in these intrigues and hopes. Peter crushed with cruel penalties this nest of conspirators. Glebof was impaled, Dositheus broken on the wheel, Lapoukhine tortured and beheaded, thirty people put to death or exiled, Eudoxia whipped and confined in New Ladoga. The affair of the Tzarévitch had changed its character after all these revelations; there could now be no question of clemency. Peter had no longer to deal with a lazy and disobedient son, but with a traitor who had become the chief of his enemies within and the ally of those without, and who had sought foreign aid. Peter had to choose between his reforms, for Alexis had openly promised to abandon St. Petersburg, the navy, the Swedish conquests, and to return to Moscow. There was no hope now of putting him in a condition where he would be harmless after the death of his father. Alexis knew they could not " nail the *khlobouque* on his head," and the seclusion of a convent had not prevented Eudoxia from indulging in secular hopes. Henceforth Alexis only found in his father an inexorable judge. Twice he suffered the knout; and a tribunal composed of the highest officials of the State condemned him to death. The difficulty seemed to lie in the execution of the sentence, but two days after the sentence was passed it became known that he had ceased to live. Divers rumors as to the manner of his death were circulated in the Memoirs of the time : some say it was caused by a sudden apoplexy, or a disarrangement of his entrails, arising from deep emotion ; some that he was beheaded with an axe, struck down with a club, suffocated under cushions, strangled with his cravat ; some reports put him to death by poison, others that his veins were opened. All that is certain is, that on the morning of the fatal day the Tzar compelled his son to appear before a commission of nine of the greatest men of the State. About what then took place these nine men were forever silent ; but it seems now to have been ascertained that in order to wring fresh confessions from the Tzarévitch the knout was again applied to him, and that he died from the consequences of the torture.

Peter had already another family. In 1702, at the sack of Marienburg, the Russians had made prisoner a young girl, about whose condition, origin, and nationality original authorities differ. It seems most probable that she was a Livonian, one of a family of serfs called Skavronski ; that she was a servant at the house of the pastor Glück, and that she had been betrothed to a Swedish dragoon. It was thus that in obscurity and dishonor her imperial destiny began. The captive passed from hand to hand, and was successively mistress of Cheremetief and of Menchikof, who ceded her to Peter the Great. Though ignorant and completely illiterate, she fascinated the Tzar by the vivacity of her mind, the correctness of her judgment, and something free and adventurous about her which contrasted with the manners of the Russian *terem*, and marked out this Lutheran slave as the future Empress of Russia. Their marriage, secretly contracted, received a final consecration under the fire of the Ottoman batteries on the Pruth. In memory of the services then rendered by Catharine to the Tzar and to the country, Peter founded the Order " for love and fidelity," and solemnly married her in 1712. He did not, however, dare to take her with him in his journey to France. The contrast would have been too obvious at Versailles between the ladies of the proud French nobility and this foreign slave ; between the cultivated wit of a Sévigné and a Deffand and this empress who could not sign her name ; between the refinements of the French fine ladies and the awkward wench described by the Margravine of Baireuth.

" The Tzarina." says the German princess, " was small and clumsily made, very much tanned, and without either grace or an air of distinction. You had only to see her to know that she was low-born. From her usual costume you would have taken her for a German comedian. Her dress had been bought at a second-hand shop; it was very old-fashioned, and covered with silver and dirt. She had a dozen orders, and as many portraits of saints or reliquaries, fastened all down her dress, in such a way that when she walked you would have thought by the jingling that a mule was passing." In 1721 Peter promulgated the celebrated edict which recognized the right of the Russian sovereign to nominate his successor, thus derogating from the hereditary principle which seems the very essence of the monarchy. Peter invoked the precedent of Ivan the Great, and the "Absalomian revolt" of Alexis. To justify this measure of the Tzar, Feofane Prokopovitch wrote his book, called 'Justice founded on the Will of the Sovereign, (*Pravda voli monarchci*). By Catharine Peter had had two sons, Peter and Paul, who died when children, and two daughters—Anne, married to the Duke of Holstein, and Elizabeth, who became Tzarina. Besides these, Alexis had left a son by Charlotte of Brunswick, afterwards Peter II., who was then named last in the public prayers. In 1723 Peter the Great published a manifesto, recalling the services Catharine had rendered, and solemnly crowned her Empress. This was the culmination of her strange destiny. Soon it began to change; the Emperor thought he had discovered proofs of her infidelity, and spoke of repudiating her. Anyhow, he had not yet exercised the right of naming his successor, claimed two years before. His health was broken by his toils and his excesses, and he no longer took any care of himself. One day he flung himself into icy water up to his waist to save a boat in distress, felt an attack of illness coming on, caught cold again in the "benediction of the waters," and died without being able either to speak or write his last wishes. He was then only fifty-three years of age.

He was above all a man of war, marked as such by his tall figure, his robust limbs, his nervous and sanguine temperament, and his arm as strong as a blacksmith's. His life was a struggle with the forces of the past, with the ignorant nobles, with the fanatical clergy, with the people who plumed themselves on their barbarism and national isolation, with the Cossack and Strelitz, representatives of the old army, and with the raskol, representative of the old superstition. This combat, which shook Russia and the world, he found repeated in his own family. It began with his sister Sophie, and continued with his wife Eudoxia and his son Alexis. Entirely given up to his terrible task, Peter all his life disdained pomp, luxury, and every kind of display. The first Emperor of Russia, the founder of St. Petersburg, forgot to build himself a palace; his favorite residence of

Peterhof is like the villa of a well-to-do citizen of Saardam. His table was frugal, and what he sought in his orgies of beer or brandy was a stimulant or a distraction. The people have preserved his memory in their songs or popular traditions; they delight in repeating, "he worked harder than a *bourlak*." This well-filled life was like a fever of perpetual activity, in which Peter, with Russia, panted and exhausted himself. Is it wonderful that he roughly hurled all obstacles out of his way? His movement was prompt and his hand heavy; the staff of Ivan IV. seems to have passed into his grasp. We have seen him strike with his cane the greatest lords, Prince Menchikof among the number. He bent to his will men, things, nature, and time; he realized his end by despotic blows. For a long while yet Russian and foreign historians will either hesitate to pass a final judgment on him, or will advance contradictory opinions.

CHAPTER IV.

THE WIDOW AND GRANDSON OF PETER THE GREAT: CATHERINE I. (1725–1727) AND PETER II. (1727–1730).

The work of Peter the Great continued by Catherine—Menchikof and the Dolgorouki—Maurice de Saxe in Courland.

THE WORK OF PETER THE GREAT CONTINUED BY CATHERINE.

At the death of Peter the Great the nation was divided into two parties: one supported his grandson, Peter Alexiévitch (then twelve years old), the other wished to proclaim Catherine the Livonian. The Galitsynes, the Dolgoroukis, Repnine, and all Old Russia desired to place the crown on the head of Peter Alexiévitch; but those who owed their elevation to Peter I., those who were involved in the trial of his son,—Prince Menchikof, Admiral Apraxine, Boutourline (Colonel of the Guard), the Chancellor Golovkine, Jagoujinski (Procurator-General of the Senate), the German Ostermann, Tolstoï (who had induced Alexis to quit the Castle of Sant' Elmo), the Bishop Feofane (author of the *Pravda voli monarchéi*), and the members of the tribunal which had condemned the Tzarévitch—all felt their only hope of salvation lay in Catherine. They were the more capable and the more enlightened; they held the power actually in their hands—directed the administration and commanded the army. Their adversaries felt that they must be content with a compromise. Dmitri Galitsyne proposed to proclaim Peter II., but only under the guardianship of the Empress-widow. Tolstoï opposed this, on the ground that it was the most certain means of arming one party against the other, of giving birth to troubles, of offering hostile factions a pretext for raising the people against the regent. He proved that, in the absence of all testamentary disposition, Catherine had the best right to succeed Peter I. She had been solemnly crowned, and had received the oaths of her subjects; she was initiated into all the State secrets, and had learned from her husband how to govern. The officers and regiments of Guards loudly declared in favor of the heroine of the

Pruth. It was at last decided that she should reign alone, and absolute, by the same title as the dead Tzar. No doubt it was a novelty in Russia—a novelty even greater than the regency of Sophia. Catherine w , not only a woman, but a foreigner, a captive, a second wife, hardly considered as a wife at all. There was more than one rotest against a decision which excluded the grandson of Peter the Great from the throne, and many raskolniks suffered torture rather than take the oath of allegiance to a woman.

Menchikof, one of the early lovers of Catherine, found himself all-powerful. He was able to stop the trial for maladministration commenced against him by the late Tzar, and obtained the gift of Batourine, the ancient capital of Mazeppa, which was equivalent to the whole principality of the Ukraine. His despotic temper and his bad character made him hated by his companions. Discord broke out among the "eaglets" of Peter the Great. Jagoujinski went to weep publicly over the tomb of the Tzar. Tolstoï was afterwards sent to Siberia. Catherine succeeded, however, in bridling the ambition of her favorite, and refused to sacrifice her other councillors to him.

This *régime* was the continuation of that of Peter. It disappointed the pessimist predictions which announced the abandonment of St. Petersburg and the fleet, and the return to Moscow. Most of the schemes of the reforming Tzar were carried out. The Academy of Sciences was inaugurated in 1736; the publication of the *Gazette* was carefully watched over; the Order of Alexander Nevski was founded; Behring, the Danish captain, was placed at the head of the scientific expedition to Kamschatka; Chafirof, recalled from banishment, was ordered to write the History of Peter the Great: Anne Petrovna solemnly married the Duke of Holstein, to whom she had been betrothed by her father. On the other hand, the Senate and the Holy Synod lost their title of "directing," and affairs of State had to be conducted in the "Secret High Council," composed of Menchikof, of the Admiral Apraxine, of the Chancellor Golovkine, Tolstoï, Dmitri Galitsyne, and of the Vice-Chancellor Ostermann, which met under the presidency of the Empress.

On her death-bed, Catherine nominated Peter Alexiévitch, her husband's grandson, as her successor, and, in default of Peter, her two daughters Anne of Holstein and Elizabeth. During the minority of the young Emperor the regency was exercised by a council composed of the two *Tzarévni*, of the Duke of Holstein, of Menchikof, and of seven or eight of the principal dignitaries of the empire.

Menchikof had taken measures to keep his high appointment

under the new reign, and even to increase his power. He had obtained from Catherine the promise that she would consent to the young prince's betrothal to his own daughter, though she was the elder by two years. He assigned his own palace on the right bank of the river as the Emperor's residence, and surrounded him by men devoted to his own interests. He caused himself to be made Generalissimo, and signed his letters to his sovereign with the words, "Your father." He had the members of his own family inscribed in the almanac with those of the imperial house, and his daughter mentioned in the public prayers. He even planned to marry Natalia Alexiévna to his son at the same time that his daughter became the wife of the Emperor. Peter II. soon began to be impatient of the government of the Generalissimo. Menchikof had given him as tutor the Vice-Chancellor Ostermann, but the young prince detested study, and preferred to hunt with his favorite, Ivan Dolgorouki. The clever Ostermann took care to make Menchikof responsible for his appointment as tutor, and to excuse himself as best he could to the prince. One day the Emperor sent a present of nine thousand ducats to his sister Natalia. Menchikof had the insolence to take them from the princess, saying that "the Emperor was young, and did not yet know how to use money properly." This time Peter rebelled, and the prince appeased him with great difficulty. Another enemy of the Generalissimo, who managed playfully to undermine his popularity, was Elizabeth, the young aunt of Peter II., and the daughter of Peter the Great. She was then seventeen years old, bright, gay, and careless, with a pink-and-white complexion and blue eyes; and she laughed the intolerable guardian out of power. An illness of Menchikof, by keeping him away from court, paved the way for his fall. Peter II. accustomed himself to the idea of getting rid of him. When the prince recovered and began as usual to oppose his wishes, Peter quitted Menchikof's palace, caused the furniture belonging to the Crown to be removed from it and placed in the imperial palace, treated his *fiancée* with marked coldness, and finally commanded the Guards to take no orders but from their colonels. This was the prelude to a public disgrace. In September 1727 Menchikof was arrested, despoiled of all his dignities and decorations, and banished to his own lands.

The Dolgoroukis profited by the revolution they had prepared, but immediately committed the same fault as Menchikof, and surrounded Peter with the same officious attentions. Like Menchikof, they banished all who offended them (even Ostermann, to whom the Emperor began to be attached; and **the old Tzarina Eudoxia Lapoukhine, who had been recalled** from the prison in Ladoga.) Using as a pretext some insulting placards recalling the services of Menchikof, they exiled him to Berezof in Siberia, where he died in 1729. Unwarned by his example, they imposed on the prince a new bride—Catherine Dolgorouki, the sister of his favorite Ivan. Their administration then assumed the character of a reaction against the reforms of Peter the Great. Ostermann and all the faithful servants, foreign or Russian, of the "Giant Tzar," saw with sorrow the return of the court to Moscow, and its indifference to all European affairs. In order the better to keep their master to themselves, the Dolgoroukis flattered his tastes for frivolity and dissipation, and organized great hunting parties which lasted for whole weeks. Peter would have wearied of them in the end as he did of Menc.ikof. He had already replied to his aunt Elizabeth, who complained that she was left without money, "It is not my fault; they never execute my orders, but I shall find means of breaking my fetters." The crisis happened, but not as had been expected. In January 1730 the young Emperor caught cold at the ceremony of the benediction of the waters, and died suddenly of small-pox. He was seventeen years old.

The two reigns of Catherine and Peter II., which only lasted in all five years, were peaceful.

In 1726 Russia had concluded a treaty of alliance with the Court of Vienna, and found herself involved, in 1727, in the war of the quadruple alliance. Notwithstanding the efforts of Kourakine and of Campredon, the failure of the projected marriage of Louis XV. and Elizabeth had produced a coldness between France and Russia. The most curious episode in the foreign relations was the attempt of Maurice de Saxe, illegitimate son of the king Augustus, to get possession of the Duchy of Courland. The offer of his hand had been accepted by the Duchess Anne Ivanovna, now a widow; he had been elected at Mittau by the deputies of the nobility. Neglecting the protest of the Polish diet and the remonstrances of France and Russia, he raised troops with the money produced by the sale of the diamonds belonging to an abbess of Quedlimburg, and a French comedian, his mother Aurora von Königsmark, and his mistress Adrienne Lecouvreur, and began to put the duchy in a state of defence. He was disavowed by his father, and Cardinal Fleury did not dare to support him even indirectly. Menchikof, left more free since the death of Catherine I., was himself a candidate for the Duchy. He sent Lascy, at the head of 8000 men, to expel the Saxon adventurers; and the future victor of Fontenoy could only collect 247 men in the isle of Usmaüs, and was obliged, in his retreat, to swim across an arm of the sea. His election was annulled, his father publicly called him a *galopin*, and Courland once more fell back under Russian influence.

A treaty with Prussia was signed under Peter II., in virtue of which the two Powers engaged at the death of Augustus to support the candidate whom they might choose for Poland. The Emperor Charles VI. and the "sergeant-king" sounded Russia about an eventual dismemberment of the republic of Poland. This is the first time the question of partition was mooted.

In Asia, Jagoujinski concluded on the Boura a treaty of commerce with the Celestial Empire, in the name of Peter II. Every three years Russian caravans might go to Pekin and trade without paying dues. Russia might keep four priests at Pekin, and six young men to learn Chinese. Kiakhta, on the Russian territory, and Maimaitchine, on the Chinese territory, were the authorized depôts.

CHAPTER V.

THE TWO ANNES: REIGN OF ANNE IVANOVNA, AND REGENCY OF ANNE LEOPOLDOVNA (1730-1741).

Attempt at an aristocratic constitution (1730): the "Bironovchtchina"—Succession of Poland (1733-1735) and war with Turkey (1735-1739)—Ivan VI.—Regency of Biren and Anne—Revolution of 1741.

ATTEMPT AT AN ARISTOCRATIC CONSTITUTION (1730): THE "BIRONOVCHTCHINA."

THE untimely death of the last male heir of Peter I. had taken all the world by surprise. It was so sudden that no party had been formed to determine the succession. Peter had left two daughters, Elizabeth and Anne, Duchess of Holstein, who died in 1728, and was represented by her son, afterwards Peter III. The Tzar's brother, Ivan Alexiévitch V., had also left two daughters, Anne Ivanovna, Duchess of Courland, and Catherine Ivanovna, Duchess of Mecklenburg; the wishes of some even turned towards the late Emperor's grandmother, the Tzarina Lapoukhine. Alexis Dolgorouki, father of the friend of Peter II., had yet a bolder idea; he claimed the throne for his daughter Catherine, although she was not even Peter's wife, but only his *fiancée*, and had the audacity to boast of a "certain will" of the sovereign, instituting her his heir. This proposal naturally found little favor in the Secret High Council, and was rejected with contempt, even by a part of the house of Dolgorouki, whose chiefs did not relish the notion of being the subjects of their niece. Another step was decided on. In the absence of the prudent Ostermann, who summoned to his aid a pretended illness, and the fact of his being a foreigner, the Secret High Council was, with the addition of the marshals Dolgorouki and Galitsyne, almost entirely composed of the great Russian nobility. It found itself, as the principal organ of government, invested with the chief power, and master of the position. It resolved to profit by these circumstances to limit the supreme authority, to give to the Russian aristocracy a sort of constitutional charter, and to impose on the sovereign who might be elected a kind of *pacta conventa*, such as existed in the republic of Poland. Elizabeth and the Duchess of Holstein, being the nearest to the throne, would no doubt manifest the greatest reluctance to accept these conditions. Thus it was necessary to turn to another branch of the family of Romanof, to the line of Ivan, and offer the crown to a princess who, having no hopes of gaining the throne, would be ready to accede to all the Council wished. The Council then resolved to open negotiations with Anne Ivanovna, and to propose to her the following terms:—1. The High Council should always be composed of eight members to be renewed by co-option, and to be consulted by the Tzarina in all affairs of Government. 2. Without the consent of the Council she was to make neither peace nor war, to impose no taxes, to alienate no crown lands, to nominate to no post nor any rank above that of colonel. 3. She was to put to death no member of the nobility, nor confiscate the property of any noble, without a regular trial. 4. She was neither to marry nor to choose a successor without the consent of the Council. "And," adds the draft of the letter laid before her for signature, and containing the points indicated, "in case of my ceasing to fulfil my engagements, I shall forfeit the crown of Russia." This was the *si non non* of the Cortez of Aragon. If this constitution had been carried out, Russia would have become an oligarchic republic instead of an autocratic empire, a sort of *pospolite* where nothing would have remained of the work of the Ivans and Peter the Great. The High Council likewise proposed to fix the seat of government at Moscow.

This constitution, which assured to the Russian nobles the inviolability of their persons and property (the English *habeas corpus* and right of taxation), raised, however, a general outcry. What! impose on Russia the same anarchic institutions that the three Northern powers had maintained in Poland? All the guarantees, all the rights, all the authority were reserved to the members of the High Council. Instead of one Tzar they would have eight. And who were these eight? Golovkine and Ostermann excepted, they were all Galitsynes and Dolgoroukis— two Galitsynes and four Dolgoroukis; the empire was to be the property of the two families. If the monarchical instincts of the greater number, and the aristocratic jealousy of many others, were excited, the partisans of reform were troubled at finding in the supreme council only the members of the old *noblesse*, and the upholders of the ancient order of things. The discontent broke forth in murmurs and turmoils; the High Council was obliged to take severe measures against meetings—a singular inauguration of the reign of liberty, which proved how little sympathy the attempt of the nobles met with from the nation.

A few days later the High Council convoked the general assembly to listen to the letter in which Anne Ivanovna announced her acceptance of all the conditions. "There was no one present," says Archbishop Feofane, "who heard the letter who did not tremble in all his limbs. Even those who had hoped much from this reunion lowered their ears like poor asses: there was a 'hush' and a general murmur, but none dared to speak or cry out." The five hundred people present silently affixed their signatures. The new Empress made, however, her solemn entrance into Moscow. Vassili Loukitch and his party constituted themselves the guards of the Empress, surrounded her jealously, and saw that no enemy of the constitution came near her. The malcontents, with Feofane at their head, agitated the clergy and the people. They found means to pass some notes to the Empress, acquainting her with the situation, and imploring her to act energetically. Children or ladies-in-waiting served as go-betweens. On the 25th of February, 1731, the members of the Council were deliberating, when they were suddenly summoned before the Empress. They were much astonished to find an assembly composed of eight hundred persons, belonging to the senate, the clergy, the nobility, and to the different administrations, who laid before Anne a petition that she would examine the complaints addressed to the High Council about the new constitution. At the lower end of the hall the officers of the guard cried out in excitement, "We do not want them to lay down the law to the Empress. Let her be an autocrat like her predecessors!" Others offered "to lay at her feet the heads of her enemies." She calmed their agitation, and prorogued the sitting till the afternoon, when the deputies presented a formal request for the re-establishment of autocracy. The Empress was astonished, and exclaimed, "What! the conditions sent me at Mittau, were they not the will of the whole nation?" "No, no," they cried. "Then," she said, turning to Vassili Loukitch, "you have deceived me."

Such was the check received by the first liberal constitution that had ever been tried in Russia. "The table was prepared," said Prince Dmitri Galitsyne, "but the guests were not worthy. I know that I shall pay for the failure of this enterprise; so be it. I shall suffer for my country, I have not long to live, and those who cause me to weep will one day weep themselves." The Galitsynes and Dolgoroukis did indeed expiate this generous attempt, in which unhappily they had taken no thought of the time nor the country. Anne's vengeance was cunning, refined and gradual She began by banishing them to their property; then, seeing that no one protested, exiled them to Siberia. Finally, encouraged by the universal silence, she crowned her revenge. The marshals Dolgorouki and Galitsyne died in prison; Vassili Loukitch and two other Dolgoroukis were beheaded; Ivan, the former favorite, was broken on the wheel at Novgorod. With these sufferings is associated the touching and tragic history of Natalia Cheremetief, betrothed wife of Ivan Dolgorouki, who, having accepted his hand in the days of his prosperity, persisted in sharing his misfortunes.

Anne Ivanovna was then thirty-five years of age. In her youth she had lived in the dreary court of Mittau, a bride sought for her duchy, the political plaything of the four Northern courts, despised by Menchikof, and receiving orders and reproaches from Moscow. The bitterness of her regrets and her disappointments was painted in her severe countenance, and reflected in her soured and coldly cruel character. A head taller than the gentlemen of her court, with a hard and masculine beauty, and the deep voice of a man, she was imposing. and even terrible. The aristocratic attempt of 1730 had made her mistrust the Russians, and she felt that a project less exclusive and more clever than that of the High Council would perhaps have had a chance with the Russian nation. By precaution, and from taste, she surrounded herself with Germans, Biren or Biron at the head of them, a Courlander of low extraction, whom the ducal nobility had refused to admit amongst them, and whom she created Duke of Courland and Prince of the Holy Empire. She made Lœwenvald manager of court affairs, Ostermann chief of the foreign administration, Korff and Kayserling of the embassies; Lascy, Münich, Bismark, and Gustaf Biren of the army. It was in Germany that she chose to seek for her successor,— Anne, daughter of Catherine Ivanovna, Princess of Mecklenburg, with her husband, the Duke of Brunswick Bevern, and their little emperor, Ivan VI. The Germans ruled in Russia, just as the Tatars had formerly done; and a new word, *Bironovchtchina*, expressive of the new *régime*, was coined on the model of the old *Tatarchtchina*. But if the Germans were triumphant, was it not the fault of the Russians themselves? The " eaglets " of Peter the Great had torn each other to pieces. Menchikof had ruined Tolstoï and Jagoujinski, and was in his turn destroyed by the Dolgoroukis, themselves victims, with the Galitsynes, of the national hate. Besides all this, the strangers who took their posts and filled the place they had left vacant were far more laborious and more exact than the natives. The Russians had still to pass through a hard school to acquire the qualities they lacked.

The new government was pitiless towards the Russians: Feofilakt Lopatinski was deposed and imprisoned in Viborg, for having edited Stephen Javorski's book against the Protestants ('The Stone (Peter) and the Faith'); and Volynski, one of those who had most loudly protested in favor of autocracy, had the misfortune to offend the favorite by his anti-German sentiments, and was cruelly tortured and beheaded. Thousands of executions and banishments decimated the upper classes, and a merciless collection of arrears of taxes, which Russian indolence had allowed to accumulate, desolated the country, while the peasants beheld their last head of cattle, their last tool, sizeed by the government for payment. The new despotism methodically organized its means of oppression. No doubt it suppressed the High Council, in order to restore the epithet of " directing " to the senate, but in reality it was the *Cabinet* composed of the ministers, and presided over by the Empress, that regulated all affairs. The old " Prikaz of Reformation " was re-established under the name of the " Secret Court of Chancery," and the cruel Ouchakof placed at the head. As the Empress had confidence only in her guards, two new regiments, the *Ismaïlovski*, and the horse guards, were created. Foreign officers were everywhere, and the brothers of the German favorites distributed among themselves the ranks of colonel and lieutenant-colonel.

Reassured as to the solidity of her throne, Anne only thought how to make up for the time she had wasted in *ennui* and regret. She surrounded herself with jesters, and, as if to humiliate the nation, she forced Nastasia and Anisia, two Russian princesses, and a Volkonski and a Galitsyne, two Russian princes, to gulp balls of pastry, or to crouch in the position of hens sitting on eggs, for the amusement of the court. Balls, fêtes, and masquerades followed each other without interruption. The Empress set the example of unbridled luxury, till then unheard of in Russia, and ruinous to a poor country. Up to that time the greatest nobles and ladies had taken no heed of the caprices of fashion; they replaced their clothes when they became old, and wore without shame the garments of their grandparents. Manstein informs us that, under Anne, a courtier with a revenue of two or three thousand roubles cut but a poor figure; costumiers got rich in two or three years; people carried their patrimony, often the price of whole villages, on their backs; they played heavily at faro and at *quinze*. In the luxury with which the court of Anne dazzled Russia, there was a mixture of antique barbarism and bad German taste which moved the mirth of Western travellers. For one well-dressed woman there were ten who made themselves frightful objects. " Among the men," says

Manstein, " the most gorgeous coat was often accompanied by an ill-combed wig ; a beautiful piece of stuff was spoilt by a clumsy tailor ; or, if the dress chanced to be successful, the equipages were defective ; a superbly dressed man would arrive in a shabby old vehicle drawn by two screws." " The favorite Biren," relates Prince Dolgoroukof, " loved bright colors, therefore black coats were forbidden at court, and every one appeared in brilliant raiment : nothing was seen but light blue, pale green, yellow, and pink. Old men like Prince Tcherkasski, or the Vice-Chancellor Ostermann, arrived at the palace in rose-color costumes." This was of slight importance. Russian taste would be formed in time, especially by the help of another school. The Germans prepared the way for the French. From the point of view of dress and domestic economy, the *Biron-ovchtchina* marks an important revolution in Russia.

Manners were still very gross. Anne amused herself with low buffoonery. Manstein says she liked Italian and German comedies for the sake of the frequent blows with a stick. Volynski, a Cabinet minister, thrashed the poet Trédiakovski. There were complaints that in the army the superior officers obliged the military doctors to serve them as cooks or hair-dressers. The exposure on poles of the heads or quarters of traitors had only just been suppressed by Peter II. Jagoujinski, the Procurator-General of the Senate, got so intoxicated that he ventured to insult the old Ostermann before the Empress, who shook with laughter. Soltykof, Governor of Moscow, denounced Tchikirine, the official who, "forgetting that he was in the house of her Majesty, had refused to get drunk."

It is an important fact that the German masters of Russia resolved to maintain the reforms of Peter. After her coronation, Anne returned to Saint Petersburg.

She abolished entail, which Peter the Great had unfortunately borrowed from Western nations, and which had produced sad results in Russia. The fathers of families taxed their peasants to wring out portions for the younger sons ; if they bequeathed the land to the eldest, they gave the cattle to the other sons. On the other hand, the time devoted to the education and the military service of the young nobles was more clearly defined. From the age of seven to that of twenty the young noble was to study, and from twenty to forty-five he was to serve the State. Examinations were established, to test the progress of the boys ; from twelve to sixteen they had to appear before a board, and whoever after the second examination was found ignorant of the catechism, arithmetic, and geometry, was forced to become a sailor. These rigorous measures prove how indifferent the mass of the nobles ther were to the advantages of education. It cannot be denied that the rule of the Germans, rough instructors though they were, had a salutary influence on Russian civilization. On the suggestion of Münich, the "corps of cadets" for 360 young nobles was founded at St. Petersburg. General education held a larger place in his programme than purely military instruction. Boys were prepared for the civil service as well as for the army. Orthography, style, rhetoric, jurisprudence, ethics, heraldry, arithmetic, fortifications, artillery, geography, general history, and the history of Germany (not Russia) were all taught. The most industrious and the most distinguished pupils might, after they had finished the preliminary courses, follow those of the Academy of Sciences.

SUCCESSION OF POLAND (1733-1735) AND WAR WITH TURKEY (1735-1739).

With regard to the East, the government of Anne Ivanovna resolved to abandon the Persian provinces conquered by Peter the Great where the climate had proved fatal to the Russian armies.

In 1733, after the death of Augustus II., the question of the succession of Poland was re-opened. Prussia, which desired to weaken Poland, did not wish to support either the French candidate, Leszczinski, or the Saxon candidate, Augustus III. Austria, on the contrary, which would gladly have beheld Poland sufficiently strong to aid her against the Turks, declared for Augustus. Russia, whose object it was to remain mistress in Poland and Courland, cared little who was elected, provided it was neither a powerful prince nor a client of France. Now Louis XV. thought himself bound in honor to maintain the cause of his father-in-law, Stanislas Leszczinski, the former *protégé* of Charles XII. The Power whose interests in this affair almost corresponded with those of Russia was therefore the house of Austria. The Austro-Russian alliance, inaugurated under Catherine I., was cemented under Anne Ivanovna. Prussia, whose project of partition had been set aside, remained neutral. The struggle between France and Russia began by a diplomatic rivalry. We find at Berlin La Chétardie pitted against Jagoujinski; at Stockholm, Saint Séverin against Michael Bestoujef; at Copenhagen, Plélo against Alexis Bestoujef; at Constantinople, Villeneuve against Neplouef; at Warsaw, Monti, against Lœwenwald. France hoped to support her candidate by Swedish and Turkish diversions, and to render the neutrality of Prussia more favorable ; in Poland she worked as hard to persuade as Russia to intimidate.

Even at St. Petersburg, the French ambassador, Magnan, neglected nothing to gain over the Empress and her favorite to a more peaceful policy, but the struggle was inevitable. Whilst a false Leszczinski, the Chevalier de Thiange, ostentatiously embarked at Brest, the real Stanislas disguised as a commercial traveller, crossed Europe, and entered Warsaw at night. Sixty thousand nobles declared in his favor on the field of election, and there were only four thousand dissidents. He was therefore legitimate King of Poland, yet the Russian army was invading the territory of the republic. Then Stanislas called the *pospolite* to arms, and retired into the maritime fortress of Dantzig to await succor from France. After his departure, the malcontents, under the protection of 20,000 Russian bayonets, proclaimed Augustus III. Stanislas found himself besieged in Dantzig by Marshal Münich, who, without waiting for the artillery, took the faubourg of Schotlandia by assault. The King of Prussia refused a passage through his territory to the Russian guns, and the French frigates were watching the sea ; but notwithstanding the blockade, Münich received his cannon, and by the capture of Sommerschantz cut off the communications of Dantzig with Wechselmünde and the mouth of the Vistula ; he then threw 1500 bombs into the town. He failed, however, in a bloody midnight attack on the fort of Hagelsberg. The French troops came up, led by Count de Plélo and Lamothe de la Peyrouse, but only numbered 2000 men. Plélo was killed, and the Count de Lamothe, who had taken refuge in Wechselmünde, had to capitulate. Dantzig opened her gates. Stanislas had already fled, disguised as a peasant. Such was the first contest between the French and the Russians. Lady Rondeau gives an account of the presentation of the Count de Lamothe and his officers to the Tzarina; the soldiers were quartered in the camp of Koporié, in Ingria ; and Anne did all she could to make them desert and to draw them into her service. Monti, the French ambassador at Warsaw, was taken prisoner at Dantzig, and in spite of his diplomatic character was retained in captivity.

The war of the Polish Succession was ended in Poland ; it began on the Rhine and in Italy, and it was the house of Austria that paid for it. The French excited against her the electors of Cologne, Mayence, Bavaria, and the Palatinate ; took Kehl and Philippsburg, and deprived her of the Duchy of Parma and the kingdom of Naples. In virtue of the treaty of alliance of

1726, the Emperor demanded help of the Tzarina. Lascy, at the head of 20,000 men, crossed Silesia, Bohemia, and Franconia, diplaying a Russian army for the first time before the eyes of Western Germany; and on the 15th of August, 1735, formed a junction with the Austrian troops between Heidelberg and Ladenberg, two miles from the French outposts. The Peace of Vienna, however, put an end to hostilities. The French had revenged themselves on Austria, which ceded Lorraine and part of Italy, not on Russia, which had taken Dantzig under their very eyes. The efforts of the French ambassador Villeneuve, of the renegade Bonneval, and of the Hungarian Ragotski, raised the Turks. The result of the war with Poland was a war in the East, to which events almost added a Swedish war.

In the East also, Russia had Austria for an ally. Campaigns against the Turks, across the desert steppes of the South, offered the same difficulties as in 1711, as everything had to be carried with the army, even wood and water. In spite of all Münich's efforts, the Russian cavalry was very second-rate. The army, encumbered with baggage, moved slowly over the interminable plains: it seemed lost among the vastness of its convoys. A simple sergeant had ten chariots, an officer thirty, the general Gustaf Biren 300 beasts of burden. There were always 10,000 sick men in the army, which, in spite of the dispensation of the Holy Synod, exhausted itself by a rigorous observance of fasts and days of abstinence.

In 1736 Lascy took Azof, Münich forced the lines of Perekop, pillaged Bakhtchi-Séraï, the capital of the khans, and laid waste the Western Crimea in such a way that the prosperity of the country has never recovered it. In 1737 Lascy devastated the eastern part of the peninsula, whilst Münich took Otchakof; in 1739, the latter gained a splendid victory at Stavoutchani, captured Khotin, crossed the Pruth, boasted of having avenged the defeat of Peter the Great, and entered the capital of Moldavia. During this time the Austrians were constantly beaten. They feared the Russians as neighbors of their orthodox provinces of Transylvania and Illyria, more than they did the Turks. They insisted on the conclusion of peace, and at Belgrade (1739) they ceded to Turkey all Servia, with Orsova and Wallachia; the Russians only obtained a tongue of land between the Bug and the Dnieper, contented themselves with the demolition of Azof, and surrendered all their conquests. This war had cost them more than a hundred thousand men. The King of France had just proved that he knew how to reach his enemies, even though separated from him by vast spaces. Anne Ivanovna found herself obliged to ask his mediation to prevent a war with

Sweden, and to conclude peace with the Turks. At the instance of Ostermann, and by orders of Louis XV., Saint Séverin negotiated at Stockholm, and Villeneuve at Constantinople. The Empress showed her gratitude to the latter by offering him 15,000 thalers. He would only accept the cross of Saint Andrew. Kantemir, Russian ambassador at Paris, still continued to warn his court that " Russia being the only Power which could counterbalance that of France, the latter would lose no opportunity of diminishing her strength."

IVAN VI—REGENCY OF BIREN AND ANNE—REVOLUTION OF 1741.

The weight of the taxes, the rigor with which they were collected, and the frequent conscriptions maddened the peasants, whilst the disgrace of Feofilakt, of Tatichtchef, of Roumantsof and Makarof (old servants of Peter the Great), as well as the sacrifice of Volynski, of Galitsyne, and the Dolgoroukis, seemed to threaten the whole nation. Soon the echoes of the general discontent reached the Secret Court of Police. The people attributed all their misfortunes to the reign of a woman, and repeated the proverb, "Cities governed by women do not endure; the walls built by women are never high." Others said the corn did not grow because a woman ruled. They began to regret the iron despotism of Peter I., and a popular song exhorts him to leave his tomb and chastise " Biren, the cursed German." The raskolniks had predicted that in 1733 the wrath of God would fall on men, and that Anne would be taken and judged at Moscow. She reigned, however, till 1740, at which time her health began to give way. Biren's scheme was to obtain from Anne Ivanovna the investiture of the regency during the minority of the little Emperor Ivan of Brunswick. Alexis Bestoujef, who owed his fortune to Biren, assured him of the support of Münich and of the Cabinet-minister Tcherkasski. The Germans of the court said, with Mengden, " If the Duke of Courland is not appointed regent, the rest of us Germans are lost." The Empress signed the nomination of Biren, and died the next day. Her last words to her favorite were, " Né boïs " (fear nothing).

Biren, however, had his own reasons for feeling uncomfortable. The Russians were indignant at having a master imposed on them who was a foreigner and a heretic, without morality and without talent, and whose only claim was a criminal union which dishonored the memory of their Empress. If a foreign regent was necessary, why not have the father of the Emperor? The long minority of a child only three months old at the death of Anne alarmed every one, and the thoughts of many turned towards the daughter of Peter the Great, and her grandson Peter of Holstein. The reign of the Germans still continued; besides Biren, the empire had to obey the Prince Antony of Brunswick Bevern, and his wife Anne Leopoldovna of Mecklenburg, governed in their turn by Anne's favorite the Saxon Lynar, and the prince's mistress, Julia Mengden. Happily, however, these foreign masters never thought of combining. The parents of the Emperor bore the authority of Biren with impatience; and the latter, discontented with their conduct, spoke of sending for Peter of Holstein, giving him his daughter in marriage, and marrying his son to Elizabeth. The fate of Menchikof and the Dolgoroukis was lost on him. His clumsy nonentity embarrassed Ostermann and Münich; and the latter, in an interview with Anne Leopoldovna, promised her to get rid of the tyrant. His aide-de-camp, Manstein, has given us a graphic account of this *coup d'état*. One night in November, Biren, who suspected nothing, and who in the evening had dined in company with Münich, was taken from his bed, the Duchess of Courland was thrust almost naked from the palace, all his friends were arrested, and he was sent to Pelim, in Siberia.

Münich had given liberty and power to the parents of the Emperor; how could they reward him? Like Menchikof, he wished to be Generalissimo, but Antony of Brunswick coveted the place. Münich then contented himself with the title of First Minister; and Ostermann was recompensed by being nominated High Admiral. Antony, Anne, and Ostermann soon united against their liberator; and Münich, filled with disgust, sent in his resignation. The Germans, when they attained the supreme power, conducted themselves exactly like the "eaglets" of Peter the Great: they mutually banished and exterminated each other. The father and mother of the Emperor, left in possession of the field, continued to dispute the authority, and to reproach each other with their mutual infidelities. Ostermann supported Antony against Anne. The incapacity of the Regent was beyond belief. Not having the energy to dress herself, Anne Leopoldovna would lie for whole days on a couch, her head covered with a hankerchief, conversing with her intimate friends. The divisions and indifference of the government threw open the way to its numerous enemies; they only wanted a chief who would attack the Brunswickers as they had successfully attacted Biren.

Elizabeth, daughter of Peter the Great, who had been narrowly watched under the hard rule of Anne Ivanovna and

Biren, raised her head under this weak government. Twenty-eight years old, tall and very pretty, with great quickness of mind though very ignorant, lively and joyous, a bold rider and fearless on the water, with soldier-like manners, she had all the qualities necessary to a party leader. Her confidants, Alexander and Peter Schouvalof, Michael Voronzof, Razoumovski, Schwartz, and the doctor Lestocq, all urged her to action. The Regent feared her, but did not dare to act on the advice of Ostermann. It was known at the palace that after the downfall of Biren three regiments of Guards had hastened to swear fealty to her, believing the next step would be the proclamation of Peter the Great's daughter; and that at Cronstadt the soldiers had said, "Will no one put himself at our head in favor of Elizabeth Petrovna?" She accepted the office of godmother to their children, visited the Guards in their barracks, and invited them to her house. When she passed through the streets in her sledge, the common grenadiers climbed on the back of the carriage and whispered familiarly in her ear. The French ambassador, La Chétardie, had orders to favor any revolution in Russia that would destroy the influence of the Germans, and break the alliance with Austria. He aided Elizabeth with advice and money, and hoped to obtain for her the support of a Swedish diversion. The Swedes had repented of their quiescence during the late wars with Poland and Turkey, and were disposed to take their own grievances and those of Elizabeth as a pretext for declaring war against the Regent. The Swedish ambassador, Nolken, only stipulated that at her accession the Tzarévna should promise to restore part of the conquests of Peter the Great. This she declined to do; but the Swedes, nevertheless, began hostilities, and issued a manifesto to the "glorious Russian nation," which they wished to deliver from German ministers, and from the "heavy oppression and cruel foreign tyranny," so as to enable it freely to elect "a legitimate and just government." This diversion precipitated the crisis. The court was by this time too well accustomed to plots for the conspirators to delay; and, besides, the regiments counted on by Elizabeth had orders to proceed to the frontier. She had only the choice between the throne and the convent. In the night of the 25th of October she went with three of her friends to the quarters of the Preobrajenski. "My children," she said to them, "you know whose daughter I am." "Mother, we are ready; we will kill *them* all." She forbade bloodshed, and added, "I swear to die for you; will you swear to die for me?" They all swore. Anne Leopoldovna, Prince Antony, the young Emperor in his cradle, Münich, Ostermann, Lœwenwald, and the Mengdens, were arrested during the night. Elizabeth was proclaimed absolute Empress, and the nobles of the empire hastened to give in their adhesion to the new revolution. Ivan VI. was confined at Schlüsselburg; Anne, with her husband and children, at Kholmogory, where she died in 1746. A tribunal was held, and the Dolgoroukis were among the judges. Ostermann was condemned to be broken on the wheel, Münich to be quartered, and the others to decapitation. The Empress, however, spared their lives. Ostermann was exiled to Berezof, and Münich to Pelim, where he lived in the house he had planned for Biren. Many of the exiles of the preceding reign were recalled, and the Birens were allowed to reside in Iaroslavl.

CHAPTER VI.

ELIZABETH PETROVNA (1741-1762).

Reaction against the Germans: war with Sweden (1741-1743)—Succession of Austria: war against Frederic II. (1756-1762)—Reforms under Elizabeth: French influence.

REACTION AGAINST THE GERMANS: WAR WITH SWEDEN (1741-1743.)

WHEN Elizabeth had been crowned at Moscow, she sent to Holstein for the son of her sister, Anne Petrovna, and of the Duke Charles Frederic. The grandson of Peter the Great embraced orthodoxy, took the name of Peter Feodorovitch, was proclaimed heir to the throne, and in 1744 the Empress married him to the Princess Sophia of Anhalt-Zerbst, afterwards Catherine II. Thus the power which had been diverted to the Ivanian branch of the Romanof dynasty, to Anne of Courland and her great-nephew of Brunswick, returned to the immediate family of Peter the Great in the person of Elizabeth as Empress, and of her nephew of Holstein as heir to the throne.

The revolution of 1741 meant much more than the substitution of the Petrovian for the Ivanian branch; it signified the triumph of the national over the German party, the reaction of the Russian element against the hard tutelage of the strangers, and thus it was understood by the people. The orthodox clergy, persecuted by the heretics, took its revenge in the sermons of Ambrose Iouchkévitch, Archbishop of Novgorod, against the "emissaries of the devil," and against "Beelzebub and his angels." The poet Lomonossof hails in Elizabeth the Astræa who "had brought back the golden age," the Moses who "had snatched Russia in one night from her Egyptian slavery," the Noah "who had saved her from the foreign deluge." Citizens and soldiers rose against the Germans; there were revolts at St. Petersburg, and in the army of Finland, against the foreign officers, on whom the men wished to inflict the punishment of Ostermann and Münich. At court, Finch, the English ambassador, Botta, the Austrian ambassador, **Lynar**, the Saxon ambassador, had compromised themselves under the preceding dynasty; therefore all the sympathies of the nation and the Tzarina were for Mardefeld, ambassador of Prussia, and especially for La Chétardie, whom they looked on as one of the authors of the revolution, and whose hands the officers of the Guard came to kiss, addressing him as "their father." The Austro-Russian alliance, consolidated under Catherine I. and Anne Ivanovna, seemed broken.

This good understanding between the courts of France and Russia was imperilled by the affairs of Sweden. The Cabinet of Versailles had not been able to persuade its Scandinavian ally into war except by hints of cessions of territory by the new Empress. Elizabeth, daughter of Peter the Great, could not renounce the conquests of her father, which even Anne Leopoldovna, a foreign princess, had maintained at the cost of war. The Swedes, who pretended to have taken up arms in favor of Elizabeth, continued the war against their former *protégée*. This war had no result except to show the weakness of the Sweden of Charles XII. against regenerate Russia. The Scandinavian armies proved themselves very unworthy of their former reputation. Elizabeth's generals, Lascy and Keith, subdued all the forts in Finland. At Helsingfors 17,000 Swedes laid down their arms before a hardly more numerous Russian force. By the treaty of Abo, the Empress acquired South Finland as far as the river Kiümen, and caused Adolphus Frederic, Administrator of the Duchy of Holstein, and one of her allies, to be elected Prince Royal of Sweden, in place of the Prince Royal of Denmark (1743).

SUCCESSION OF AUSTRIA: WAR AGAINST FREDERIC II. (1756-1762).

The war of the Austrian Succession had broken out in Europe. For whom would Russia declare—for Maria Theresa, or for France and her allies? Bestoujef, disgraced by Biren, who had returned to his post under the protection of Lestocq, Vice-Chancellor, and later Chancellor, of the empire, was on the side of Austria. Voronzof, Vice-Chancellor, trimmed between both parties; La Chétardie and Mardefeld, ambassadors of Louis XV. and Frederic II., intrigued with Lestocq and the mother of Sophia of Anhalt (now become the Tzarévna, or Grand Duchess Catherine) to draw Elizabeth into the Franco-Prussian Alliance, and to overthrow Bestoujef. The Chancellor neglected nothing to destroy his enemies. He had his *black cabinet*, where he looked over the despatches of the foreign ambassadors; he found means to place under the eyes of the sovereign extracts from the letters of La Chétardie proving that Lestocq was a pensioner of France, and that La Chétardie had spoken insultingly of Elizabeth in his political correspondence. The French ambassador received orders to quit the capital within twenty-four hours, and Russia within eight days, and the Grand Duchess's mother was sent back to Germany. Later Lestocq was summoned before a commission, put to the torture, and banished to Ouglitch. Bestoujef triumphed; it seemed as if Russia was going to interfere on behalf of Maria Theresa: but in his turn, Botta, the Austrian ambassador, allowed himself to be drawn into an affair which was quite as disastrous; compromised by the conduct of the malcontents, he saw his accomplice, Madame Lapoukhine, knouted and mutilated, and was sent back to Austria. Times passed on. Russia, satisfied with the sort of intimidation that she exercised over all the European courts, did not care to go into action. Bestoujef and the Vice-Chancellor Voronzof played with the various courts, the one holding out hopes to Austria, the other allowing himself to be cajoled by D'Allion, La Chétardie's successor.

France, abandoned by her allies, had transported the war into the Low Countries, where Maurice de Saxe, the former Duke of Courland, gained a series of victories. In 1746 an Austro-Russian treaty of alliance was concluded; England promised subsidies to Elizabeth, but it was not till 1748 that 30,000 Russians under Repnine, crossed Germany and took up a position on the Rhine. They only served to hasten the Peace of Aix-la-Chapelle (1748), and returned to Russia without having fired a shot or risked the *prestige* of the empire.

D'Allion had been recalled in 1747, and had no successor at St. Petersburg. However, the same Bestoujef who had caused La Chétardie to be expelled, and concluded the Austrian alliance, had proclaimed as far back as 1744 that Prussia was more dangerous than France, " because of her near neighborhood and her late accession of strength." Elizabeth hated Frederic : "The King of Prussia," she said to Lord Hyndford, " is certainly a bad prince, who has no fear of God before his eyes; he turns holy things into ridicule, he never goes to church, he is the Nadir-Shah of Prussia." He had no religion, he had not been consecrated, he did not spare epigrams about the Empress. The " self-sufficient neighbor " had shown off his importance at Aix-la-Chapelle, and had opposed the admission of a Russian plenipotentiary to the congress. Other things led to a sort of diplomatic rupture. Finally, on the 6th—17th of May, 1756, the Chancellor read to the Empress a statement of foreign affairs. He reminded her that the new growth of the Prussian power was unfavorable to Russia, and pointed out how Frederic II., who had raised his army from 80,000 to 200,000 soldiers, who had deprived Austria of Silesia, who from the "great revenues" of the latter province and the "millions levied on Saxony" had constituted a great war fund for himself, who coveted Hanover and Courland, and hoped for the dismemberment of Poland, had consequently become "the most dangerous of neighbors." He concluded by proving the necessity of reducing the forces of the King of Prussia, and of supporting the States menaced by him. This patriotic disgust, this wholesome mistrust of Bestoujef, might well have become the traditional policy of Russia.

At this moment it was still believed at St. Petersburg that in this war, as in the last, Prussia would be the ally of France, against Austria and England. The reversal of French policy had not been expected. Bestoujef was in too great haste to conclude a treaty of subsidies with England. Voronzof warned the Empress to beware lest the Russian troops should be employed in favor of that very Prussia whom she wished to fight. The event justified his prediction, confounded the plans and the provisions of Bestoujef, and paved the way for his fall. When Prussia allied herself to England, and Austria to France, Russia found herself indirectly also allied to the latter Power. Diplomatic relations between the courts were renewed. It was then than the secret missions of Valcroissant, of the Scotch Douglas, and the mysterious Chevalier d'Eon took place; that L'Hôpital became the French ambassador in Russia, and that a private correspondence was exchanged between Louis XV. and the Empress Elizabeth.

Frederic was alarmed on hearing the decision of Russia; he feared nothing so much as the invasion of her "undisciplined hordes." It was to secure the friendship of "these barbarians" that he had arranged in 1744 the marriage of Peter Feodorovitch and of Sophia of Anhalt. His invasion of Saxony put the Russian army in motion. In 1757, the year of Rosbach, 83,000 Muscovites, under the Generalissimo Apraxine, crossed the frontier of Prussia, occupied the province of Eastern Prussia, slowly advanced in the direction of the Oder, and crushed the corps of Lewald at Gross-Jägersdorff. The Prussian loss was 4600 killed, 600 taken prisoners, and 29 guns. Instead of following up his advantages, Apraxine retraced his steps, and recrossed the Niemen. The ambassadors of France and Austria suspected treachery, and clamored for his dismissal from the chief command. His papers were examined, and were found gravely to compromise the Grand Duchess Catherine and the Chancellor Bestoujef-Rioumine. The latter was exiled, and his place filled by Voronzof.

In 1758 Fermor again invaded the Prussian states, took Königsberg, and bombarded Küstrin on the Oder. Frederic II. hastened to Silesia, made a junction with Dohna, and thus found himself at the head of 32,000 men, in presence of 89,000 Russians, near the village of Zorndorff. In spite of the stoical bravery of the Muscovites, and the defeat of the Prussian left wing, their inexperience, the weakness of their commander, and, the superiority of the cavalry of Zeidlitz caused them to be beaten. They lost 20,000 men, 100 cannon, and 30 flags. But Frederic II. had not yet reached his aim, as his enemies were by no means annihilated, and were able to make an imposing retreat.

In 1759, Soltykof, Fermor's successor, returned to the Oder, defeated the Prussians at Paltzig, near Züllichau, and made his entry into Frankfort. Frederic again came to the help of his lieutenants, and encountered the Russians near Künersdorff. This time his army was simply crushed under the enormous weight of the Muscovite masses. He lost 8000 men and 172 guns. He himself escaped with great difficulty from the field of battle, with forty hussars. Only 3000 men remained to him of an army of 48,000. "A cruel misfortune," he wrote to Finkenstein: "I shall never survive it. The consequences are worse than the battle itself. I no longer see any resource, and, to say the truth, I think all is lost." It was at this moment that he thought of suicide. The disaster of Künersdorff weighed on him during the remainder of the war. Henceforth he could only hold himself on the defensive, without daring to descend into the plain.

The allies were not less exhausted than Frederic. Elizabeth alone declined to speak of peace till she had "reduced the forces" of Frederic, and secured the annexation of Eastern Prussia. In 1760 the Russians entered Berlin after a short resistance, pillaged the State coffers and the arsenals, and destroyed the manufactories of arms and powder. The following year they conquered Pomerania, and Roumantsof took Kolberg. Frederic II. would have been lost if this terrible war had continued; he was saved by the sudden death of Elizabeth. Still his power was much weakened. The Empress had left Prussia less dangerous and threatening than she had found it.

REFORMS UNDER ELIZABETH : FRENCH INFLUENCE.

The reign of Elizabeth was marked by an increase of orthodox zeal. In spite of her dissolute manners, she was much influenced by the priests, though she still clung to her old superstitions. In 1742 the Holy Synod ordered the suppression of the Armenian churches in the two capitals, and hoped likewise to suppress the dissenting churches on the Nevski Prospect. In the Tatar regions some of the mosques were closed, and the erection of new ones forbidden. The intolerance of the bishops and missionaries caused the Pagan or Mussulman tribes of the Mordvians, the Tcheremisses, the Tchouvaches, and the Mechtcheraks to revolt. The Jews were expelled on the ground that they were "the enemies of Christ our Saviour, and did much evil to our subjects." To the observation of the Senate that she was ruining commerce and the empire, Elizabeth replied, "I desire no gain from the foes of Christ." The fanaticism of the raskolniks rose by contact with the fanaticism of the officials. Fifty-three men burned themselves at once near Oustiougue, and 172 near Tomsk in Siberia.

On the other hand, the morals of the clergy were corrected, and attention paid to their education. The monasteries were enjoined to send pupils to the Ecclesiastical Academy of Moscow, which complained that at present its number consisted of five. Rebellion and drunkenness were repressed by stripes and chains. The fair of the priests was put down, and all popes who hired themselves out in public were whipped. The laws of Peter I. against persons who walked about and talked in church were revived. The tobacco pouches of those who smoked were confiscated. Inspectors nominated by the bishops besought the peasants to clean their holy images, whose dirtiness shocked strangers. Catechisms were distributed in the churches, and a new corrected edition of the Bible exposed for sale. Theological studies, when they were not absolutely neglected, were still very puerile. At the Ecclesiastical Academy of Moscow they discussed whether the angels think by analysis or by synthesis, and what is the nature of the light of glory in the future life.

The Senate was re-established with the functions given it by Peter the Great, of which it had been deprived by the High Council of Catherine I., or the Cabinet of Anne Ivanovna. Trade was encouraged. Tchins, or ranks of assessors, of secretaries of colleges, and of councillors of State, were distributed to manufacturers of cloth, linen, silk, and cotton. In 1753 the customhouses of the interior were suppressed, as well as many toll-duties. Agricultural banks were founded where they lent to landholders at 6 per cent. ; whilst private individuals raised usurious interest to 15 or even 20 per cent. Sons of merchants were sent to study trade and book-keeping in Holland. New mines were discovered, and the commerce with the far East increased rapidly. Siberia began to be peopled. Attempts were made to colonize Southern Russia, now freed from the prospect of Tatar incursions, with Slavs who had fled from the Turkish or Tatar provinces. On the territory acquired by Anne Ivanovna, between the Bug and the Oder, the agricultural and military colony of New Servia was founded, which furnished four regiments of light cavalry.

Legislation was less severe. Elizabeth imagined that she had abolished the penalty of death, but the knout of her executioners killed as well as the axe. Those who survived flagellation were sent, with their nose or ears cut, to the public works. Torture was only employed in the gravest cases. If the civil code did not advance, a code of procedure and a code of criminal investigation were completed. The police had hard work to maintain even a show of order in this rude society. Moscow and St. Petersburg were like woods of ill-fame. Thieves had lost none of their audacity, and one of them, Vanka Kaïne, the Russian Cartouche, is the hero of a whole cycle of songs. Edicts were required to prevent the keeping of bears in both capitals, and to hinder them from being allowed to roam at night through the towns of the provinces. Public baths common to both men and women were forbidden in the large towns. The government was powerless to stop brigandage on the great highways ; pirates captured ships on the Volga, and armed bands gave battle to regular troops.

The real minister of literature and the fine arts, under the reign of Elizabeth was her young favorite, Count Ivan Schouvalof. He founded, in the centre of the empire, the University of Moscow, whose small beginnings have excited the contempt of German historians, but of which Nicholas Tourguénief has been able to say, that " never in any country has any institution been more useful and more fruitful in good results; even to-day (1844) it is rare to find a man who writes his own language correctly, a well-educated and enlightened official, an upright and firm magistrate, who has not been at the University of Moscow." Schouvalof desired that every student, whatever his origin, should carry a sword, and bear the rank of the tenth degree of the Tchin ; doctors were given the eighth degree. Ten professors taught the three branches of jurisprudence, medicine, and philosophy. He likewise wished to open two Universities at St.

Petersburg and at Batourine, and gymnasia and schools in all the governments; he established schools on the military frontier of the south, and one at Orenburg for the children of the exiles. He sent young men abroad to finish their studies in medicine. He was the creator of the Academy of Fine Arts at St. Petersburg, over which he set French masters. The painter Lorraine, the sculptor Gilet, the architect Valois and later Dévely and Lagrenée, were among them.

St. Petersburg, which as yet contained only 74,000 inhabitants, began to look like a capital. The Italian Rastielli built the Winter Palace, the monastery of Smolna, which became under Catherine II. an institution for the daughters of the aristocracy, and the Palace of the Academy of Sciences, and traced the plan of Tzarskoe-Selo, the Russian Versailles.

Under the presidency of Cyril Razoumovski, son of a former favorite of Elizabeth, the Academy of Sciences, which had been founded by Peter the Great and Catherine I., began to make itself known. In spite of the interminable contests excited by Lomonossof between its German and Russian professors, it continued to publish both books and translations.

The Academicians Bauer and Miller devoted themselves to the origin of Russia. Tatichtchef, formerly governor of Astrakhan, wrote the first history of the monarchy. Lomonossof, Professor of Physic, made himself the Vaugelas and the Malherbe of his country. The son of a fisher in the neighborhood of Arkhangel, he had the colossal frame of the ancient *bogatyrs*, and certain vices of the people. He was sent abroad to complete his studies, and there became the hero of a hundred adventures. He married the daughter of a Magdeburg tailor, was kidnapped for the King of Prussia, and imprisoned. Even in Russia his drunkenness and turbulence would have drawn him into many scrapes, but for the intervention of his protectors. He published a grammar, a book of rhetoric and poetics, and labored to free the modern Russian language from the Slavonic of the Church. His "panegyrics" of Peter and Elizabeth, and, above all, his Odes, are the master-pieces of the time. Soumarokof wrote dreams, comedies and satires and published the first Russian review, 'The Busy Bee.' Kniajnine was very successful in comedy, though his tragedies were poor. Prince Kantemir, son of the Hospodar of Moldavia, ambassador at Paris and London, published letters and satires. Trediakovski, author of the tragedy of 'Deidamia' and of another inferior epopee, called the 'Telemachid,' imitated from Fénelon, is chiefly known as a reformer of the language, and an indefatigable translator. He translated all Rollin's 'Ancient History,' Boileau's 'Art Poétique,' the *libretti* of Italian operas, and works of science and politics. His biography proves the small estimation in which a poet was then held. Anne Ivanovna had employed him to make rhymes for her masquerades, and we have seen how brutally he was treated by Volynski. He did not know how to make himself respected like a Kantemir or a Lomonossof.

Elizabeth, like Anne Ivanovna, loved the theatre. The Italian company of Locatelli acted *ballets* and *opéras-bouffes*. Sérigny, director of a French theatre, made 25,000 roubles a year. The Empress furnished spectators, willing or reluctant, sending lackeys to beat up the laggards, and imposing a fine of fifty roubles on all who would not come. The Russian theatre had begun to exist. Soumarokof led his actors, who were members of the corps of cadets, into the apartments of the Empress. At Iaroslavl, Volkof, the son of a merchant, and a *protégé* of the voïevode Moussine-Pouchkine, was at once author, actor, manager, decorator, and scene-painter, to a company whom the Empress summoned to St. Petersburg. Soumarokof afterwards became the manager, and wrote twenty-six pieces for them, among which were ' Khorev,' ' Sineous and Trouvor,' ' Dmitri the Impostor,' and some translations of Shakespeare and of French pieces.

The characteristic feature of the reign of Elizabeth is the establishment of direct relations with France, which had been, since the 17th century, the highest representative of European civilization. Up to this time French civilization had been only known at second hand in Russia. The people were Dutch under Peter I., German under Anne Ivanovna. The Russians had made themselves the pupils of those who were themselves but pupils of the French. Now the barriers were thrown down. French *savants* were members of the Academy of Sciences, French artists of the Academy of Fine Arts. The French representations of Sérigny were thronged, and Soumarokof caused translations from French works to be put on the stage. The writings of Vauban on Fortifications, and of Saint Rémy on Artillery, were translated, and the Russians learned to know Corneille, Racine, and Molière. The favorite Ivan Schouvalof had his furniture brought from France, his dresses from Paris, loved everything French, and caused Elizabeth, once betrothed to Louis XV., to share his tastes. La Chétardie and L'Hôpital made the manners of Versailles fashionable. The Russians perceived they had more affinity with the French than with the Germans. Trediakovski and Cyril Razoumovski went to perfect themselves in Paris, where the Russian students were sufficiently numerous to have a chapel of their own, under the protection of the ambassador. A Voronzof entered the service of Louis XV., and in the uniform of the light cavalry stood on guard in the galleries of Versailles. The Ambassador Kantemir was a friend of Montesquieu. A generation French in ideas and culture grew up at the court of Elizabeth. Catherine II., Princess Dachkof, and the Voronzofs wrote French as easily as their own language. In 1746, De l'Isle communicated to the Academy of Sciences the wish expressed by Voltaire to become a corresponding member. The following year, by means of D'Allion and Cyril Razoumovski, Voltaire entered into relations with Schouvalof, who furnished him with documents as well as with advice and criticism for his 'History of Russia under Peter the Great.'

In her internal policy, then, Elizabeth continued the traditions of the great Emperor. She developed the material prosperity of the country, reformed the legislation, and created new centres of population; she gave an energetic impulse to science and the national literature; she prepared the way for the alliance of France and Russia, emancipated from the German yoke; while in foreign affairs she put a stop to the threatening advance of Prussia, vanquished and reduced to despair the first general of the age, and concluded the first Franco-Russian alliance against the military monarchy of the Hohenzollerns. Better appreciated by the light of later discoveries, Elizabeth will hold an honorable place in history, even between Peter the Great and Catherine II.

CHAPTER VII.

PETER III. AND THE REVOLUTION OF 1762.

Government of Peter III. and the alliance with Frederic II.—Revolution of 1762: Catherine II.

GOVERNMENT OF PETER III.: ALLIANCE WITH FREDERIC II.

THE successor of Elizabeth was her nephew, the grandson of Peter the Great, son of Anne Petrovna and of Charles Frederic, Duke of Holstein-Goltorp, then thirty-four years of age. His accession was looked forward to with feelings of mistrust, because he affected to think himself a stranger in Russia, and to act more as the Duke of Holstein than as heir to the imperial throne. Without education and without training, his youth had been passed in puerile amusements; he only seemed to care for minute military details, occupied himself in drilling his battalion of Holsteiners—known by the name of "long suffering"—and showed himself the fanatical admirer of Frederic II. and of the Prussian tactics. His aunt suspected him of communicating to the King the secret deliberations of the government, and thought herself obliged to exclude him from conferences which were concerned with affairs of war and administration.

The first measures of Peter III. caused, however, a delightful surprise. In February, 1762, he published a manifesto which freed the nobility from the obligation imposed on them by Peter the Great, of consecrating themselves to the service of the State. He reminded them that this law of his grandfather had produced most salutary effects, by forcing the nobles to educate themselves and interest themselves in the public welfare, by giving birth to an enlightened generation, and by furnishing the State with distinguished generals and administrators. But now that the love of the sovereign and zeal for his service was spread abroad, he no longer thought it necessary to maintain the law. The Russian nobles, overcome with gratitude, thought of raising a statue of gold to him. Peter III. answered that the most beautiful monuments were those possessed by a sovereign in the memory of his people. Another reform was the abolition of the Secret Court of Police,—"an abominable tribunal," writes the English ambassador, "as bad, and in some respects worse than the Spanish Inquisition." Peter III. respected the raskolniks; they had been so cruelly persecuted during the preceding reign that their number had fallen from forty thousand to five thousand in the government of Novgorod alone; and thousands of these unhappy creatures had fled to the deserts, or emigrated into the neighboring countries. He commanded that they should be brought back to Russia, offering them at the same time lands in Siberia; "for," says the oukaze, "the Mahometans and even idolaters are tolerated in the empire. Now, the raskolniks are Christians." He took up his grandfather's project of the resumption of conventual property, allowing the monks a pension in its stead. He even thought of the peasants, on whom the modern State founded by Peter the Great weighed so heavily, and proclaimed a pardon to those who, misled by false intelligence, thought they were able to rise against their masters. The greater part of these acts were inspired by his Secretary of State, Volkof. The culprits of the last reign—the Mengdens, Madame Lapoukhine, old Marshal Münich and his son, Lestocq, the Duke of Courland, and all the Birens—were recalled.

Unhappily, the Emperor's personal conduct almost neutralized any wisdom in his laws. Not only did he plunder the clergy, but he did not hide his contempt for the national religion, which he had been forced to embrace instead of Lutheranism. The people were scandalized by his attitude in the funeral chamber where the corpse of his aunt was exposed. "He was seen," says Princess Dachkof, "whispering and laughing with the ladies-in-waiting, turning the priests into ridicule, picking quarrels with the officers, or even with the sentinels, about the way their cravats were folded, the length of their curls, or the cut of their uniforms." The reforms that he introduced into the dress and drill, so as to assimilate them to those of Prussia, irritated the army; the Guards were jealous of the favor shown the battalions of Holstein, which he wished to raise to 18,000 men, and proposed as models for the national troops. The suppression of the body-guard of Grenadiers, formed by Elizabeth in 1741, announced to the regiments of Preobrajenski, Semenovski, and Ismaïlovski the lot that awaited them. The Emperor had already observed that "the Guards were dangerous, and held the palace in a state of siege."

The court was discontented with the foolish innovations he introduced into etiquette, obliging the ladies to curtsey in the

German fashion. He seemed to have taken an aversion to all the tastes of his aunt; and one of his first cares had been to dismiss the French company of actors. The manners of the upper classes had become sufficiently refined to look upon Peter's gross habits with disgust. "The life led by the Emperor," writes the French ambassador, De Breteuil, "is shameful. He smokes and drinks beer for hours together, and only ceases from these amusements at five or six in the morning, when he is dead drunk. . . . He has redoubled his attentions towards Mademoiselle Voronzof. One must allow that it is a strange taste; she has no wit; and as to her face, it is impossible to imagine anything uglier: she resembles in every way a servant at a low inn."

The foreign policy of Peter III. only widened the breach between himself and his subjects. Frederic II. was almost reduced to extremity by the battle of Künersdorff; the slow movements of Boutourline in the campaign of 1761 had indeed procured him a little respite, but if the war with Russia was prolonged, he was ruined. We may imagine with what joy and hope he hailed the accession of Peter III. He addressed his congratulations to the new Emperor through the English ambassador in Russia, and the friendship between the great king and his admirer was soon renewed. Tchernichef received orders to detach himself from the Austrians in Silesia, and the King of Prussia sent Goltz to make proposals of peace to the Tzar. He authorized his envoy even to cede Eastern Prussia if it was exacted by Peter, merely reserving to himself an indemnity. On his arrival Goltz found a prince who swore only by Frederic II., wore his portrait in a ring, and remembered all that he had suffered for him in the reign of Elizabeth, when he had been dismissed from the "Conference." There was no longer any question of annexing Eastern Prussia, as the late Tzarina had so ardently wished; Peter III. restored to his "old friend" all the Russian conquests, and formed an offensive and defensive alliance with him. The two princes promised each other help to the amount of 12,000 infantry and 8000 horses, and the Prussians, who had till that moment been fighting the Russians, now joined them against Austria. Frederic guaranteed to the Emperor his States of Holstein, and confirmed the uncle of Peter in the duchy of Courland. undertaking to come to an understanding with him on the subject of Poland. Such a sudden change in State policy had never before been seen. Breteuil and Mercyd'Argenteau. the French and Austrian ambassadors, found themselves all at once in disgrace. The envoy of Frederic II. was not only a favorite, he was really the first minister of the Emperor of Russia, pointing out suspicious characters, banishing his enemies, accusing Voronzof and the Shouvalofs of French sympathies. The treaty being concluded, Peter III., at a grand dinner, proposed the health of the King of Prussia, amidst the thunders of the guns of the fortress. He carried his extravagances, by which he testified his admiration for the great man, to such a point as to disquiet Goltz himself. "Let us drink to the health of the king our master," he cried in one of his orgies; "he has done me the honor to confide to me one of his regiments. I hope he will not dismiss me; you may be assured that if he should order it, I would make war on hell with all my empire."

REVOLUTION OF 1762: CATHERINE II.

The Russians would have hailed with pleasure the end of a tedious war, though they regretted the abandonment of the conquests of Elizabeth, but a new war succeeded the old one; the empire was to exhaust herself anew, combating her allies of yesterday, and to fight against Denmark for the pretensions of the house of Holstein. The hearts of the people softened towards the Empress Catherine on account of the harsh treatment she had received, her intelligence and obtrusive demonstrations of piety throwing into relief the incapacity and extravagances of her husband. Peter III. wished to divorce her and to marry Elizabeth Voronzof; he was said to meditate disinheriting his son Paul in favor of Ivan VI.; once he gave an order, which was not executed, to arrest his wife, and to confine her in a convent.

Sophia of Anhalt, now the Empress Catherine, was not a woman to pardon these threats, nor to wait till they were carried into effect. As Breteuil remarks, "All this, joined to daily humiliations, fermented in a head like hers, and only wanted an occasion to break out." She bided her time and acted.

Numerous contemporary documents exist about the revolution of June 1762. The accounts best known are those of Rulhière, of Princess Dachkof in her Memoirs, of Keith and Breteuil in their despatches, and of Catherine II. herself in her letter to Poniatowski. The order given to the Guards to leave for Holstein precipitated the revolution of 1762, as a similar order precipitated that of 1741. Peter III. had no idea of his danger; he did not see conspirators silently increase and multiply in the Senate, in the court, and in the army. Their number was great, and their aims often different. Some wished to proclaim Paul I., under the guardianship of his mother; others desired to crown Catherine herself. The group which had then all the confidence of the Empress was composed of young officers: Gregory Orlof, her lover, Alexis Orlof, and three others of the same name, Bariatinski, and Passek. The Orlofs were acquainted with all the details of the affair, and concealed it with care from the other conspirators, among them the Princess Dachkof, whom they considered wanting in discretion. Put on her guard by the arrest of Passek, Catherine resolved to act. Peter III. was then at Oranienbaum with his Holsteiners, and Catherine at Peterhof, between Oranienbaum and St. Petersburg. She abruptly quitted her residence, accompanied by Gregory and Alexis Orlof and two servants. On her arrival in the capital the three regiments of Foot Guards rose and took the oaths to her at the hands of their priests. Peter's uncle, George of Holstein, was arrested by his own regiment of Horse Guards. From Our Lady of Kazan Catherine went to the Winter Palace, whence Admiral Talysine was sent to secure the allegiance of Cronstadt, and whence proclamations were issued to the people and the army. Then, at the head of nearly 20,000 men, besides artillery, she marched on Oranienbaum.

Peter III., suddenly aroused from his tranquil repose, embarked for Cronstadt to put himself at the head of the garrison. "I am the Emperor," he cried to Talysine. "There is no longer any Emperor," replied the admiral, and, menaced by the artillery of the fortress, Peter had to return to his residence. There in spite of the counsels of the warlike old Münich and the presence of his 1500 Holsteiners, he quietly abdicated,— "like a child being sent to sleep," as Frederic II. remarked. He visited his wife with his mistress and his most intimate friends: "after which," relates the Empress, "I sent the deposed Emperor, under the command of Alexis Orlof, accompanied by four officers and a detachment of gentle and reasonable men, to a place named Ropcha, fifteen miles from Peterhof, a secluded spot, but very pleasant." Here he died in four days, of a "hæmorrhoidal colic," his wife assures us, which was complicated by "flying to the brain." This was the version officially adopted. The English ambassador relates that he received the following note from the Russian Cabinet:—"The imperial minister of Russia thinks it his duty to inform the foreign ministers that the late Emperor having been taken ill with a violent colic, to which he was subject, died yesterday."

The unhappy son of Anne Leopoldovna and of Antony, the great grandson of the Tzar Ivan V., the Emperor imprisoned since his childhood by Elizabeth and confined at Schlüsselburg, had been brought by Peter III. to St. Petersburg. He was now twenty-one years old, and had lost his reason.

Catherine II. imprisoned him anew at Schlüsselburg. He was no dangerous character, but merely a name. A memorandum of the Empress on the subject still exists. "It is my opinion that he should not be allowed to escape, so as to place him beyond the power of doing harm. It would be best to tonsure him, and to transfer him to some monastery, neither too near nor too far off; it will suffice if it does not become a shrine."

Revolutions are almost invariably followed by revolts. The frequency of these military *coups de main* encouraged audacious spirits; but two years after Catherine's usurpation, Mirovitch, lieutenant of the Guards, conceived the project of delivering Ivan VI. His warders seeing no other means of preventing his escape, put him to death at the moment that Mirovitch entered his chamber, and the conspirator found nothing but his corpse. He was himself arrested and condemned to death. The day of the execution, the people, who during the twenty years' reign of Elizabeth had seen no one beheaded, uttered such a cry and were seized with such emotion, that when the executioner held up the head of Mirovitch the bridge over the Neva almost gave way under the pressure of the crowd, and the balustrades broke. Catherine had now no rival for the throne of Russia, except her own son.

"I know," writes Voltaire some years later, speaking of Catherine—"I know that she is reproached with some trifles about her husband, but these are family affairs with which I do not meddle. And, after all, it is often as well to have a fault to repair; it obliges people to make greater efforts to wrest esteem and admiration from the public." We shall see what efforts were used by Catherine II. to force the Russians to forget the **means by which she had mounted the throne.**

CHAPTER VIII.

CATHERINE II.: EARLY YEARS (1762–1780).

End of the Seven Years' War: intervention in Poland—First Turkish war: first partition of Poland (1772): Swedish Revolution of 1772--Plague at Moscow—Pougatchef.

END OF THE SEVEN YEARS' WAR; INTERVENTION IN POLAND.

In the first moments that followed her triumph, Catherine II. had published a manifesto in which Frederic was treated "as perturber of the public peace," and "perfidious enemy of Russia." She soon, however, altered her sentiments. This princess, who had punished Peter III, for his alliance with Prussia and his designs upon the Church property, was herself destined to realize, both in her foreign and domestic policy, the plans of her husband. Tchernichef had received the order to detach himself from the Prussians, as he had formerly received the order to detach himself from the Austrians. Frederic managed to retard the departure of the general for three days, and Tchernichef consented to occupy with grounded arms a position which covered the Prussian army. Frederic profited by this to defeat Daun at Burkersdorff and Leutmannsdorff. The final withdrawal of Russia from the Seven Years' War hastened the conclusion of peace. During all the early part of her reign, the policy of Catherine II. consisted in what is known as the "system of the North"; that is, a close alliance with Prussia, England, and Denmark, against the two great Powers of the South, the house of Bourbon and the house of Austria. The diplomatic struggle with France especially was very lively in the secondary courts; that is to say, at Warsaw, at Stockholm, and at Constantinople.

The duchy of Courland, legally a dependency of the Polish crown, but in reality annexed to the Russian empire, found itself at that time without a sovereign. Anne Leopoldovna had exiled the Duke Biren; Peter III. had destined the crown to George of Holstein; Augustus III. had coveted it for his son

Charles of Saxony; Catherine put an end to the competition by establishing Biren. It was a union in disguise of Courland and the empire.

A more important event soon absorbed all her attention: this was the approaching death of the King of Poland, and the consequent opening of the whole question of succession. Two parties then disputed the power at Warsaw; the court party, with the minister Brühl and his son-in-law Mniszek, and the party supported by Russia, headed by the Czartoriski. The former wished to secure the succession for the Prince of Saxony, which was also the policy of France and Austria; the latter intended to elect a *piast*, that is, a native noble of their own party, and their choice had fallen on Stanislas Poniatowski, a nephew of Czartoriski. Thus France, which in 1733 had made war for a piast against the Saxon candidate, now supported the Saxon candidate against Poniatowski. Circumstances had changed, and the kingdom of Poland, becoming every day more feeble, could only be sustained at all by the forces of a German state, Saxony. Now Frederic II. feared an increase of power for Saxony quite as much as for Poland; Saxony was the old rival of Prussia in the empire, as Poland had been in the country of the Vistula. Russia, on her side, which, by fighting Stanislas Leszczinski, had fought the father-in-law of Louis XV., now fought for the Saxon, the client of France and Austria. Further, she had no intention that a Polish noble should become too powerful, and meant to get rid of the Czartoriskis. The candidature of Stanislas Poniatowski, a man without any personal power, therefore satisfied both the desires of Frederic II., the interests of the Russian empire, and the sentiments of Catherine, happy to be able to crown one of her early lovers. When Augustus III. really died, the country was violently agitated by the diets of convocation and election. Power was fiercely disputed by the two parties. The Czartoriskis called in the Russian arms to put down their enemies, and under the protection of foreign bayonets Poniatowski inaugurated his fatal reign, in which Poland was thrice dismembered, and erased from the list of the nations.

Three principal causes led to the ruin of the ancient royal republic; 1. The national movement of Russia which tended to complete itself on the Western side, and to "recover," to use the expression of her historians, the provinces which had formed part of the territory of St. Vladimir; that is White Russia, Black Russia, and Little Russia. The national question was complicated by the same religious question which had led, under Alexis Mikhaïlovitch, to a first dismemberment of the

Polish State. The complaints of the agitations of the Uniates had multiplied in Lithuania, and Russia had often tried to interfere diplomatically. In 1718 and 1720 Peter the Great had written to Augustus II. to inform him of the ill-treatment suffered by his co-religionists. Augustus had published an edict which insured the free exercise of the orthodox religion, but which remained unexecuted, as the king was never sufficiently strong to restrain the zeal of the clergy and the Jesuits, to repress the abuses of power on the part of his officers, and to protect the peasants belonging to the Greek Church against their lords. In 1723 Peter had written to the Pope to entreat his interference, threatening reprisals against the Roman Church in his dominions. The Pope declined the proposals of Peter, and the annoyances continued.

2. The second cause of the ruin of Poland was the insatiable greed of Prussia. Poland possessed Western Prussia, that is, the Lower Vistula between Thorn and Dantzig, separating Eastern Prussia from the rest of the Brandenburg monarchy. It thus spoilt the construction of the latter State by dividing it into two parts. Poland also occupied the side of the country where German colonization had greatly developed, especially in the towns. Lastly, the government of Warsaw was so foolish as to annoy the Protestant dissenters in the same way as she did those of the Greek Church.

3. Poland could not escape the spirit of reform which was the spirit of the eighteenth century. Poniatowski and the more enlightened Poles were well aware of the contrast that existed between the national anarchy and the order of the neighboring States. Whilst Prussia, Russia, and Austria tried to constitute themselves into modern States, to build up the central Powers on the ruins of the forces of the Middle Ages, to realize the reforms proclaimed by French philosophers and physiocratists, Poland had up to that time, followed the opposite plan, despoiling the kingly power at each accession, weakening the national strength, persisting in the traditions of feudalism. In the midst of European monarchies which attained, on her very frontiers, the maximum of their power, Poland remained a state of the eleventh century. She had allowed them to get such a start, that even the effort to reform herself hastened her dissolution.

From a social point of view she was a nation of agricultural serfs, overlaid by a numerous class of small nobility, themselves subject to a few great families, against whom the king was absolutely powerless. There was no middle class at all, unless we give that name to some thousands of Catholic citizens and to a million of Jews, who had no interest in maintaining a state of things which condemned them to eternal opprobrium. Economically, she had a primitive system of agriculture worked by a serf population, little commerce, no retail trade, no public finances. Politically, the country was only legally composed of nobles. The rivalry of the great families, the anarchy of the diets, the weakness of the royal power, the *pacta conventa* the *liberum veto*, the *confederations* or *diets under the shield*, the inveterate habit of invoking the intervention of strangers, or of selling them their votes, had extinguished in Poland the very idea of law and a State. From a military point of view the Polish soldiers were merely the lawless soldiers of the Middle Ages; she had only the cavalry of her nobility, no infantry, little artillery, and scarcely any fortresses on her frontiers, which were everywhere exposed. Maurice de Saxe affirms, in his 'Reveries,' that it only needed 48,000 men to conquer Poland. What could she do, divided against herself, long ago corrupted by the gold of her enemies, enclosed by three powerful monarchies, who hardly thought they were violating her frontiers by occupying her territory, and whose ambassadors had more power in her diets than the king?

Catherine and Frederic had come to an understanding on two essential points: to vindicate the rights of the dissenters, and to prevent all reform of the anarchic institution, which was giving Poland into their hands. While affecting to espouse the cause of tolerance, they made Europe forget that it was to be gained at the price of the independence and integrity of the country. The noisy fanaticism of the Poles helped them to conceal their object.

In 1765 Koninski, the orthodox bishop of White Russia, presented a petition to the King of Poland recalling all the vexations to which the Greek Church in the kingdom was subject. Two hundred churches had been taken away from them and given to the Uniates; they were forbidden to rebuild those which had fallen into ruin, or to construct new ones; their priests were ill-treated, sometimes put to death. "The Missionary Fathers," says the petition, "are specially distinguished for their zeal: seconded, when they are engaged on a mission, by the secular authority, they assemble the Greco-Russian people of all the neighboring villages, as if they were a flock of sheep, keep them for six weeks together, force them to confess to them, and, to frighten those that resist, raise impaling poles, display rods, thorny branches, erect scaffolds, separate children from their parents, women from their husbands, and seek to astound them by imaginary miracles. In cases of stout resistance men were beaten with rods, or with thorny branches, their hands were burned, and they were kept in prison for months together."

Russia supported the complaints of the dissenters before the Polish Diet, and Stanislas promised to sustain them. It was necessary to secure to the people the free exercise of their religion, and to the orthodox nobles the political rights of which they had been deprived by former legislatures. The Diet of 1766 made a frantic opposition to this proposal; the deputy Gourovski, who attempted to speak in favor of the dissenters, narrowly escaped being put to death.

Repnine, Catherine's ambassador, got the dissenters to promise that they would resort to the legal means of confederations. The orthodox assembled at Sloutsk, the Protestants under the patronage of the Russian ambassador at Thorn; there was also a confederation of Catholics at Radom, enemies of the Czartoriski, and of those who feared a reform of the constitution, and the abolition of the *liberum veto*. Russia, which with Prussia had guaranteed the maintenance of this absurd constitution, likewise took them under her protection. Eighty thousand Muscovites were ready, at a sign from Repnine, to enter Poland. Under these auspices opened the Diet of 1767: the Poles did not appear to feel the insult to their independence, and only exerted themselves to support the system of intolerance. Soltyk, bishop of Cracow, Zalusski, bishop of Kief, and two other nuncios showed themselves most warm in opposition to the project. Repnine had them removed and taken to Russia, and the Poles had done so much evil themselves that Europe applauded this violation of the law of nations, as it seemed to secure liberty of conscience. The Diet yielded, and consented that the dissident nobles should have political rights equal to those of the Catholics, but Romanism remained the religion of the State, and that which the king must always profess. In 1768 a treaty was made between Poland and Russia, in virtue of which the constitution could never be modified without the consent of the latter Power. This was to legalize foreign intervention, and to condemn Poland to die of her abuses. The Russian troops evacuated Warsaw, and the Confederates sent deputies to thank the Empress.

In spite of this, the Confederation of Radom, the most considerable of the three, which had taken up arms to hinder the reform of the constitution, and in no wise to support reforms in favor of the dissenters, was much discontented with the result. When it was dissolved, there sprang from its remains the Confederation of Bar, in Podolia, more numerous still, and which had adopted as its programme not only the maintenance of the *liberum veto*, but also that of the exclusive privileges of the Catholics. In Gallicia and Lublin two other confederations were formed with the same objects in view. The insurgents took for their motto, "*Pro religione et libertate;*" but the word "liberty" was heard with indifference by the mass of the peeple, who only saw in the "liberty" of the Poles that of the nobles. The confederates of Bar sent deputies to the courts of Dresden, Vienna, and Versailles, to interest them in their cause. In the West opinion might well be perplexed. On which side, men asked, was the nation ranged? Whither did the forces of the future tend? Were right and justice at Warsaw with the king and the senate, and all the men who had voted for the enfranchisement of the dissenters, and who meditated in secret the reform of the constitution and the revival of Poland? Were they at Bar, where turbulent nobles, guided by fanatical priests, revolted in the name of the *liberum veto* and religious intolerance? Voltaire and the greater part of the French philosophers declared in favor of King Stanislas; but M. de Choiseul, minister of Louis XV., supported the Confederates. It did not strike him that by weakening the authority of the Polish king he was weakening Poland herself. The Polish government, in presence of the insurrection, found herself forced to commit a fresh fault. The royal army did not amount to 9000 effective men, and according to the treaty of alliance with Russia, they appealed to her for troops. The Muscovite columns wrested Bar, Berdichef, and Cracow from the Confederates. The orthodox monks replied by their sermons to those of the Catholic priests. Gontaï and Jeliéznak called to arms the Cossacks of the Ukraine, the Zaporogues, and the *haïdamaks*, or brigands. A savage war, at once national, religious, and social, desolated the provinces of the Dnieper; the land-owners and the Jews saw the return of the bloody days of Khmelnitski. The massacre of Ouman, a town of Count Potoçki's, horrified the Ukraine.

The Confederates, repulsed by the Russian columns, had obtained some support from the court of Vienna. They had established the council of the Confederation at Teschen, their head-quarters at Eperies in Hungary, and still held three places in Poland. Choiseul sent them money, and sent also the Chevalier de Taulés, Dumouriez, and the Baron de Viomesnil, to organize them. In the Memoirs of Dumouriez, we find that the forces of the Confederation, scattered through the whole extent of Poland, did not exceed 16,000 or 17,000 horsemen, without infantry, and divided into five or six bands, each with its independent chief. Zaremba in Great Poland, the Cossack Sava, Miaczinski, Walevski, and many others, usually acted without combination. Pulavski was the open enemy of Potoçki; Dumouriez was beaten at Landskron, with his undisciplined troops; but Viomesnil, Dussaillans, and Choisy, three French officers, surprised the Castle of Cracow (1772), shortly afterwards recaptured by Souvorof. An attempt made by some of the Confederates, on the 3rd of November, 1771, to secure the person of the king—whose wounds and remote residence rendered him an easy prey—excited the ostentatious and insincere indignation of the European courts, and increased Voltaire's dislike of the Confederates.

FIRST TURKISH WAR (1767-74): FIRST PARTITION OF POLAND (1772): SWEDISH REVOLUTION OF 1772.

Choiseul imagined that the best way of aiding the Confederates was to induce the Turks to declare war against Russia. Vergennes, the French ambassador at Constantinople, set to work energetically to bring it to pass; but unhappily France greatly exaggerated the power of Turkey, and was ignorant how far her strength had diminished since her last war with Austria The mistake made by Choiseul when he linked the fate of his ally on the Vistula with the success of the Ottoman arms only rendered the partition of Poland inevitable. On the news of the violation of the frontier at Balta, not by the Russian troops but by the *haïdamaks*, when pursued by the former, the Sublime Porte declared war on Russia. The Baron de Tott had been sent by Vergennes to Krim-guérai, Khan of the Crimea, to persuade him to second the Turks. In the winter of 1768, the Tatars devastated the New Servia of Elizabeth. Catherine, whose forces were occupied in Poland, had only a feeble army to oppose to the Turco-Tatar invasion. "The Romans," she writes to her generals, "did not concern themselves with the number of their enemies; they only asked, 'Where are they?'" Galitsyne, with 30,000 men, was therefore ordered to check the Grand Vizier at the head of 100,000, who was on the point of entering Podolia to join the Polish Confederates; Roumantsof was to occupy the Ukraine and watch the Crimean Tatars and the Kalmucks. Galitsyne took the initiative, defeated the Grand Vizier on the Dnieper, near Khotin, which capitulated (1769), and took up a position in Wallachia and Moldavia, to the great joy of the orthodox populations of the Danube. The following year, his successor, Roumantsof, defeated the Khan of the Tatars, although the latter had 100,000 men, and was entrenched on the banks of the Larga. He then gained over the Grand Vizier in person the victory of Kagoul, where 17,000 Russians defeated 150,000 Mussulmans (1770). In 1771 Prince

Dolgoroūki forced the lines of Perekop, ravaged the Crimea, took Kaffa, Kertch, and Ienikale, and put an end forever to the Turkish rule in the peninsula. During this time the army of Wallachia captured the fortresses on the Danube, successfully completed the conquest of Bessarabia by taking Bender, and penetrated into Bulgaria.

Catherine II. had prepared a yet more terrible surprise for the Turkish empire, disturbed as it was by the revolt of the Pacha of Egypt. A Russian fleet left the Baltic under the orders of Alexis Orlof, and, after having put in at the English ports and made the tour of Europe, suddenly appeared on the coast of Greece. The Christian populations of the Western Morea and of Magnesia revolted; Voltaire already announced the regeneration of Athens and the resurrection of Sparta; but Orlof abandoned the Greeks after he had compromised them, and hastened to seek the Turkish fleet. With the help of his lieutenants Spiridof and Greig, he defeated it at the harbor of Chios, and totally annihilated it in the port of Tchesmé, aided by fire-ships led by the English Dugdale. At this news the terror of Constantinople exceeded all bounds; they pictured the Russians arriving in the Bosphorus. Alexis Orlof lost his time in the conquest of the islands, while Baron de Tott rallied the courage of the Sultan and the Turkish people, drilled the Ottoman soldiers, cast cannon, and put the Dardanelles in a state of defence. When the Russians at last presented themselves at the entrance of the Straits, they were too late (1770).

Russia, however, had none the less conquered Azof, the Crimea, the shore of the Black Sea between the Dnieper and the Dniester, Bessarabia, Wallachia, Moldavia, a part of Bulgaria, and of the islands of the Archipelago. She would willingly have kept her conquests, but Austria took fright at her close neighborhood and the rupture of the equilibrium of the East. It was at this point that the Turkish and Polish questions became involved in each other : Poland was to serve as the ransom of Turkey.

Of the three Northern States, Prussia was the most interested in the dismemberment of Poland; she had a geographical necessity to lay hands on Western Prussia, and, if possible, on the cities of the Vistula. It was Frederic II. who had denounced to Catherine the projects of the Czartoriski for the reform of the constitution, and brought to light the wrongs of the dissenters; in a word created the Polish question. It was he who, in the interviews of Neiss (Silesia) and of Neustadt (Moravia), had disquieted Joseph II. and Kaunitz on the subject of the Russian ambition in the East, and had suggested the idea of a partition of Poland; and it was he who had sent his brother Prince Henry to St. Petersburg, to gain over Catherine II. He made her clearly comprehend that her pretensions in the East would cause Austria and France to side against her; that her ally the King of Prussia, weakened by the Seven Years' War, would be unable to stand a war against united Europe; that no doubt she had a right to an equivalent for the expenses of the double war, but that it could matter little to her whence she procured this indemnity, from the Vistula or from the Danube; that she could therefore aggrandize herself at the expense of Poland, and that to re-establish equilibrium in the North she must suffer Prussia and Austria to aggrandize themselves also.

Catherine II., who had already on her hands the wars with Poland and Turkey, could not dream of fighting both Austria and Prussia. Although she would have preferred to maintain the integrity of Poland, on condition of holding a preponderating influence over its affairs, she was forced to submit to the proposal of Frederic II. The King of Prussia knew how to play off Russia and Austria against each other. Even now he was acting as master in Great Poland, taking away the wheat for his own subjects, and the inhabitants for his own army. Once he occupied Dantzig. Austria on her side, in vindication of her ancient rights, invaded the county of Zips. The partition was almost carried out, when it was legalized by the treaty of Feb. 17, 1771, between Prussia and Russia, accepted by Austria in April, and signified to the King of Poland on the 18th of September in that same year. Russia obtained White Russia (Polotsk, Vitepsk, Orcha, Mohilef, Mstislavl, Gomel), with 1,600,000 inhabitants; Austria had Western Gallicia and Red Russia, with 2,500,000 people; while Prussia got possession of the long-coveted Western Prussia, with a population of 900,000 souls.

Russia had still to treat with the Porte. After the rupture of the Congress of Fokchany in 1772, the war had broken out again. The Russians had been forced to raise the siege of Silistria, but they had surrounded the Grand Vizier in his camp of Shumla, and a single victory might open them the way to Constantinople. Sultan Abdul Hamid consented to sign the Peace of Koutchouk-Kairnadji (1774). He undertook: 1, to recognize the independence of the Tatars of the Bug, of the Crimea, and of Kuban; 2, to cede Azof on the Don, Kinburn at the mouth of the Dniester, and all the strong places in the Crimea; 3, to open the Straits of the Bosphorus and the Dardanelles to the merchant ships of Russia; 4, to treat the Russian merchants in the same way as the French, who were then the most favored nation; 5, to grant an amnesty to all the Christian populations engaged in the last insurrection ; 6, to allow the Russian ambassador to interfere in favor of his subjects in the Danubian principalities ; 7, to pay a war indemnity of 4,500,000 roubles, and to recognize the imperial title of the Russian sovereign. Not only did Russia acquire important territories and numerous strategical points, but she established a sort of protectorate over the Christian subjects of the Sultan, and prepared the way for the annexation of the Crimea, of the Kuban, and of all the northern shore of the Black Sea.

France, indirectly defeated in Poland and Turkey, had lately obtained a great diplomatic success in Sweden. Frederic II. and Catherine II. had a tacit understanding to guarantee in the latter country the maintenance of the oligarchic constitution, which was practically the maintenance of anarchy. This was in order to reserve to themselves a pretext for interference, and even to prepare for a dismemberment, which would have given Finland to Russia, and Swedish Pomerania to Prussia ; the *rôle* of third partitioner, played by Austria in the Polish question, was here assigned to Denmark. Gustavus III., who had grown up amidst the clamors and intrigues of the Diet, had determined to reestablish the royal power, as being the only hope for the independence of the country. In 1771, while he was still prince royal, he went to France, visited the philosophers, frequented the fashionable *salons*, amongst others that of Madame Géoffrin, and received encouragement and promises of help from the French government. The spectacle of the anticipated partition of Poland had strengthened him in his patriotic resolutions, and a favorable opportunity seemed offered by the embarrassing situation of both Russia and Prussia. Recalled to Sweden by the death of his father, he prepared his *coup d'état* with the utmost secrecy, having previously gained over the army and the nation. On the 19th of August, 1772, he assembled the Guard, dismissed the senators, made the people of Stockholm rise in revolt, and imposed on the Diet a constitution of fifty-seven articles, which guaranteed the public liberties, at the same time that it restored to the Crown its essential prerogatives. He then abolished torture and the State inquisition, shut up the "cave of roses," a hole full of reptiles used for "the question," and set on foot useful reforms which placed Sweden, already impregnated with French ideas, in the current of the 18th century. The success of this bloodless revolution which doubled the real power of Sweden, and put her beyond the pale of foreign intrigue, caused great mortification to Frederic II. and Catherine ; but the affairs of Poland deprived them of the power or desire to interfere.

THE KREMLIN (IMPERIAL PALACE IN MOSCOW

PLAGUE AT MOSCOW (1771)—POUGATCHEF (1773).

Catherine II., victorious in Poland and in Turkey, found herself face to face with terrible difficulties in her own empire. In 1771 the plague broke out at Moscow, and during the months of July and August the deaths amounted to a thousand a day. The people, wild with fright, thronged to the feet of the holy image of the Mother of God at Bogolioubovo, and many died of suffocation in the crowd. Archbishop Ambrose, an enlightened and educated man, wished to remove the image. This was the signal for a terrible insurrection. "The archbishop is an infidel," cried the people; "he would deprive us of our protectress; he is in a conspiracy with the doctors to make us die. It is not the part of an orthodox nation to suffer the injustice of authority; if he had not caused the streets to be fumigated, the plague would have long ago ceased. To the Kremlin! to the Kremlin! Let us demand of Ambrose why he forbids us to pray to the Mother of God!" Ambrose was put to death, and his palace pillaged. It was necessary to use muskets and cannon to disperse the crowd, which was ready to commit new deeds of violence. Catherine sent Gregory Orlof to appease the revolt, and to reassure the people. At last the plague ceased, and peace was restored.

The insurrection of Moscow proved in what gross darkness the lower classes of the capital (domestic serfs, lackeys, small tradesmen, and working men) then lived. The revolt of Pougatchef shows what elements of disorder had fermented in the distant provinces of the capital. The peasants, on whom were laid the burden of all the State expenses, all the needs of the proprietors, and all the exactions of the officials, forever dreamed of impossible changes. In their profound ignorance they were always ready to follow any impostors, and there were now plenty; false Peters III., Ivans VI., even a Paul I., who were eagerly welcomed by the debased classes, always prejudiced against "the rule of women." The raskolniks, made wild and fanatical by many persecutions, remained in their forests or in the scattered villages of the Volga, irreconcilable enemies of the second Roman empire, stained with the blood of the martyrs. The Cossacks of the Jaïk and the Don, and the Zaporogues of the Dnieper, chafed under the new yoke of authority. The tribes of the Volga (Pagan, Mussulman, or Christian in spite of themselves) only awaited a pretext to recover their lawless liberty, or to reclaim the lands which the Russian colonists had usurped.

How little these ungovernable elements accommodated themselves to the laws of a modern State was seen when, in 1770, the Kalmuck-Torgaouts (men, women, and children), to the number of about 300,000, with their cattle, their tents, and their chariots, abandoned their encampments. Ravaging everything in their road, they crossed the Volga, and retired to the territory of the empire of China. When we add to these malcontents the vagabonds of all kinds, the ruined nobles, the disfrocked monks, the military deserters, fugitive serfs, highwaymen, and Volga pirates, we shall see that Russia, especially in her Oriental part, contained all the materials necessary for an immense Jacquerie, like those which the false Dmitri or Stenko Razine had let loose. The Jaïk, whose Cossacks had risen in 1766, and had been cruelly repressed, was destined to furnish the expected chief to this servile war. Emilian Pougatchef, a Cossack deserter and a raskolnik, who had been already confined in the prison of Kazan, and had escaped from Siberia, gave himself out as Peter III., and asserted that he was saved under the very hands of the executioner. Displaying the banner of Holstein, he proclaimed that he would march to St. Petersburg to punish his wife and to crown his son. He besieged the small fortress of Jaïk with only 300 men. This was an insignificant affair, but all the troops sent against him passed over to his side and delivered up their chiefs. He always hung the officers, and cut the hair of the soldiers in the Cossack style. In the villages the nobles were also hung. All who resisted him were punished as rebels, convicted of the crime of high treason. He thus gained possession of many little fortresses on the Steppe. Whilst his intimate friends who knew his origin treated him when alone as a simple Cossack, the people began to receive him with bells, and the priests to present him bread and salt. Some of the Polish Confederates, captives in those regions organized his artillery. For almost a year he made Kazan and Orenburg tremble, and defeated all the generals sent against him. Everywhere proprietors fled, and the barbarous tribes hastened to his head-quarters. The peasants rose against the nobles, the Tatars and Tchouvaches against the Russians: a war of race, a social war, a servile war, was let loose in the basin of the Volga. Moscow, with its 100,000 serfs, was agitated: the lower orders, seeing the frightened land-owners pour in from Eastern Russia, began openly to speak of liberty and the extermination of the masters. Catherine II. charged Alexander Bibikof to check the progress of the scourge. Bibikof, on his arrival at Kazan was alarmed at the universal demoralization, but he rallied his courage, reassured and armed the nobles, restrained the people, and affected the greatest confidence, while he wrote to his wife, "The evil is great—it is frightful! Ah! all will go ill." He thoroughly comprehended that all this disorder was not the work of a single man. "Pougatchef," he said, "is only a bugbear worked by the Cossacks; it is not Pougatchef that is important, but the general discontent." Although very uncertain of his own troops, he attacked the impostor, defeated him both at Tatichtcheva and at Kargoula, dispersed his army and took his guns. Bibikof died in the midst of his victories, but his lieutenants, Michelson, de Collonges, and Galitsyne, gave chase to Pougatchef. Tracked to the Lower Volga, he suddenly ascended the river, threw himself into Kazan which he pillaged and burned, received a check before its Kremlin, and was beaten on the Kazanka. Then he returned down the river, boldly entered Saransk, Samara, and Tzaritsyne, and, though closely followed by his enemies, had time to hang the imperialists, and to establish new municipalities. During his retreat to the south the people awaited him on the road to Moscow, and, in order not to disappoint them, false Peters III. and false Pougatchefs sprang up on all sides, and at the head of savage bands put proprietors to death and burned castles. Moscow was nearer revolt than ever. It was time that Pougatchef was arrested. Shut in between the Volga and the Jaïk, by Michelson and the indefatigable Souvorof, he was pinioned and surrendered by his own accomplices, at the very moment he intended flying into Persia. He was brought to Moscow, so that the people might witness his punishment. Many declined to believe in the death of the false Peter III., and if the revolt was put down the spirit of revolt existed some time longer.

It was a warning for Catherine II., and she remembered it when in 1775 she extinguished the Zaporogue republic. This brave tribe, expelled by Peter the Great, and recalled by Anne Ivanovna, no longer recognized their former territory in the Ukraine. Southern Russia, freed from Tatar incursions, was rapidly colonized; cities rose everywhere, the boundaries of property were fixed, and the vast herbaceous steppes, through which their ancestors had roamed as freely as the Arabs in the desert, were transformed into cultivated fields with a beautiful black soil. The Zaporogues were much discontented with this transformation; they intended to reclaim their lands, and reestablish the desert; they protected the *haïdamaks*, who illtreated the colonists. Potemkine, the creator of New Russia, became weary of these inconvenient neighbors. By order of the Empress he occupied the *sétcha* and destroyed it. The malcontents fled to the territory of the Sultan; the rest were organized like the Black Sea Cossacks, and in 1792 the Isle of Phanagoria and the eastern shore of the Sea of Azof were assigned them. Such was the end of the great Cossack power. It **no longer** existed save in the songs of the *kobzars*.

CHAPTER IX.

CATHERINE II.: GOVERNMENT AND REFORMS.

The helpers of Catherine II.: the great legislative commission (1766-1768)—Administration and justice: colonization—Public instruction—Letters and arts—The French Philosophers.

THE HELPERS OF CATHERINE II.: THE GREAT LEGISLATIVE COMMISSION (1766-1768).

CATHERINE II. surrounded herself with distinguished fellow-workers, some of whom were her favorites. In the early part of her reign, the influence of the Orlofs was predominant; these were Gregory Orlof, the favorite *par excellence*, grand master of the artillery, by whom she had a recognized son, Alexis, created Count Bobrinski; Alexis Orlof, the admiral, who received the name of Tchesmenski after the expedition to the Archipelago, and was involved in the tragic history of the Princess Tarankof; Theodore Orlof, who became procurator-general of the Senate; Vladimir Orlof, who was director of the Academy of Sciences at the age of twenty-one. Later, the favor of the Orlofs was outweighed by that of Potemkine, creator of New Russia, organizer of the Crimea, conqueror of the Ottomans in the second war with Turkey, and who, as Prince of the Taurid, displayed his Asiatic luxury in his palace of the same name at St. Petersburg. Of all the favorites who, in the latter part of the reign, succeeded each other so rapidly, only one had any real influence over affairs. This was Plato Zoubof, whose brother Valerian conducted the war with Persia. In the direction of foreign affairs were distinguished Nikita Panine, and later Bezborodko, Ostermann, Markof, and Voronzof. Repnine and Sievers in Poland, Budberg at Stockolm, Semen Veronzof in London, and Dmitri Galitsyne at Paris, have made themselves a name in diplomacy. The army was commanded by Alexander Galitsyne, Dolgorouki, Roumantsof, and Souvorof; the fleet by Greig, Spiridof, and Tchitchagof; Ivan Betski had charge of the fine arts and of benevolent institutions.

From 1766 to 1768 Catherine II. assembled first at Moscow and afterwards at St. Petersburg the commission for the compilation of the new code. This commission was composed of deputies from all the services of the State, from all the orders and all the races of the empire. Besides the delegates from the Senate, the synod, and the colleges and the courts of Chancery, the nobles elected a representative for each district, the citizens one for every city, the *odnovortsi* or free colonists one for every province, the soldiers, militia, and other fighting men, also one for each province; the Crown peasants, the fixed tribes, whether Christians or not, equally elected one for each province; the deputation of the Cossack armies was fixed by their atamans.

Six hundred and fifty-two deputies assembled at Moscow; officials, nobles, citizens, peasants, Tatars, Kalmucks, Lapps, Samoyedes, and many others. Each man was to be furnished with full powers and with papers compiled by at least five of the electors. Each received a medal with the effigy of Catherine, and the motto, "For the happiness of each and of all, Dec. 14, 1766." The were exempted forever from all corporal punishments, and were declared inviolable during the session. In the 'Instructions for the arrangement of the New Code,' Catherine II. had, according to her own expression, "pillaged" the philosophers of the West, especially Montesquieu and Becaria. "It contained," says the prudent Panine, "axioms enough to knock a wall down." Catherine II. assures Voltaire that her 'Instruction' was interdicted at Paris. Among the ideas of which she boasted, we meet with the following, which were certainly calculated to enrage Louis XV.:—"The nation is not made for the sovereign, but the sovereign for the nation. Equality consists in the obedience of the citizens to the law alone, liberty is the right to do all that is not forbidden by law. It is better to spare ten guilty men than to put one innocent man to death. Torture is an admirable means for convicting an innocent but weakly man, and for saving a stout fellow even when he is guilty," Other maxims loudly condemned intolerance, religious persecutions, and cruel punishments.

The assembly nominated many committees, and held more than two hundred sittings. The most vexed questions were openly discussed. Nobles of the Baltic claimed their provincial rights, merchants brought forward municipal organization and all economical questions, gentlemen proposed to restrain the rights of masters, and to pronounce the pregnant word "enfranchisement of the peasants." It was not, however, an assembly so numerous, so divided by the interests of classes, and of such various races that could arrange a new code. It was a work almost impossible in the Russia of that period, which contained within itself so many divers forces. The Empress, forced by the Turkish war to break up the assembly, expressed herself satisfied with her experiment. "The Commission for the Code has given me hints for all the empire. I know now what is necessary, and with what I should occupy myself. It has elaborated all parts of the legislation, and has distributed the affairs under heads. I should have done more without the war with Turkey, but a unity hitherto unknown in the principles and methods of discussion has been introduced." These States-general of Russia influenced the laws of Catherine II., as the French States-general of 1356, of 1413, or of the 16th century influenced the laws of Charles V., Charles VII., or the later Valois.

In the course of the discussions the deputy noble Korobine had proposed to suppress the rights of property over the serfs, and only to leave the masters the right of superintendence. Protapof, another deputy, then observed that "in that case nothing would remain but to set the peasant free, but that, if this was the intention of the Empress, it was necessary to proceed gradually." The Economical Society founded, under the auspices of Catherine II., by the care of Gregory Orlof and other "patriots," had put the question to the assembly. A paper, dated from Aix-la-Chapelle, pronouncing for emancipation, obtained the prize, but other influences were at work to efface the recollection of this essay from the mind of the Empress. The Russian aristocracy were then little disposed to abdicate their rights, as is shown by the conversations of Princess Dachkof with Diderot, and the correspondence of Dmitri Galitsyne. Catherine confined herself to repressing the most crying abuses. The trial of Daria Saltydof, convicted of having caused the death of forty of her servants by torture, shows to what a point slavery, which degrades the serf, could demoralize the masters. She was condemned in 1768 to be publicly pilloried, and to perpetual imprisonment; her memory still lives in the legends of the people. The same reasons which had caused the establishment of serfage in the time of Boris Godounof seemed to operate in favor of its continuance. Catherine II., in spite of a few generous impulses, finally aggravated the existing state of things. More than 150,000 Crown peasants were transformed into serfs of nobles, by being distributed among her favorites. In 1767 an edict forbade peasants to complain of their masters, who were authorized to send them at will to Siberia, or to force them to become recruits. Catherine II. established serfage in **Little Russia**, where it had hitherto had no legal existence.

ADMINISTRATION AND JUSTICE : COLONIZATION.

The Empress's "Council" deprived the Senate of part of its political importance; but the latter, divided into six departments, had under its jurisdiction all the branches of the public administration. Catherine II. attacked the *viesiatski*, exactions and peculations—the most inveterate evil of this administration. "I consider it," says a oukaze of 1762, " as my most essential and necessary duty to declare to the people, with the profoundest sorrrw, that corruption has progressed so rapidly that it is hardly possible to cite an administration or a tribunal that is not infected by it. If anyone asks for a place, he must pay for it; if a man has to defend himself against calumny, it is with money; if you wish falsely to accuse your neighbor, you can by gifts insure the success of your wicked designs. Many judges have transformed the sacred place where they should administer justice in the name of the Almighty into a market. My heart trembled when I learned that a *registrar* of the Government Court of Chancery at Novgorod found an opportunity, while receiving the oath of allegiance from my subjects, to accept from each a piece of money."

One means of securing the administration of the laws was, perhaps, to diminish the extent of the governments, which placed the seat of justice too far from the people governed. By an edict of 1775 Catherine modified all the territorial divisions of the empire. Instead of fifteen provinces she created fifty governments, each with a population of from 300,000 to 400,000 souls, and subdivided into districts of 20,000 to 30,000 inhabitants. Every province had its governor and its vice-governor; the governor-generals, or *namiéstniki*, were invested with authority over two or three governments. Thus Livonia, Esthonia, and Courland had each a governor, with a governor-general between them. Administration was definitely separated from justice; each governor was aided by a council of regency for administration and the police, by a chamber of finance for taxes, property, mines, the census, and a college of provision for hospitals and the assistance of the public.

The judicial system increased the profound separation of classes. There were, in the first instance, *district tribunals* for gentlemen, *city magistrates* for the townspeople, *inferior justices* for the *odnovortsi* or free colonists, and for the Crown peasants. There was nothing for the serfs of the nobles. No text of law positively authorized the repression of the most cruel seignorial abuses ; the sense of two articles of the military code had to be wrested before even the lives of the agricultural slaves could be protected. As courts of appeal, a supreme tribunal, a government magistracy, and a superior court of justice were to be found in the head-quarters of each division of government. All this hierarchy led to a court of final appeal in the Senate. In the towns of the government there were juries for certain criminal causes which acted as justices of the peace in civil actions.

The nobility had received a sort of provincial organization. In each government there existed an assembly of the nobles, which elected a marshal and other dignitaries; and as Catherine II. could not revoke the law of Peter III., she forced gentlemen to serve by depriving those nobles of the right of suffrage in the elections who had not obtained the rank of officers, and also refused them certain prerogatives of their own order.

Special privileges had been accorded to the merchants and citizens (*miéchtchanes*) of the towns; among them were the election of their magistrates, an individual jurisdiction, and a kind of municipal self-government. They were divided, like the merchants, into three guilds: to the first belonged men with a capital of less than 10,000 roubles; to the second, those who had at least 1000; to the third, those with a property worth more than 500 roubles. Below this, all the citizens were confounded in the appellation of *miéchtchanes*. In the matter of commerce and trade Catherine had renounced the system of protection and surveillance adopted by Peter the Great, except in the case of cereals, the consumption of which she tried to regulate by establishing granaries in abundance. She finally suppressed the three colleges of mines, manufactures, and commerce.

To people the uninhabited though fertile lands of the Volga and the Ukraine, Catherine called in foreign colonists; she offered them a capital to aid in their settlement, for which no interest was to be asked for the space of ten years, and exempted them from all taxes for thirty years. These colonists were chiefly Germans, the greater part from the Palatinate. Like Frederic II., she offered an asylum to the Moravians, and to all persecuted religious sects. In the province of Saratof alone, she induced 12,000 families to take up their abode, whose descendants, now very numerous, still inhabit the country, and preserve unbroken the German language and customs. In the single year of 1771 as many as 26,000 people answered her appeal. The suppression of the hetmanate of Little Russia, and the extinction of the *setcha* of the Zaporogues, favored colonization. The Empress founded nearly 200 new towns, many of which, as Ekaterineburg and Ekaterinoslaf ("glory of Catherine"), bore her name. They have not all prospered, but in 1793 Pallas reckoned a population of 33,000 at Saratof.

One reform projected by Peter I., and clumsily pushed forward by Peter III., was accomplished by Catherine II. : this was the secularization of the Church property. The number of peasants belonging to the clergy, regular as well as secular, amounted to nearly a million. The monastery of St. Cyril, on the White Lake, possessed 35,000; that of St. Sergius, at Troitsa, 120,000. The abbots of these monasteries may be compared to the sovereign prelates, to the priest-kings on the banks of the Rhine. Catherine II., who was afterwards to protest so loudly against the resumption of Church property during the French Revolution, effected this important change with the greatest quietness. She formed a commission of churchmen and functionaries, who managed to carry out the operation. The property of the Church was placed under the administration of an "economical commission," charged with the collection of the revenues, in the proportion of a rouble and a half for every male peasant. The monasteries, thus converted from proprietors to Crown-pensioners, were indemnified according to their importance, and were divided into three classes. Their surplus revenues were applied to the foundation of ecclesiastical schools, homes for invalids, and hospitals.

Catherine II. had written an account of the work of the commission in compiling the code, to Voltaire. "I think you will be pleased by this assembly, where the orthodox man is to be found seated between the heretic and the Mussulman, all three listening to the voice of an idolater, and all four consulting how to render their conclusion palatable to all." This was the restoration of religious tolerance in Russia, after the reign of the pious Elizabeth. In the provinces taken from Poland, a natural reaction from the Polish system obtained many converts to orthodoxy; in the latter years of the reign they amounted to 1,500,000 souls. Catherine II. was so far from persecuting the Catholics, that she allowed the Jesuits, notwithstanding their legal suppression by Pope Clement XIV., to purchase the right of existence in White Russia. She authorized the Volga Tatars to rebuild their mosques, and thus checked the Mussulman emigration provoked by the severity of Elizabeth. The raskolniks were protected, reassured, and freed from the double tax imposed on them by Peter the Great, and the "bureau" of the raskolniks was suppressed.

The population of the empire increased during this reign to 40,000,000, but it was still far too small to cultivate the enormous plains. One great obstacle to the multiplication of the inhabitants has always been the want of hygiene, the lack of doctors, the absence of all assistance from science, and the mortality of children, which counterbalanced the fruitfulness of the marriages. Catherine II. did everything that could be done at that period. She encouraged the study of medicine, sent for foreign physicians, founded a "department of the College of Pharmacy" at Moscow, helped to build manufactories of chirurgical instruments, introduced inoculation into Moscow, and vanquished the popular outcry by being herself the first subject. She desired Dimsdale, the Englishman, to inoculate her as well as her son by Gregory Orlof. This was at the time that smallpox carried off Louis XV. and the children of the King of Spain. "That is very foreign," writes Catherine to Voltaire; and again "more people have been inoculated here in one month than have been inoculated in Vienna in a year." Even the natives of Siberia recognized the benefits of the new invention, but the Mussulmans, the raskolniks, and part of the Russian people energetically defended themselves against it.

PUBLIC INSTRUCTION—LETTERS AND ARTS—FRENCH PHILOSOPHY.

The Empress displayed the same eagerness to instruct the upper and middle classes, if she did not seek to touch the people, properly speaking, whose masses could not be penetrated by a culture that was still superficial. "To triumph over secular superstitions," she dictated to Betski, "to give a new education, and in one sense a new life to the people, is a work demanding incredible toil, and of which posterity alone will reap the fruits." From the lack of a national education, "Russia wanted the class of men known in other countries as the third estate." Betski thought it necessary that the children should be taught by Russians, as strangers would fail to understand how much in their pupils belonged to the religion, habits, and manners of the country. The moment had not yet come when Russia could do without foreign teachers. The scheme of national education for children of all classes, presented by Betski, could only partially be realized; secondary schools were founded in the great cities alone. Catherine II. also interested herself in the instruction of women. At the monastery or institute of Smolna, she assembled 480 young girls, under the direction of a Frenchwoman, Madame Lafond. "We want them to be neither prudes nor coquettes," she writes to Voltaire. French and other foreign languages and accomplishments were taught there; but the line between the pupils of noble birth and tradesmen's daughters was sharply drawn. A splendid foundation of Catherine's was the "Vospitatelnyi Dom," or house of education at

Moscow,—a large establishment, which was to extort admiration from Napoleon I., and where nearly 40,000 children in need of assistance, or girl-pupils, were received in Catherine's reign. The serf who married one of these orphans became free.

The influence of French genius over Russian civilization greatly increased during the reign of Catherine II. The national poets translated and imitated the French classics of the 17th century. The great Russian nobles, like the Voronzofs and the Galitsynes, esteemed it an honor, as did the French nobility on their side, to correspond with the writers and thinkers of the West. Catherine II. quotes, in the preface to her laws, some of Montesquieu's most audacious maxims. This French influence was beneficial, although it was only exercised on the upper classes of society, and often stopped at the exterior without modifying either the character or the manners. It was this that introduced or strengthened in the Russian nobility those ideas of religious tolerance, of moral dignity, of respect for the human body, even in the person of a slave,—those habits of courtesy and politeness, those aspirations after social justice and political liberty, which must, in the long run, perform their work, soften the hardness of the old boyards, prepare for the emancipation of the agricultural classes, and bring about the regeneration of Russia. We shall, however, see the Russian nobility, who had apparently followed the French philosophers into their most audacious deductions, suddenly frightened at the most moderate reforms of 1789, and declaring loudly against revolutionary France. We shall find characters in which a slight varnish of Parisian civilization scarcely hides the ancient barbarism, but it was not in vain that Catherine's contemporaries had been fascinated by Montesquieu, by Voltaire, and by the American revolution. The social state of Russia, divided into an aristocracy of proprietors and a people of serfs, prevented the country from advancing with the same rapidity as France, bu French ideas did not delay her progress.

Catherine II. was not less eager than her nobles in seeking the sympathy of French writers ; her correspondence with philosophers added not a little to her *prestige* in the Europe of the 18th century, and to her fame with posterity. She attracted Grimm, once a friend of Rousseau, to her service, and he sent her regular letters from Paris on the affairs of France. She affected a gracious familiarity towards the Prince de Ligne, and the French ambassador, Count de Ségur, both men distinguished for wit and literary talents : admitted them into her travelling-carriage during a long journey to the South, and was able to respond to their ingenious flatteries and to their lively sallies. She wished to employ Mercier de la Rivière, and to secure the services of Beccaria, author of the 'Treatise on Crimes and Penalties;' she declared herself the "good friend" of Madame Géoffrin, whose Parisian *salon* was one of the intellectual powers of that epoch. She offered to D'Alembert, who refused it, the superintendence of the education of the Grand Duke Paul, heir to the throne; later, she placed the Swiss Laharpe, celebrated for his republican opinions, with her grandsons Alexander and Constantine. She thanked Marmontel for sending her his 'Belisarius,' "a book which deserves to be translated into all languages," caused a translation of it to be made by her friends during a voyage down the Volga, and even undertook the ninth chapter herself. She bought the library of Diderot, yet allowed him to enjoy it; subscribed to the 'Encyclopædia,' which was forbidden to appear in Paris; admired the 'Pensees Philosophiques,' condemned by the Parliament to be burned, and the 'Lettre surles Aveugles,' which had consigned the philosopher to the Bastile. She sent for the author to St. Petersburg, and entertained him for a month with the most brilliant hospitality. The great sculptor Falconet, the friend of Diderot and the Encyclopædists, was already there, working at the statue of Peter the Great. It was with Voltaire, above all, that Catherine kept up a close correspondence, beginning in 1763, and continuing to the death of the great man in 1778. She wished herself to keep him informed, not only of her victories, but of her reforms, her efforts at legislation and labors for the colonization of Russia, knowing that the hermit of Ferney had fame in his gift. She gave money to his *protégés*, the families of Sirven and Calas, victims of the judicial abuses of the 18th century; and, after the expedition of Alexis Orlof to the Archipelago, caused him to hope for the resurrection of Greece. She multiplied the purchases of pictures and works of art, and endowed the capital of Peter the Great with artistic splendors hitherto unknown.

In spite of her devotion to the arts and letters of the West, Catherine piqued herself on being, above everything, a Russian empress; and jestingly bade her doctor to bleed her of her last drop of German blood. She has a place of her own in Russian literature of the 18th century, having compiled for the use of her grandsons Alexander and Constantine the 'Grandmother's A.B.C.,' stories from Russian history, and a whole 'Alexandro-Constantine Library,' which had the honor to be printed in Germany. The prefaces to her laws, her correspondence in Russian, French, and German with her ministers, her governors, and friends in France and Germany, prove her literary activity. She also worked for the new-born Russian theatre: in her lyric drama called ' Oleg,' the first expedition of the Russians against Constantinople is celebrated ; in her comedy of ' Goré Bogatyr' (the Knight of Misfortune), she turns into ridicule the adventurous Gustavus III. ; in those of the ' Charlatan ' and the 'Mystified Man,' she chastises Cagliostro, who sought for dupes even in Russia ; while the ' Birthday of Madame Vortchalkina,' ' O Time,' and many others, are satires on contemporary manners. Against the French Abbe Chappe d'Auteroche, and his voyage to Siberia, she published an amusing pamphlet, called ' The Antidote.' Finally, she has left in French some curious memoirs about her arrival in Russia and her life as a Grand Duchess.

The Russian Academy, modelled in some degree after the French, was founded in 1783, on the suggestion of Princess Dachkof, then President of the Academy of Sciences. The task of "fixing the rules of the orthography, grammar, and prosody of the Russian language, and of encouraging the study of Russian history," was confided to her. She then undertook the publication of a dictionary which appeared from 1789 to 1799, which included in its six volumes 43,257 words, and was re-edited from 1840 to 1850. Indeed the Russian Academy was so much in fashion that the most illustrious men of letters and the highest ladies of rank—Princess Dachkof, the poets Derjavine, Fon-Vizine, Kniajnine, and Count Ivan Schouvalof—insisted on working at the dictionary. Catherine II. herself compiled ' Complementary Notes ' for the first volume. In 1835, the minister Ouvarof amalgamated the Russian Academy with the Academy of Sciences, under the title of " Second Class."

Catherine II. made herself the patroness of Russian *literati*. If she imposed the recital of a certain number of lines from the Telemachid of Trediakovski as a penance on her friends of Tsarkoe-Selo, or the Hermitage, she encouraged Fon-Vizine, the comic author, the Russian Moliere, who in his comedy of the ' Brigadier ' derided those whose only reading were the French romances, and ridiculed in his ' Fop' (the *niedorosl*) the indolence and frivolity of the young Russian nobles, the foolish infatuation of their parents, and the strange choice of their preceptors. The taste for the pleasures of wit was spread by the theatre of Soumarokof, in many ways an imitation of the French theatre, whose plays were often acted by the corps of cadets, at the court and in public places. Kniajnine wrote ' The Miller,' a comedy which has kept its place on the boards, ' The Boaster,' ' The Originals,' ' The Fatal Carriage,' and attempted an historical drama in ' Vadim of Novgorod.' Kheraskof composed ' The Russiad,' an epic poem. Bogdanovitch reproduced, in the light poetry of the " Douchenka," the antique subject of Psyche.

Chemnitzler translated the fables of Gellert, and invented others in Russian, whose natural ease recalled La Fontaine and predicted Krylof. Derjavine, in hi odes ' To God ' on ' The Capture of Ismail,' ' The Death of Prince Mechtcherski,' ' The Cascade,' ' My Idol, ' The Great Noble,' continued the lyrical traditions of Lomonossof. His piece of ' Felitsa,' a lively satire of high society, full of malicious allusions to different people of the court, which might have cost him dear under the preceding reigns, gained him a golden tobacco-box and a rich gift from the Empress, who took care to send copies of the ' Felitsa ' to all alluded to, underlining the passages applied to them. Although a poet, Gerjavine was Minister of Justice.

The ardent and laborious Novikof, in order that the new culture might penetrate to the silent masses of the smaller tradespeople, and also to the people, took up the ' Moscow Gazette,' : e-cured for it 4000 subscribers (an enormous number for the time), perfected the Russian typography, created new libraries, and published a series of reviews and magazines for home readings for the young and for nearly illiterate workmen. Among these were the ' Pilgrim's Staff,' the ' Painter,' the ' Purse,' the ' Ancient Library of Russia,' the ' Couriers of Russian Antiquities,' the ' Morning Aurora,' the ' Evening Aurora,' the ' Edition of Moscow,' and the ' Rest of the Worker.' He founded some philanthropical societies, and that of the Friends of Instruction, and took in hand the cause of national education.

The aged Müller edited the first ' National History of Russia,' by Tatichtchef ; and the ' Kernel of Russian History,' by Mankief. Pallas of Berlin performed his celebrated travels in the Crimea, in Siberia, and on the frontiers of China, and was given by the Empress an estate in the Taurid. Golikof, pardoned by Catherine II. on the occasion of the inauguration of Falconet's bronze, vowed at the feet of Peter's statue to raise an historical monument to the glory of the Russian hero, and published in twelve volumes the ' Actions of Peter the Great.' Prince Chtcherbatof wrote the ' History of Russia from the most Remote Times.' Boltine discussed the recent history of Russia by the French Leclerc. Moussine-Pouchkine discovered the unique manuscript of the ' Song of Igor.' Khrapovitski (confidential secretary of Catherine II.), Porochine (one of the masters of the Grand Duke Paul), Nikita Panine (the diplomatist), the great nobles, Semen and Alexander Voronzof, their sister Catherine Dachkof, and the old soldier Bolotof, collected or prepared valuable memoirs on the reigns of Elizabeth and Catherine. The historian Karamzine, and the dramatic poet Ozerof, the glories of the following reigns, were yet only boys.

CHAPTER X.

CATHERINE II. : LAST YEARS (1779-1796).

Franco-Russian mediation at Teschen (1779)—Armed neutrality (1780)—Reunion of the Crimea (1783)—Second war with Turkey (1787-1792) and war with Sweden (1788-1790)—Second partition of Poland : Diet of Grodno—Third partition : Kosciuszko—Catherine II. and the French Revolution—War with Persia.

FRANCO-RUSSIAN MEDIATION AT TESCHEN (1779)—ARMED NEUTRALITY (1780)—REUNION OF THE CRIMEA (1783).

THE second part of the reign of Catherine II. is characterized by the abandonment of the "System of the North"; that is, of the English and Prussian alliance, and by a marked reconciliation, first with Austria and then with France. The dominant influence in foreign affairs of Nikita Panine was to give place to that of Bezborodko, and especially of Potemkine, who became all-powerful. It was at this epoch that the French ambassadors (the Marquis de Juigné, Bourée de Corberon, the Marquis de Vérac, and above all the Comte de Ségur) were again taken into favor in Russia.

In 1777, the Elector of Bavaria being dead, his succession occasioned a conflict between the house of Austria and Frederic II. In order to stop this war, which had already begun in Bohemia, the Courts of France and Russia agreed to offer their mediation, and in 1779 assembled a Congress at Teschen, where M. Breteuil represented Louis XVI., and the Prince Repnine Catharine II. Peace was signed on the 10th of May. Bavaria passed to the Elector Palatine, and Austria only acquired some districts upon the Danube, the Inn, and the Salza.

In 1780, during the American War, the Empress, moved to indignation by the wrongs committed by the English Admiralty against foreign merchantmen, joined with Sweden, Denmark, Prussia, Austria, and Portugal to proclaim an armed neutrality. The celebrated act embodied the principles of a new maritime law, agreeing with the French code of 1778. It was settled:

1. That neutral ships could freely navigate the coasts of the nations at war. 2. That the goods belonging to the subjects of the belligerent powers should be safe in neutral vessels, except in the case of contraband merchandise. 3. That "contraband goods" only included arms and munition. 4. That a port should only be considered in a state of blockade when the blockade was effectual—that is, when the vessels attacking it should be so near as to render it dangerous to pass out. 5. That these principles should serve as a rule in trials and judgments on the legality of captures.

These principles were opposed at all points to those which the English Admiralty wished to see prevail. The latter held the theory that the blockade exists from the moment that it is declared by an act of the Admiralty, and considered as contraband even grain, and all that could be, however indirectly, of use to the belligerents. France, who had at first laid down these principles, and to whom the armed neutrality brought a moral support in her struggle with Great Britain, adhered to this declaration. Her allies, Spain and the Two Sicilies, imitated her. Holland even began a war with England to maintain the rights of the neutral Powers.

The Crimea had been declared independent by the Treaty of Kaïrnadji; and since 1774 anarchy had been the normal state of the peninsula. The Sultan, deprived by the treaty of his temporal sovereignty, continued, as successor of the Khalifs, to claim the religious supremacy. The Mourzas, abandoned to themselves, were divided into two, the Russian party and the Turkish party, which in turn made and unmade a Khan of the Crimea. Nearly 35,000 Christians, Greeks, Armenians or Catholics, disturbed by these civil discords, quitted the ravine of Tchoufout-Kalé and the wonder-working sanctuary of the Assumption, dug out of the hard rock, and emigrated in a body to the territory of Russia. In 1775, the Khan Sahib-Ghirei, who was devoted to Russia, was overthrown and replaced by Devlet-Ghirei. He in his turn was dethroned by Catherine, and Chahin-Ghirei reigned in his stead, but, by his attempts at European reforms, caused a general revolt. Russia interfered; she proclaimed the union of the empire and the peninsula, which had been since the 13th century the home of banditti, and whose gullies had so often sent forth Tatar squadrons to bring fire and flame to Moscow. Thus Catherine finished the work of the conqueror of Kazan, of Astrakhan, and of Siberia, by the extinction of the last kingdom that recalled the Mongol yoke.

The two military States which formerly disputed the steppes of the South, the Tatar khanate and the equally warlike republic of the Zaporogues, succumbed almost at the same time. In face of the advent of civilization, these old enemies were alike condemned to total ruin. Representatives of the ancient anarchy, children of the desert and the steppe, knights of pillage and of prey, they constituted a dangerous anachronism and an intolerable anomaly on the frontier of a prosperous Russia. The Porte protested against the annexation of the Crimea, and threatened a rupture ; but France, which had formerly excited the war, tried this time to smooth matters. Catherine II. recognized the good offices of the ambassador Saint-Priest, and addressed her thanks to Louis XVI. The Sultan acknowledged the cession of the Crimea and of the Kuban by the Treaty of Constantinople (1783).

In 1784 the Grand Duke Paul and his wife, under the names of the Count and Countess du Nord, had made a tour in the West, and received a brilliant reception in Paris. In 1787 the Comte de Ségur, thanks to the good terms on which he stood with Potemkine, and the latter's desire to hasten the development of Odessa, by trading with the French ports on the Mediterranean, concluded a treaty of commerce, an important negotiation in which all his predecessors had hitherto failed.

SECOND WAR WITH TURKEY (1787–1792) AND WAR WITH SWEDEN (1788–1790).

All this time Russia maintained a close alliance with Joseph II., whom she had gained over to her ambitious projects in the East. The Cabinet of St. Petersburg proposed to that of Vienna a plan for the dismemberment of Turkey. "There ought to exist between the Russian, Austrian, and Turkish monarchies, an intermediate State, independent of each, which, under the name of Dacia, should comprehend Moldavia, Wallachia, and Bessarabia, and have a sovereign of the Greek Church. Russia was to acquire Otchakof and the seaboard between the Bug and the Dnieper, besides one or two isles in the Archipelago. Austria was to annex the Turkish provinces on her frontiers. If the war were crowned with such success that the Turks were expelled from Constantinople, the Greek empire was to be re-established in complete independence, and the throne of Byzantium to be filled by the Grand Duke Constantine Pavlovitch, who was to renounce all claims to the throne of Russia, so that the two kingdoms might never be united under the same sceptre." Joseph II. accepted these propositions, but further stipulated that besides Servia, Bosnia, and the Herzegovina, the Slav provinces of the Turkish empire, he should have the Venetian possessions in Dalmatia. Venice was to receive in exchange the Morea, Candia, and Cyprus. England, France, and Spain might share in the spoils of Turkey. Such was the celebrated scheme of partition, known under the name of the "Greek project," which would have fulfilled all the wishes of Voltaire, who had died five years previously.

The attitude of Russia became each day more threatening to the Porte. The second son of Paul I. bore the significant name of Constantine, and had been given a Greek nurse. The Taurid, annexed by Catherine II., who had alleged the security of the empire as the reason of her act, became, in the hands of Potemkine, a menace to the Turks. Already Cherson had a formidable arsenal; Sebastopol was being built; there was a Russian fleet on the Black Sea, and in two days it might cast anchor under the walls of the Seraglio. Catherine's agents continued to agitate in the Roumanian, Slav, and Greek provinces, and even in Egypt; she was preparing to incorporate the Caucasus, and had taken the Tzar of Georgia under her protection. The triumphal journey made by the Empress in 1787 to the governments of the South and the newly-conquered provinces; her interviews with the King of Poland and Joseph II.; the military equipment arrayed by Potemkine, prince of the Taurid; the arches with the famous inscription, "The way to Byzantium," still further alarmed and irritated the Porte. France, which too well knew the weakness of her old ally, held her back; but England, and even Prussia, acted in the contrary way, in order to spite Russia. Sweden, which the French ambassador also tried to moderate, had promised to aid the Sublime Porte.

In the summer of 1787, Boulgakof, the Russian envoy, received the ultimatum of Turkey. She demanded the extradition of Mavrocordato, hospodar of Wallachia; the recall of the Russian consuls of Iassy, Bucharest, and Alexandria; the abandonment of the protectorate over Heraclius, the vassal of the Sultan; the right of the Turks to inspect all Russian vessels navigating the Straits; and the admission of Turkish consuls or commissaries into the ports of the Russian territory. On the refusal of Boulgakof, he was confined in the Seven Towers, and the Porte declared war.

Russia found herself taken by surprise. Potemkine had not finished his preparations, and the fleet at Sebastopol had suffered severely from a recent tempest. His despairing letters to Catherine show how deeply he was discouraged; and he even spoke of evacuating the Crimea. The Empress shows in her replies a manly and dauntless soul; she managed to prove to her favorite that the evacuation of the Peninsula would be the certain ruin of the great port of Sebastopol and the infant fleet which had been created at such cost. Without waiting for the enemy it was necessary to assume the offensive, and march on Otchakof or Bender. "I implore you to take courage and reflect," she writes; "with courage all can be repaired, even a disaster."

Catherine had more than one enemy to cope with. Whilst Turkey menaced her on the South, Prussia was scheming to force Poland to cede her Dantzig and Thorn, and to oblige the two other co-partitioners to give up Gallicia. Gustavus III. likewise abruptly laid claim to South Finland, declared his intention of mediating between Russia and Turkey, and, without awaiting a reply to his ultimatum, laid siege to Nyslot and Fredericksham. If he had acted promptly, instead of wasting the ardor of his troops against the fortresses, he might have conquered Livonia, then defended by only two regiments, or surprised St. Petersburg, deprived of its troops. Although the roar of the Swedish cannon might be heard in the Winter Palace, Catherine practised the courage that she enjoined on Potemkine. She declined to desert her capital, and assembled in a few days 12,000 men for its defence. The Swedish fleet was arrested on its way by the indecisive battle of Hogland. An aristocratic revolt broke out even in the camp of Gustavus III., who was accused by his officers of violating his own constitution by declaring war without consulting the Senate. The King of Sweden was obliged to return to Stockholm, where he punished the conspirators, and by a new *coup d'état* gave to the constitution a still more monarchical character. A diversion of the Danes in Sweden forbade his assuming the offensive, but in 1789 he got rid of them through the threatened intervention of England and Prussia, and took up arms against Russia; his fleet, however, suffered considerable loss. Though he gained the naval battle of Svenska-Sund, where he captured 30 vessels, 600 cannon, and 6000 men (July 9, 1790), he found himself unable to pursue his advantage, which was compromised by a second battle on the same seas. The affairs of France gave another direction to the ideas of this strange prince. He hastened to sign the Peace of Verela, on the basis of *statu quo ante bellum*, and passed from open hostilities to propositions of an alliance with Russia against the Revolution.

In the South, Catherine had ready in 1788 an army of 40,000 men to protect the Caucasus, 30,000 to defend the Crimea, and 70,000 under Roumantsof to operate on the Dniester; while 80,000 Austrians, under Joseph II., threatened the line of the Danube and the Save. The Emperor was unfortunate in this war. He was forced to fall back beyond the Save, and was defeated at Temesvar; and feeling the growing discontent of Hungary, where the people had been irritated by his religious innovations and the nobles by encroachments on their privileges, he resigned the command to Laudon. During this time Souvorof defended Kinburn against superior forces, and was wounded in a *sortie*. Potemkine, after a siege which seemed very long to the Prince de Ligne (*vide* his correspondence), and a premature attack of Souvorof, took the strong city of Otchakof by assault, with a loss of 20,000 on the side of the Turks. Catherine II., accustomed up to that date to see French volunteers in the enemy's camp applauded the prowess of the Baron de Damas and Count de Bombelles, who fought under her own standard. Khotin, on the Dniester, the key of Moldavia, had been taken by Soltykof.

In 1789 Souvorof, who had combined with the Prince of Coburg, the Austrian general, defeated the Turks at Fokchany (July 31st), and on the Rymnik near Martinestie (September 22nd). In the latter battle 100,000 Turks gave way before 25,000 Christians. Souvorof earned by this victory the surname of Rymnikski. On the west Laudon took Belgrade and conquered Servia; while on the east Potemkine successfully besieged Bender and subdued Bessarabia.

Freed from the war with Sweden, Catherine II. carried on hostilities with the Turks with greater vigor in 1790. Ismail, on the northern side of the Danube, was formidable from its position, and was defended besides by 40,000 men. Koutouzof had abandoned all hope of taking it, and Potemkine entreated the impetuous Souvorof to be prudent. Souvorof, however, carried it by assault, with a loss of 10,000 men on the Russian, and 30,000 on the Turkish side. "Never," he writes to Potemkine, "was a fortress stronger than Ismail, and never was a defence more desperate! But Ismail is taken."

Joseph II. died; and his successor, Leopold II., signed a peace at Sistova, which only gave him the old town of Orsova and the territory of the Unna (August 1791). Catherine still continued the war for some months. The fall of Akkerman and Kilia made her mistress of the mouths of the Danube. Repnine, with 40,000 men, defeated the Grand Vizier with 100,000 at Matchin, whilst Ouchakof dispersed the Turkish fleet and surrounded Varna, so as to cut off the Grand Vizier's communications with Constantinople, and the Sultan, in alarm, implored peace. On the other hand, Catherine's attention was claimed by the affairs of France and Poland. By the separate

Peace of Iassy, she retained only Otchakof and the sea-board between the Bug and the Dniester, and stipulated for guarantees in favor of the Danubian Principalities (January 1792). This war had been more severe than the preceding one, and the success more disputed. The Turks, thinking themselves on the eve of being driven into Asia, managed to make a better fight than the struggle of 1767.

SECOND PARTITION OF POLAND: DIET OF GRODNO—THIRD PARTITION: KOSCIUSZKO.

The years between 1773 and 1791 had been, for Poland, years of valiant efforts and needful reforms. Tyzenhaus had founded a school of medicine in Warsaw, the old universities of Wilna and Cracow had been re-organized, and a number of secondary schools created, for which the French philosopher Condillac had compiled a manual of logic. Stanislas Poniatovski, the correspondent of Voltaire, the friend, the "dear son" of Madame Géoffrin, had induced French and Italian artists to visit the country. National historians and poets adorned with their talents the last years of independence. It was a real Polish renaissance, under the salutary influence of the universal French genius. "Progress was rapid," says Lélével: "in a few years no more was seen of those sombre superstitious practices, of that hideous bigotry, which had laid its bloody finger on the piety of the faithful; charlatanism could no longer seduce them; they spoke with a smile of the ancient faith in sorcery; the phenomena of nature were explained in a reasonable way; hatred gave place to fraternity amongst the worshippers at different shrines. The characters of the people, degraded for centuries by a fatal education, became elevated by the rational instruction given them at the new schools. A generation of men grew up strangers to the fanaticism and corruption of the preceding age, possessed with a passion for liberty and the country, whose crowning glory they were to be. To give an idea of the work accomplished, we have only to compare the Zamoïski, the Kosciuszkos, the Niemcevitches, and the Dombrovskis with the men of the first partition. Poland wished to live, and made a last effort for her regeneration.

It was necessary first to reform the hateful and anarchic constitution, which had been perfidiously guaranteed by strangers, and made Poland the laughing-stock and prey of her enemies. In 1788 the Diet of Warsaw established a committee for this purpose, raised the number of the army to 60,000 men, and imposed new taxes. Circumstances seemed favorable to the boldest measures: if France, occupied with her revolution, could not come to the aid of Poland, England showed herself openly hostile to Russia; Turkey and Sweden were making war on her, while Prussia sought the friendship of the Poles, persuaded Poniatovski to despise the Russian guarantee, and negotiated a treaty of alliance offensive and defensive. The Diet of 1791 was formed into a confederation, and, deciding this time by a majority, undertook the reform of the constitution. It declared the throne hereditary, and nominated the house of Saxony heirs to Poniatovski; it abolished the *liberum veto*, which was legal anarchy and organized venality; it divided the legislative power between the king, the senate, and the Chamber of Nuncios; it centred the executive power in the king, assisted by six ministers, responsible to the Chambers, and invested him with the command of the armies and the appointment of the officials. The towns obtained the right of electing their judges, and of sending deputies to the Diet. None dared touch the rights of nobles over their peasants, for the nobles were then the fighting part of the nation, the "legal country"; and it was owing, in fact, to their patriotism that the revolution was accomplished. All the Diet could do was to sanction beforehand individual compacts made between the owners and their serfs, to the advantage of the latter. Such was the memorable Constitution of the 3rd of May, 1791. A similar transformation which took place in Sweden at the royal *coup d'état* of 1772 had saved the monarchy of the Vasas from dismemberment—would the parliamentary *coup d'état* of 1791 save Poland? Would the Northern Courts, which thought it a crime on the part of the French liberals to weaken, by the constitution of the same year, the powers of the Bourbon kings, permit the Polish patriots to restore to their sovereign the essential prerogatives of royalty, the force necessary to subdue anarchy within, and cause the nation to be respected without?

Catherine II. feared to protest as long as she had the Turkish war on her hands; but when the Peace of Iassy was signed, she received at St. Petersburg a deputation of Polish malcontents, who regretted the *liberum veto*, and were alarmed at the promises made to the peasants. Amongst these unworthy citizens, we may remark Felix Potocki, the hetman Brianski, Rjevuski, and the two brothers Kossakovski. Catherine II. authorized them to form the Confederation of Targovitsa. In her manifesto of the 18th of May, 1792, she reminded men that Russia had guaranteed the Polish constitution, and signalized the reformers of the 3rd of May as accomplices of the Jacobins. Enlightened Russians were indignant at the perfidious language held by their government. Sémen Voronzof, ambassador in London, writes, "The manifesto had no right to enter into ridiculous eulogies of the ancient form of government, *under which the Republic has flourished and prospered for so many centuries.* That has an air of stupidity, if it is said in good faith, or of insulting contempt, if they believe, like the rest of the world, that it is the most absurd and detestable of all governments." The epithet Jacobin is besides singularly inapplicable to the Poles, who wished to strengthen the royal power.

On the request of the Confederates of Targovitsa, 80,000 Russians and 20,000 Cossacks entered the Ukraine. Poniatovski turned to Prussia, and recalled to her the promises of help. Frederick William II. replied that he had not been consulted about the change of the constitution, and that he considered himself absolved from all engagements. He was already arranging with Russia a second treaty of partition, from which Austria was to be excluded. Austria would have to content herself with any provinces she might wrest from revolutionary France. Russia likewise promised to help her to acquire Bavaria, in exchange for the Low Countries. The Poles, deserted by all, tried in vain to resist the Russian invasion. Their army of Lithuania retreated without fighting, while the Polish army properly so-called gave battle at Ziélencé, under Prince Joseph Poniatovski; and at Dubienka on the Bug, under Thaddeus Kosciuszko. Then King Stanislas pronounced himself ready to accede to the Confederation of Targovitsa, thus disavowing his glorious work of the 3rd of May. The reformers Ignatius Potoçki, Kollontaï, and Malakhovski had to withdraw, and their places in the council of the king were taken by Confederates of Targovitsa, who abolished the constitution. The *liberum veto* was re-established.

The Polish patriots, remaining in ignorance of the treaty of partition, were unconscious of half their misfortunes. The King of Prussia in his turn crossed the western frontier, announcing in his manifesto that the troubles of Poland compromised the safety of his own States, that Dantzig had sent corn to the French revolutionaries, and that Great Poland was infested by Jacobin clubs, whose intrigues were rendered doubly dangerous by the continuation of the war with France. The King of Prussia affected to see Jacobins whenever it was his interest to find them. The part of each of the Powers was marked out in advance. Russia was to have the eastern provinces with a population of 3,000,000, as far as a line drawn from the eastern frontier of Courland, which, passing Pinsk, ended in Gallicia, and included

Borissof, Minsk, Sloutsk, Volhynia, Podolia, and Little Russia. Prussia had the long-coveted cities of Thorn and Dantzig, as well as Great Poland, Posen, Gnezen, Kalisch, and Czenstochovo. If Russia still only annexed Russian or Lithuanian territory, Prussia for the second time cut Poland to the quick, and another million and a half of Slavs passed under the yoke of the Germans.

It was not enough to despoil Poland, now reduced to a territory less extensive than that occupied by Russia; it was necessary that she should consent to the spoliation—that she should legalize the partition. A diet was convoked at Grodno, under the pressure of the Russian bayonets. This same pressure, enforced by pecuniary corruption, had been exercised in the elections, and the King was in some sense dragged to Grodno to preside over the ruin of his country. Sievers, Catherine's ambassador, displayed all the resources of an unscrupulous diplomacy, which had seduction, intimidation, and violence at its service. In spite of the support of bought deputies and Targovitsan traitors, he gained nothing for a long while. At last the Diet, in the deceitful hope of dividing its enemies, consented that the treaty of cession to Russia should be ratified, but showed herself more stubborn with regard to Prussia. Sievers was forced to surround the Hall of Session by two battalions of grenadiers, point four pieces of cannon, and install General Rautenfels in a chair beside the King. Twenty days passed without his being able to extract a word of assent from the defenceless assembly. The Poles hated the Prussians above everything. Catherine might have delivered Great Poland from a hated yoke, and united all the kingdom under her authority, which would have been almost gratefully accepted. Like Sémen Voronzof, Sievers felt the enormous fault that was committed by aggrandizing Prussia at the expense of a Slav country. Unhappily, his instructions were positive. In order to triumph over this *vis inertiæ* he had four deputies carried off by his dragoons, and closely blockaded the assembly in the hall of deliberations. The day of September 23, 1793, and the following night, were occupied by a "silent sitting," while the King sat on his throne, and the deputies on their benches, gloomy and dumb. At three in the morning, Rautenfels left to fetch his grenadiers; then the Marshal of the Diet, Bielinski, put the question. Ankiévitch proposed to the nuncios a compromise which would give satisfaction to Prussia, while leaving to a "more happy posterity" the task of raising up the country. Bielinski asked three times, without taking breath, if the Diet authorized the delegate to sign the treaty. No one replied;

then a voice was heard declaring the silence to be equivalent to consent. It was four o'clock in the morning—the nuncios left the hall in profound grief, with streaming eyes.

On the 16th of October, the Diet concluded with Russia a treaty of alliance, or rather a compact of slavery, by which Catharine II. guaranteed "the liberty of the republic"; that is, all the abuses of the old constitution. The Polish troops who were encamped on the provinces ceded to the Empress, received orders to swear allegiance to her; the army that remained to the republic consisted only of 15,000 men.

By her fanaticism and electoral corruption, Poland had merited her misfortunes in 1772; she did not merit those of 1793. History will not forget the generous efforts of the Czartoryskis, of the greater part of the nobility, and of the patriotic "third estate," for the reform of the country.

The citizens of the large towns, inspired by French ideas, were indignant at this new attempt against their country. The army, still 25,000 men strong, had received with fury the order to disband. Part of the noblemen shared these sentiments, while the others, through fear of new taxes or social reforms, resigned themselves to foreign rule. The country proper remained apathetic and indifferent. Poland expiated cruelly the harsh servitude that her *prospolite*, in the full current of eighteenth-century civilization, had allowed to weigh on the rural classes. George Forster writes in 1791, "The Polish nobles alone in Europe have pushed ignorance and barbarism so far that they have almost extinguished in their serfs the last lingering sparks of thought." This is one of the extenuating circumstances invoked by Russian or German historians to excuse the dismemberment: the lot of the peasants was not to grow worse under Russian domination, and was to improve under German rule.

The Polish patriots had, however, placed all their hopes on Thaddeus Kosciuszko, the hero of Dubienka. Born in 1752, admitted in 1764 to the military school founded by the Czartoryskis, he had distinguished himself by unceasing labor. In Poland he had received hard lessons in equality; he had seen his father assassinated by exasperated peasants, and he himself had been put to shame by the powerful noble Sosnovski, whose daughter he, a simple portionless gentleman, had dared to ask in marriage.

He had fought in the American War, and returned invested with the republican decoration of Cincinnati. After the second partition he had quitted Warsaw and retired into Saxony, where he found the men of the 3rd of May—Malakhovski, Ignatius Potoçki, the ex-Chancellor Kollontaï, Niemcevitch, all of Poland that was honorably devoted to liberty. Sent into France, he received promises of help from the Committee of Public Safety, and now he was working in Dresden to organize in Poland a vast conspiracy. He was soon able to reckon thousands of nobles, priests, citizens, and disbanded soldiers; but in spite of the number of the conspirators, General Igelstrom, who commanded in Warsaw for Catherine II., failed to seize the principal threads of the plot.

The order to disband the army hastened the explosion. Madalinski refused to allow the brigade that he commanded to be disarmed, crossed the Bug, threw himse'f on the Prussian provinces, and then fell back on Cracow. At his approach, this city, the second in Poland, the capital of the ancient kings, rose and expelled the Russian garrison. Kosciuszko hastened to the scene of action, and put forth the "act of insurrection," in which the hateful conduct of the co-partitioners was branded, and the population called to arms. Five thousand scythes were made for the peasants, the voluntary offerings of patriots were collected, and those of obstinate and lukewarm people were extracted by force. Igelstrom, who was very uneasy in Warsaw, detached, nevertheless, Tormassof and Denissof against Cracow. Deserted by Denissof, Tormassof came up near Raclavitsa with Kosciuszko and Madalinski, the number of whose troops—4000 men, one-half of whom were peasants—was almost equal to his own. The cavalry of the nobles gave way at the first shock, and fled, announcing everywhere the defeat and capture of Kosciuszko, but the steadiness of the peasants preserved the Polish army, and twelve guns were taken from the Russians. To punish the cowardice of the cavalry officers, the dictator took off the dress of a gentleman, and assumed that of a peasant.

The news of this success soon reached Warsaw, and the representation of the 'Cracovians,' which seemed an allusion to the events in Gallicia, still further increased the excitement. Igelstrom had posted his regiments so injudiciously that their communication could easily be cut off by the Polish regiments in the town. The arsenal had not yet been delivered to the Russians, and remained in the hands of the patriots.

On the 17th of April, at 3 o'clock in the morning, the tocsin sounded in all the churches, and the insurrection broke out. The people, excited by the shoemaker Kilinski and the binder Kapostas, fell everywhere on the isolated detachments of Russians. Igelstrom found himself blockaded in his palace, unable to communicate with the scattered regiments, and assailed at once by the citizens and the Polish troops. On the 18th he left the town with great difficulty, abandoning twelve cannon, 4000 killed and wounded, and 2000 prisoners. Wilna, the capital of Lithuania, followed the example of Warsaw, and expelled the general Arsenief.

A provisional government installed itself at Warsaw, and sent a courier to Kosciuszko. It was composed of men of the 3rd of May, amongst whom Ignatius Potoçki represented the moderate and Kilinski the extreme party. King Stanislas remained in his palace, respected but watched, and taking no active part in public affairs, of which he was kept informed only by the courtesy of the government. To sum up, the revolution of the 17th of April, 1794, had a national and monarchic character like the Constitution of the 3rd of May, 1791. It sought the support of France, without following all the advice of the Convention. A tribunal extraordinary gave some satisfaction to the public conscience by seeking out the wretches who had betrayed their country, and whose connection with foreigners had been proved by the papers seized at the Russian embassy. Ankiévitch, the hetmans Zabiello and Ozarovski, and Kossakovski, bishop of Livonia, were hung; the brother of the latter, Kossakovski, hetman of Lithuania, had been punished at Wilna.

In spite of the agitation caused by Kollontaï and the democrats, Kosciuszko dared not settle the question about the peasants, and his manifesto of the 7th of May, 1794, was not put in force. He feared to risk the alienation of the military class, without gaining the rural masses, brutalized by centuries of oppression; still he tried to win the clergy and the orthodox populations, by proclaiming liberty of conscience, and the equality of different religions in the eye of the law.

The Prussians, however, managed to take Cracow, which was only feebly defended by its commander. The government of Warsaw declared war against Frederic William II. The people, attributing the loss of Cracow to treason, rushed to the prisons, and promptly executed the seven men who were detained there. They merited the fate that befell them; they had been amongst the promoters of the Confederation of Targovitsa, or agents of Russia. Kosciuszko condemned this bloody justice, and insisted on the punishment of the rioters, but at the same time hastened the trial of the guilty prisoners.

General Zaïontchek had been defeated in the battle of Golkof by the Russians, and the Prussians were marching on the Vistula. The King of Prussia had quitted his army on the Rhine in order to direct the siege and bombardment of Warsaw. Catherine affected to be indignant at this abandonment of the holy war against the Revolution, for the common cause of kings and religion. The pretensions of Prussia to Cracow disturbed the good understanding between the three Powers of the North, disquieted Austria, and threatened to break the coalition formed against France. Frederic William, greatly disgusted with his Russian ally, General Krouchtchof, countermanded the order for assault, and raised the siege, being recalled to his own dominions by an insurrection in Great Poland.

The Poles had hardly time to congratulate themselves on this success. The Russians had recaptured Wilna; the Austrians had entered Lublin. Still more threatening was the fact that the Russian general, Fersen, had crossed to the right bank of the Vistula in spite of Poninski, and was advancing to meet Souvorof, who was coming up with the army of the Ukraine, and had already beaten Siérakovski at Krouptchitse and at Brest-Litovski. If the two Russian armies, each of which was superior to the whole Polish force, managed to effect a junction, the insurrection was crushed.

Kosciuszko, who had hastened to console Siérakovski, speedily returned to take up a position on the Vistula, equidistant from Warsaw and Lublin, to oppose Fersen. Around him were gathered his bravest lieutenants—Potoçki, Kaminski, Kollontaï, Niemcevitch, poet and general. The evening before the battle, Kaminski pointed out to Niemcevitch the crows that were flying on their right. " Remember your Livy," he said ; " it is a bad omen." " A bad omen for the Romans, not for us," replied the brave poet. On the 10th of October, Krouchtchof attacked the van of the Poles, while Fersen ordered Denissof to lead the assault on the right, and Tormassof on the left. The Polish army, shaken by a violent cannonade, could not resist the charge of the bayonets. They gave way, and twenty-one guns and 2700 prisoners remained in the hands of the Russians. All the generals were captured ; Kosciuszko had been carried off half-dead by the hetman Denissof. The Russian generals treated their prisoners well, and the officers tried to console the wounded Niemcevitch by complimenting him on the 'Return from the other World,' a poem in manuscript which they had found in his pocket (1794.)

Warsaw was horror-stricken by this calamity. Vavrjevski took the place of Kosciuszko, but proved no adequate substitute for the popular hero who had been the soul of the revolt. Souvorof had already appeared before Praga, and the whole Russian army occupied its positions to the sound of drums and music. The impetuous general at once divided his army into seven columns. The Russian soldiers, on the eve of the assault, put on white shirts, as if for a wedding, and the holy images were placed at the head of the columns. At 3 o'clock on the morning of the 4th of November the signal was given, and in an instant the fosses were filled and the ramparts scaled. "The Poles," says a Russian witness, "defended themselves like heroes, with desperate recklessness." Praga suffered all the horrors of a capture by assault. In vain Souvorof renewed his orders to spare the inhabitants, to give quarter to the vanquished, not to slay without a motive. The soldiers were too much exasperated against the Poles, whom they believed to be republicans, atheists, accomplices of the French Jacobins, murderers of their comrades, disarmed in the revolt of the 17th of April. The dead numbered twelve thousand ; the prisoners only one. "The streets are covered with corpses ; blood flows in torrents," says the first despatch of Souvorof. The massacre of Praga terrified Warsaw, which was ill protected by the width of the Vistula from the Russian bullets. Souvorof refused to treat with Potoçki and the men of the 17th April, and King Stanislas had to act as mediator. Souvorof guaranteed to the inhabitants their property, a pardon, and passports to all compromised persons. He made his entrance into Warsaw, and was created Field-marshal by the Empress. The King was sent to Grodno. The third treaty of partition, forced on the Empress by the importunity of Prussia, and in which Austria also took part, was put in execution. Russia took the rest of Lithuania as far as the Niemen (Wilna. Grodno, Kovno, Novogrodek, Slonim,) and the rest of Volhynia to the Bug (Vladimir, Loutsk, and Kremenetz). She thus reached the extreme limit of the countries formerly governed by the princely descendants of Rurik, except in the case of Gallicia, for the empress, whose policy had abandoned Poland to the Germans, had allowed Austria to take Red Russia after the first partition. Besides the Russian territory, Russia also annexed the old Lithuania of the Jagellons, and finally acquired Courland and Samogitia.

Prussia had all Eastern Poland, with Warsaw; Austria had Cracow, Sandomir, Lublin, and Chelm. Her possessions extended towards the north, as if to rejoin Warsaw. (1795.)

The Polish army of Vavrjevski had refused to be included in the capitulation of Warsaw, but agitated by the quarrels of its leaders, and weakened by want of discipline and desertion, it was obliged to accept an honorable convention at Radochitse. The officers kept their swords, and obtained passports for foreign travel. The prisoners made at Maceiovitsy had been divided amongst the governments which had seized the places of their birth. Madalinski was sent to Prussia ; Kollontaï and Zaïontcheck to Austria ; Kosciuszko, Kapostas, Kalinski, Potoki, and

Vavrjevski to St. Petersburg. Poland was not yet dead: out of the remains of the army dispersed at Radochitse, Dombrovski was to form the famous Polish legions, for twenty years inseparable from the banners of the French Republic and the Empire. We shall find Dombrovski in Egypt, Joseph Poniatovski at Borodino. The Poles, defeated at Maceiovitsy, will meet their conquerors on all the battle-fields in Europe—in Italy, in Switzerland, in Austria, in Prussia, in Poland, in Lithuania. Napoleon will satiate their vengeance against the robber Powers, and, two hundred years after Vladislas, will land the Polish troops into the holy city of Moscow.

CATHERINE II. AND THE FRENCH REVOLUTION—WAR WITH PERSIA.

Just before the breaking out of the Revolution, the two governments of Louis XVI. and Catherine II. had entered into negotiations for the purpose of forming a quadruple alliance, including Russia, Austria, and both houses of Bourbon, which was destined to keep in check the naval pretensions of England and the encroachments of Prussia. After the taking of the Bastile, Catherine understood that she could no longer look to France, which was then occupied with her internal transformation, for support. She followed, however, events in Paris with much anxiety, showed the most lively antipathy to the new principles, was one of those who advised the flight to Varennes, and fell ill at the news of the 21st of January. The correspondent of Voltaire and Diderot allowed herself to be carried away by terror into reaction. She caused Russians suspected of liberal ideas to be watched, and their letters to be inspected; she mutilated Kniajnine's tragedy of 'Vadim at Novgorod,' and spoke of having it burned by the executioner; Radichtchef, the author of the 'Journey from St. Petersburg to Moscow,' a curious book with many reflections on serfage, was dismissed and sent to Siberia; Novikof was arrested and confined in Schlüsselburg, his libraries and his printing press closed, and all his enterprises ruined. She dismissed Genest, the French ambassador, and refused to recognize, first the Constitution of 1791, and then the Republic; put forth an edict announcing the rupture of diplomatic relations with France; forbade the Russian ports to the tricolor flag; expelled all French subjects who refused to swear fidelity to the monarchic principle; received the *émigrés* with open arms, and hastened to acknowledge Louis XVIII.

In 1792 she wrote the celebrated note on the restoration of

the royal power and aristocratic privileges in France, assuring every one that 10,000 men would be sufficient to operate a counter-revolution. She encouraged Gustavus III. (shortly to be assassinated by his nobility, at a masked ball, March 16, 1792) to put himself at the head of the crusade against democracy; urged England to aid the Count of Artois in a scheme for a descent on France; and stimulated the zeal of Austria and Prussia. In spite of all this, though she had many times consented to negotiate treaties of subsidies and promised troops, she took care never to engage in a war with the West. "My position is taken," she said, "my part assigned; it is my duty to watch over the Turks, the Poles, and Sweden" (which was reconciled with France after the death of Gustavus III.) The punishment of the Jacobins of Warsaw and Turkey was indeed more easy, and certainly more lucrative work. Perhaps we must also take into account an admission that she made, in 1791, to her Vice-Chancellor, Ostermann: "Am I wrong? For reasons that I cannot give to the Courts of Berlin and Vienna, I wish to involve them in these affairs, so that I may have elbow-room. Many of my enterprises are still unfinished, and they must be occupied so as to leave me unfettered." She excused herself for not taking part in the anti-revolutionary contest, alleging the war with Turkey; and when obliged to hasten the Peace of Iassy on account of the revolution of the 3rd of May, she made the Polish war another excuse. When the war was ended, she pretended to excite the zeal of Souvorof and his soldiers against the "atheists" of the West, but in reality only dreamed of forwarding her schemes in the East. Mohammed, the new king of Persia, had invaded Georgia and burnt Tiflis, the capital of Heraclius, Catherine's *protégé*. The Empress sent for an exiled brother of Mohammed to her court, and ordered Valerian Zoubof to conquer Persia.

In reality Catherine had been, against her will, more useful to France than to the coalition. By her intervention in Poland and her projects against the East, she had raised the jealousy and suspicions of Prussia and Austria. She took care to play off one against the other; made the second partition with Frederic William in spite of Austria; and with Francis II. the third partition, which disgusted Prussia. She contributed indirectly to agitate and dissolve the coalition, whilst the Polish insurrection, encouraged by France, prevented her from joining it. She died on the 6th–17th November, 1796, aged 67 years. No sovereign since Ivan the Terrible had extended the frontiers of the empire by such vast conquests. She had given Russia for boundaries the Niemen, the Dniester, and the Black Sea.

CHAPTER XI.

PAUL I.

(17th November, 1796—24th March, 1801.)

Peace policy : accession to the second coalition—Campaigns of the Ionian Islands, Italy, Switzerland, Holland, and Naples—Alliance with Bonaparte : the League of Neutrals, and the great scheme against India.

PEACE POLICY : ACCESSION TO THE SECOND COALITION.

Paul I. was forty-two years of age when he ascended the throne. He was intelligent and had some natural gifts, but his character had been soured by the close dependence in which he had been held by his mother, who had even deprived him of the education of his children, and forbade him to appear before the army, by the humiliations forced on him by the favorites, and by the isolation to which he was abandoned by the courtiers, in their haste to pay court to the risen sun. The mystery surrounding his father's death troubled and disquieted him. There was a touch of Hamlet in Paul I. Like Peter III., his taste for military minutiæ amounted to a mania. He had a high idea of his authority, and was born a despot. He is supposed to have uttered the famous saying, " Know that the only person of consideration in Russia is the person whom I address at the moment that I am addressing him." He hated the Revolution with a blind hate, unknown to Catherine II. Many of his eccentricities of conduct may be explained by his desire always to act in the contrary way to his mother, whom he secretly accused of having usurped his crown. Without being cruel, he caused much unhappiness, being as prompt to chastise as to pardon, and was as prodigal of exiles to Siberia as of unexpected favors.

He began by abolishing the edict of Peter III. about the succession, and re-established the monarchic principle of inheritance by primogeniture, from male to male in the direct line. He profited by his mother's obsequies to cause the remains of his father to be exhumed, and to render the same honors to both coffins in the Church of the Fortress. Alexis Orlof had to march in procession by the coffin of his father, and to carry his crown. He did not punish the favorites of his mother, but removed them from about his own person, giving his confidence to Rostopchine and the austere Araktchéef. Bezdorodko he confirmed in his place as Minister of Foreign Affairs.

To re-establish the principle of authority, which he thought had been shaken in Russia, he revived the rude old manners, compelled the carriages of his subjects to halt when he passed, and made women as well as men salute him by throwing themselves on their knees in the mud or snow. He issued decrees full of minute provisions, forbidding the wearing of round hats, frock-coats, waistcoats, high collars, large neckties, and everything which savored of Jacobinism. He banished from the official language the words " society," " citizen," and other terms which his mother had delighted to honor. He made the censorship of the theatre and the press more rigorous than ever, forbade the importation of European books and music, forced the Russians who were travelling abroad to return, and forbade any Frenchman not provided with a passport signed by the princes of the house of Bourbon to enter his territory.

In the last years of Catherine grave abuses must have crept into the army, and no one but an emperor with a genius for war could accomplish the reforms which were necessary if Russia were to keep pace with Western improvements in tactics and in arms. Paul unfortunately took up the reforms in his usual narrow spirit. He had a craze for Prussian methods, and abolished the Russian national uniform, convenient, soldier-like, and well suited to the climate as it was. The Russians did not recognize themselves in their Prussian costume, with pigtails, powder, shoe-buckles, shoes, gaiters, heavy caps, and uncomfortable hats. Old Souvorof shook his head and said, "There are powders and powders! Shoe-buckles are not gun-carriages, nor pigtails exactly bayonets ; we are not Prussians, but Russians." This epigram was punished by the exile of the martial humorist to his village of Koutchevskoe. There he could ride-a-cockhorse with the small boys of the district, ring the church bells, read the epistle, and play the organ to his heart's content. Paul showed more method and common-sense when he tried to reform the finances, which had been impaired in the last year of Catherine by endless wars, the dishonesty of officials, the luxury of the court, and the prodigal gifts bestowed on favorites.

As to foreign affairs, Paul's early policy was peaceful. He discontinued the levying of recruits in his mother's manner—

that is, in the proportion of three men to every five hundred souls. He withdrew his forces from Persia, and left Georgia to its own levies. To the Poles he even showed some pity, recalled prisoners from Siberia, transferred King Stanislas from Grodno to St. Petersburg, visited Kosciuszko at Schlüsselburg, and set him, with the other captives, at liberty. He bade Kolytchef, Envoy Extraordinary at Berlin, tell the King of Prussia that he was neither for conquest nor aggrandizement. He dictated a circular to Ostermann, which was to be communicated to foreign Powers, in which he declared that Russia, and Russia alone, had been engaged in ceaseless wars since 1756; that these forty years of war had exhausted the nation; that the humanity of the Emperor did not allow him to refuse his beloved subjects the peace for which they sighed; that nevertheless, though for these reasons the Russian army would take no part in the contest with France, " the Emperor would remain as closely as ever united with his allies, and oppose by all possible means the progress of the mad French republic, which threatened Europe with total ruin, by the destruction of her laws, privileges, property, religion, and manners." He refused all armed assistance to Austria, then alarmed by Bonaparte's victories in Italy; he recalled the vessels sent by Catherine to join the English fleet, to blockade the coasts of France and Holland. He even received the overtures made by Caillard, the French envoy in Prussia, to the Russian envoy Kolytchef, and caused the latter to observe " that the Emperor did not consider himself at war with France, that he had done nothing to harm her, that he was disposed to live in peace with her, and that he would persuade his allies to finish the war, offering to this end the mediation of Russia."

Difficulties soon arose between France and Russia. The treaty of Campo Formio had given the Ionian Islands to the French, who thus acquired a position threatening to the East, and a greater influence over the Divan. The directorate authorized Dombrovski to organize Polish legions in Italy. Panine at Berlin intercepted a letter from the Directorate to the French envoy, in which there was a question of the restoration of Poland, under a prince of Brandenburg. Paul, on his side, took into his pay the corps of the Prince of Condé, and stationed 10,000 *émigrés* in Volhynia and Podolia. He offered an asylum to Louis XVIII., who was expelled from Brunswick, established him in the ducal palace of Mittau, and gave him a pension of 200,000 roubles. The news that a French expedition was being mysteriously organized at Toulon caused him to tremble for the security of the coasts of the Black Sea, which were immediately put into a state of defence. The capture of Zagourski, Russian Consul at Corfu; the reduction of Malta by Bonaparte, and the arrival at St. Petersburg of the banished knights, who offered Paul the protectorate of their order, with the title of Grand Master; the invasion of the Swiss territory by the Directorate; the expulsion of the Pope and the proclamation of the Roman Republic—all precipitated the rupture.

Paul further concluded an alliance with Turkey, which was irritated at the invasion of Egypt, with England, Austria, and the kingdom of Naples. It was thus that, owing to Bonaparte's double aggression against Malta and Egypt, Russia and Turkey were forced, contrary to all traditions, to make common cause. Paul undertook that his fleet should join the Turkish and English squadrons, to furnish a body of troops to make a descent in Holland, and another to conquer the Ionian Islands, besides a great auxiliary army for the campaigns in Switzerland and Italy.

CAMPAIGN OF THE IONIAN ISLANDS, ITALY, SWITZERLAND, HOLLAND, AND NAPLES.

In the autumn of 1798 a Turco-Russian fleet captured the French garrisons of the Ionian Islands. The King of Naples caused the territory of the Roman Republic to be invaded, but Championnet conducted the Neapolitan troops back to their native land, entered Naples himself, proclaimed the Parthenopean Republic, and made St. Januarius work his annual miracle.

The Russian army in Holland was put under the orders of Hermann, that of Switzerland under those of Rymski-Korsakof while, at the request of Austria and the suggestion of England, the victor of Fokchany and Rymnik was appointed to the Austro-Russian army of Upper Italy. Paul I., flattered by this mark of deference, recalled Souvorof from his village exile. "Souvorof has no need of laurels," wrote the Tzar, "but the country has need of Souvorof."

The Directorate, taken by surprise, having not only France to protect, but likewise the Batavian, Helvetian, Cisalpine, Ligurian, Roman, and Neapolitan republics—that is to say, the vast line of country that extends from the Zuyder Zee to the Gulf of Tarento—had very inferior numbers to oppose to those of the coalition: in Holland 20,000 men, under Brune, against 40,000 Anglo-Russians, under York and Hermann; on the Rhine, 50,000, under Bernadotte and Jourdan, against the 70,000 of the Archduke Charles; in Switzerland, 30,000, under Masséna, against Hotze and Bellegarde, who had 70,000 Austrians in the

Vorarlberg and the Tyrol; in Upper Italy, 50,000, under Scherer, against the 60,000 Austrians of Kray; at Naples, 30,000, under Macdonald, against 30,000 English, Russians, and Sicilians.

At last the Russians arrived in Switzerland, 40,000 in number, under Rymski-Korsakof; in Italy, to the number of 40,000, divided into two corps, that of Rosenberg and that of Rebinder, with Souvorof in chief command. Consequently the French had only 170,000 to oppose to 350,000 allies.

In his passage to Vienna, Souvorof refused to communicate his schemes to Thugut, the acting minister, and to receive the advice of the *Hof-Kriegsrath*, the Aulic council of war. When the Austrians questioned him as to his plan of campaign, he showed a blank paper signed by the Emperor Paul. His object he declared, was Paris, where he would restore the throne and the altar. To his soldiers he repeated the formulæ of his military catechism : " A sudden glance, rapidity, impetuosity! The van of the army is not to wait for the rear! Musket balls are fools; bayonets do the business! The French beat the Austrians in columns, and we will beat them in columns." He scoffed at the slowness and pedantry of the *Hof-Kriegsrath*. " Parades, manœuvres! too much confidence in their talents! To know how to conquer, well; but to be always beaten is not smart! The Emperor of Germany desires that, when I have to give battle next day, I should first address myself to the Court of Vienna. The accidents of war change rapidly; one cannot be tied down to a fixed plan. Fortune flies like the lightning: one must seize opportunity by the forelock; it will never come back."

The Austrians had already defeated Jourdan at Stokach (March 29), and Scherer at Magnano (April 9). Masséna, although victorious at the first battle of Zurich, had been obliged to retreat behind the Limmat and the Linth, on the heights of the Albis. On the 28th of April, Austria, believing that where the French were concerned she might violate with impunity the law of nations, had assassinated their plenipotentiaries at Rastadt. Souvorof, on his arrival at Verona, had taken the command of the allied forces.

The Austro-Russians numbered about 90,000; the French no more than 30,000, under Moreau, which included the Italian legions and three or four thousand men of the Polish legions. These Poles represented the Slav element in the French army, as the Russians did in that of the coalition. This quarrel of kinsmen, which began at Maceiovitsy and Warsaw, was to be continued on the bank of the Adda. Souvorof surprised the passage of this river at Cassano, penetrated the centre of Moreau, and surrounded the right wing; Serrurier and about 3000 men were made prisoners (April 28).

Moreau retired into Piedmont; imperilled next by the loss of Ceva and of Turin, he was forced to take refuge in the Alps. Souvorof made his entry into Milan amidst the acclamations of the nobles, the priests, the excited populace, of all the enemies of the Revolution, and abolished the Cisalpine Republic. Instead of attacking the 15,000 men who remained with Moreau Souvorof, harrassed by the advice of the *Hof-Kriegsrath*, amused himself by laying siege to Mantua, Alessandria, and the citadel of Turin.

Macdonald hastened from the end of the Peninsula with the army of Naples. After having opened communications with Moreau, he conceived the project of throwing himself between Alessandria and Mantua, and separating the two principal bodies of the allied army. He defeated the Austrians on the Tidona, but came up with Souvorof on the Trebbia. The battle lasted three days (17th–19th June): the ferocity of the French, Russians, and Poles rendered it extremely bloody. On the 17th the French only amounted to 28,000 against 40,000; the next day 24,000 against 36,000: numbers were sure to tell. Each army lost ten or twelve thousand men, and Macdonald hastened to rejoin Moreau in the gorges of the Alps. Mantua had capitulated. In the south the Anglo-Russians, allied with the banditti of Cardinal Ruffo and of the brigand Fra Diavolo, expelled the French garrisons from Neapolitan territory. A frightful reaction flooded the streets of Naples with blood, and 2000 houses were burned by the bandits and lazzaroni (July 1799).

The Directorate made a last effort to reconquer Italy. The army of the Alps, increased by new reinforcements to 40,000 men, was placed under the command of General Joubert, who had said to his young wife, "You will see me either dead or victorious." Joubert wished to relieve Alessandria, and to prevent this Souvorof marched quickly up with 70,000 men, and gave him battle at Novi. Joubert was killed at the beginning of the action. The two armies each lost 8000 men (August 15), and the remains of the Polo-French troops fell back into the mountains of Genoa. Italy was lost to France: the Cisalpine, Roman, and Neapolitan republics were extinguished.

The Russians and Austrians separated after the victory. The German generals could not endure the vanity of Souvorof; Thugut was even less friendly towards him; the new *Prince Italiiski* imagined that he had fought for the restoration of sovereigns, and not for the private ambition of the house of Austria. He wished therefore to establish a national government in Piedmont, and to reorganize the Piedmontese army under his special standard. Now, Thugut cared nothing about the restoration of Victor-Amadeus, or of the Pope. The misunderstanding increased; it was decided that Souvorof should abandon Italy, and join Rymski-Korsakof in Switzerland, so as to defend the snowy mountains of Helvetia with a purely Russian army. Souvorof, who already saw himself in Franche-Comté and on the route to Paris, accepted the work.

In Switzerland, after the first battle of Zurich, Masséna had retired to the heights of the Albis, behind the line formed by the Linth, the lake of Zurich, and the Limmat. He had been opposed in his movements by the Archduke Charles, with 25,000 men; by Korsakof, with 28,000 Russians; and by Hotze, with 27,000 Austrians. The Archduke had to evacuate Switzerland and lay siege to Philippsburgh, and was to be replaced by Souvorof with 20,000 men. It would be a critical moment for the allies when the Archduke should have evacuated Switzerland and Souvorof should not yet have arrived, and this was the moment eagerly awaited by Masséna. He had now 60,000 men against 55,000, who were to be raised by the army of the *Prince of Italy* to 75,000. On the 25th of September he surprised the passage of the Limmat near to Diétikon, and cut the Russian army in two. The Russian grenadiers who defended Diétikon fought till their powder was exhausted, refused to surrender, and died in their ranks. The other corps were defeated successively. Korsakof, forced back upon Zurich, caused the gates to be closed. In the night Masséna sent him envoys, who were captured or repulsed by musketry. On the 26th of September Korsakof formed an immense square of 15,000 men and attacked the French. "This dense and impenetrable mass," says Major Masson, "made the enemy retire at every point." But this policy, which had been successful against the Poles and the Turks, was certain to fail against the French. Decimated by the sharpshooters and light cavalry, shaken by a general charge of cavalry, and infantry with bayonets, the Russians had to fall back on Zurich, leaving the field of battle covered with dead, and with wounded, who pressed *icons* and relics to their breasts. They had lost 6000 men, their guns, the army treasure, the official papers, and sacred plate. Korsakof fled to Eglisau. Then Masséna made Oudinot attack Zurich and the Swiss legion, and took all the Russian stores and baggage. It was here that the celebrated Lavater perished, killed by a drunken Swiss soldier. On the 25th Soult, on his side, had crossed the Linth, and defeated Hotze, who was killed. The allies retreated in disorder on Schaffhausen, with a loss of 10,000 prisoners, of twenty Austrian cannons, and nearly all the Russian artillery.

Such was the victory of Zurich. "Bonaparte," says M. Duruy, "has no more glorious battle, for the victories which insure the salvation of a country are worth more than those which only add to her power or the glory of her chiefs."

Souvorof had, however, arrived by dint of forced marches at Taverno, near Bellinzona. The Austrian administration had neglected to gather together a sufficient number of sumpter mules for the passage of the Alps, and Souvorof lost four precious days in impressing them from the surrounding country. He only reached the St. Gothard on the 21st, and crossed it under unheard-of difficulties, and after a sharp skirmish with some French detachments stationed on the mountains. He plunged at once into the narrow valley of the Reuss, enclosed between mountains so precipitous that the road many times crosses the torrent, notably at the Pont du Diable.

"In this kingdom of terrors," writes Souvorof in his despatch to Paul, "abysses open beside us at every step, like tombs awaiting our arrival. Night spent among the clouds, thunder that never ceases, rain, fog, the noise of cataracts, the breaking of avalanches, enormous masses of rocks and ice which fall from the heights, torrents which sometimes carry men and horses down the precipices, the St. Gothard, that colossus who sees the mists pass under him,—we have surmounted all, and in these inaccessible spots the enemy has been forced to give way before us. Words fail to describe the horrors we have seen, and in the midst of which Providence has preserved us." The impression produced on the native of the great Russian plains by the grandeur of the Swiss Alps is graphically sketched in the curious 'Narrative of an Old Soldier,' the memoirs of an eye-witness and companion of Souvorof.

The tenacious Lecourbe, charged by Masséna to retard the Russian advance, had only 11,000 men, but with them he expected to "crush Souvorof in the mountains." At Hospital he disputed the passage of the Reuss, cannonaded the Russians till his ammunition was exhausted, threw his artillery into the stream, went down to defend the Pont du Diable, which he blew up, and finally fell back on Seedorf, where he broke down the bridge. Souvorof crossed the precipitous chain of Schachenthal, and only reached Altdorf and Multenthal on the 26th, having lost 2000 men on the way. It was here that he heard of the disaster of Zurich and the flight of Korsakof, and that he grasped the full horror of his situation, lost in the heart of the mountains, betrayed by the carelessness of his allies, enclosed in Multenthal as it were in a mouse-trap, surrounded on all sides by a victorious army, with numbers superior to his own. On his rear Gudin had again occupied the Upper Reuss; on the road to Stanz Lecourbe had taken up a position at Seedorf; on that of Schwitz Masséna had concentrated the corps of Mortier; on that of Glarus Molitor was posted, whom Soult was about to reinforce. This was the most splendid moment of Souvorof's life. His heroic retreat is more glorious than his victories in Italy gained with superior forces; no general in such a desperate situation has shown more indomitable energy than this little man nearly seventy years old. He resolved to cross Mont Bragel in sixty five centimetres of snow, and to cut away by the Kleinthal and the route to Glarus. His rear-guard, left in the Multenthal, resisted for three days the assaults of Masséna, thus protecting the retreat of the army, while the vanguard took Glarus, and forced Molitor back on Naefels. There Molitor checked the Russians, who were obliged to retire on the Rindskopff, on whose glaciers many hundreds of men perished. Thence they succeeded in gaining Illanz, Coire, and Feldkirch. Souvorof, with the gallant remnant of his army, took up his winter-quarters between the Iller and the Lech.

On the 27th of August the Anglo-Russians had disembarked on the Texel, and captured the Dutch fleet, but the Batavian populations remained faithful to the cause of liberty, and on the 19th of September Brune, reinforced, defeated the allies at Bergen. He then fought them in four other battles, besieged them in Zyp, and made Alkmaer and the Duke of York capitulate (October 18). The Anglo-Russian army obtained leave to march out. The remains of the Russian forces re-embarked; but being coldly received in England, they were, so to speak, "interned" in the islands of Jersey and Guernsey.

Masséna and Brune had saved the frontiers of the republic, prepared the ruin of the coalition, and deprived the *coup d'état* of Brumaire of all excuse.

ALLIANCE WITH BONAPARTE: THE LEAGUE OF NEUTRALS, AND THE GREAT SCHEME AGAINST INDIA.

Paul I., Souvorof, and all Russia accused Austria of treason. The Emperor Francis, by the advice of England, humbly consented to explain the misunderstanding which had lost Korsakof, and almost lost Souvorof. The Tzar, a little softened, suspended the retreat of the Russian army, but insisted in return on the recall of Thugut, and the restoration of the Italian princes to their reconquered States. Austria could not relish this disinterested policy, or renounce her plans. Thugut, threatened with the loss of his post, labored to complete the rupture. It was insinuated to the Russian Emperor that the maintenance of his troops in Bohemia constituted a heavy charge for the hereditary States. The irritable Tzar learnt in addition that a conflict had taken place at the siege of Ancona. This maritime station was besieged by the Austrians, Russians, and Turks; the Austrian general secretly concluded a capitulation with the French, stipulated that his soldiers alone should be admitted into the fortress, and caused the Turkish and Russian flags, which had been fixed on the ramparts beside his own, to be removed. This insult to his banner completed the exasperation of Paul.

The same diplomatic results followed after Bergen and Zurich; a quarrel with England, which was likewise accused of treason, soon succeeded to the dispute with Austria. Bonaparte, who promptly destroyed at Marengo all the fruits of Souvorof's victories, who appeared to the Russians almost as an avenger against the perfidy of the Austrians—Bonaparte, whose despotic principles reassured the Tzar, and whose glory blinded him, cleverly turned to account the irritation of Paul. He began by declaring that he returned, without exchange, all the Russian prisoners, newly equipped at the expense of France. Paul was the more touched by this action, as Austria and England had refused to exchange the Russian soldiers for the French prisoners whom they held. Negotiations were opened by means of Berlin, and the French and Russian agents at Hamburg. Bonaparte took care to attack the Tzar on his weak sides, his gloomy dignity and his affectation of chivalrous disinterestedness. He offered to indemnify the King of Sardinia, to re-establish the Pope in Rome, and to recognize Paul as Grand Master of Malta, and owner of the island. Malta was at that time blockaded by the English, who in September 1800 made themselves masters of it. Their refusal to relinquish this important post to Paul I. greatly irritated him. Disturbed by the maritime tyranny of Great Britain, which had declared the ports of France and her allies in a state of siege, and recommenced her system of vexations against the neutral ships, Paul renewed the famous Act of Armed Neutrality, and sought the support of Prussia, Sweden, and Denmark. Bonaparte hastened to express his assent to the Russian principles. During this time General Sprengtporten, who, under pretext of taking command of the Russian prisoners in Paris, had been sent on a secret mission, was followed there by Kolytchef, charged with more precise instructions. Kolytchef was particularly to persuade Bonaparte to take the title of King himself, and to make it hereditary in his family, as the only means " of changing the revolutionary principles which have armed all Europe against France." On this point the First Consul was only too well disposed. Negotiations began on the following bases: France was to respect the integrity of Naples and Wurtemburg, to re-establish the King of Sardinia in Piedmont, while reserving Savoy for herself, and to retain the left bank of the Rhine, subject to an understanding with Russia, for the indemnification of the depossessed princes. It was under the Franco-Russian mediation that secularization was to take place in Germany.

Paul, with his usual impetuosity, was possessed by a daily increasing passion for Bonaparte; he surrounded himself with his portraits, drank his health publicly, and abruptly ordered Louis XVIII. to quit Mittau.

It was then that the two sovereigns arranged together the great scheme that had for its object the complete overthrow of the English rule in India. France still occupied Egypt; she was authorized to keep garrisons in the southern ports of the kingdom of Naples; her agents traversed Arabia and the Indian States. Paul on his side, to secure himself a basis of operations, ordered his troops to the Caucasus, and, at the request of the son of Heraclius, pronounced Georgia to be united to the empire. The expedition against English India was to be undertaken by two different ways—the command of a Russian army, destined for the Upper Indus by way of Khiva and Bokhara, was given to Knorring. Orlof-Denissof, Ataman of the Don Cossacks, received letters from Paul, desiring him to begin his movement on Orenburg. " The English are preparing for an attack by land and sea against me and my allies, the Swedes and the Danes; I am ready to receive them. But it is necessary to be beforehand with them, and to attack on their most vulnerable point, and on the side were they least expect it. It is three months' march from Orenburg to Hindostan, and it takes another month to get from the encampments of the Don to Orenburg, making in all four months. To you and your army (*voïsko*) I confide this expedition. Assemble therefore your men, and begin your march to Orenburg; thence, by whichever of the three routes you prefer, or by all, you will go straight with your artillery to Bokhara, Khiva, the river Indus, and the English settlements in India. The troops of the country are light troops, like yours; you will therefore have over them all the advantage of your artillery. Prepare everything for this campaign. Send your scouts to reconnoitre and repair the roads. All the treasures of the Indies shall be your recompense. . . . Such an enterprise will cover you with immortal glory, will secure you my goodwill in proportion to your services, will load you with riches, give an opening to our commerce, and strike the enemy a mortal blow" (12th-24th January).

" India, to which I send you, is governed by a supreme head (the Great Mogul) and a quantity of small sovereigns. The English possess commercial establishments there, which they have acquired by means of money, or conquered by force of arms. The object of this campaign is to ruin these establishments, to free the oppressed sovereigns, to put them with regard to Russia in the same state of dependence that they now are with regard to the English, finally to secure for ourselves the commerce of those regions. . . ." (12th-24th January). " Be sure to remember that you are only at war with the English, and the friend of all who do not give them help. On your march you will assure men of the friendship of Russia. From the Indus you will go to the Ganges. On the way you will occupy Bokhara, to prevent her going over to China. At Khiva you will deliver some thousands of my subjects who are kept prisoners there. If you need infantry, I will send it to follow in your footsteps. There is no other way, but it will be best if you can be sufficient for yourselves" (13th-25th January). " The expedition is urgent; the earlier the better" (7th-19th February).

Such were the instructions, a little premature and inconsequent, that Paul sent daily with incomplete maps to Orlof-Denissof. These letters abound in contradictions. He promised his Cossacks all the wealth of the Indies, and forbids them to attack princes who remain neutral; in the same line he enjoins them to free the princes, and to place them under the sovereignty of Russia. To go from the Don to the Volga, from the Oural to the Indus, from the Indus to the Ganges, is far from being an easy undertaking, and he entrusts the Ataman besides with missions to Khiva and Bokhara. These letters of Paul, published by the *Rousskaïa Starina*,* made some noise in the Russian press at the beginning of the present quarrels with England.

This plan really began to be executed, as we see by the 'Memoirs of the Ataman Denissof,' nephew of the late Ataman, published in the same collection. He assembled eleven *polks* of Cossacks, and succeeded in crossing the Volga on the floating ice, in the midst of unheard-of difficulties. This vanguard of the great Cossack army had reached the left bank of the river,

---

* *Rousskaïa Starina* of 1873, vol. viii. p. 209. See also vol. xii. p. 237, and vol. xv. p. 216; the *Novoïé Vrémia* of the 14th-16th Nov. 1876; and the *Univers Pittoresque*, by Dubois de Jancigny, p. 105.

when in March 1801 its chief suddenly received the news of the death of the Emperor, and the order to return.

The other expedition was to be composed of 35,000 French and 35,000 Russians, at whose head Paul, with noble and chivalrous feeling, insisted on placing the victor of Zurich, Masséna. The 35,000 French were to start from the banks of the Rhine, descend the Danube in ships furnished them by the Austrian Government, embark at the mouth in Russian ships, which would transport them to Taganrog, then go up the Don as far as Piati-Isbanskaïa, cross the Volga at Tzaritsyne, drop down as far as Astrakhan, and thence, navigating the Caspian in Russian vessels, arrive at Asterabad on the Persian shore, where the 35,000 Russians would await them. The combined army was then to march by way of Herat, Ferah, and Kandahar to the Upper Indus, and begin the war against the English. This project, on the margin of which are scrawled the criticisms of Bonaparte and the reply by the Emperor of Russia, enters into the most minute details. Twenty days were reckoned to descend the Danube, fifty-five days to reach Asterabad, and forty-five to arrive at the Indus—120 days in all from the Rhine to Scinde. Aërosticians, artificers, and a body of *savants* such as went to Egypt, were to accompany the expedition. The French Government was to send precious objects, the produce of the national industry.

"Distributed with tact among the princes of these countries, and offered with the grace and courtesy natural to the French," says the Russian note, "these gits will enable these races to form the highest idea of the magnificence of French industry and power, and will in consequence open an important branch of commerce." To inspire the people with the most exalted conception of France and Russia, brilliant fêtes were to be given, accompanied by such military evolutions " as celebrate in Paris great events and memorable epochs." Paul I. seemed to be reconciled to the anniversaries of the Revolution.

It does not appear that Paul ever doubted the success of this hazardous expedition. Bonaparte naturally made this objection: "Supposing the combined army to be reunited at Asterabad, how do you propose that it should get to India through countries almost barbarous, and without any resources, having to march a distance of 300 leagues, from Asterabad to the frontiers of Hindostan?" The Tzar replied that these countries were neither barbarous nor arid, that caravans traversed them every year and made the journey in thirty-five or forty days, and that in 1739 and 1740 Nadir Shah had marched through the reverse way, from Delhi to the Caspian.

Paul ended by saying, "The French and Russian armies are eager for glory; they are brave, patient, and unwearied; their courage, their perseverance, and the wisdom of their leaders will know how to surmount all obstacles. . . . What a *really Asiatic* army did in 1739 and 1740, we cannot doubt that an army of French and Russians can do to-day!"

On the Continent Paul did his best to make Prussia declare against England. The League of Neutrality made the British Government so uneasy, that, notwithstanding the peace, Admirals Parker and Nelson seized the Danish Fleet (Naval Battle of Copenhagen, 2nd of April, 1801). An event still more extraordinary broke up the coalition, the death of the Emperor Paul in the night of the 23rd-24th of March, 1801 (11th or 12th March, O.S.). On the 24th of March Alexander was proclaimed.

England could not help being satisfied by the simultaneous news of the destruction of the Danish fleet and the terrible death of the Tzar, who was the soul of the coalition. In France the consternation was great. Bonaparte, who saw the downfall of his vast projects, could not contain himself. He caused the following lines, full of rage and hate against England, to be printed in the *Moniteur*, making himself the mouthpiece of an absurd suspicion: "It is for history to clear up the secret of this tragic death, and to say what national policy was interested in provoking such a catastrophe."

CHAPTER XII.

ALEXANDER I.: FOREIGN AFFAIRS (1801–1825).

First war with Napoleon: Austerlitz, Eylau, Friedland, and Treaty of Tilsit—Interview at Erfürt: wars with England, Sweden, Austria, Turkey, and Persia—Grand Duchy of Warsaw: causes of the second war with Napoleon—The "Patriotic War": battle of Borodino; burning of Moscow; destruction of the Grand Army—Campaigns of Germany and France: treaties of Vienna and Paris—Kingdom of Poland; congresses at Aix-la-Chapelle, Carlsbad, Laybach, and Verona.

FIRST WAR WITH NAPOLEON: AUSTERLITZ, EYLAU, FRIEDLAND, AND TREATY OF TILSIT.

WITH the new reign began a new foreign policy.* Immediately after his accession, Alexander addressed a letter of reconciliation to George III. He ordered the embargo on English vessels to be raised, and the sailors who had been captured to be set at liberty; he also entreated Admiral Parker to cease hostilities against Denmark. Those acts announced the dissolution of the League of Neutrality. On the 17th of July, 1801, a compromise was agreed on by which England consented to define more strictly what articles should be understood to be contraband in war, admitted that a blockade must be effective before it could be considered binding, and gave up boarding foreign men-of-war.

The concessions of Russia were of a much graver kind. They consisted in the abandonment of the principles of the armed neutrality, and the disavowal of the naval policy of Catherine II. and Paul I. Alexander allowed that the flag was not to cover the merchandise; vessels of war were not to have the right to hinder the inspection, nor even the seizure of the merchant ships that they escorted. England restored the islands taken

---

* A short time after Alexander's accession, Pahlen, Zoubof, and Panine, the "men" of the 24th of March, 1801, had been successively disgraced. Alexander surrounded himself with young men,—Czartoryski, Novossiltsof, Strogonof, and Kotchoubey, who were supposed to be English partisans.

from the Swedes and Danes. Denmark and Sweden, considering the common cause betrayed, confined themselves to making peace with Great Britain without touching the disputed points.

Alexander affected, nevertheless, a desire to remain on good terms with France, and instructed Count Markof to continue at Paris the negotiations begun by Kolychef. Affairs had gone on so rapidly under Paul, that the two States had arranged an offensive alliance without ever having concluded a formal treaty of peace. The First Consul was greatly irritated at the abrupt change in the Russian policy. On the other hand, the instructions given by Alexander to Markof breathed defiance towards Bonaparte, who, "by flattering the deceased Emperor, had chiefly in view the use of him as a weapon against England, and who doubtless only thought of gaining time."

Bonaparte, however, sent Duroc to represent him at Alexander's coronation. He received Count Markof courteously, assuring him of his esteem for Alexander, but he made him understand that the situation was no longer the same, and that Russia had not the right to exact so much from France. "My obligations towards the Emperor Paul, whose great and magnanimous ideas corresponded perfectly with the views of France, were such that I should not have hesitated to become the lieutenant of Paul I." He complained that Russia insisted on such important trifles as that of the "little kinglet" of Sardinia, and that she wished to treat France "like the republic of Lucca."

In his demands in favor of the kingdom of Sardinia, Alexander did not feel that he had the support of England, who, in negotiating herself for peace, had advised Cornwallis "not to embarrass himself with questions foreign to purely British interests." On the 8th of October, then, a treaty was signed between France and Russia, and on the 11th of October there was a secret convention, of which the principal articles were as follow:

1. The common mediation of the two Powers for the Germanic indemnities stipulated by the Peace of Luneville. 2. An agreement about Italian affairs. 3. The mediation of Russia for the establishment of a peace between France and Turkey. 4. The neutrality of Naples, and the evacuation of her territory by the French, after the latter had evacuated Egypt. 5. The indemnity of the King of Sardinia "according to present circumstances." 6. A suitable indemnity to the sovereigns of Bavaria, Wurtemberg, and Baden. 7. Independence and neutrality of the Ionian Isles.

The two parties also bound themselves to do all that lay in their power to strengthen the general peace, to re-establish the equilibrium of the different parties of the world, and to insure liberty of navigation.

The treaty of the 8th of October followed that of Luneville between France and Austria, and prepared that of Amiens, with England. It secured the dictatorship of France and Russia in the regulation of continental affairs. Common mediation for the indemnities, and joint action in Italian affairs,—these were the principles that the late Tzar would have wished to see prevail; but circumstances were changed. Out of regard for Paul I., Bonaparte might have renounced Piedmont, Naples, and Italy, but Paul I. fought for the liberty of the seas, threatened England in the Baltic and India, and assured the revenge of the French against Great Britain. The first act of Alexander had been, on the contrary, to desert his allies, and seek a reconciliation with England.

In the regulation of German affairs, the will of France naturally preponderated. If Bonaparte increased the dominions of the houses of Bavaria, Wurtemberg, Baden, and Darmstadt, which were related to the imperial family of Russia, it was doubtless to please Alexander, but above all because he wished to recompense their fidelity to the French alliance. It was the influence of France, and not that of Russia, that was increased on the left bank of the Rhine. This was plainly to be seen in 1805, when all these princes hastened to conclude separate treaties with France, which already announced the Confederation of the Rhine. For the moment it was the self-esteem of Alexander that was specially wounded; he saw that everything was worked from Paris, that Bonaparte was all-powerful, and that his envoy, Markof, was only sought by the German princes after they had paid court to Talleyrand.*

In Italy the question of the King of Sardinia's indemnity dragged on slowly. On the 11th of September, 1802, Bonaparte had announced the union of Piedmont to France, but he always declined to fix the promised equivalent. He had at first suggested Parma and Piacenza, then had given them to an Infant of Spain. He had no longer offered anything beyond Siena, Orbitello, and a pension of 500,000 livres, saying, "As much money as you like, but nothing more;" and again, "This affair ought not to interest the Emperor Alexander more than the affairs of Persia interest me, the First Consul."

In Switzerland, in that Helvetia which Souvorof had hoped to march through as victor, it was Bonaparte who laid down the law, accepting the title of mediator, and occupying cantons trou-

* Rambaud, ' Les Français sur le Rhin' and ' L'Allemagne sous Napoleon I.'

bled by intestine discords. It is true that in the Ionian Islands, ceaselessly agitated by small civil wars, it was a Russian plenipotentiary that arrived to appease the popular excitement, while the Emperor of Russia guaranteed the constitution.

The Peace of Amiens was on the eve of being broken, and, to hinder the rupture between France and England, Russia would have wished to offer her mediation. She feared above everything the French occupation of Naples and Hanover. The occupation of Naples meant the humiliation of another Italian client of Russia; that of Hanover brought the French very near to the Elbe and Hamburg. The fears of Alexander were realized. In a war against England, Bonaparte could not neglect such important points. Gouvion Saint Cyr occupied Tarento, Otranto, and Brindisi; Mortier invaded Hanover and got a loan from Hamburg; Holland and Tuscany were also garrisoned with French troops (June–July, 1803).

The choice of Markof as the Russian representative at Paris had not been happy. Like almost all the Russian aristocracy, he hated equally new France, the Revolution, and Bonaparte. He was the declared friend of the *émigrés*, at the very moment when the royalist plots put the life of the First Consul in danger. His Austrian sympathies were notorious. He proved to be proud, excessively obstinate, and even impertinent. When the consular court and all the diplomatic body went into mourning on the death of General Leclerc, Bonaparte's brother-in-law, he alone declined to wear it. He was compromised by the seizure of some pamphlets published against the Government, his name being found at the head of the list of subscribers. He had the audacity to say, " The Emperor of Russia has his will, but the nation also has hers." The Russian Government refused to recall him, in spite of Talleyrand's declaration that since the renewal of the war with England " the presence of so ill-disposed a man was more than unpleasant to the First Consul." Bonaparte also complained of some French *émigrés* whose intrigues were protected by Russia; of Christin, formerly secretary to Calonne, at Paris, of Vernègues at Rome, of D'Entraigues at Dresden. At last, after an angry scene, Markof appeared no more at the Tuileries, and was finally recalled. The French were, however, no better contented with D'Oubril, who remained at Paris as *chargé d'affaires*.

The seizure and execution of the Duc d'Enghien increased the misunderstanding between the two cabinets. The news of this murder reached St. Petersburg on the eve of a diplomatic reception; when the reception itself took place, the Emperor and all his court were in mourning. Alexander passed General

Hédouville, the French Ambassador, without speaking to him. D'Oubril presented to the French Government a note protesting against the violation of international law and of neutral territory. Alexander, in his character as guarantor of the German Empire—a title which he maintained that he had acquired by the Treaty of Teschen—caused a similar note to be laid before the Diet at Ratisbon, which Sweden and England hastened to ratify, but which terribly embarrassed the Diet and all the Germanic body. Bonaparte retorted by recalling Hédouville. He replied officially to D'Oubril's note by complaining of the unfriendly acts of the Russian Government towards him, of the ill-will of all her agents, of the embarrassing situation which they sought to create for France by everywhere patronizing the *émigrés*, contested the right of Russia to interfere in the affairs of Germany, and declared that in the affair of Ettenheim the Government had only acted in self-defence. "The cry raised by Russia to-day compels us to ask if, when England meditated the assassination of Paul I., men had been aware that the authors of the conspiracy were lurking within a league from the frontiers, they would not have hastened to capture them?" After such an interchange of letters, the *chargés d'affaires* themselves were recalled, and all diplomatic relations broken.

Napoleon had just been crowned Emperor; he had taken at Milan the crown of Italy, united Genoa to the French territory, and modified the constitution of Holland. From the camp at Boulogne he threatened England, but a coalition was already formed against him. Novossiltsof, one of the favorite ministers of Alexander, had left for London with special instructions drawn up by the Emperor; we find in them all kinds of Utopian schemes, sometimes generous, often incoherent, which he still cherished at this epoch. He proposes to wrest from the French, who gave themselves out as the champions of liberty, the dangerous weapon of propaganda; to give to the troubled world a good example by restoring the King of Sardinia; to render back to Switzerland and Holland the liberty to choose their own rulers; to declare to the French nation, which would gladly welcome the allies, that the war was directed, not against her, but against her Government, from which she suffered as severely as the rest of Europe. In this note Alexander renewed the question of the reconstitution of Europe: taking count of natural frontiers, of crests of mountains, of groups of nationalities, he added a scheme for the partition of the Ottoman empire, in the case of its existence becoming incompatible with the present state of Europe. The British Cabinet received these communications somewhat coldly, but concluded a treaty of subsidies in the proportion of £1,200,000 for every 100,000 men put under arms by Russia.

Sweden and Naples entered the coalition; Austria had already attacked Bavaria, the ally of Napoleon. Alexander also wished to assure himself of Frederic William III., who always vacillated between France and Russia, and who had undertaken engagements towards both. Alexander thought to gain him by announcing that his army was about to cross Silesia and Pomerania, but the King of Prussia instantly mobilized his troops, to cause his neutrality to be respected. The violation of the territories of Anspach and Baireuth by the French soon changed the course of his ideas. Alexander had his famous interview near Frederic the Great's tomb, with the King and Queen of Prussia. By the Treaty of Potsdam, Prussia undertook to furnish 80,000 men to the coalition if Napoleon did not accept its ultimatum. The ultimatum stipulated for the independence of Germany and Italy, and the indemnity to the King of Sardinia. Haugwitz was ordered to carry it to Napoleon.

During these negotiations the Russian army was put in motion. Behind the three great Austrian armies (those of the Archduke Charles in Italy, the Archduke John in the Tyrol, and Mack with the Archduke Ferdinand against Bavaria) were ranged the Russian troops. Besides the 20,000 men (under Tolstoï) who were to join the Swedes and disembark at Stralsund, and the 20,000 (under Admiral Seniavine) who were to join the English and disembark at Naples, there were the troops who guarded the frontiers of Turkey and Prussia, and the great army of Germany. The latter had as its vanguard Koutouzof, who, with 45,000 men, hastened to the Inn to unite with Mack. In Moravia strong forces were gathering under the orders of Buxhœwden and the eyes of the Emperor. Alexander had with him his three ministers—Czartoryski, Novosiltsof, and Strogonof. All the Imperial Guard was there—the Horse Guards, the Knights, the Preobrajenski, the Semenovski, the Ismaïlovski, the Pavlovski, and the flower of the army.

Koutouzof had already reached Braunau on the Inn, when he heard of the Capitulation of Ulm, and the annihilation of Mack's army. He found his own position very critical, being at a great distance from the main body. He had under him excellent troops, and three admirable lieutenants: Prince Bagration, one of the heroes of the campaign of 1799, the favorite pupil of old Souvorof; Doktourof, the intrepid leader of the Grenadiers; Miloradovitch, surnamed the Murat of the Russian army, and of whom it was said, "Whoever wishes to follow Miloradovitch must have a spare life." To escape being cut

off on the right bank of the Danube by Murat's cavalry, by
Oudinot and by Lannes, and on the left bank by the corps of
Mortier, Koutouzof retreated, giving battle to Oudinot at Lambach in Amstetten. He then crossed the Danube at Krems,
fought the battle of Dirnstein with Mortier, and marched to the
north to join the great Russian army. The surprise of the
bridge of Vienna by Lannes and Murat endangered him on his
left flank during his retreat into Moravia. To save his army,
his rear-guard must be sacrificed. The dogged Bagration was
charged to check the pursuit of the French. He intrenched
himself at Hollabrunn and Schöngraben. Murat came up first,
and desired to gain time in order to allow Lannes to join him;
Bagration wished to give Koutouzof time to escape. He received Murat's envoy favorably, and sent to propose an armistice
in the name of the Tzar. Ten hours passed while they awaited
the answer of Napoleon. The latter, furious at Murat's credulity,
sent orders that he was to attack immediately. Bagration's
10,000 men fought desperately during twelve hours. At night
Bagration retreated, having lost 2000 men and all his guns.
Koutouzof, who had been saved by his devotion, embraced him
and exclaimed, "You live, and that is enough for me."

The junction of Koutouzof, Buxhœweden, and the Austrians
took place at Olmütz, and Napoleon was concentrating his forces
at Brünn. He had collected about 70,000 men, the Emperors
of Russia and Austria about 80,000. The greatest exultation
reigned in the Russian head-quarters. The young Emperor and
his young officers, proud of the splendid battles fought by Koutouzof and Bagration, spoke with profound contempt of the Austrians, who had allowed themselves to be so easily trapped at
Ulm; they had only hatred and disdain for "Buonaparté the
Corsican," who owed his victories to the imbecility of his adversaries. A small success of the vanguard at Wischau, the apparent timidity of Napoleon, and the arrival of General Savary as
envoy, completely turned their heads. Alexander sent the
young Prince Dolgorouki to the French head-quarters, with a
note addressed to the "head of the French nation." It was
necessary, said the Prince to Napoleon, that France should
abandon Italy, if she wanted immediate peace. If she were
vanquished, she would have to lose not only the Rhine, but
Piedmont, Savoy, and Belgium, which would be formed into
barriers against her. "What! Brussels also?" exclaimed
Napoleon, and coldly dismissed him. "These people are
mad," he said. "What would they do with France if I were
defeated!"

"It is difficult," relates a Russian eye-witness, Jirkiévitch, the lieutenant of artillery, "to picture the enthusiasm that animated us all, and the strange and ridiculous infatuation that accompanied this noble sentiment. It seemed to us that we were going straight to Paris. No one spoke of anything but Dolgorouki, a young man of twenty-five, who presented himself to Napoleon with a letter from the Emperor, and all admired the cleverness of the superscription, in which the imperial title of Napoleon had been so skilfully avoided. It was even added that when Dolgorouki gave the letter to Napoleon, as the latter remained covered, Dolgorouki replaced his hat. A few days passed, and our ideas became greatly changed." The scheme conceived by Weirother the Austrian, and approved by Alexander, was that Bagration on the right should keep Lannes in check; the two Imperial Guards would be sufficient to watch the plateau of Pratzen; Doktourof, Langeron, Prjébichevski, even Koutouzof and Miloradovitch, were to descend into the valley of Goldbach to turn Napoleon, cut him off from the Danube, and force him back on the mountains of Bohemia.

The evening before the battle it was still believed that Napoleon would retreat. Dolgorouki recommended his soldiers " to watch well which way the French retired." On the morning of the 2nd of December, 1805. the valley of Goldbach was covered by a fog, from the waves of which emerged, as from the bosom of a milky sea, the mountain summits gilded by the early rays of the sun; on the west lay the heights of Schlapanitz, where Napoleon had taken up his position; on the east, the hills of Pratzen, where the allied emperors were encamped. Napoleon distinctly saw the Russian columns descend the plateau of Pratzen, and lose themselves in the fog; and from the side of Lakes Sokolnitz, Satchan, and Menitz—that is to say, to the right—he heard the noise of their artillery carriages. He was therefore certain that, as he had foreseen, the allies hoped to turn this wing. When the plateau of Pratzen, the centre of the Russian army, seemed to him sufficiently bare, he gave the signal. In twenty minutes the corps of Soult scaled the slopes in heavy masses, and attacked Koutouzof and Miloradovitch, whose divisions alone remained on the plateau. There a desperate battle was fought. The Emperor of Russia found himself under fire, his men were dispersed, and he himself was obliged to retire at a gallop, attended only by his doctor, a single company, and two Cossacks. A little to the right of the plateau, the Tzarévitch Constantine with the Guards tried to oppose the cavalry of Murat and the French Guards. It was an epic struggle, where fought on one side the famous Russian regiments of the Foot Guards, the Horse Guards, the *élite* of the Russian nobility, the Uhlans, the *chasseurs* of the Guard, the Cossacks and the Cuirassiers of Lichtenstein; on the other, the Mamelukes of Rapp, the mounted Grenadiers of Bessières, the light cavalry of Kellermann, the Cuirassiers of Hautpoul and of Nansouty. At the extreme right of the Russians, Bagration could easily beat a retreat before Lannes; but on their left, the columns of Doktourof, Langeron, and Prjébichevski, entangled in the network of lakes, engaged since morning by the corps of Davoust, and suddenly attacked in their rear by the victorious troops returning from the plateau of Pratzen, found themselves in a frightful situation: 2000 men perished on the ice, which Napoleon had broken by shots from the guns. Doktourof protected the retreat. "It was impossible," says Dumas, "at the end of a lost battle, to put a better face on things."

Such was "the battle of the three emperors." The Russians fell back on Austerlitz. Without reckoning the Austrian loss, their own amounted to 21,000 men, 133 cannon, and 30 flags. They were furious against their allies. As happened after the battle of Zurich, they accused them of incapacity, and even of treason. It was the Austrians who had sketched the plan of the battle: now, fighting in their own country, on a soil which they had studied at leisure in the manœuvres on parade, they had wholly failed in strategy, and had provided neither forage nor ammunition. Dolgorouki, in a report to the Emperor, remarks: "They conducted the army of your majesty rather to deliver it to the enemy than to fight; and what puts the finishing touch to this infamy is, that our dispositions were known to the enemy, a fact of which we have certain proof." Rostopchine echoes him: "The plan had been treacherously communicated to Bonaparte; forty-eight hours before we were ready, the latter began the attack at break of day. From the beginning, half of the Austrians took up arms; the other half crossed over to the enemy, and some even fired on us."

On the 4th the Emperor Francis had an interview with Napoleon, and obtained for the Russian army, which was greatly imperilled after its disaster, and was closely pressed by Davoust, leave to retire, on condition that it should return to Russia by stages, to be regulated by Napoleon. On the 26th the Treaty of Presburg was signed, which deprived Francis II. of Venice, the Tyrol, and Austrian Swabia; he was likewise to give up the title of Emperor. This new intervention of the Russians in Europe ended in a formidable growth of French power. The King of Naples was dethroned and replaced by Joseph; the kingdom of Italy was increased by Venice; Murat became Grand Duke of Berg; the sovereigns of Bavaria, Wurtemburg, and

Baden, strengthened by the spoils of Austria, decorated with the titles of king and grand duke, formed, with the new Prince-Primate Charles of Dalberg, the Grand Duke of Hesse-Darmstadt, and fifteen other sovereign princes, the Confederation of the Rhine (*Rheinbund*). There was no longer a Russian *clientèle* in Germany. Already Napoleon's family was contracting matrimonial alliances with those of Bavaria, Wurtemburg, and Baden. The German vassals of the successor of Charles the Great, of the new Emperor of the West, could add to his army from 100.000 to 150,000 men. Haugwitz, who had been ordered to inform Napoleon of the ultimatum stipulated by the Treaty of Potsdam, found himself at Schönbrunn in the presence of a defiant and invincible conqueror; he was forced to sign a treaty imposing on Prussia the acceptance of Hanover, in exchange for Anspach and Baireuth, and irrevocably embroiling her with England. The coalition was therefore beaten in the field and dissolved in the cabinet. Russia, isolated by the ruin of Naples, the desertion of Austria, and the defection of Prussia, found herself almost alone on the Continent.

We all know how from this same Treaty of Schönbrunn, which appeared to attach Prussia to Napoleon, sprang a new war. The coalition was renewed between Russia, England, Sweden, and Prussia. The Prussians showed in 1806 the same precipitation as the Austrians in 1805; like them, they did not allow time for the Russians to join them; and when Alexander found himself able to undertake a second campaign, he learnt the twofold catastrophe of Jena and Auerstadt, as he had formerly learnt that of Ulm. For the second time, her principal ally being beaten, the whole weight of the war fell upon Russia. On this occasion the disaster was even greater, for the Prussian monarchy had ceased to exist. The French occupied Berlin, and took the fortresses on the Oder and the Vistula. Nothing remained to Frederic William in the north but three fortresses, Dantzig, Königsberg, and Memel, and a small body of 14.000 men under Lestocq.

These events had followed one another with a rapidity so startling that Russia found herself taken unawares. After Austerlitz she had tried to negotiate with Napoleon, and sent D'Oubril to Paris; but D'Oubril, who had consented to the evacution of Cattaro and the Ionian Isles, and the recognition of the principle of Ottoman integrity, had been disavowed at St. Petersburg, like Haugwitz at Berlin. Russia found herself in a terrible plight; and she had in addition the prospect of a double war against Persia and Turkey. Czartoryski, Minister of Foreign Affairs, addressed a memorial to the Emperor, counselling peace. He showed that Russia had two vulnerable points.—Poland, and the serfage of the peasants. Invasion must be avoided at all costs, for the invader would not fail to proclaim the re-establishment of Poland, and the freedom of the serfs. It was of little consequence that Germany was subject to Napoleon, if the latter would consent not to pass the Weser or even the Elbe. It was necessary to consent to the evacuation of Cattaro and the Ionian Isles, to guarantee Sicily only to the King of Naples, and to obtain some sort of an indemnity for the King of Sardinia. It would be better to secure the co-operation of Napoleon for regulating the affairs of Turkey. Only one thing was important, the safety of the empire.

But Alexander, secure of Prussia, at this moment still intact, inclined to war. He demanded a new conscription of one man in every hundred, lowered the regulation height one inch, ordered muskets even from private manufacturers and foreigners, created new regiments, summoned students and young nobles, promising them the grade of officer after six months' service, for the fight at Pratzen had made terrible havoc with the Guards. A plan of organizing militia was talked of, which would have given them 612,000 men. The priests were ordered to proclaim everywhere that war was made, "not for vain glory, but for the salvation of the country." England was asked for a loan of £6,000,000. Austria was once more appealed to. When Prussia was crushed, the 14,000 Prussians of Lestocq were sent for.

Buxhœwden had 28,000 men; another army of 60,000 men was confided to Bennigsen, a learned man of boundless energy (one of the conspirators of 1801), with a certain genius for tactics. He has, however, been reproached with indecision at the critical moment, with neglecting discipline, and not knowing how to repress pillage; the marauders did not respect even his head-quarters or his own house. These defects were, however, partially atoned for by a tenacity destined to astonish Napoleon. The old Field-marshal Kamenski, nominated Generalissimo, had concentrated all his forces on the Vistula. When his infirmities obliged him to resign his command, Bennigsen succeeded him.

Murat, Davoust, and Lannes had entered Warsaw, then a Prussian possession, and had established themselves on the Bug, forming the right of the Grand Army. Soult and Augereau crossed the Vistula at Modlin, and formed the centre; on the left Ney and Bernadotte occupied Thorn and Elburg. In the rear Mortier acted in Pomerania against the Swedes; Lefèbvre besieged Dantzig; and Jerome Bonaparte, with Vandamme, finished the conquest of Silesia. Pressed by the Grand Army,

Bennigsen was obliged to evacuate Poland, after some severe fighting, especially at Pultusk (December 26), and retired by way of Ostrolenka, leaving in the mud of Poland eighty field-pieces and nearly 10,000 men; he stopped on the Alle to cover Königsberg.

Winter had arrived: the Grand Army reposed in camp, when Bennigsen conceived the audacious project of moving his left wing, passing between the two forces of Bernadotte and Ney, crushing Bernadotte and forcing Ney into the sea; of relieving Dantzig and carrying the war into Brandenburg on the rear of Napoleon. Bernadotte, however, resisted so stubbornly at Mohrungen and Osterode, that Napoleon had time to come up, and Bennigsen himself was on the point of having his left wing turned, and seeing his lines of communication cut. An intercepted despatch warned him of the risk he ran; it was necessary to sound a retreat, and Bagration was again called on to protect it. As at Schöngraben, he covered himself with glory, and allowed himself to be sacrificed for the salvation of the army; his "incomparable regiment of Kostroma" was almost annihilated, and he himself severely wounded. During this time Bennigsen marched to Eylau and took up a position to the east of the town, on a line of heights which extended from Schloditten to Serpallen; behind his centre lay the village of Sansgarten, his front was covered by 250 pieces of cannon.

When Napoleon arrived at Eylau, which was taken on the 7th of February, he had only with him Soult, Augereau, Murat, and the Guard; Davoust, who was to form his right wing, and Ney, who was to form his left wing, and who had been delayed by his pursuit of Lestocq, were still wanting. Bennigsen, on his side, awaited Lestocq, who was to compose his right. The battle, however, began (February 8), and was one of the bloodiest of the century. A thick snow was falling, which ever and anon hid the battle-field from sight: the sky was of a livid gray; the landscape was as gloomy as the action. The battle began by a formidable cannonade, which lasted all the day. The French, sheltered by the buildings of the town of Eylau, and disposed in thin lines, suffered from it less than the Russians, who had little cover, and were ranged in compact masses. The corps of Augereau and the division of St. Hilaire, entrusted with the attack on the Russian left wing, went astray, blinded by a snowstorm; when the sky cleared, the two divisions of Augereau found themselves opposite the Russian centre, forty paces from a battery of seventy-two guns; mown down at the cannon's mouth, they lost in a few minutes 5200 men. Augereau and his two generals of division were wounded. At the same moment an enormous mass of cavalry, uhlans, and cuirassiers dashed themselves against St. Hilaire's infantry, upsetting everything in their passage. The infantry of the Russian centre advanced almost to the cemetery of Eylau, where stood Napoleon. It was then that Murat, in his turn, assembled eighty squadrons, and led against this infantry the most frightful charge mentioned in the annals of these wars; solid squares were broken by his cuirassiers. Then the two armies continued to watch and to fire at each other. The battle made little progress till Davoust at last joined the right wing of the French army, turned the Russian left and threw it back upon the centre, and reached Sansgarten on their rear. The Prussians of Lestocq arrived in their turn at the other extremity of the line, but they were followed by Ney, who in the darkness of night, at half-past nine o'clock, began to break Bennigsen's right wing. The Russians now ran the risk of being surrounded. They had suffered cruel losses: one of their divisions, that of Count Ostermann Tolstoï, no longer counted more than 2500 men. "The general in chief," says M. Bogdanovitch, "trembled as he read the reports of the generals of divisions." He had not 30,000 men under arms; 26,000 were killed or wounded; among the latter were Barclay de Tolly, Doktourof, and seven other generals. He profited by the darkness to beat a retreat, and did not hesitate to claim as a victory what in reality had only been a glorious resistance.

The French had more right to call themselves victorious, as they remained masters of the field of battle. Unlike the Russians, some of their troops were still intact, such as Ney's corps and the Foot Guards, but they had likewise suffered terribly, and a gloomy sadness hung over the survivors. Such efforts, so much blood shed, yet such small results, so few trophies! This melancholy impression is reflected even in Napoleon's despatch, where he allows himself to describe the funereal aspect of the battlefield, the thousands of heaped-up corpses, the gunners killed on their pieces, "all thrown into relief by a background of snow." Ney shrugged his shoulders on seeing the carnage. "What a massacre," he said, "and without result!" The French suffered hunger and cold; the immense spaces, the broken roads, the marshy plains, the stoical resistance of the Russians, had disconcerted the calculations of Napoleon. Eylau gave him a foretaste of 1812; the delay of Ney a foretaste of Waterloo. Fortune took care to warn him that she would not always be punctual to her rendezvous. The effect produced on Europe was unlucky for France; in Paris the Funds fell. Bennigsen boldly ordered the *Te Deum* to be sung.

In order to confirm his victory, re-organize his army, reassure France, re-establish the opinion of Europe, encourage the Polish insurrection, and to curb the ill-will of Germany and Austria, Napoleon remained a week at Eylau. He negotiated: on one side he caused Talleyrand to write to Zastrow, the Prussian foreign minister, to propose peace and his alliance; he sent Bertrand to Memel to offer to re-establish the King of Prussia, on the condition of no foreign intervention. He also tried to negotiate with Bennigsen; to which the latter made answer, "that his master had charged him to fight, and not negotiate." After some hesitation, Prussia ended by joining her fortunes to those of Russia. By the convention of Bartenstein (25th April, 1807), the two sovereigns came to terms on the following points:—

1. The re-establishment of Prussia within the limits of 1805. 2. The dissolution of the Confederation of the Rhine. 3. The restitution to Austria of the Tyrol and Venice. 4. The accession of England to the coalition, and the aggrandizement of Hanover. 5. The co-operation of Sweden. 6. The restoration of the house of Orange, and indemnities to the kings of Naples and Sardinia. This document is important; it nearly reproduces the conditions offered to Napoleon at the Congress of Prague, in 1813.

Russia and Prussia proposed then to make a more pressing appeal to Austria, Sweden, and England; but the Emperor Francis was naturally undecided, and the Archduke Charles, alleging the state of the finances and the army, strongly advised him against any new intervention. Sweden was too weak; and notwithstanding his fury against Napoleon, Gustavus III. had just been forced to treat with Mortier. The English minister showed a remarkable inability to conceive the situation; he refused to guarantee the new Russian loan of a hundred and fifty millions, and would lend himself to no maritime diversion.

Napoleon showed the greatest diplomatic activity. The Sultan Selim III. declared war against Russia; General Sebastiani, the envoy at Constantinople, put the Bosphorus in a state of defence, and repulsed the English fleet; General Gardane left for Ispahan, with a mission to cause a Persian outbreak in the Caucasus. Dantzig had capitulated, and Lefebvre's 40,000 men were therefore ready for service. Massena took 36,000 of them into Italy.

In the spring, Bennigsen, who had been reinforced by 10,000 regular troops, 6000 Cossacks, and the Imperial Guard, being now at the head of 100,000 men, took the offensive; Gortchakof commanding the right and Bagration the left. He tried, as in the preceding year, to seize Ney's division; but the latter fought, as he retired, two bloody fights, at Gutstadt and Ankendorff.

Bennigsen, again in danger of being surrounded, retired on Heilsberg. He defended himself bravely (June 10); but the French, extending their line on his right, marched on Eylau, so as to cut him off from Königsberg. The Russian generalissimo retreated; but being pressed, he had to draw up at Friedland, on the Alle.

The position he had taken up was most dangerous. All his army was enclosed in an angle of the Alle, with the steep bed of the river at their backs, which in case of misfortune left them only one means of retreat, over the three bridges of Friedland. The French vanguard arrived at two in the morning, filled the woods of Posthenen with sharpshooters, and held the Russians in check till the arrival of the Emperor. The Russian army was almost hidden in the ravine of Alle. " Where are the Russians concealed?" asked Napoleon when he came up. When he had noted their situation, he exclaimed, " It is not every day that one surprises the enemy in such a fault." He put Lannes and Victor in reserve, ordered Mortier to oppose Gortchakof on the left and to remain still, as the movement which " would be made by the right would pivot on the left." As to Ney, he was to cope on the right with Bagration, who was shut in by the angle of the river; he was to meet them " with his head down," without taking any care of his own safety. Ney led the charge with irresistible fury; the Russians were riddled by his artillery at 150 paces: he successively crushed the *chasseurs* of the Russian Guard, the Ismailovski, and the Horse Guards, burnt Friedland by shells, and cannonaded the bridges which were the only means of retreat. In a quarter of an hour the Ismailovski lost 400 men out of 520. Bagration, surrounded by the grenadiers of Moscow, had to use his sword: his lieutenants, Raievski, Ermolof, and Baggowut, wasted their strength in useless efforts. The Russian left wing was almost thrown into the river; Bagration, with the Semenovski and other troops, was hardly ably to cover the defeat. On the Russian right, Gortchakof, who had advanced to attack the immovable Mortier, had only time to ford the Alle. Count Lambert retired with 29 guns by the left bank; the rest fled by the right bank, closely pursued by the cavalry. Meanwhile Murat, Davoust, and Soult, who had taken no part in the battle, arrived before Konigsberg. Lestocq, with 25,000 men, tried to defend it, but on learning the disaster of Friedland he hastily evacuated it. Only one fortress now remained to Frederic William—the little town of Memel. The Russians had lost at Friedland from 15.000 to 20,000 men, besides 80 guns (June 14 1807).

Alexander, who was established at Jurburg, received a report from Bennigsen merely announcing that he had been obliged to evacuate the banks of the Alle, and that he would wait in a more advantageous position till Lobanof Rostovski brought him reinforcements. Now, Lobanof had only a few thousand Kalmucks, and it was to these badly-armed savages that they looked for the salvation of Russia. More explicit accounts reached Alexander from the Tzarévitch Constantine and other officers. The situation was desperate : Alexander had no longer an army. Only one man, Barclay de Tolly, proposed to continue the war ; but in order to do this it would be necessary to re-enter Russia, to penetrate into the very heart of the empire, to burn everything on the way, and only present a desert to the enemy. Alexander hoped to get off more cheaply. He wrote a severe letter to Bennigsen, and gave him powers to treat. Prince Lobanof left for the head-quarters of Napoleon, who sent in his turn the Captain de Talleyrand-Périgord. Alexander had at that time a common sentiment with Napoleon—hatred of the English. He neither pardoned them for their refusal to guarantee a Russian loan, nor for the calculated insufficiency of their diversions, nor for their mercantile selfishness.

On June 25th the interview on the raft at Tilsit took place. Alexander and Napoleon conversed for nearly two hours. The King of Prussia was not admitted to a conference on which depended the fate of his dynasty. On horseback on the shore, he pushed his steed into the stream, or sat with his eyes fixed on the fatal raft. Even the personal graces of the Queen of Prussia could not soften the severity of the treaty. It was from " respect for the Emperor of Russia, and desire to unite the two nations in a bond of eternal friendship," that Napoleon " consented " to restore to Frederic William III. Old Prussia, Pomerania, Brandenburg, and Silesia (July 8, 1807).

These articles consummated the fall of Prussia. On the west, Napoleon deprived her of all her possessions between the Rhine and the Elbe, with Magdeburg ; he dethroned her allies of Brunswick and Cassel, and on the east confiscated all Poland. He thus broke the two wings of the Prussian eagle. On its right he established the kingdom of Westphalia ; on its left the Grand Duchy of Warsaw. Dantzig was declared a free town ; the district of Belostok, part of the dismembered Black Russia, again became Russian soil. The States of the princes of Mecklenburg and Oldenburg were restored to them ; but they had to suffer the occupation of their territory for the carrying out of the continental blockade, and, like Saxony, the States of Thuringia, and all the small princes of Germany, they were forced to accede to the Confederation of the Rhine. The King of Prussia adhered to the continental blockade. His dominions were not to be given back to him till after the complete payment of a war indemnity.

Besides the conditions relative to Prussia, the Treaty of Tilsit established : (1) Russian mediation between France and England, French mediation between England and Turkey; (2) Alexander's recognition (likewise that of Frederic William III.) of the kings Joseph of Naples, Louis of Holland, Jerome of Westphalia, as well as the recognition of the Confederation of the Rhine, and of all States founded by Napoleon; (3) reciprocal guarantees for the integrity of the present possessions of Russia and France.

A second treaty with secret articles stipulated that Cattaro should be restored to France ; that the Ionian Isles should be hers in perpetuity; that if Ferdinand were deprived of Sicily, he should have no other equivalent than the Balearic Isles, or Cyprus and Candia ; that in this case Joseph should be acknowledged King of the Two Sicilies ; that an amnesty should be accorded to the Montenegrins, Herzegovinians, and other peoples who had revolted at the call of· Russia ; that if Hanover were united to the kingdom of Westphalia, Prussia should receive in exchange a territory on the left bank of the Elbe, with 300,000 or 400,000 inhabitants.

A third treaty, offensive and defensive, provided that (1) an ultimatum should be addressed to England on the 1st of November, and that if it had no results war should be declared against her by Russia on the 1st of December ; (2) that Turkey should be allowed a delay of three months to make her peace with the Tzar, and that then " the two high contracting Powers should come to an understanding to withdraw all the Ottoman provinces in Europe, Constantinople and Roumelia excepted, from the yoke and tyranny of the Turks " ; (3) that Sweden should be summoned to break with England, and if she refused Denmark was to be invited to take part in the war against her, and Finland was to be annexed to Russia ; (4) that Austria should be invited to accede to the system of continental blockade at the same time as Sweden, Denmark, and Portugal.

In certain respects this peace deserved the name of the " treacherous peace " that the English agent Wilson applied to it in his disappointment. Turkey was abandoned, delivered over, by her old friend France, though it is true that Napoleon alleged in excuse the revolution which had just overthrown his friend the Sultan Selim. He acted in the same way with regard to Sweden, another old ally. He made all these sacrifices to have the right of executing his Macchiavellian designs against

Spain, whose troops fought loyally under his banners. Alexander did not make fewer sacrifices of honor and interest to the new combination. He abruptly consented to go to war with his former ally, England; he renounced the principle of the integrity of Prussia, and even accepted as spoil the province of Belostok; he did not hesitate to wrest Finland from his brother-in-law Gustavus IV.; he consented to see, under the euphemism of the Grand Duchy of Warsaw, a nucleus of Poland formed on the frontier. This strange treaty might, however, if it had been loyally executed, have contented the two States. The part of Russia was more brilliant on the whole than that of Napoleon: while France was to exhaust herself in a barren war with Spain, splendid vistas opened in the East and on the Danube to the ambition of Alexander. Thanks to the French alliance, he could follow on this side the glorious traces of Sviatoslaf, of Peter the Great, and his grandmother Catherine. During some days, at least, Alexander seemed enthusiastic about his ally. They exchanged the ribbons of their orders; each decorated one of the bravest soldiers of the other army; the grenadier Lazaref received the cross of the Legion of Honor; a battalion of the Imperial Guard offered a fraternal banquet to the Preobrajenski.

INTERVIEW AT ERFURT; WARS WITH ENGLAND, SWEDEN, AUSTRIA, TURKEY, AND PERSIA.

The change in the foreign policy was to bring with it a change in the composition of the Government. Alexander separated himself from the friends of his youth—Novossiltsof, Kotchoubey, Strogonof, and Adam Czartoryski—who had been his counsellors in the preceding war. Partisans of the new policy were called to his cabinet—Roumantsof to foreign affairs, and Speranski to the Council of State. The latter did not conceal his admiration for the genius of the Emperor of the French, for the principles born of the Revolution, and embodied in the Civil Code. He seriously desired the maintenance of the French alliance; and M. Pogodine, one of the Slavophils of our time, has not the courage to condemn this policy. "It proves, on the contrary," he says, "his perspicacity as a statesman. The conditions imposed by Napoleon I. would certainly have been more easy to bear than those imposed by Napoleon III. at Sebastopol. The destinies of Europe would have been different. Sebastopol would still have shone on the shores of the Black Sea, and the Continent would not lately have been inundated with blood by two cruel wars." "The Eastern question," says another Slavophil (M. Oreste Müller), "had in this case been settled, and English preponderance been extinguished in the Levant."

We must recognize the fact that in 1807 Russian opinion was hostile to this peace. The aristocracy were not yet reconciled with the state of things to which the Revolution had given rise. The Empress-mother surrounded herself with French *émigrés*; her court was the centre of the English and Austrian party. It was not only the sudden abandonment of the ancient alliances that was blamed, but it was also the partial restoration of the hereditary enemy, Poland; yet the question of the Grand Duchy of Warsaw seemed secondary—" it was considered as a consequence of the subjection to Napoleon." The dismissal of Louis XVIII., who was forced to leave Mittau for England, and the attempt at Bayonne against the Bourbons of Spain, exasperated passions still further.

Savary, Napoleon's ambassador, had to bear this emotional reaction. The selection of him was by no means happy, as Savary was supposed to have been more or less concerned in the affair of the Duc d'Enghien. "Opinion ran so high against the French," says Savary, "that no furnished hotel would take me as a lodger. . . . The general reception of myself and my companions was in inverse proportion to the kindness of the Emperor Alexander. During the first six weeks of my stay here I could not get a single door opened to me. The Emperor of Russia saw all this, and wished it had been otherwise. At the moment of my arrival at St. Petersburg, prayers were publicly recited against us, and particularly against the Emperor Napoleon." The shops and libraries were full of pamphlets against France, against Napoleon, and against the French ambassador, "Nothing," continues Savary, "was equal to the irreverence with which the youthful population of Russia dared to express itself about its sovereign. For some time I was much disturbed at the consequences this licence might have in a country where revolutions in the palace were only too common." Napoleon's envoy thought it even his duty to place in Alexander's hands a correspondence lately seized, in which the writer sent letters of this kind from Prussia to his friends in the interior: "Have you no longer any Pahlens, any Zoubofs, and Bennigsens?"

Stedingk, the Swedish ambassador, also wrote to Gustavus IV.: "The discontent against the Emperor Alexander increases daily, and things are said at this moment which are frightful to hear. The partisans of the Emperor are in despair, but there is no one among them who dares to remedy the evil, or to reveal to him the full horror of the situation. A change of government is spoken of, not only in private conversations, but in public meetings." Some echo of the public discontent did, however, reach the ears of Alexander Admiral Mordvinof wrote to him: "Though the days of glory may be passed, those in which Russia laid down the law; though she may have lost the bright hopes which she cherished in our youth, the sons of Russia are ready to shed the last drop of their blood rather than bow ignominiously before the sword of him whose only advantage over them is that he has known how to use weakness, treachery, and incapacity." The historian Karamsin was already preparing for the Emperor his work on 'Ancient and Modern Russia.'

In general, the literature of this epoch has a very pronounced anti-French character. The national tragedies of Krioukovski and Ozérof, the patriotic odes of Joukovski, even the comedies and fables of "grandfather" Krylof; the productions of the press, represented by Glinka, Gretch, Batiouchkof, and Schichkof —all breathe hate against Napoleon; aversion for that new France which the Russians, accustomed to admire and imitate the old France of Versailles, looked on with the eyes of the *émigrés* themselves. The most impetuous of the Gallophobes of this epoch was the Count Rostopchine. About 1807 he published his new satire 'Oh, the French!' and a comedy entitled the 'News,' or the 'Living-dead,' in which he attacked the alarmists, and the exaggerated partisans of Western customs. In his 'Spoken Thoughts on the Red Staircase,' in 1807, he exclaims, "How long shall we go on imitating monkeys? . . . As soon as a Frenchman arrives who has escaped the gallows, we fly to welcome him, and he represents himself as a prince or a gentleman who has lost his fortune for faith or loyalty, when in reality he is only a lackey, a shopman, or a tax collector, or a suspended priest who has fled in fear from his country. What do they teach children to-day? To pronounce French properly, to turn their toes out, and to frizz their hair. He alone is a wit whom a Frenchman takes for his countryman. How can men love their country when they do not even know their native tongue? Is it not a shame? In every country French is taught to children, but only that they may understand it, and not in order that it may replace their native language." He continues with violent invectives against French ambition, and invokes the brave soldiers of Eylau. "Glory to thee, victorious Russian army, bearing the sword in the name of Christ! Glory to our Emperor and to our mother Russia! Salutation to you, Russian heroes, Tolstoï, Kojine, Galitsyne, Doktourof, Volkonski, Dolgorouki! Eternal peace to you in heaven, young and gallant

Galitsyne! Triumph, Russian empire! the enemy of the human race recoils before thee; he cannot struggle against thy invincible strength. He came as a savage lion, thinking to devour everything; he flies like a hungry wolf, grinding his teeth."

By a contradiction, explained by his education, it is chiefly in his correspondence, and his works written in French, that Rostopchine attacks the nation so bitterly; it is in French that the Russian nobles, pupils of the French of the 18th century, curse France. Miss Wilmot, with an obvious intention of disparaging both nations, scoffs, about 1805, "at the absurdity of Bruin the bear, when he gambols with a monkey on his shoulders." "In the midst of this adoption of French manners, habits, and language, there is something stupidly puerile in declamation against Bonaparte and the French, when the Russians cannot dine without a French cook to make ready their repast; when they cannot bring up their children without the help of adventurers come from Paris, under the names of tutors and governors; in a word, when all their notions of fashion, luxury, and elegance are borrowed from France. What arrant folly!"

Such was Russian society after Tilsit. From these evil dispositions towards France, the indignation raised by the abominable attempt of England against Denmark, and the bombardment of Copenhagen in a time of peace (September 1807), only made a diversion of short duration. At one moment we might almost believe that the Peace of Tilsit had only three partisans in Russia—the Emperor, the Chancellor Roumantsof, and Speranski. Yet Alexander began to learn the worth of more than one illusion: all the acts of his ally wounded his convictions. After the exile of the kings of Sardinia and of Naples, he had to see the expulsion of the house of Braganza, the dethronement of the Bourbons of Spain, the forced flight of the Pope of Rome; the Confederation of the Rhine, increased beyond all measure, now extended to the other side of the Elbe, and had set foot on the Baltic by way of Lübeck and Mecklenburg; on the Vistula, the Grand Duchy of Warsaw received a formidable organization. Tolstoï, who certainly had done nothing to make himself liked at Paris, who quarrelled with Ney, and entered into relations with the Faubourg St. Germain, was not able in any way to soften the lot of Frederic William III., or to obtain the promised evacuation of the Prussian States. Scanty was the compensation for all these sacrifices. The first campaign against Sweden had been far from brilliant. The naval war with England had ruined Russian commerce. At Constantinople, Guilleminot, Napoleon's ambassador, had managed to conclude an armistice between Turkey and Russia, in virtue of which the latter had to evacuate the Danubian principalities. There was no longer any question of the partition of the Ottoman empire, that brilliant prospect which had led astray the lively imagination of Alexander.

The famous Franco-Russian alliance was shaken. Napoleon, who had on his hands a terrible war in Spain, and who descried on the horizon another war with Austria, felt that he must give his ally some satisfaction. Then the interview at Erfürt took place. Alexander came accompanied by his brother Constantine, the ministers Tolstoï, Roumantsof, Speranski, and the French ambassador Caulaincourt; Napoleon brought with him Berthier, the diplomatists Talleyrand, Champagny, Maret, and the Russian ambassador Tolstoï. There was also another court, formed by his German vassal; the Prince-Primate of the *Rheinbund;* the Kings of Saxony, Bavaria, Wurtemberg, and Westphalia; the Grand Dukes of Baden, Darmstadt, Oldenburg, and Mecklenburg; and the sovereigns of Thuringia. Prussia was represented by Prince William, who came to plead for the interests of his brother; Austria by Baron Vincent, charged to salute the two emperors in the name of his master. The irritable self-respect of the Russians did not fail to take notice of the superior influence of the French. " I seem to see my country degraded in the person of her sovereign," says Nicholas Tourguénief with passionate exaggeration. "There was no need to know what was passing in European cabinets; you could tell at a glance which of the two emperors was master at Erfürt and in Europe." It is true that Napoleon wished to receive the Tzar in a town that was his own property, at Erfürt; it is true that it was around him that this assemblage of sovereigns specially pressed, but these appearances really answered to a superiority of power. Napoleon neglected nothing to make the young Emperor forget all that was unequal in their respective situations, but he could not undo the fact that Alexander had not been the victor at Friedland.

In turn with fêtes, banquets, balls, theatrical representations, and hunting parties, serious interests were discussed between the two sovereigns and their ministers. On the 12th of October, 1808, Champagny and Roumantsof signed the following convention, which was to remain secret:—1. The Emperors of France and Russia renewed their alliance with all solemnity, and engaged to make peace or war in common. 2. They were to communicate to each other all proposals that might be made to them. 3. They were to propose an immediate peace to England, in a manner as public and as conspicuous as possible, so as to render refusal on the part of the British Cabinet more difficult (this proposition took the form of a letter addressed to the British Government, and signed by the two emperors). 4. They were to negotiate on the base of *uti possidetis*: France was only to consent to a peace which secured Finland, Wallachia, and Moldavia to Russia; Russia to a peace which confirmed France in all her actual possessions, and to Joseph Bonaparte the crown of Spain and the Indies. 5. Russia might act immediately to obtain the Danubian provinces from Turkey, whether by peace or war; but the French and Russian plenipotentiaries had come to an agreement about the language to be held, "so as not to compromise the existing friendship between France and the Porte." 6. If Russia, by the acquisition of the Danubian provinces, or France about its Italian or Spanish affairs, found themselves exposed to a rupture with Austria, the two allies were to make war in common. Talleyrand touched on the question of a Russian marriage for Napoleon. The recall of Tolstoï was demanded, and he was replaced by Prince Kourakine. Prussia obtained a remission of twenty millions of her war indemnity, and the evacuation of her territory, on condition that she should reduce her army to 42,000 men. To recapitulate: Alexander guaranteed to Napoleon the tranquillity of the Continent during his operations in Spain, while Napoleon ratified the seizure of Finland and the Danubian provinces. Napoleon accompanied his guest some way on the road from Erfürt to Weimer; they then embraced and separated. This was the last time they saw each other (September–October 1808).

The alliance concluded at Tilsit and confirmed at Erfürt was to involve Russia in three new wars—against England, against Sweden, against Austria. Besides these, the wars still continued which had begun with Turkey in 1806, and against Persia and the populations of the Caucasus, since Alexander's accession.

The war with England only presents one fact worth recording. The Russian fleet of the Archipelago, commanded by Admiral Seniavine, was forced, when it regained the ocean, to seek refuge in the Tagus, where, according to the Convention of Cintra, signed by Junot, it was obliged to surrender to Admiral Cotton. It was convoyed to England; the officers and crews were treated there with diplomatic courtesy, and instantly sent back to Russia at England's expense. Five years later Russia recovered her ships. The embargo over English ships was kept up, and Russia in a certain measure took part in the system of continental blockade.

The King of Sweden, Gustavus IV., was not quite in his right mind; his fury against Napoleon equalled his powerlessness to harm him; a great reader of the Bible, he saw in the

Emperor of the French the beast of the Apocalypse. He caused a contemptible pamphlet called the ' Nights of St. Cloud ' to be translated into Swedish. After having concluded an armistice with Mortier in 1806, he had broken it at the moment of the negotiation of Tilsit, so that his last Pomeranian fortresses were taken from him. He neither knew how to live in peace with England, whom he defied, nor with Prussia, whose misfortunes he insulted, nor with his brother-in-law Alexander. He alone of the European sovereigns applauded the bombardment of Copenhagen, and he regaled Admirals Gambier and Jackson at Helsingfors. When Alexander had to make him the first overtures, relative to the peace with France and the adoption of the continental system, Gustavus IV. impertinently returned the ribbon of St. Vladimir. On the 18th of February, 1808, he signed a treaty with England. Then 60,000 Russians, under Buxhœwden, crossed the Kitmen, which had been, since the time of Elizabeth, the boundary between the two States. A proclamation was addressed to the Finns, advising them not to resist " their friends, their protectors," and to appoint deputies for the diet which Alexander intended to assemble. The Swedish troops were dispersed, and retreated to the north ; Finland was almost conquered in March 1808 : Helsingfors, the impregnable Svéaborg, Abo, and the Isles of Aland fell into the hands of the Russians. Fortune seemed for one moment to hesitate when Klingspor gained two important successes over the Russians, but he was immediately after obliged to retire into the deserts of Bothnia. Another proclamation was issued to the Finnish soldiers serving in the Swedish army, inviting them to desert with arms and baggage, promising them two roubles for every gun, one rouble for a sabre, and six for a horse. During the winter the Russians fortified themselves in the Isles of Aland ; and three corps, commanded by Kulner, Bagration, and Barclay de Tolly, crossed the Gulf of Bothnia on the ice, and carried the war into the Swedish country. A military revolution broke out in Stockholm (13th of March, 1809). No blood was shed, but Gustavus IV. was arrested, and confined at Drottingholm with his family. Later he was set at liberty, and travelled in Europe under the name of Colonel Gustaffson. His uncle, the Duke of Sudermania, assumed the crown under the title of Charles XIII. He signed the peace of Fredericksham, which ceded Finland as far as the Tornea. In 1810, when Christian Augustus of Holstein-Augustenburg, the prince royal elected by the States, died, Bernadotte, marshal of France, was chosen to fill his place. Napoleon had little sympathy with this proceeding ; he would have preferred a Danish prince, whose accession would have brought about a Scandinavian union. The success of the Swedish war caused scant enthusiasm in St. Petersburgh. "Poor Sweden! poor Swedes!" said the people. Finland, coveted for so long, had lost its value in the eyes of the Russians; it seemed too much a gift of Napoleon. According to his promise, Alexander had convoked the Diet of Finland, and guaranteed to the "grand duchy" its privileges, its university, and its constitution.

In April, 1809, began Napoleon's war with Austria (fifth coalition). Alexander, whom the Treaty of Erfürt obliged to furnish a contingent, had done all he could to prevent this war. He had warned the Cabinet of Vienna that he had made an alliance with Napoleon, and offered, on the part of himself and his ally, to guarantee the integrity of the Austrian possessions. Forced to put a contingent under arms, he gave the command of 30,000 men to Prince Sergius Galitsyne, to act in concert with Poniatovski and Dombrovski, generals of the Grand Duchy of Warsaw, against the Archduke Ferdinand. This war of the Russians against the Austrians was a comedy; they detested their Polish allies, and feared their success in Gallicia above everything. In the whole campaign there were only two encounters between the Russians and Austrians: at the battle of Oulanovka there was only one killed and two wounded, and the Austrian major sent excuses to Galitsyne, saying he thought he was attacking the Poles; at the battle of Podgourjé, under Cracow, there were two killed and two wounded.

The conflicts between the Russians and Poles were much more frequent. Galitsyne allowed Sandomir to be taken by the Austrians under his very eyes, and Poniatovski in vain denounced to Alexander this "traitorous conduct." On the other hand, the Russians entered Lemberg when the Poles had already taken it, and attempted to prevent the people swearing allegiance to Napoleon. At Cracow, the Russian and Polish armies actually came to blows. The Poles were uneasy at seeing the Muscovites in Gallicia, and the Russians attributed all kinds of dangerous projects to the Poles. "Our allies disturb me more than the Austrians," writes Galitsyne to his master. He complains that Poniatovski, after having taken the title of commandant of the "Warsaw troops," or of "the ninth corps of the Grand Army," appropriated that of "commandant of the Polish army." "There is no Polish army," he said; "there is only an army of Warsaw." "The Emperor of the French is at liberty to give what names he chooses to the corps which are under his orders," replied Poniatovski.

Galitsyne announced that Poniatovski had reinforced his

army with Polish soldiers, deserters from Austrian regiments, and Lithuanian nobles, subjects of Russia. In the theatres of the Gallician towns, the King of Poland was represented leaving his tomb, the Dwina and the Dnieper forming the frontiers of new Poland. Galitsyne counselled Alexander to take from the French this weapon of Polish propaganda, by proclaiming himself restorer of Poland. The Tzar refused, alleging the inconstancy of the Poles, and the necessity of preserving the Lithuanian provinces from all contagion.

At the Congress of Schönbrunn, which preceded the Treaty of Vienna, the Emperor of Russia declined to have himself represented. He did not intend to sanction the results, but by so doing he left Austria unsupported. She was obliged to cede her Illyrian provinces and all Gallicia. Western Gallicia (1,500,000 souls) Napoleon added to the Grand Duchy of Warsaw, while he gave Eastern Gallicia and a population of 400,000 to Russia (October 14, 1809). This gift was not, however, sufficient to compensate Alexander for the danger of an aggrandized Poland.

The war with Turkey had already gone on for many years. In 1804 Russia had proposed to the Divan an alliance against France, but she demanded at the same time that the subjects of the Sultan professing the orthodox religion should be placed under the immediate protection of her diplomatic agents. Selim III. repelled a proposal that threatened the very integrity of his empire. He tried to make advances to France, applauded the victories of Napoleon, and after Austerlitz acknowledged his imperial title and sent an envoy to Paris with presents, in spite of the efforts of the Russian ambassador Italinski. After Jena an Ottoman ambassador left for Berlin, to strengthen the alliance with the *padishah* of the French. Ypsilanti and Morousi, hospodars of Wallachia and Moldavia, who were devoted to Russia, were stripped of their dominions. This was an infraction of the Peace of Iassy with Catherine II.

About this time began the troubles of Servia. The Janissaries of this country formed a turbulent militia, like that of Egypt and Algiers, oppressed the Christian populations, entered into a contest with the Pasha of Belgrade, the *spahis*, or noble cavalry, and other Mussulmans, and even trod under foot the authority of the Sultan. They would only obey their chiefs, four in number, who were called *dakhié* or *deys*. Against these insubordinate subjects Selim III. authorized the resistance of the rayahs.

Many of the Christians had learned to bear arms in the last war of Catherine II. and Joseph II. against the Turks, and many had served with the Russian or Austrian troops. Pushed to extremity by the murder or torture of a certain number of their *knezes*, they rose against the Janissaries and the deys; put Tchernyi George, or George the Black, a rich pork merchant, at their head; and expelled the Mussulmans from Belgrade and the rest of the fortresses, affecting all the time to be only executing the orders of the Sultan. When Selim wished to recall them to obedience and demanded the restitution of the strong places, they broke with the Sultan himself, and declared themselves independent. They would have been crushed by the superior forces of the neighboring pachas, if the Russians had not taken up arms in 1806, which freed the frontiers. Alexander sent them an auxiliary corps under Colonel Bala.

The Russian ambassador had protested against the deposition of Ypsilanti and Morousi, and against the violation of the Treaty of Iassy. The English ambassador had almost induced the Divan to yield on October 17, 1806, when without a declaration of war the Russian general Michelsen crossed the frontier, invaded Moldavia with 35,000 men, took Khotin and Bender, entered Bucharest, and advanced towards the Danube. The British ambassador wished to interpose his good offices, but he was not listened to, and left Constantinople with *éclat*. It was then that the English fleet under Admiral Duckworth passed the Dardanelles, burnt the Turkish vessels in the Sea of Marmora, and appeared at the entrance of the Bosphorus. The demonstration failed before the firmness of the Sultan Selim and the military preparations of the French ambassador Sebastiani. Engineer and artillery officers hastened from the French army of Dalmatia. The English vessels retraced their path, and the Turkish fleet, crossing the Dardanelles in its turn, gave battle to the Russian Admiral Seniaviné, in the waters of Tenedos. It was beaten. A short time after Selim III. was deposed in consequence of a revolt of the Janissaries, and Napoleon used his fall as a pretext for sacrificing Turkey at Tilsit.

Guilleminot, Sebastiani's successor, had received an order to aid the Russians " in everything, not officially, but effectively." In spite of the armistice concluded by his exertions, the Russian troops continued to occupy the principalities, whose administration was confined to a divan composed of Russians and Roumanian boyards. After Erfürt, the Sultan having refused to subscribe to the dismemberment of his empire, the war recommenced. The campaign of 1809 was partially successful; the Russians conquered nearly all the fortresses of the Danube, but were defeated in Bulgaria by the Grand Vizier. In 1810 Field-marshal Kamenski reconquered Bulgaria as far as the Balkans, and gained a brilliant victory at Batynia, near Kouch-

ASTRAKHAN IN RUSSIA

Russia, vol. two.

tchouk. In 1811 his successor, Koutouzof, managed to draw the Grand Vizier to the left bank of the Danube, and crushed him at Slobodzei. The imminence of a rupture with France forced the Tzar to withdraw five divisions of the army of the Danube. A congress assembled at Bucharest in 1812: Russia renounced Moldavia and Wallachia, but kept Bessarabia, a Roumanian district, with the fortresses of Khotin and Bender; the Pruth and the Lower Danube, where Russia acquired Ismaïl and Kilia, formed the limit of the two empires. The hospodars of Wallachia and Moldavia were to be restored, and all the ancient privileges of those countries confirmed. The eighth article stipulated for an amnesty in favor of the Servians, who were to remain subjects of the Sultan, but to be governed by George the Black, assisted by the *skoupchtchina* or national assembly. Turkey took no part in the wars of 1812 and 1813; she profited by them to violate the eighth article, to crush the Servian army, and to re-establish the ancient order of things. George the Black, and the greater part of the Servian voïevodes, fled to Austrian soil; others were put to death; one alone remained in the country, and managed to gain the respect and even confidence of the Turks. This was Miloch Obrénovitch. When the oppression became too intolerable, he gave the signal for a new insurrection (1815), reconquered the independence of his country, and made the Porte accept a treaty in 1817 which recognized the autonomy of Servia under the sceptre of the Sultan, with a national government composed of Miloch, the hereditary prince, and a *skoupchtchina*, but with the occupation of the principal fortresses by Ottoman garrisons. This system lasted till 1817.

At the same time as the Turkish war, hostilities began in 1806 against Persia, which wished to regain its authority over Georgia, and against the tribes of the Caucasus. Prince Titsianof, Count Goudovitch, Tormassof, and Kotliarevski all distinguished themselves in this campaign. In 1803 Titsianof had caused Maria, the Tzarina-mother of Georgia, to be transported to St. Petersburg, as she refused to recognize the legitimacy of the cession made by her eldest son to Paul I. He subdued the Chirvan, but was treacherously assassinated by the khan Hussein-Kouli, under the walls of Bakou. Glasénop punished Ali-Khan, an accomplice in the crime, by depriving him of Derbend. Persia attempted to come to the aid of the Caucasian tribes; Prince Abbas-Mirza passed the Araxes with 20.000 men, but was defeated. This laborious war prolonged itself till 1813. A more serious struggle already absorbed all the attention and forces of Russia.

GRAND DUCHY OF WARSAW: CAUSES OF THE SECOND WAR WITH NAPOLEON.

The misunderstanding between Alexander and Napoleon became more bitter day by day. The most important of the causes leading to it were the following :—1. The growth of the Grand Duchy of Warsaw ; 2. The discontent of Napoleon at the conduct of the Russians in the campaign of 1809 ; 3. The abandonment of the project of a Russian marriage, and the substitution of an Austrian marriage ; 4. The increasing rivalry of the two States at Constantinople and on the Danube ; 5. The Napoleonic encroachments of 1810 in northern Germany ; 6. Irritation produced by the continental blockade ; 7. Mistrust occasioned by the respective armaments.

At the Treaty of Tilsit, Napoleon had formed the Grand Duchy of Warsaw out of the Prussian provinces (Warsaw, Posen, and Bromberg), with a population of 2,500,000. At the Treaty of Vienna he had increased it by Western Gallicia (Cracow, Radom, Lublin, and Sandomir), inhabited by 1,500,000 people. He had reserved to himself all the means for reconstituting Poland; he had given Dantzig to no one, and had declared it a free city; the Illyrian provinces of Austria might in his hands soon be exchanged for the rest of Gallicia ; the treaty of 1812 with the Emperor Francis was to realize this calculation. There was no need even to take away the acquisitions of the third partitioner, Russia, for at that time Russia only possessed Lithuania and White Russia. Now we know that these provinces are not Polish. It sufficed to take back what he had himself ceded to Alexander out of the spoils of Prussia and Austria— Belostok and Western Gallicia, the latter being still in great part Little Russia. The name of Poland was not pronounced officially, but in fact she already existed. No doubt she had a stranger, the King of Saxony, for the sovereign, but the ancestors of Frederic Augustus had reigned over Poland, and it was to the house of Saxony that the patriots of the 3rd of May, 1791, had wished to secure the succession after Stanislas Poniatovski.

The Constitution of 1807, compiled by a Polish commission and approved by Napoleon, was almost that of the 3rd of May 1791. Napoleon had advised the King of Saxony to dismiss the Prussian officials, and to govern Poland with the Poles. The executive power belonged to the king, who was assisted by a council of responsible ministers with a president at their head. **The** legislative power was divided between the king, the senate, and the legislative body. The senate was composed of six bishops, six palatines, and six castellans; the legislative body, of sixty deputies elected in the district, from the nobility, and forty deputies from the towns; their chief work lay in the imposition of taxes and the compilation of the laws. After the annexation of Western Gallicia, the number of members of parliament was increased. Napoleon could boast of having "raised a tribune in the midst of the silent atmosphere of the neighboring governments" (Bignon). The *Zamok*, the old royal castle in which the Parliament sat, was the centre of the Polands still disunited. Napoleon had given the Grand Duchy his Civil Code, which did not express the actual social state of the country, but on which the social state was to model itself. He had proclaimed the freedom of the serfs, while preserving to their former masters the right of property over the lands. With regard to this, the present Russian government has proceeded in a more radical fashion. Napoleon created parliamentary Poland,—a Poland whose liberty was more based on equality than in former times.

The army of the Grand Duchy was raised to 30,000 men after 1807, to 50,000 after 1809; at its head was Joseph Poniatovski, nephew of the last king, the man who was vanquished at Ziélencé, the hero of many a Napoleonic battle. Under him served Dombrovski, a soldier of the campaign of 1799; Zaïontchek, who had fought with the French in Egypt; and Chlopiçki, the intrepid leader of the Polish legions in Spain. The sentiments which animated the army are still reflected in the recently published 'Memoirs of a Polish Officer' (which are those of General Brandt).

In a country where every peasant is born a horseman, the cavalry was always admirable; the infantry had lately been improved; the artillery had been organized by the Frenchman Bontemps and Pelletier; the fortresses of Ploçk, Modlin, Thorn, and Zamosc restored by Haxo and Alix. The army, where the former serf elbowed the gentleman, was a school of equality. The famous legions of the Vistula, made use of by Napoleon for his own private ends, acquired an imperishable glory in the wars of Prussia, Austria, and Russia.

The ministers of the Grand Duchy—Stanislas Potoçki (president of the council), Joseph Poniatovski (war), Lubienski (justice), Matuszevicz (finance), Sobolevski (police), &c.—were upright and intelligent men. Bignon, Napoleon's representative, was full of devotion to Poland. Unfortunately he was replaced, on the eve of a supreme crisis, by the Archbishop of Malines, **Abbé** of Pradt, a noisy and vain character, complicated by literary vanity. No doubt Warsaw had its parties. The Czartoryskis had with reason made up their minds, in case of need, to have recourse to Alexander's generosity; but in 1811, when the guns of Warsaw announced the birth of the King of Rome, all thought themselves in safety under the protectorate of France. Never had the lively and witty Polish society been so brilliant. The growth of the Warsaw army, which was in reality the vanguard of the Grand Army of the Vistula, was always an object of disquietude for Alexander and anger for the Russians. The " mixed subjects "—that is, the nobles who held lands in the Grand Duchy and in Lithuania, and who passed from one service to the other—were the pretext for perpetual diplomatic intrigues. Alexander remarked bitterly that they worked " the spectre of Poland " on the uncertain frontier of Lithuania.

Napoleon had not hesitated to complain to Kourakine of the way in which the Gallician campaign had been conducted. "You were lukewarm," he said; "you never drew the sword once."

The projected marriage with Anna Pavlovna, Alexander's sister, had met with difficulties in more than one direction. The Empress-mother, Mary of Wurtemberg, had been invested by the will of Paul, which was kept at the Assumption in the Kremlin, with absolute power to dispose of the hands of her daughters. Now, she alleged that the laws of the orthodox church did not allow marriage with a divorced man. Anna was already betrothed to the Prince of Saxe-Coburg, as her sister Catherine, perhaps with a view to a request of this nature, had been married to the Grand Duke of Oldenburg. The first marriage of Napoleon had been barren, and he might a second time repudiate his wife. The difference of religion was another barrier. Anna could not embrace Catholicism, and the idea of seeing a Russian priest and chapel at the Tuileries was repugnant to Napoleon. Alexander took little pains to press the negotiation; he complicated it by another negotiation for a formal promise that Poland should never be re-established. Napoleon lost all patience, and, as the house of Hapsburg seemed to be ready to meet his wishes, the Austrian marriage was concluded.

Alexander felt both anger and regret. A closer alliance between France and Austria was prejudicial to the essential interests of Russia in the East and on the Danube. In 1809 Talleyrand had submitted to Napoleon a project which consisted in indemnifying Austria by putting her in possession of the Roumanian principalities and of the Slav provinces of Turkey, which would have created a permanent conflict of interests between Russia and Austria. The former, repulsed from the Danube, would have been forced to turn towards Central Asia, towards Hindostan. In this emergency she would in her turn have found herself at perpetual war with England, and all germs of coalition against the French empire would by this means have been extinguished. In the same year Duroc laid before Napoleon another memorial, in which he showed—1, that the Russian alliance was contrary to French traditional policy; 2, that the French possessions in Italy and Dalmatia were threatened by the action of Russia in Servia and Greece; 3, that Russia only defended Prussia, because she reckoned on the use of her army if needed; 4, that she favored the Spanish enterprise, in the hope of seeing 200,000 Frenchmen perish in the Peninsula; 5, that the interest of the Napoleonic dynasty demanded that Russia should be pushed as far as possible to the East; 6, that the dismemberment of Poland had been the shame of the old dynasty, and that her re-establishment was necessary to the greatness of France and the security of Europe. Prince Kourakine managed to procure a copy of this memorial, and sent it to the Emperor Alexander (March 1809), pointing out "how dangerous it was for Russia to permit the ruin of Austria." Alexander remembered this in the campaign of 1809.

In 1810 the Senatus Consultum of July pronounced the union of the whole of Holland to the French empire; that of December, the future union of three Hanseatic towns, of Oldenburg, and other German territories. It was not a simple occupation to secure the execution of the continental blockade; it was an annexation. In the *jus gentium* as understood by Napoleon, these decisions of the Senate were to replace treaties. Where were these encroachments to stop? Hamburg, Bremen, and Lübeck—free towns, whose existence was an object of interest to the commerce of the whole world, and especially to Russia—had become French. By means of Lübeck, the French empire would strengthen her hold on the Baltic, on that "Varangian Sea" where the Russians, since Peter I., disputed the preponderance of the Scandinavians. Another of these annexations, that of Oldenburg, wounded Alexander yet more deeply. He saw his sister Catherine and her husband, robbed of their crowns, fly to St. Petersburg. The wrong to his interests and his affections was yet further increased by the want of respect towards him. He had neither been consulted nor informed of the step. Like the rest of the world, Alexander heard of this conquest, in the height of peace, through the *Moniteur*. It is true that since that time many other German allies of the imperial house have been deprived of their crowns or their essential prerogatives, without any remonstrance from Russia.

Kourakine was charged to communicate with Champagny, who talked of necessity, and assured him that the Grand Duke should receive an indemnity. The Russian court sent a note to all the other cabinets, in which, while affirming the maintenance of her alliance with Napoleon, she protested against the annexation of Oldenburg. The conqueror was deeply irritated at the publicity of this note, as well as at the remarks accompanying the protest.

As to the continental blockade, although it was observed by Russia less strictly than by France, she still suffered cruelly from it. The commerce with England was stopped. In 1801 the Russian aristocracy had made a plot to re-open the sea to her hemp, her grains, and other natural productions of the country. The rouble which was worth 67 kopecks in 1807, was not worth more than 25 in 1810. In December of this same year, Alexander promulgated an edict which, with the apparent design of preventing specie from leaving the country, proscribed the importation of objects of luxury from whatever country they came, particularly of silks, ribbons, embroideries, bronzes, and porcelains: wine was heavily taxed. This chiefly struck at French commerce. The forbidden goods were ordered to be burnt. Napoleon was exasperated, and said, "I would rather have received a blow on the cheek."

During some time Kourakine, the Russian envoy at Paris, while recognizing the fact that Russia could not cope with Napoleon, advised a policy of intimidation by collecting great armaments. Accordingly five divisions of the army of the Danube were recalled; a levy of four men in every five hundred was to be raised, and the fortresses of the Dwina and the Dnieper were to be repaired. These preparations provoked those of Napoleon. Such an emulation in threatening measures naturally led to a rupture. Soon the "army of Warsaw" was put on a warlike footing, the army of occupation in Northern Germany was reinforced; Napoleon summoned some regiments from Spain, and notably the Polish legions; the army of Naples advanced towards Upper Italy, the army of Italy towards Bavaria; in the vast military establishment known as the Grand Army, and which covered the entire Continent, from Madrid to Dantzig, a movement from the West to the East was felt. The grievances of the two emperors against each other were brought forward in some lively interviews of Napoleon, first with the ambassador Kourakine, and then with the aide-de-camp Tchernichef, Alexander's envoy extraordinary. Napoleon received Tchernichef courteously, and even pinched his ear, but passionately discussed all the questions relative to Poland, to the Danubian principalities, to Oldenburg, to the continental blockade, to the oukaze of December, to the menacing preparations of Alexander. He at once rejected the idea of giving Dantzig as an indemnity for Oldenburg. The mission of Tchernichef was unsuccessful ; he even compromised himself seriously : an *employé* of the War Minister was shot for allowing himself to be bribed, and for having delivered to him the estimates of the Grand Army. It was about this period that Napoleon ordered the publication in the newspapers of a series of articles wherein he proved " that Europe found herself in train to become the prey of Russia," and spoke of " the invasion that must be checked, of the universal domination that must be extinguished." It was then that Lesur published the famous book entitled 'Of the Progress of the Russian Power,' in which we meet for the first time with the apocryphal document called the ' Will of Peter the Great.'

Napoleon recalled Caulaincourt, whom he thought too Russian, and who, being conciliatory, was much embarrassed with the part he had to play. He replaced him by Lauriston, who could not reckon on the confidence of Alexander. Everything proved that war was inevitable. Alexander, like Napoleon, only negotiated in order to gain time and finish his preparations. The rupture of the alliance was patent to all. At the court of Murat the French envoy, Durand, fought a duel with the Russian envoy Dolgorouki. Alexander suddenly disgraced Speranski, the friend of France ; he sent for Stein, the great German patriot, Napoleon's mortal foe, placed by him under the ban of the Confederation. Russia hastened to conclude peace with Turkey ; she negotiated with Sweden for an alliance, with England for a treaty of subsidies. Napoleon, on his side, signed two conventions with Prussia and Austria, which assured him the help of 20,000 Prussians and 30,000 Austrians in the projected expeditions. Sweden and Turkey would have been more certain allies, but the treaties of Tilsit and Erfürt had alienated them from the French ; Sweden had suffered, like Russia, from the continental blockade, and the Prince Royal Bernadotte had not pardoned Napoleon for his refusal to give him Norway, and for having occupied Swedish Pomerania. On the 9th of May, 1812, Napoleon left Paris for Dresden, for the centre of his army. The ambassadors, Kourakine and Lauriston, demanded their passports.

THE "PATRIOTIC WAR:" BATTLE OF BORODINO; BURNING OF MOSCOW: DESTRUCTION OF THE GRAND ARMY.

With the military resources of France, which then counted 130 departments, with the contingents of her Italian kingdoms, of the Confederation of the Rhine, of the Grand Duchy of Warsaw, and with the auxiliary forces of Prussia and Austria, Napoleon could bring a formidable army into the field. On the 1st of June the Grand Army amounted to 678,000 men, 356,000 of whom were French, and 322,000 foreigners. It included not only Belgians, Dutchmen, Hanoverians, Hanseats, Piedmontese, and Romans, then confounded under the name of Frenchmen, but also the Italian army, the Neapolitan army, the Spanish regiments, natives of Germany, Badois, Wurtemburgers, Bavarians, Darmstadt Hessians, Jerome's Westphalians, soldiers of the half-French grand duchies of Berg and Frankfort, Saxons, Thuringians, and Mecklenburgers. Besides Napoleon's marshals, it had at its head Eugène, Viceroy of Italy; Murat, King of Naples; Jerome, King of Westphalia; the princes royal and heirs of nearly all the houses in Europe. The Poles alone in this war, which recalled to them that of 1612, mustered 60,000 men under their standards. Other Slavs from the Illyrian provinces, Carinthians, Dalmatians, and Croats, were led to assault the great Slav empire. It was indeed the "army of twenty nations," as it is still called by the Russian people.

Napoleon transported all these races from the West to the East by a movement similar to that of the great invasions, and swept them like a human avalanche against Russia.

When the Grand Army prepared to cross the Niemen, it was arranged thus:—To the left, before Tilsit, Macdonald with 10,000 French, and 20,000 Prussians under General York of Wartenburg; before Kovno, Napoleon with the corps of Davoust, Oudinot, Ney, the Guard commanded by Bessières, the immense reserve cavalry under Murat—in all a total of 180,000 men; before Pilony, Eugene with 50,000 Italians and Bavarians; before Grodno, Jerome Bonaparte, with 60,000 Poles, Westphalians, Saxons, &c. We must add to these the 30,000 Austrians of Schwartzenberg, who were to fight in Gallicia as mildly against the Russians as the Russians had against the Austrians in 1809. Victor guarded the Vistula and the Oder with 30,000 men, Augereau the Elbe with 50,000. Without reckoning the divisions of Macdonald, Schwartzenberg, Victor, and Augereau, it was with about 290,000 men, half of whom were French, that Napoleon marched to cross the **Niemen and threaten the centre** of Russia.

Alexander had collected on the Niemen 90,000 men commanded by Bagration; on the Bug, tributary of the Vistula, 60,000 men, commanded by Barclay de Tolly; those were what were called the Northern army and the army of the South. On the extreme right, Wittgenstein with 30,000 men was to oppose Macdonald almost throughout the campaign; on the extreme left, to occupy the Austrian Schwartzenberg, as harmlessly as possible, Tormassof was placed with 40,000. Later this latter army, reinforced by 50,000 men from the Danube, became formidable, and was destined, under Admiral Tchitchagof, seriously to embarrass the retreat of the French. In the rear of all these forces was a reserve of 80,000 men—Cossacks and militia (*opoltchénié*). Only a few contingents of the *opoltchénie*, brave mougiks with long beards, were to figure in the campaign, but its imposing total of 612,000 men could hardly have existed except on paper. In reality, to the 290,000 men Napoleon had mustered under his hand, the Emperor of Russia could only oppose the 150,000 of Bagration and Barclay de Tolly. He counted on the devotion of the nation. "Oh that the enemy," says a proclamation of the Tzar, "may encounter in each noble a Pojarski, in each ecclesiastic a Palitsyne, in each citizen a Minine. Rise, all of you! With the cross in your hearts and arms in your hands, no human force can prevail against you."

At the opening of the campaign the head-quarters of Alexander were at Wilna. Besides his generals, he had there his brother Constantine, his ministers Araktchéef, Balachef, Kotchoubey, and Volkonski. There were also collected refugees of all nations—Stein from among the Germans, the generals Wolzogen and Pfuhl, the Piedmontese Michaux, the Swede Armfelt, and the Italian Paulucci. They deliberated and argued much. To attack Napoleon was to furnish him with the opportunity he wished; to retire into the interior, as Barclay had advised in 1807, seemed hard and humiliating. A middle course was sought by adopting the scheme of Pfuhl—to establish an intrenched camp at Drissa, on the Dwina, and to make it a Russian Torres Vedras. The events in the Peninsula filled all minds. Pfühl desired to act like Wellington at Torres Vedras. Others proposed a guerilla warfare like that of Spain. When they heard of the passage of the Niemen, Barclay had to fall back on the Dwina, and Bagration on the Dnieper.

Napoleon made his entry into Wilna, the ancient capital of the Lithuanian Gedimin. He had said in his second proclamation, "The second Polish war has begun!" The Diet of Warsaw had pronounced the re-establishment of the kingdom of Poland, and sent a deputation to Wilna to demand the adhesion of

Lithuania, and to obtain the protection of the Emperor. We can understand with what ardor the Lithuanian nobility crowded around Napoleon. The decision of the Polish diet was solemnly accepted by the Lithuanians. "This ceremony," relates Fezensac, "took place in the cathedral of Wilna, where all the nobility had assembled together. The men were dressed in the ancient Polish costume, the women adorned with red and violet ribbons, the national colors." As to the Poles, properly so called, although Napoleon, by dispersing the army of 60,000 men among the divisions, had rendered it invisible, nothing could equal their enthusiasm; boundless hope filled all hearts. The work begun at Tilsit at the expense of Prussia, continued at Vienna at the expense of Austria, was to be finished at the expense of Russia! At last they were to taste the revenge which France had prepared for eighteen years for the faithful legions of Dombrovski! This was the splendid gift with which the Emperor was going to reward the zeal of his grumblers of the Vistula! "The young officers had recovered their confidence in the star of Napoleon," relates Brandt. "Our elders might well laugh at our enthusiasm, and call us mad and possessed; we only dreamed of battles and victories; we feared only one thing, a too great anxiety for peace on the part of the Russians. . . . We had in our ranks numerous descendants of the Lithuanians who had fought a hundred years before, under the banners of Charles XII.—Radzivills, Sapiehas, Tysenhauses, and Chodskos." However, the enormous incapacity of Pradt at Warsaw, and the somewhat reserved answers of Napoleon at Wilna,* caused a little hesitation. In Lithuania the movement could not be truly national, since the people were not Poles. Napoleon, whether to please Austria, whether to preserve the possibility of peace with Russia, or whether he was afraid to make Poland too strong, only took half-measures. He gave Lithuania an administration distinct from that of Poland; assembled a commission, which voted the creation of a Lithuanian army, formed of four regiments of infantry and five of cavalry; and spent 400,000 francs in aid of their equipment. A national guard—of infantry in the towns, of horse in the country—was to watch over the security of the convoys, and to help the French

---

* "If I had reigned during the partitions of Poland," replied Napoleon to the deputation from Warsaw, "I should have armed all my subjects to support you. I applaud all that you have done; I authorize the efforts that you wish to make: all that depends on me to second your resolutions I will do. But I have guaranteed to the Emperor of Austria the integrity of his States. Let Lithuania, Samogitia, Volhynia, the Ukraine, and Podolia be animated by the same spirit that I have seen in Great Poland, and Providence will crown with success the sanctity of your cause."

gendarmerie to maintain discipline. A last attempt to negotiate a peace had failed. To gain time, Alexander had sent Balachef to Wilna. Napoleon had proposed two unacceptable conditions —the abandonment of Lithuania, and the declaration of war against Great Britain. If Napoleon, instead of plunging into Russia, had contented himself with organizing and defending the ancient principality of Lithuania, no power on earth could have prevented the re-establishnent of the Polish-Lithuanian State within its former limits. The destinies of France and Europe would have been changed.

The road which led to Wilna passed through a sort of natural pass, due to the configuration of the Dwina and the Dnieper, the one making an angle near Vitepsk, the other near Orcha, thereby ceasing to bar the way to the invader. There were still the raised works at Drissa on the Dwina, the Torres Vedras of the learned Pfühl; but the place of the camp was so badly chosen, with the river at the back, and only four bridges in case of retreat, and was so easily turned from Vitepsk, that it was resolved to abandon it. There existed in the army immense irritation against Pfühl, against the Germans, against the division of commands. The Tzar seemed out of place with the army; they remembered Austerlitz. The Russian nobles made up their minds to induce him to depart; Araktchéef himself, and Balachef, the Minister of Police, respectfully represented to him that his presence would be more useful at Smolensk, at Moscow, or at St. Petersburg, where he could convoke the orders of the State, demand sacrifices both in men and money, and keep up the patriotic enthusiasm. From that time Barclay and Bagration commanded their armies alone.

Napoleon feared to penetrate into the interior; he would have liked to gain some brilliant success not far from the Lithuanian frontier, and seize one of the two Russian armies. The vast spaces, the bad roads, the misunderstandings, the growing disorganization of the army, caused all his movements to fail. Barclay de Tolly, after having given battle at Ostrovno and Vitepsk, fell back on Smolensk; Bagration fought at Mohilef and Orcha, and in order to rejoin Barclay retreated to Smolensk. There the two Russian generals held council. Their troops were exasperated by this continual retreat, and Barclay, a good tactician, with a clear and methodical mind, did not agree with Bragration, impetuous, like a true pupil of Souvorof. The one held firmly for a retreat, in which the Russian army would become stronger and stronger, and the French army weaker and weaker, as they advanced into the interior; the other wished to act on the offensive, full of risk as it was. The army was on the side of Bagration, and Barclay, a German of the Baltic provinces, was suspected and all but insulted. He consented to take the initiative against Murat, who had arrived at Krasnoé, and a bloody battle was fought (August 14). On the 16th, 17th, and 18th of August another desperate fight took place at Smolensk, which was burnt, and 20,000 men perished. Barclay still retired, drawing with him Bagration. In his retreat Bagration fought Ney at Valoutina; it was a lesser Eylau: 15,000, men of both armies remained on the field of battle.

Napoleon felt that he was being enticed into the interior of Russia. The Russians still retreated, laying waste all behind them. " Tell us only when the moment is come, we will set fire to our *isbas*," they said. The French lost three days at Smolensk; but the Russians on their side were astonished that the ancient fortress, which had sustained so many lengthy sieges in the 16th and 17th centuries, had only resisted Napoleon that time. The Grand Army melted before their very eyes. From the Niemen to Wilna, without every having seen the enemy, it had lost 50,000 men from sickness, desertion, and marauding; from Wilna to Mohilef nearly 100,000. Ney was reduced from 36,000 men to 22,000; Oudinot from 38,000 to 23,000; Murat from 22, 000 to 14,000; the Bavarians, attacked by dysentery, from 27,000 to 13,000; the Italian division Pino from 11,000 to 5,000; the Italian Guard, the Westphalians, the Poles, the Saxons, and the Croats had not suffered less. The " ignoble and dangerous crowds of marauders " (Brandt) encumbered all the roads, pillaged the convoys and the magazines, plundered by actual force the villages and towns, not even respecting isolated officers. They had devoured Poland and Lithuania in their passage through them. At Minsk, whilst the *Te Deum* was being chanted for the deliverance of Lithuania, Cuirassiers had broken into the magazines. In this offensive march, the miseries of the retreat might be clearly foreseen. Napoleon did what he could to fill the voids which were already so sensible. He ordered Victor's army to advance into Lithuania, Augereau to pass the Elbe and the Oder, and the hundred cohorts of the national guards to make themselves ready to cross the Rhine. In the north Macdonald repulsed Wittgenstein, took Polotsk after a battle (18th of August), occupied Dünaburg, threatened to invest Riga, and disquieted St. Petersburg; and in the south Tormassof obtained some success over Reynier and Schwartzenberg.

In the Russian army, the discontent grew with the retreating movement; they always retired, now on Dorogobouge, now on Viasna: they began to murmur as much against Bagration as against Barclay. It was then that Alexander united the two armies under the supreme command of Koutouzof. Koutouzof had on his side the reminiscences of Amstetten, Krems, and Dirnstein; it was not to him that Austerlitz was imputed. He was a true Russian of the old school, indolent and sleepy in appearance, but very judicious and very patriotic. No one understood better than he did the Russian soldier and the national character. Men needed hope above all things. His appointment excited general enthusiasm: the rumor immediately spread in the army that "Koutouzof had come to beat the French." Happy sayings raised his popularity to the skies. Passing his regiments in review, "With such soldiers," he exclaimed, "who would think of beating a retreat?" He ordered, however, a retrograde movement; but "all felt that in retiring they were marching against the French." They "recoiled," but only to reinforce themselves, to await the troops Miloradovitch was to bring them, the Cossacks that Platof was to recruit on the Don, the bearded militia which rose at the voice of the Tzar, the famous *droujina* of Moscow, promised by the Governor Rostopchine.

Koutouzof halted at Borodino. He had then 72,000 infantry 18,000 regular cavalry, 7000 Cossacks, 10,000 *opoltchénié* or militiamen, and 640 guns served by 14,000 artillerymen or pioneers; in all 121,000 men. Napoleon had only been able to concentrate 86,000 infantry, 28,000 cavalry, and 587 guns, served by 16,000 pioneers or artillerymen. This was about equal to the effective force of the Russians, but his army, now tempered by the long march of 800 leagues, was still the most admirable of modern times. On the 5th of September the French took the redoubt of Chevaradino; the 7th was the day of the great battle: this was known as the battle of Borodino among the Russians, as that of the Moskowa in the bulletins of Napoleon, though the Moskowa flows at some distance from the field of carnage.

The front of the Russian army was bounded on the right by the village of Borodino on the Kolotcha; on the centre by the Red Mountain, where rose what the French called the Great Redoubt, and the Russians the Raïevski battery, on the spot where now stands the memorial column; and on the left by three little redoubts or outworks of Bagration's, on the site of the monastery since founded by Madame Toutchkof. Between the Red Mountain and Bagration's outworks ran the ravine of Semenevskoé, with the village of the same name. During the battle Napoleon remained near the redoubt of Chevardino; Koutouzof at the village of Gorki. Barclay de Tolly commanded on the right, and through Miloradovitch he occupied Borodino, and through Doktourof, Gorki. Bagration commanded the left, and by Raïevski he occupied the Red Mountain and Semenevskoé, by Borosdine the three redoubts. Napoleon had placed Eugène, with the army of Italy and the Bavarians, opposite the great redoubt; Ney, with Junot and the Wurtembergers, opposite the three small ones; Davoust with the Poles and Saxons, and Murat with his numerous cavalry, were to turn the Russians by their left. On the extreme right Poniatovski was to clear the woods of Oustitsa. In the rear, the division of Friant and the Guard formed an imposing reserve.

Profound silence reigned in the Russian camp on the eve of the battle; religious fervor and patriotic fury inflamed all hearts: they passed the night confessing and communicating; they put on white shirts as if for a wedding. In the morning 100,000 men were blessed on their knees, and sprinkled with holy water by their priests; the wonder-working Virgin of Vladimir was carried in procession round the front of the troops in the midst of sobs and enthusiasm; an eagle hovered over the head of Koutouzof, and a loud "hurrah" saluted this happy omen. The battle began by a frightful cannonade of 1200 guns, which was heard at 30 leagues round. Then the French, with an irresistible charge, took Borodino on one side, and the redoubts on the other; Ney and Murat crossed the ravine of Semenevskoé, and cut the Russian army nearly in two. At ten o'clock the battle seemed won, but Napoleon refused to carry out his first success by employing the reserve, and the Russian generals had time to bring up new troops in line. They recaptured the great redoubt, and Platof, the Cossack made an incursion on the rear of the Italian army; an obstinate fight took place at the outworks. At last Napoleon made his reserve troops advance; again Murat's cavalry swept the ravine; Caulaincourt's cuirassiers assaulted the great redoubt from behind, and flung themselves on it like a tempest, while Eugène of Italy scaled the ramparts. Again the Russians had lost their outworks. Then Koutouzof gave the signal to retreat, and collected his troops on Psarévo. Napoleon refused to hazard his last reserves against these desperate men, and to "have his Guard demolished." He contented himself with crushing them with artillery during the flight. The French had lost 30,000 men, the Russians 40,000; the former had 49 generals and 37 colonels killed and wounded, the Russians almost as many, and they numbered Bagration, Koutaïzof, and the two Toutchkofs among their dead. Napoleon still concentrated 100,000 men under his own eye, Koutouzof only 50,000; but Napoleon's losses were irreparable at this distance: the Grand Army was condemned to gain nothing by its victories. The novelist Tolstoï uses this expression, " The beast is wounded to death." " Napoleon," says Brandt, the Pole, " had succeeded, but at what a price ! The great redoubt and its surroundings offered a spectacle which surpassed the worst horrors that could be dreamed of. The ditches, the fosses, the very interior of the outwork had disappeared beneath an artificial hill of dead and dying, six or eight men deep, heaped one upon another."

Koutouzof retired in good order, announcing to Alexander that they had made a steady resistance, but were retreating to protect Moscow. He called a council of war at Fily, on one of the hills which overhangs Moscow ; and the sight of the great and holy city extended at their feet, condemned perhaps to perish, caused inexpressible emotion to the Russian generals. The only question was this, Was it necessary to sacrifice the last army of Russia in order to save Moscow ? Barclay declared that " when it became a matter of the salvation of Russia and of Europe, Moscow was only a city like any other." Others said, like the artillery officer Grabbe, " It would be glorious to die under Moscow, but it is not a question of glory." "But," said Prince Eugène of Wurtemberg, " many hold that honor forces them to put a stop to all retrograde movements : as the tomb is the end of all earthly journeys accomplished by man, Moscow ought to be the aim, the tomb of the Russian warrior ; beyond her another world already begins." Bennigsen, Ermolof, and Ostermann were in favor of a last battle. Koutouzof listened to all, and then said. " Here my head, be it good or bad, must decide for itself," and ordered a retreat through the town. Yet he felt that Moscow was not " only a city like any other." He would not enter it, and passed the faubourgs weeping. Even for the retreat there were two alternative paths. Barclay advised that of Vladimir, which allowed St. Petersburg to be covered. Koutouzof preferred that of Riazan, by which he could place himself on the right flank of Napoleon to draw up reinforcements from the south, and to bar the way to the most fertile provinces of the empire to the French. The event proved that he was right.

Alexander, however, had only raised the *opoltchénié* in sixteen governments: those of Moscow, Tver, Iaroslavl, Vladimir, Riazan, Toula, Kalouga, and Smolensk were to furnish 123,000 men; St. Petersburg and Novgorod 25,000. Alexander had said to Michaux. "We will make of Russia a new Spain." The Metropolitan of Moscow and all the priests called men to arms against the "impious Frenchman, the bold Goliath," who was to be thrown to the earth by the sling of a new David.

Alexander had appointed Count Rostopchine as Governor of Moscow. This French wit was well acquainted with the nobles and the people, affected the picturesque language of the peasants, and understood, as he says, "how to throw dust in their eyes." The patriot Glinka compared him to Napoleon. His correspondence with Semen Voronzof, his proclamation of 1812, his Memoirs written in 1823, his pamphlet of the same year entitled 'The Truth about the Burning of Moscow,' may be counted amongst the most curious sources of history. "I do *everything*," he writes to the Emperor, "to gain the goodwill of *every one*. My two visits to the Mother of God at Iberia, the free access of all towards myself, the verification of the weights and measures, fifty blows with a stick applied in my presence to a sub-officer who, charged with the sale of salt, had caused the mougiks to wait too long, have won me the confidence of your devoted and faithful subjects." "I have resolved," he says, "at every disagreeable piece of news to raise doubts as to its truth; by this means I shall weaken the first impression, and before there is time to verify it others will come which need to be examined." He organized a regular system of spies to watch over the propagators of false news, the Martinists, the Freemasons, and the Liberals. He was jealous of Glinka, who nevertheless admired him, and who in the *Russian Messenger* "unchained the furies of the patriotic war." When Alexander came to Moscow and convoked the three orders at the Kremlin, Rostopchine caused *kibitkas* to be prepared to carry into Siberia any who might ask the Emperor indiscreet questions. These precautions were useless. The nobles gave their peasants, the merchants their money; the reading of the imperial manifesto was received with enthusiasm. "At first," relates Rostopchine, "they listened with the greatest attention, then they gave some signs of anger and impatience; when they came to the phrase which declared that the enemy came with 'flattery on their lips and irons in their hands,' the general indignation burst forth. They beat their heads, they tore their hair, they bit their hands, and tears of rage fell down their faces, which recalled those of the ancients. I saw one man grind his teeth." At bottom, the Government mistrusted the people, who, being serfs, might allow themselves to be tempted by the proclamations of liberty put forth by the invader. It was for this reason that Rostopchine placed 300,000 roubles at the disposal of Glinka, the popular writer. There was no need of the money, and Glinka restored the 300,000 roubles. When Alexander left the city, he gave full powers to Rostopchine.

Rostopchine invented good news; one day he posted up

"Great Victory of Ostermann," another day "Great Victory of Wittgenstein." Sensible people ended by never believing him. His bulletins had always firm hold on the people. "Fear nothing," he said: "a storm has come; we will dissipate it; the gain will be ground, and become meal. Only beware of drunkards and fools; they have large ears, and whisper folly one to the other. Some believe that Napoleon comes for good, whilst he only thinks of flaying us. He makes the soldiers expect the field-marshal's staff, beggars mountains of gold, and while they are waiting he takes every one by the collar and sends him to his death. And for this reason I beg you, if any of our countrymen or foreigners begin to praise him and to promise this or that in his name, seize him, whoever he may be, and take him before the police. As to the culprit, I shall know how to make him hear reason, were he a giant." "I will answer with my head that the scoundrel does not enter Moscow. And see on what I base my prophecy. . . . If that is not enough, then I shall say, ' Forward, *droujina* of Moscow! let us march likewise. And we shall be 100,000 soldiers. Let us take with us the image of the Mother of God, 150 guns, and we shall finish the affair together.'" After Borodino he again puts forth this proclamation, " Brothers, we are numerous, and ready to sacrifice our lives for the salvation of the country and to prevent that wretch from entering Moscow; but you must help me. Moscow is our mother; she has suckled us, nourished us, enriched us. In the name of the Mother of God, I invite you to the defence of the temples of the Lord, of Moscow, of Russia! Arm yourselves in any way you can, on foot or on horseback: take only enough bread for three days, go with the cross, preceded by the banners that you will take from the churches, and assemble at once on the three mountains. I shall be with you, and together we will exterminate the invaders. Glory in heaven for those who go there! Eternal peace to those who die! Punishment in the last judgment to those who draw back!"

It was necessary, however, to carry to Kazan forty Frenchmen or foreigners settled at Moscow. Domergue, the director of the French theatre at Moscow, describes their sad journey. Rostopchine made a certain Leppich or Schmidt work mysteriously at a wonderful balloon, which would cover with fire the whole French army. He removed all the archives and the treasures of the churches and palaces to Vladimir. When the Russian army left Moscow, he also quitted it, after cruelly slaying Verechtchaghine, who was accused of having spread the proclamation of Napoleon. He caused the prisons to be opened; distributed among the people the muskets of the arsenal, took away the pumps, and ordered Voronenko to set on fire the stores of brandy, and the boats loaded with alcohol. The burning of Moscow no doubt arose from this. By his own confession it was "an event which he had prepared, but which he was far from executing." He contented himself with "inflaming the spirits of men." Already the barriers of the capital were crowded with vehicles of all sorts; every one emigrated who could leave the town.

The people who remained at Moscow steadily nursed their illusions. When the first soldiers of the Grand Army appeared they thought that it was the Swedes or English who had come to their help. The pillage of the deserted houses began, and the populace rivalled the zeal of the invaders. Napoleon arrived, and tried to quell the disorder; he appointed Mortier governor of the town. "Above all, no pillage!" he said; "you will answer for it with your head." The troops defiled through the streets of Biélyi-gorod and Kitaï-gorod, singing the *Marseillaise* (Sept. 14). Napoleon ascended the Red Staircase, and established himself in the ancient palace of the Tzars. Almost immediately the fires broke out in many places. The night of the 15th–16th September was especially terrible. The Kremlin itself, with the artillery wagons of the Guard, was in danger. Napoleon had to leave it, and force his way through the flames; he almost perished on the road, and finally reached the Petrovski park. The courts-martial condemned about four hundred incendiaries, real or suspected, to death. All was over with the French conquest; only a fifth of the houses and churches remained standing. From that time it was impossible to prevent the plunder of the cellars, and of the buildings which were intact. The German allies were, according to the Muscovites, incomparably more greedy than the true Frenchmen.* They deserved the name of "The merciless army" (*bezpardonnoe voïsko*).

During the thirty-five days that the troops remained at Moscow, their disorganization was brought to a climax, and probably 10,000 or 12,000 men perished from hunger. The troops began to eat the horses. Napoleon, however, got together a *troupe* of comedians in the house of Posniakof, held concerts in the Kremlin, and promulgated the decree of Moscow about the Théâtre Français of Paris; but in spite of all this he was a prey to disquietude. The plan of a march to St. Petersburg on the approach of winter was rejected as impracticable. His attempts to open negotiations with Alexander were unsuccessful. He thought of declaring himself King of Poland, of

* See the new accounts in M. Rambaud's book called ' Francais et Russes, Moscou et Sévastopol '

re-establishing the principality of Smolensk, and of dismembering Western Russia ; he studied papers relative to the attempt of 1730, to see if he could not seduce the nobles by the bait of a constitution, and dreamed of decreeing the liberty of the serfs and of raising the Tatars on the Volga. He was powerless ; without means of action ; without news ; almost blockaded in Moscow. To the south the way was barred by Koutouzof, who had reinforced himself in his camp of Taroutino ; by the battle of Vinkovo (October 18) against Murat, the road to Riazan was shut ; and by the battle of Malo-Iaroslavets (23rd–24th Oct.) that to Kalouga was to be blocked, only leaving free the road to Smolensk, which had been laid waste. Even this was no longer safe. The war of guerillas, the war of peasants, the Cossack war had begun. Gerasimus Kourine, a peasant of the village of Pavlovo, assembled 5800 men " to fight for the country and the holy temple of the Mother of God against an enemy who threatened to burn all the villages, and to take the skin off all the inhabitants."

The mougiks fell on foraging parties and marauders ; they killed them by blows with pitchforks ; they hung them. they drowned them. Wilson the Englishman relates that they buried men alive. In the single district of Borovsk, 3500 soldiers were killed or taken. The guerilla chiefs Figner, Sesslavine, Davydof, Benkendorff, and Prince Kourakine captured the convoys on the road to Smolensk. Dorokhof, with a band of 2500 men and a party of Cossacks, took Vereïa by assault. The peasant Vassilissa and Mademoiselle Nadéjda Dourova gave warlike examples to the Russian women. Cossacks already appeared disguised in Moscow.

On the 13th of October, in the first snow, Napoleon had made the ambulances and the first convoys leave Moscow. From the 18th to the 23rd, 90,000 combatants quitted Moscow. They took with them 600 guns, 2000 artillery wagons, and 50,000 non-combatants—invalids, workmen, women, and inhabitants of the towns who feared the first excesses of the Cossacks. Mortier left Moscow the last, having sprung mines under the Kremlin. The palace of Elizabeth was blown up ; the gate of the Saviour, that of the Trinity, and the tower of Ivan the Great were cracked by the explosions ; there were many gaps in the walls of the Kremlin. It was a cruel, useless revenge, which might call down horrible reprisals on the wounded who were left behind.

The only road to Smolensk was opened by the battle of Viasma (3rd November), where Ney and Eugène, cut off from Davoust by Miloradovitch, defeated 40,000 Russians. At Smolensk they found the magazines empty (November 12). It was there that hunger and 18 degrees of cold began to decimate the remains of the Grand Army. What it suffered is eloquently described in the memoirs and accounts of Ségur, Labaume, Brandt, Fezensac, Denniée, Chambray, Fain, René Bourgeois, Domergue, Madame Fusil (actress at the French theatre at Moscow), Madame de Choiseul-Gouffier, and Wilson. A repetition here would be superfluous.

At Krasnoé Napoleon was obliged to send the Guard to rescue Davoust; Ney, who commanded the rear-guard, was forced with a body of 6000 fighting men and 6000 stragglers to give battle to 60,000 Russians (19th November), but from Smolensk to Krasnoé 26,000 stragglers and wounded, 208 cannon, and 5000 carriages fell into the hands of Koutouzof.

The old general, who had collected all these trophies almost without a blow, triumphed in his success. They brought him a French flag, where amidst the names of immortal battles might be read that of Austerlitz. "What is that?" he asked "Austerlitz! It is true it was hot work at Austerlitz. But I wash my hands of it before the whole army. They are innocent of Austerlitz." This was at the camp of the Semenovski, and one of his officers exclaimed, "Hurrah for the Saviour of Russia!" "No," said Koutouzof; "listen, my friends! It is not to me that the honor belongs, but to the Russian soldier." And, throwing his cap into the air, he cried with all his strength, "Hurrah! hurrah for the brave Russian soldier!" Then, made communicative by the joy of success, he said to his officers, "Where does the son of a dog lie this night? I know already that he will not sleep quietly at Liady: Sesslavine has given me his word of honor. Listen, gentlemen, to a pretty fable that Krylof the good story-teller has sent me. A wolf entered into a kennel and tormented the dogs. As to his entrance, he had managed that very well; but it was quite another affair to get out! All the dogs were after him, and he was driven into a corner with his hairs standing on end, and saying, 'What is the matter, my friends? What is your grievance against me? I simply came to see what you were doing, and now I am going away.' The huntsman by this time had hastened to the spot, and replied, 'No, friend Wolf, you will not impose upon us! It is true you are an old rascal with gray hair, but I am also gray, and not more stupid than you.'" And, taking off his cap and showing his gray locks, Koutouzof continued, "You shall not go as you have come, for I have set my dogs on your traces" ('Memoirs of Jirkiévitch').

The situation of the French army was critical. In the north St. Cyr, after a bloody battle at Polotsk (19th October), had evacuated the line of the Dwina. Macdonald was therefore left without support, expecting the desertion of some of his Prussians. In the south, Schwartzenberg had retreated on Warsaw, more occupied with Poland than with the safety of Napoleon. Thus, Wittgenstein on the north, and Tchitchagof on the south, could hang on the flanks of the Grand Army; both hoped to come up with it at the passage of the Berezina, and to enclose it between themselves and Koutouzof. Koutouzof himself reckoned on this, and restrained the ardor of the most impatient of the Cossacks, and of Wilson the Englishman, who said, "What a shame to let all these ghosts roam from their graves!" They all believed that a breath would scatter what had been the Grand Army, but Koutouzof would not hazard what he had gained in a battle; he left it to time, to hunger, and to winter. The cold was to reach 26 degrees.

In spite of Koutouzof, in spite of Wittgenstein, in spite of Tchitchagof, the ice, the breaking down of the bridges, the French army crossed the Berezina near Stoudianka (26th–29th November). The world knows what a price the passage cost, but still it was a great success, a victory of the desperate. Surrounded by 140,000 Russians, these 40,000 men with the Emperor managed to cross. A third among them were Poles. They continued their journey. At Smorgoni, Napoleon quitted the army to hasten to Paris, leaving the command to Murat. It stopped at Wilna, where some months previously splendid fêtes had received the restorer of Poland, the liberator of Lithuania. The starving soldiers rushed eagerly into the houses. Suddenly the cannon sounded on three sides: it was the three Russian armies which had come up. Ney, with his 4000 "braves," protected the flight of this tumultuous crowd. After his departure, there happened in Wilna a scene more frightful, perhaps, than the passage of the Berezina. Wilna was filled with sick and wounded French; nearly every house had its guests. The Jews, who were very numerous in this town, through fear of the Russians and hatred of the French and Polish conscriptions, threw these unhappy wretches out of the windows. The Jewish women could easily kick to death the men who had taken the bridge of Friedland or the great redoubt of Borodino. The Cossacks, first to enter the town, fell furiously upon the defenceless camp-followers, on the women and the sutlers. Then a frightful carnage took place. Thirty thousand corpses were burned on piles. The remains of the army, always protected by the intrepid Ney, at last recrossed the Niemen. They left behind them 330,000 French or allies dead or prisoners.

CAMPAIGNS OF GERMANY AND FRANCE: TREATIES OF PARIS AND VIENNA.

After the extinction of the Grand Army, Koutouzof and the Chancellor Roumantsof were agreed not to tempt fortune, but simply to take the eastern provinces of Prussia and Poland, to make the Vistula the frontier of Russia, and to conclude a peace with Napoleon.

"But," says M. Bogdanovitch, "they did not reflect that Napoleon could easily repair his losses, thanks to the strong concentration of France in a confined space, to the rapidity with which French conscripts were taught, to the great magazines, and the vast financial resources. We, on the contrary, had to assemble our recruits over immense spaces, and our finances were in great disorder. Consequences proved that even with the help of Prussia, then exerting all her strength, we could not make head against Napoleon in the battles of Lützen and Bautzen. What then would have happened if the Prussians, irritated at our pretensions, had allied themselves with France? Obviously Napoleon, reinforced by Prussian armies and the Polish contingents, would have reappeared on the Dwina, and, profiting by the lesson of 1812, would have acted with more precaution and perhaps with more success." Alexander, therefore, resolved to find in the nations which were said to be oppressed by Napoleon the forces necessary to vanquish him, to make the security of Russia rest on the "liberation" of the whole of Europe; and following the example of Napoleon, who had provoked a general movement from West to East against Russia, to raise the nations from East to West against France. The burning of his palace and his capital rendered him inaccessible to all proposals of peace; Stein and the other German refugees did not allow him to forget his vengeance.

Whilst the Russian troops invaded Poland, and gave battle to the remnants of the Grand Army at Elbing and Kalisch; whilst Czartoryski entreated the Tzar to re-establish Poland, under the sceptre of the Grand Duke Michael, Alexander opened negotiations with Prussia. Frederick William negotiated at once both with him and Napoleon. He disavowed York of Wartenburg, whose defection at Tauroggen had given the signal for the Germanic movement, and who raised Eastern Prussia. He sent, however, Knesebeck, disguised as a merchant, to the head-quarters of the Tzar. Alexander in his turn sent him Stein and Anslett, who induced him to sign the Treaty of Kalisch (February 28, 1813), by which the two princes formed an offensive and defensive alliance, "for the re-establishment of the Prussian monarch within limits which may assure the tranquility of the two States." Russia furnished 150,000 men, Prussia 80,000; they were only to treat with Napoleon in concert, and Russia was to try to obtain a subsidy from England, for Prussia. It was only on the 17th of March, when Wittgenstein had made his entry into Berlin, that the King of Prussia declared war against Napoleon, and put forth proclamations "To my people! to my army!" On the 19th of March, when Blücher entered Saxony, the two princes concluded the convention of Breslau: they decided to summon all the princes and all the people of Germany to hasten to set free their common country; the princes who refused within a specified time were to be deprived of their territories. The Confederation of the Rhine was broken: a central council of government was created to administer the countries which were to be reconquered, from Saxony to Holland, to recollect the revenues assigned from that time to the allied Powers, and everywhere to organize levies.

Napoleon had displayed his ordinary activity; he had set on foot 450,000 men; his good cities of Paris, Lyons, Rome, Amsterdam, and Hamburg had made him patriotic presents of thousands of horses. The Confederation of the Rhine, with the exception of Saxony, which was at that time being invaded, prepared contingents. It was with 180,000 men and 350 guns that Napoleon reappeared on the line of the Elbe, and he might well count on crossing it, for in his strong places on the Vistula and the Oder—Dantzig, Thorn, Plock, Modlin, Kustrin, Glogau, Settin, and Stralsund—he had left garrisons amounting to nearly an equal number. The weak point of this new army was the great number of conscripts, the youth of the soldiers, and the feebleness of the cavalry. The veterans, the innumerable squadrons of Murat, were buried beneath the snows of Russia.

On the 2nd of May, at Lutzen, and on the 20th of May, at Bautzen, Napoleon gained two brilliant victories, but could not pursue the vanquished for want of cavalry. He entered Dresden and re-established his ally the King of Saxony; even Silesia was entered. In the north Davoust had recaptured Hamburg and Lübeck, which an insurrection had lost to the French: the guerillas who had shown themselves in Westphalia and Hanover had been driven back.

The King of Prussia was singularly discouraged. Never able to put aside the recollections of 1806, he remarked after Lützen, "It is just as it was at Auerstadt." "The loss of these two battles," says M. Bogdanovitch, "had loosened the bonds of the alliance. The Prussian generals complained that their country was ravaged by the Russians as well as by the French. The ideas of Barclay de Tolly and most of the Russian leaders did not agree with those of Blücher and his officers. In proportion as the Russians increased the distance from their country, did they find it difficult to get ammunition, and even food. In all the space included between the Elbe and the Vistula there were as yet no magazines. The soldiers were badly clothed and badly shod. The habitual discipline of the troops relaxed. The condition of the Prussian army was no better." Alexander and even the King of Prussia might say to themselves that their stakes were heavy.

It was then that the Emperor Francis interfered and persuaded his son-in-law to sign the armistice of Pleswitz, of which Napoleon said, " If the allies do not really wish for peace, this truce may be fatal to us." During this time the Russian army was in fact re-organized; Prussia created its Landwehr; the Prince of Sweden became a member of the Coalition for the promise of Norway; Moreau, another Frenchman, brought his talents to the help of the allies; Dantzig, Stettin, Küstrin, and Glogau were besieged. A piece of exciting news reached Germany. Spain was lost to Napoleon, and the English threatened the Bidassoa. As to Austria, her tendency to defection showed itself more and more; after Lützen, she had sent at the same time Stadion to Alexander, and Bubna to Napoleon. She prolonged negotiations. Discontented with her attitude, Napoleon had tried in vain to approach Alexander; Caulaincourt was not received.

Austria at last transmitted to Napoleon the conditions of the allies: 1. The destruction of the Grand Duchy of Warsaw, and the partition of Poland between the three courts of the North; 2. The re-establishment of Prussia, as far as possible, within the limits of 1805; 3. Restitution to Austria of her Illyrian provinces; 4. Restoration of the Hanseatic towns; 5. Dissolution of the Confederation of the Rhine. Napoleon manifested the most lively irritation, but nevertheless consented that a congress should assemble at Prague to discuss the conditions. He gave his instructions to Narbonne and Caulaincourt. To punish Austria's disloyalty, he determined that " not one single village" should be ceded to her; with Russia he wished for a glorious peace, but on the principle of *uti possidetis*. Pretensions so opposite could not be reconciled, and the allies increased their claims still further, by demanding that the Italian provinces should be restored Austria, and Holland abandoned. When Napoleon finally consented to sacrifice the Grand Duchy of Warsaw and the Illyrian provinces, Austria declared that it was too late, and that she had entered into the Coalition (August 15).

The allies had now three armies in Germany: that of the North, under Bernadotte, encamped on the Havel, with 130,000 men (Russians, Swedes, and Prussians); that of Silesia, under Blücher, posted on the Oder, numbering 200,000 men (Russians and Prussians); that of Bohemia, under Schwartzenberg, consisted of 130,000 Austrians and Russians, and had taken up its position in the neighborhood of Prague. Thus of the three commanders-in-chief not one was Russian. The Grand Duke Constantine, Barclay, Ostermann and Ermolof served Schwartzenberg, Sacken under Blücher, and Wintzingerode under Bernadotte. The old Koutouzof had died at Buntzlau during the summer campaign.

On the other hand, the Emperor of Russia, before whom the pale sovereigns of Austria and Prussia were eclipsed, seemed to direct the armies and the diplomacy of the Coalition. It was he who to the end was to be the firmest against Nopoleon, the most convinced of the necessity of his downfall, and who, after having transported the war from Russia to Germany, would transport it from Germany to France.

To all these forces Napoleon opposed the 30,000 men of Davoust who occupied Hamburg, 70,000 under Oudinot at Wittenberg, and the 180,000 which he had concentrated under his hand from Dresden to Liegnitz, with Vandamme, St. Cyr, Ney, Macdonald, Mortier, and Murat. He fought a great battle with the army of Bohemia in the very faubourgs of Dresden (26th and 27th of August), in which the latter was forced to fall back in disorder on Bohemia, with the loss of 40,000 men and 200 guns. The allies henceforth resolved to avoid all encounters with Napoleon, and only to fight his lieutenants.

Napoleon had posted Vandamme, with 25,000 men, in the defiles of Peterswald, to bar the way to the fugitives, and in the events which followed forgot to recall him. Vandamme descended as far as Töplitz, to cut off the allies, but he came up with the Russian Guard, which made a desperate resistance; even the musicians, the drummers, and the clerks demanded muskets. Ostermann lost one arm. Vandamme, still without orders, retreated to Külm. He there found himself attacked and surrounded by forces four times as numerous as his own, and was taken with half of his *corps* (30th of August). Külm was almost entirely a Russian victory, due above all to Barclay, Ostermann, and Ermolof. It cost dear, for the Russians lost 6000 men, 2800 of whom belonged to the Guard. In his joy Alexander covered the Preobrajenski, the Ismaïlovski, the sailors, and the *chasseurs* of the Guard with decorations and caused St. George's cross to be attached to their standards. At last the Coalition had gained a success. Nearly at the same time Macdonald was defeated by Blücher on the Katzbach; Oudinot at Gross-Beeren, and Ney at Dennewitz, by Bernadotte. The Cossacks threw themselves into Westphalia, and Tchernichef took Cassel and the archives of King Jerome.

From that time the three armies pressed closer to Napoleon. Bennigsen had just brought the Russian army a reinforcement of 60,000 men. The French army, reduced to 160,000 men, found itself surrounded by 300,000 allies and 1200 guns; these formed a half-circle round her, and only left free the way to the West. Then Napoleon, whose *corps d'armée* were stationed at each gate of Leipzig, so as to command all the routes, fought the celebrated "battle of nations," which lasted four days. Alexander showed great personal bravery, remaining almost under the fire of the French batteries, and hastening the arrival of reinforcements on the most threatened places. On the 16th of October the French still maintained their position, on the 17th they watched, while the allies reached their maximum of concentration. On the 18th the battle began with renewed fury: the cannonade was more terrible than that of Borodino, says Miloradovitch; it was on this day that the Saxons deserted. On the 19th the French army began to retreat towards the west, Victor and Augereau at the head; Ney, Marmont, the Guard, and Napoleon in the centre, while Lauriston, Macdonald, and Poniatovski formed the rear-guard. It was this rear-guard that was destroyed by the premature explosion of the bridges over the Elster. Macdonald saved himself by swimming; Lauriston was captured with 30,000 men and 150 guns; Poniatovski was drowned. With him perished the hope of the regeneration of Poland by the hand of Napoleon : intrepid, disinterested, and patriotic, Poniatovski did not care for the staff of a marshal of France : he wished only to remain "the chief of the Poles."

The Prussians, who detested Saxony, wished to take the town of Leipzig by assault. Alexander had to interfere, and managed to negotiate a capitulation with the remains of the French troops. As to the King of Saxony, a prisoner in his own palace, Alexander received him coldly; he refused to treat with him under the pretext that he had rejected the appeal made by the Coalition to the German princes, and had persisted in his devotion to Napoleon. Perhaps he also wished to punish the last Saxon prince who had reigned over Poland. We shall see, besides, that the schemes of Alexander with regard to this part of Europe did not allow him to hold out any hopes to the King of Saxony.

The battle of Leipzig was the overthrow of the French rule in Germany; there only remained, as evidence of what they had lost, 150,000 men, garrisons of the fortresses of the Vistula, the Oder, and the Elbe. Each success of the allies had been marked by the desertion of one of the peoples that had furnished its contingent to the Grand Army of 1812: after Prussia, Austria; at Leipzig the Saxons: the French had not been able to regain the Rhine except by passing over the bodies of the Bavarians at Hanau. Baden, Wurtemberg, Hesse, and Darmstadt declared their defection at nearly the same time; the sovereigns were still hesitating whether to separate themselves from Napoleon, when their people and regiments, worked upon by the German patriots, had already passed into the allied camp. Jerome Bonaparte had again quitted Cassel; Denmark found itself forced to adhere to the Coalition.

Napoleon had retired to the left bank of the Rhine. Would Alexander cross this natural frontier of revolutionary France? "Convinced," says M. Bogdanovitch, "by the experience of many years, that neither losses inflicted on Napoleon, nor treaties concluded with him, could check his insatiable ambition, Alexander would not stop at setting free the involuntary allies of France, and resolved to pursue the war till he had overthrown his enemy." The allied sovereigns found themselves reunited at Frankfort, and an immediate march to Paris was discussed. Alexander, Stein, Blücher, Gneisenau, and all the Prussians were on the side of decisive action. The Emperor Francis and Metternich only desired Napoleon to be weakened, as his downfall would expose Austria to another danger, the preponderance of Russia on the Continent. Bernadotte insisted on Napoleon's dethronement, with the ridiculous design of appropriating the crown of France, traitor as he was to her cause. England would have preferred a solid and immediate peace to a war which would exhaust her in subsidies, and augment her already enormous debt. These divergencies, these hesitations, gave Napoleon time to strengthen his position. After Hanau, in the opinion of Ney, "the allies might have counted their stages to Paris."

Napoleon had re-opened the negotiations. The relinquishment of Italy (when Murat on his side negotiated for the preservation of his kingdom of Naples), of Holland, of Germany, and of Spain, and the confinement of France between her natural boundaries of the Rhine and the Alps; such were the "Conditions of Frankfort." Napoleon sent an answer to Metternich, "that he consented to the opening of a congress at Mannheim: that the conclusion of a peace which would insure the independence of all the nations of the earth had always been the aim of his policy." This reply seems evasive, but could the proposals of the allies have been serious? Encouraged by disloyal Frenchmen, they published the declaration of Frankfort, by which they affirmed "that they did not make war with France, but against the preponderance which Napoleon had long exercised beyond the limits of his empire." Deceitful assurance, too obvious snare, which could only take in a nation weary of war, enervated by twenty-two years of sterile victories, and at the end of its resources! During this time Alexander, with the deputies of the Helvetian Diet summoned at Frankfort, discussed the basis of a new Swiss Confederation. Holland was already raised by the partisans of the house of Orange, and entered by the Prussians. The campaign of France began.

Alexander issued at Freiburg a proclamation to his troops: "Your heriosm has led you from the banks of the Oka to those of the Rhine; it will conduct you still further; we will cross the Rhine, we will penetrate to the territory of the people against whom we have sustained such a fierce and bloody struggle. Already we have saved and glorified our country; we have given back to Europe her liberty and her independence. Oh that peace and tranquillity may reign over the whole earth! that each State may prosper under its own government and its own laws! By invading our empire, the enemy has done us much harm, and has therefore been subjected to a terrible chastisement. The anger of God has overthrown him. Do not let us imitate him. The merciful God does not love cruel and inhuman men. Let us forget the evil he has wrought; let us carry to our foes, not vengeance and hate, but friendhip, and a hand extended in peace. The glory of Russia is to hurl her armed foe to the earth, but to load with benefits her disarmed enemy and the peaceful populations." He refused to receive Caulaincourt at Freiburg, declaring that he would only treat in France. "Let us spare the French negotiator the trouble of the journey," he said to Metternich. "It does not seem to me a matter of indifference to the allied sovereigns, whether the peace with France is signed on this side of the Rhine, or on the other, in the very heart of France. Such an historical event is well worth a change of quarters."

Without counting the armies of Italy and the Pyrenees, Napoleon had now a mere handful of troops, 80,000 men, spread from Nimeguen to Bâle, to resist 500,000 allies. The army of the North (Wintzingerode) invaded Holland, Belgium, and the Rhenish provinces; the army of Silesia (Blücher) crossed the Rhine between Mannheim and Coblentz, and entered Nancy;

the army of Bohemia (Schwartzenberg) passed through Switzerland, and advanced on Troyes, where the Royalists demanded the restoration of the Bourbons. Napoleon was still able to bar for some time the way to his capital. He first attacked the army of Silesia; he defeated the vanguard, the Russians of Sacken, at St. Didier, and Blucher at Brienne; but at La Rothière he encountered the formidable masses of the Silesian and Bohemian armies, and after a fierce battle (1st February, 1814) had to fall back on Troyes. After this victory had secured their junction, the two armies separated again, the one to go down the Marne, the other the Seine, with the intention of reuniting at Paris. Napoleon profited by this mistake. He threw himself on the left flank of the army of Silesia, near Champeaubert, where he dispersed the troops of Olsoufief and Poltaratski, inflicted on them a loss of 2500 men, and took the generals prisoners. At Montmirail, in spite of the heroism of Zigrote and Lapoukhine, he defeated Sacken; the Russians alone lost 2800 men and five guns (11th February). At Château Thierry, he defeated Sacken and York reunited, and again the Russians lost 1500 men and five guns. At Vauchamp it was the turn of Blücher, who lost 2000 Russians, 4000 Prussians, and fifteen guns. The army of Silesia was in terrible disorder. "The peasants, exasperated by the disorder inseparable from a retreat, and excited by exaggerated rumors of French successes, took up arms, and refused supplies. The soldiers suffered both from cold and hunger, Champagne affording no wood for bivouac fires. When the weather became milder, their shoes wore out, and the men, obliged to make forced marches with bare feet, were carried by hundreds into the hospitals of the country" (Bogdanovitch).

Whilst the army of Silesia retreated in disorder on the army of the North, Napoleon, with 50,000 soldiers full of enthusiasm, turned on that of Bohemia, crushed the Bavarians and Russians at Mormans, the Wurtembergers at Montereau, the Prussians at Méry: these Prussians made part of the army of Blucher, who had detached a corps to hang on the rear of Napoleon. This campaign made a profound impression on the allies. Castlereagh expressed, in Alexander's presence, the opinion that peace should be made before they were driven across the Rhine. The military chiefs began to feel uneasy. Sesslavine sent news from Joigny that Napoleon had 180,000 men at Troyes. A general insurrection of the eastern provinces was expected in the rear of the allies.

It was the firmness of Alexander which maintained the Coalition, it was the military energy of Blucher which saved it.

Soon after his disasters he received reinforcements from the army of the North, and took the offensive against the marshals; then, hearing of the arrival of Napoleon at La Ferté Gaucher, he retreated in great haste, finding an unexpected refuge at Soissons, which had just been taken by the army of the North. At Craonne (March 7) and at Laon (10th to 12th March), with 100,000 men against 30,000, and with strong positions, he managed to repulse all the attacks of Napoleon. At Craonne, however, the Russian loss amounted to 5000 men, the third of their effective force. The battle of Laon cost them 4000 men. Meanwhile, De Saint Priest, a general in Alexander's service, had taken Rheims by assault, but was dislodged by Napoleon after a fierce struggle, where the *émigré* commander was badly wounded, and 4000 of his men were killed (13th March).

The Congress of Châtillon-sur-Seine was opened on the 28th of February. Russia was represented by Razoumovski and Nesselrode, Napoleon by Caulaincourt, Austria by Stadion and Metternich. The conditions proposed to Napoleon were the reduction of France to its frontiers of 1792, and the right of the allies to dispose, without reference to him, of the reconquered countries. Germany was to be a confederation of independent States, Italy to be divided into free States, Spain to be restored to Ferdinand, and Holland to the house of Orange. "Leave France smaller than I found her? Never!" said Napoleon. Alexander and the Prussians would not hear of a peace which left Napoleon on the throne. Still, however, they negotiated. Austria and England were both agreed not to push him to extremities, and many times proposed to treat. After Napoleon's great success against Blücher, Castlereagh declared for peace "It would not be a peace," cried the Emperor of Russia; "it would be a truce which would not allow us to disarm one moment. I cannot come 400 leagues every day to your assistance. No peace, as long as Napoleon is on the throne." Napoleon, in his turn, intoxicated by his success, enjoined Caulaincourt only to treat on the bases of Frankfort—natural frontiers. After Montereau he forbade him to treat at all without authority. It was then that he addressed a letter to his father-in-law, the Emperor of Austria, trying to make him ashamed of his alliance with the "Tatars of the desert, who scarcely deserve the name of men," and tempting him by the offer of a separate and advantageous peace. He afterwards again permitted Caulaincourt to treat, but only on the bases of Frankfort. Caulaincourt likewise demanded that Eugène should be maintained in Italy, Elisa Borghese at Lucca, the sons of Louis Napoleon at Berg, and the King of Saxony at Warsaw. These conditions proved unacceptable ; and, as fortune returned to the allies, the congress was dissolved (19th of March). The Bourbon princes were already in France ; Louis XVIII. was on the point of being proclaimed.

Alexander, tired of seeing the armies of Bohemia and Silesia fly in turn before thirty or forty thousand French, caused the allies to adopt the fatal plan of a march on Paris, which was executed in eight days. Blücher and Schwartzenberg united, with 200,000 men, were to bear down all opposition on their passage. The first act in the drama was the battle of Arcis-sur-Aube, where the Russians took six guns from Napoleon. The latter conceived a bold scheme, which perhaps might have saved him if Paris could have resisted, but which was his ruin. He threw himself on the rear of the allied army, abandoning to them the route to Paris, but reckoning on raising Eastern France, and cutting off their retreat to the Rhine. The allies, uneasy for one moment, were reassured by an intercepted letter of Napoleon's, and by the letters of the Parisian royalists, which revealed to them the weakness of the capital. " Dare all ! " writes Talleyrand to them. They, in their turn, deceived Napoleon, by causing him to be followed by a troop of cavalry, continued their march, defeated Marmont and Mortier, crushed the National Guards of Pacthod (battle of La Fère-Champenoise), and arrived in sight of Paris.

Barclay de Tolly, forming the centre, first attacked the plateau of Romainville, defended by Marmont ; on his left, the Prince of Wurtemberg threatened Vincennes ; and on his right, Blücher deployed before Montmartre, which was defended by Mortier. The heights of Chaumont and those of Montmartre were taken ; Marmont and Mortier with Moncy were thrown back on the ramparts. Marmont obtained an armistice from Colonel Orlof, to treat for the capitulation of Paris. King Joseph, the Empress Marie-Louise, and all the Imperial Government had already fled to the Loire. Paris was recommended " to the generosity of the allied monarchs " ; the army could retire on the road to Orleans. Such was the battle of Paris ; it had cost, according to M. Bogdanovitch, 8400 men to the allies, and 4000 to the French (30th March).

In the morning of the 31st, Alexander received the deputies of Paris. He promised that the allied armies should behave with the utmost propriety in Paris, that the security of the capital should be confided to the National Guards, and that the inhabitants should be asked for provisions only. He made his entry between the King of Prussia and Schwartzenberg (the Emperor of Austria being absent) ; but the Parisians had only eyes for him, the only question being, "Which is the Emperor Alexander?" The allied troops maintained a strict discipline, and were not quartered on the inhabitants. Alexander had not come as a friend of the Bourbons—the fiercest enemy of Napoleon was least bitter against the French; he intended leaving them the choice of their government. He had not favored any of the intrigues of the *émigrés*, and had scornfully remarked to Jomini, "What are the Bourbons to me?" He reproved by a witty speech the baseness of a Royalist: "We have waited for your Majesty a long while." "I should have come earlier if I had not been prevented by the bravery of your soldiers," said Alexander. He sent a detachment of the Semenovski to protect the column of the Grand Army against the attempts of the *émigré* Maubreuil. He repeated in the senate that he did not make war on France, that he was the friend of the French, and that he would protect the freedom of discussion, which tended to the establishment of liberal and lasting institutions, in accordance with the progress of the century. He yielded when Talleyrand assured him that "the republic was an impossibility, the regency and Bernadotte an intrigue, the Bourbons alone a principle." On the 2nd of April the senate proclaimed the dethronement of Napoleon; on the 11th he abdicated at Fontainebleau. Alexander had promised Caulaincourt to defend the interests of his ally at Tilsit; he chiefly contributed to secure him the sovereignty of the Isle of Elba. Count Schouvalof was ordered to accompany the fallen Emperor to this place of exile. "I confide to you," said Alexander, "a great mission; you will answer to me with your head for a single hair which falls from that of Napoleon." He confessed to Caulaincourt that the imbecile conduct of the Royalists did not seem to him less dangerous for the peace of Europe than the unreasonable wars of the Empire.

Everyone knows what the French lost by the first Treaty of Paris. On the 3rd of May, Louis XVIII. made his entry into the Louvre. He affected, even with Alexander, the lofty ceremonial of the ancient court; only gave him a chair, while he seated himself on a throne; preceded his guests, the King of Prussia and the Emperor of Russia, to the dining-hall, and, seated in the place of honor, caused himself to be helped before them. Alexander paid no attention to these points. Like his ancestor, Peter the Great, he inspected with interest the monuments and great institutions of the capital. It was at Vienna that the destinies of Europe were to be regulated.

At the Congress of Vienna Alexander was represented by Razoumovski, Nesselrode, Capo d'Istria, and Stackelberg; he had confided the discussion of Polish affairs to Czartoryski and Anslett. On one point he and his ally, the King of Prussia, were agreed ; the latter only asked to get rid of his Polish provinces, and Alexander desired to unite the whole of Poland under his own sceptre, and to fulfil the promise he had made to Czartoryski and to the gallant remnant of the legions of the Vistula. In exchange, Prussia demanded Saxony, whose king was to receive an indemnity elsewhere. We cannot see what interest the Restoration could have secured by sacrificing Poland to the King of Saxony, and by opposing a combination which, by establishing this prince on the left bank of the Rhine, would have given France a neighbor infinitely less dangerous than Prussia. Talleyrand, however, only used the influence that he had acquired in the congress to combat the views of Russia and Prussia, and to support the resistance of England and Austria. On the 21st of October Alexander took a decisive step : he ordered Prince Repnine, Governor of Saxony, to hand over that country to the Prussian government, and to announce its incorporation with the territories of Frederick William III. By his orders the Tzarevitch Constantine entered Poland, assembled an army of 79,000 men, and summoned Poland to the defence of the national integrity. Then Talleyrand, with the consent of Castlereagh, concocted a scheme of alliance between France, Austria, and England. This convention was signed January 3, 1815, but remained secret. Discord reigned in the Congress of Vienna ; Europe was on the eve of a general war. In one way or another France would regain her place in Europe ; but was it on the side of England and Austria that her interests were to be found, Razoumovski having formally proposed to establish the King of Saxony in her Rhenish provinces?

At last the storm rolled away : Alexander declared that he would content himself with only a part of Poland, and Prussia that she would be satisfied with only a third of Saxony, with 700,000 inhabitants. The other decisions of the Congress of Vienna—the organization of the Germanic Confederation, of Italy, and the kingdoms of the Low Countries—belong to general history. Nevertheless, the formation of Germany into a confederation in which the clients of Russia, the allies of the imperial house, enjoyed an independent existence, and a considerable influence on the diet, was far more advantageous to Russian power and security than the state of things resulting from the war of 1870. Poland was again divided between Russia, Prussia, and Austria : this was the fourth partition. The treaties of Vienna, however, provided that " the Poles, the subjects of **Russia, Austria, and Prussia** respectively, should be given a representation and national institutions; whose political existence was to be regulated in the way that the government to which each belonged should judge the most suitable." Cracow was pronounced free and independent. In all these treaties Russia only gained 3,000,000 of souls (kingdom of Poland), whilst Prussia obtained 5,392,000 (Western Poland, Saxony, Swedish Pomerania, Westphalia, and the Rhenish provinces), and Austria 10,000,000 (Gallicia, Germany, and Italy). The Power which had struck hardest for the " freedom of Europe " was the most poorly recompensed.

The event which had suddenly smoothed the difficulties of the Saxo-Polish conflict, and hastened the signing of the treaties, was the news of the return of Napoleon to Paris. The bad government of the Bourbons had realized the unfavorable predictions of Alexander. The sovereigns and plenipotentiaries at Vienna did not hesitate for a moment; Alexander was resolved to pursue the common enemy to his fall, " down to his last man and his last rouble." Bonaparte's couriers, the bearers of pacific assurances, were arrested on the French frontier, and were prevented from reaching the sovereigns. In vain did Napoleon try to sow mistrust between the allies, and to win over Alexander by sending him a copy of the convention signed between Talleyrand, England, and Austria on the subject of the Saxo-Polish affair. "The only result of this movement was to irritate Alexander a little more against the Bourbons and Talleyrand. Napoleon did not profit by it, and France suffered."* Out of the 800,000 men that the Coalition had prepared to march against France, the Russian contingent amounted to 167,000: Barclay de Tolly, field-marshal since the battle of Paris, was commander-in-chief; under him were Doktourof, Raievski, Sacken, Langeron, Sabanéef, Ermolof, Wintzingerode, and Pahlen. In spite of the news of Waterloo and the abdication of Napoleon, the Russians still invaded France. When Alexander reached Paris, he found Blücher already established there, treating it as a conquered city, exacting a tribute of a hundred millions, and preparing to blow up the bridge of Jena. Alexander was hailed as a deliverer by the inhabitants, who were terrified by the Prussian violence. He protested against the outrageous demands of the Germans, and found support in the wise policy of Wellington. Both felt that to restore the Bourbons to a greatly weakened France would be to render this unlucky dynasty still more powerless. They could not this time prevent the pillage of the museums, but the exactions of Russia and England were relatively

* Albert Sorel, ' La Traité de Paris.'

the most moderate. There was a reason for this: these two sovereigns understood that in the regulation of European affairs, and especially of the affairs of the East, France would be an ally in the future, an obstacle to the exaggerated pretensions of either side, at once "a menace and a protection;" she was essential to the equilibrium of Europe. On the other hand, Alexander did not care to obtain for Germany the "territorial guarantees" which she demanded. "He wished," says Sybel, "to allow some danger to exist on this side, so that Germany, having need of Russia, might thus remain dependent." "A Russian diplomat," says Pertz, "avowed ingenuously that it was not the policy of Russia to give Germany secure frontiers against France." Capo d'Istria said openly to Stein that it was Russia's interest to strengthen France, so that the other Powers should not employ all their forces against Russia. If Stein used all his influence with Alexander to cause the claims of the Russian patriots to prevail, other influences were at work to oppose him. First there was the Duc de Richelieu, who had been the governor of New Russia, the founder of Odessa, and whom Alexander desired to see replace the wily Talleyrand with Louis XVIII. Then came Capo d'Istria, Pozzo di Borgo, and his Greek advisers, who, seeing the Eastern question appearing on the horizon, wished to secure for the Hellenic interest an alliance with Russia against the narrow policy of Austria and England. Last came the mystic Madame de Krüdener, who placed before Alexander the ideas of absolute justice, of greatness of soul, of forgiveness for offences, of universal brotherhood, and who in her drawing-room, one of the most brilliant in Paris, surrounded the Emperor with every one France could boast who was brilliant and seductive—Chateaubriand, Benjamin Constant, Madame Recamier, and the Duchesses de Duras and d'Escar.

It is an incontestable fact, that of all the allies Russia showed herself the least grasping. Here is the table of propositions made officially by each member of the Coalition: Russia —temporary occupation of France, war indemnity; England— the same conditions, and the return of the frontiers to those of 1790; Austria—the same, *plus* the dismantling of the fortresses of Flanders, Lorraine, and Alsace; Prussia—occupation, indemnity, return to the frontier of 1790, cession of the fortresses of Flanders, Lorraine, and Alsace. The secondary States of Germany and the Low Countries demanded the cession of Flanders, Lorraine, Alsace, and Savoy. "Such," says M. Sorel, "were the *official* propositions; the *oral* demands were quite another thing." "Look here, my dear Duke," said Alexander to Richelieu in 1818, "this is France as my allies wished to make her:

they only wanted my signature, and that I promise you they shall want always." The map that he showed the Duke presented a line of frontiers which would deprive France of Flanders, Metz, Alsace, and the east of Franche-Comté. We do not mention Carlovitz (who proposed to Stein that France should be divided into Langue d'Oc and Langue d'Oïl, after being robbed of her Flemish- and German-speaking provinces), nor the demoniacs who clamored for Burgundy and the ancient kingdom of Arles.

Richelieu had just succeeded Talleyrand as Minister of Foreign Affairs. He found himself in the presence of a collective ultimatum of the Powers, demanding the cession of Savoy, Condé, Philippeville, Marienburg, Givet, Charlemont, Landau, Fort-Joux, Fort-l'Ecluse, the demolition of Huningue, the payment of eight hundred million francs, and the occupation of the north and east for seven years. He discussed this ultimatum point by point. "The Russians," writes Gagern, "without openly opposing them, labor secretly for the modification of the articles." Richelieu ended by saving Condé, Givet, Charlemont, the forts of Joux and l'Ecluse, and obtained the reduction of the indemnity to seven hundred millions, of the occupation to five years, with the addition of this clause, that "at the end of three years the sovereigns reserved to themselves to cut short the term of occupation, if the state of France permitted it" (November 20, 1815). Alexander left Paris. In the army of occupation Champagne and Lorraine were entrusted to Russia; Voronzof commanded 27,000 men and 84 guns; Alopeus had charge of the political affairs, and both lived at Nancy. Nicholas Tourguénief, a member of the official staff, has given us some curious details about the Russians in Lorraine.

KINGDOM OF POLAND: CONGRESSES AT AIX-LA-CHAPELLE, CARLSBAD, LAYBACH, AND VERONA.

With regard to Poland, Alexander accomplished more loyally and more completely than the two other co-partitioners, the somewhat vague obligations imposed on them by the Treaty of Vienna. After the farewells of Fontainebleau, Dombrovski, commander-in-chief of the legions of the Vistula, placed his troops at the disposal of the Emperor Alexander, from whom the Poles hoped for the restoration of their country. The Tzar assigned Posen as their place of assembly, and gave them his brother Constantine as head. On the 11th of December, 1814, the Tzarévitch addressed them a proclamation in French: "Gather around your banners; arm yourselves to defend your country and to maintain your political existence. Whilst this august monarch prepares the happy future of your country, show yourselves ready to second his noble efforts, even at the price of your blood. The same chiefs who for twenty years have led you on the path of glory, will know how to bring you back to it. The Emperor appreciates your courage. In the midst of the disasters of a fatal war, he has watched your honor survive events for which you were not responsible. Great feats of arms have distinguished you in a struggle whose cause was often not your own. Now that your efforts are consecrated to your country, you will be invincible.... Thus you will reach that happy position which others may promise, but the Emperor alone can secure to you." This proclamation, by which Russia adopted all the glories of the ancient army of Warsaw, was the most magnificent of amnesties. In a letter of Alexander to Oginski, President of the Polish Senate, dated the 30th of April, 1815, he takes the title of King of Poland, and speaks of the efforts he had made to "soften the rigors of separation, and even to obtain for the Poles all possible enjoyment of their national institutions."

On the 21st of June, 1815, the cannon at Warsaw announced the restoration of Poland. As a delicate attention to Polish loyalty, the act of the King of Saxony's abdication was published, as well as the manifesto of the new King of Poland. The army, assembled in the plain of Vola, took the oath of allegiance. The warlike blazon of the kingdom was wedded to the arms of Russia. The new constitution was almost the reproduction of that of the Napoleonic grand duchy. It contained a senate and a chamber of deputies: the senate was composed of bishops, voïevodes, castellans, nominated as life members by the king; the chamber, of seventy-seven noble deputies, and fifty-one deputies of towns. The necessary qualification was property rated at fifteen roubles for the deputies, and 300 for a senator; the former must have reached the age of thirty, the latter that of thirty-five. The electors of the deputies were proprietors above the age of twenty-one, priests, professors, learned men, and artists. The diet was to meet every two years, and to sit thirty days. Laws had to be passed by both chambers, and sanctioned by the king. The constitution declared the liberty of the press, with the exception of one law which restrained its abuses. Amongst the responsible ministers, we find some men of the former *régime*. Sobolevski was Minister of Finance, Matuszevicz of the Interior, Stanislas Potoçki of Education, Vavrjevski of Justice, Viéléhorski of War. The *namiestnik*, or viceroy, was Zaïontchek, a veteran of the Napoleonic wars.

Constantine, the Emperor's brother, was commander-in-chief of the Polish army; Novossiltsof, imperial commissioner. They had thus taken the places of Poniatovski, leader of the Poles, and of Bignon, the envoy of Napoleon. The ministers formed the council of government, and, united to the principal dignitaries, they formed the general council of the kingdom. Czartoryski could not console himself for not having been chosen *namiestnik*.

Alexander's mystic notions soon, however, began to obscure his liberal ideas. The act of the Holy Alliance, which, inoffensive though it was, made such a noise in Europe, is a singular monument and a curious proof of his temper at this period. The King of Prussia signed it willingly, the Emperor of Austria without knowing why, Louis XVIII. surely with a smile; Castlereagh refused his signature " to a simple declaration of biblical principles, which would have carried England back to the epoch of the Saints, of Cromwell, and the Roundheads." Notwithstanding, Russia had then in Europe a preponderating influence, out of proportion with her real strength and the number of her army. But it was she who had given the signal for the struggle against Napoleon, and had shown the most perseverance in pursuit of the common end. Alone, she could never have crushed the man of destiny, but without her example the States of Europe would never have dreamed of arming against him. Her skilful leniency towards France finished the work begun by the war. Alexander was incontestably the head of the European areopagus. Nicholas had to commit many faults before Russia lost this place, which *prestige* and public opinion had given her.

Alexander's influence showed itself in the congresses in which the European States tried to arrange together the affairs of the Continent. The first in date after the Congress of Vienna is that of Aix-la-Chapelle (1818), which regulated the relations of Europe with France; this country appeared sufficiently quiet for the occupation to cease. This was not the fault of the Court of Artois and of the "pavillon de Marsan;" but their famous secret note only made Alexander indignant. In a visit which he paid to Louis XVIII., he said, " If any of my subjects had committed a similar crime, I should have put him to death." Richelieu had gained his object, the entrance of France into the European assembly.

The second congress was that of Carlsbad (1819), where the tone of mind prevalent in Germany was discussed. The disloyalty of the German princes, who had forgotten the promises of liberty made in 1813; that of Frederick William III., who had caused himself to be absolved from his engagements by the Prussian bishop Eylert ; and the reactionary influence of Metternich on the Diet of Ratisbon, had provoked a general stir in German public opinion. The young men and University professors, the liberal writers, and the former members of the Tugenbund, demanded the promised constitutions. The ecstatic demonstrations of the German students, and the murder of Kotzebue by Maurice Sand, shook all the cabinets. It is from this moment that Alexander's character seems to change : the liberator of Europe, the champion of liberal ideas, submits in his turn to the influence of Metternich ; he subscribes to measures which have for their aim to deprive Germany of the liberties which he himself had promised in 1813. The press is subjected to a rigorous *censure;* the Universities are closely watched and the liberal professors expelled ; and the patriots of the war of independence, and Alexander's companions in arms, are obliged to seek refuge in the France they had despoiled.

Soon the stir in men's minds spread through Europe. Spain rose and imposed a constitution on her king : this constitution became an object of envy to the neighboring peoples ; then broke out the revolutions of Portugal, Naples, and Piedmont. As champion of divine right Alexander now defended the detestable kinglets of the South, Ferdinand VII. of Spain and Ferdinand IV. of Naples, who had perjured themselves to their people. He who wished to give Poland a constitution, and to guarantee that of France, opposed to the utmost the constitutional measures of Spain and Italy. By an aberration similar to that of Paul I. he thought himself obliged to interfere in these remote regions, about questions foreign to the interests of Russia. He convoked a congress at Troppeau (1820), then transferred it to Laybach, so that the King of Naples might more easily be present at it, be absolved from his constitutional oath, and provoke vengeance against his too credulous subjects. Alexander was on the point of sending an army to Naples under the command of Ermolof, the hero of Borodino and of Külm ; but Austria, always uneasy at Russian interference in Italy, hastily despatched Frimont, who put an end to the Neapolitan and Piedmontese constitutions. The Russian flag thus escaped the doubtful honor of protecting, as in 1799, the bloody Neapolitan reaction, and of sanctioning the vengeance of Austria against Pellico, Pallavicini, and Maroncelli. Ermolof rejoiced at it. "There is no example," he writes, "of a general appointed to command an expedition being so delighted as I am that there is no war. It is by no means advantageous to one's reputation to appear in Italy after Souvorof and Bonaparte, who will be the admiration of future centuries."

In 1822 the Congress of Verona took place. Russia sent, like the other Powers, a threatening note to the constitutional cabinet of Madrid. The latter returned a proud answer; it was the French army which was entrusted to carry out the wishes of Europe beyond the Pyrenees.

Still graver events were at hand in the East. The Balkan peninsula, almost entirely peopled by the co-religionists of the Russians, began to move. The Ottoman yoke bore heavily on all. The Wallachians and Moldavians complained of the violations of the Treaty of Bucharest. The Servians, whose independence Alexander had guaranteed, and who had been crushed by the Porte while the eyes of Europe were turned another way, had taken up arms under Miloch Obrenvitch. The *hetairia* propagated itself in all the provinces, in all the isles of Greece; it counted already one martyr, Rigas, delivered up by the Austrians and executed by the Turks. What was Alexander to do in the presence of this awakening universe? Would he burn with something of that crusading ardor which hurried Peter the Great to the banks of the Pruth? Would he act here "according to the principles and after the heart of Catherine," as he said in his manifesto at his accession? Would Servia find in him the liberator of 1813, or the president of the Congress of Carlsbad, the man of legitimacy at all costs, the champion of absolute monarchical rights, the theorist of the passive obedience of subjects? This seemed so impossible to the nations, that the Greeks refused to believe Capo d'Istria when he asserted that they would not be supported. Ypsilanti could not imagine that the Emperor would seriously disavow him; he crossed the Pruth, raised the Roumanian populations, and succumbed at Rymnik, which had witnessed the triumph of Souvorof. Alexander might multiply his disavowals, but the Peloponnesus rose under Kolokotroni, and the Mainotes under Mavromichalis. The war of extermination had already begun by the Mussulman riot at Constantinople. At the feast of Easter the Greek population were assaulted, and, as if the better to insult the orthodox religion, the Patriarch was seized at the altar, and hung at the doors of the church in his sacerdotal robes. The Grand Vizier amused himself for an hour by seeing his corpse illtreated by the Turkish populace, and dragged through the mud by the Jews. Three metropolitans and eight bishops were slain (1821). Russia trembled with indignation. Diébitch drew up an admirable plan of campaign, which still deserves to be studied, and which he executed in the following reign. Alexander exchanged diplomatic notes with the Porte, and allowed himself to be lulled to sleep by England and Austria, which did not desire intervention. The massacres continued. Alexander occupied himself about them at Verona, at the same time as the affairs of Spain. The Russian people were astounded, and attributed to the wrath of God, irritated at the impunity accorded to the assassins of the Greek patriarch, first the terrible inundation of St. Petersburg, and soon the premature and mysterious death of Alexander.

To sum up, the grandson of Catherine had added to the empire, Finland, Poland, Bessarabia, and part of the Caucasus (Daghestan, Chirvan, Mingrelia, and Imeritia).

CHAPTER XIII.

ALEXANDER I.: INTERNAL AFFAIRS.

Early years: the triumvirate; liberal measures; the ministers; public instruction—Speranski; Council of the Empire; projected civil code; ideas of social reform—Araktchéef: political and university reaction; military colonies—Secret societies: Poland—Literary and scientific movement.

EARLY YEARS: THE TRIUMVIRATE; LIBERAL MEASURES; THE MINISTERS; PUBLIC INSTRUCTION.

In the home affairs of the empire, the early years of Alexander's reign, succeeding to the hard rule of Paul I., had been a period of emancipation, of generous ideas, and liberal reforms. The Emperor had announced in his manifesto on his accession that he would govern "according to the principles and after the heart of Catherine II." When he managed to free himself from the guardianship of the conspirators of the 24th of March, 1801, he surrounded himself either with the ministers of his grandmother, or with new men, young like himself, who shared his great hopes and his schemes of regeneration. Like him, they brought to the regulation of affairs much inexperience, but immense good-will. Those who at that time most influenced Alexander were Prince Adam Czartoryski, Novossiltsof, Strogonof, and Kotchoubey. The first three were closely united, and were known by the name of the triumvirate. They knew Western Europe better than Russia: the English constitution was their ideal. Czartoryski, a great Polish lord, whose family had given kings to Poland, cherished a dream of the re-organization of his native country, under the sceptre of the Emperor of Russia. Guardian or *popetchitel* of the scholarly circle of Wilna, he profited by this situation to favor the teaching of the Polish language in White Russia. As Minister of Foreign Affairs, or intimate adviser of Alexander, he never lost sight of the interests of his nation, at whose head he may have hoped one day to place himself, in the capacity of viceroy or *namiestnik* of the Emperor.

The tyrannical measures of the preceding reign were reversed; the Russians were again permitted to travel abroad freely, and foreigners were allowed to penetrate into Russia. European books and papers entered the country freely, the *censure* was mitigated, and new instructions ordered the doubtful passages of a book to be interpreted in the sense most favorable to the innocence of the author. The "secret expedition," another form of the secret court of police, or of the State inquisition, was abolished, and its functions handed over to the senate. Priests and deacons, gentlemen and citizens of guilds, were declared exempt from corporal punishments.

Grander designs were brought forward in the council of the young sovereign. As an introduction to the code of the empire, a sort of constitutional scheme was discussed, in which the privileges of the supreme power were defined, its obligations spoken of, and where the *rights* of subjects, and of the four orders of the State, were in question. A sort of civil list was established, under the name of "his Majesty's cabinet." The emancipation of the serfs, as in the brightest period of the reign of Catherine II., was the topic of the day. The situation of the Crown peasants, who were much more free and happy than those belonging to individuals, was assured by the resolution taken by the Emperor to make no more donations of " souls." A million of roubles were even devoted yearly to the acquisition of land with serfs for the Crown. While waiting for a more general measure, Alexander put forth the edict of February 1803, which legalized contracts of freedom voluntarily entered into between the owners and their slaves; the individuals or the communes who thus acquired liberty while they kept their land formed in Russia a new class, the "free cultivators," who, with the ancient *odnodvortsi*, became the nucleus of a rural third estate. The German nobility of Esthonia in 1816, that of Courland in 1817, and that of Livonia in 1819, resolved to anticipate the needs of the new century, so as not to be obliged to submit to them entirely; they took the initiative in the emancipation of Lett or Tchoud serfs, in order that they might consult their own interests in the operation. "All the serfs of these provinces," says M. Bogdanovitch, "were gradually to pass in an interval of fourteen years to the condition of free persons. It was forbidden to sell them with or without land, individually or by families, to give them away, to hire them out, or to make them slaves by any means whatever. Their right to acquire land, houses, and other property was recognized. In civil cases they were in the first two instances amenable to judges elected by themselves and partly drawn from among them. Thus they had now only civil relations with their former masters; but as the latter had distributed no lands among them, the serfs were kept in a burdensome state of dependence upon them." Formerly they were slaves body and soul, but possessed lands; now they were free, but forced for their livelihoods to continue to cultivate for others, as farmers or day-laborers, the soil which had belonged to their warlike ancestors.

The prohibitions of the former reigns against the sale of slaves at auctions, and the separation of the members of one family, were renewed. The abuse, however, still continued, and Nicholas Tourguénief assures us that there was a public slave-market almost under the windows of the imperial palace.

Alexander also gave evidence of his good intentions towards the *raskolniks*. "Reason and experience," says the edict, "have for a long while proved that the spiritual errors of the people, which official sermons only cause to take deeper root, cannot be cured and dispelled except by forgiveness, good examples, and tolerance. Does it become a government to employ violence and cruelty to bring back these wandering sheep to the fold of the church?" These inoffensive sects were, on the other hand, protected; Alexander visited their settlements more than once in the course of his travels. A sect of dancing *raskolniks* were allowed to celebrate their rites in the Mikhail Palace, and Prince Galitsyne, Minister of Worship, was seen honoring with his presence the absurdities of the priestess Tatarinof, and the sacred dances of her adherents.

In political institutions, two great innovations took place in 1802. The collegiate organization of the branches of the administration was set aside; the colleges of Peter the Great, which had succeeded the prikazes of the ancient Tzars, were now replaced by ministers, after the European custom. Here is a list of the first ministry of Alexander I.: War, General Vismiatinof; Marine, Admiral Mordvinof, a bold patriot and distinguished administrator; Foreign Affairs, the Chancellor Alexander Voronzof, nephew of Elizabeth's great Chancellor; Home Office, Count Kotchoubey; Justice, Derjavine, the poet; Finance Count Vassilief; Commerce, Count Roumantsof celebrated for his patronage of arts and sciences; Public Education, Count Zavadovski. The number and functions of the ministers were more than once modified. Ministers of domains, of the Crown, of general control, of roads and bridges, and of the Emperor's household, were afterwards created.

The second innovation bore upon another great institution of Peter I., the Senate, whose importance had been lessened by the formation of an imperial council, presided over by the Emperor or by an appointed minister. Ministers and the general council lacked, however, one essential thing,—responsibility. Autocracy abdicated none of its rights. "Sire," remarked, on one occasion, one of the councillors of Alexander, "if a minister refuse to sign an edict of your Majesty, would the edict be binding without this formality?" "Certainly," replied Alexander; "an edict must be executed under all circumstances."

Alexander and his young fellow-laborers undertook a vast re-organization of public education. The empire was divided into six scholastic circles. That of St. Petersburg included eight governments; that of Moscow, eleven; that of Dorpat, three (the three German provinces); that of Kharkof, sixteen (with the Caucasus and Bessarabia); that of Kazan, twelve (with Siberia); that of Wilna, six (White Russia). At the head of each circle was placed a *popetchitel*, or guardian, ordinarily a considerable personage, like Novossiltsof, Potoçki, or Adam Czartoryski, charged with the protection of the schools and their general direction.

For the instruction of the clergy, ecclesiastical schools were founded, whose revenues were obtained from the exclusive sale of tapers in the churches. Above these schools were seminaries; next the ecclesiastical Academies of Moscow, St. Petersburg, Kazan, and Kief. For the laity were established parish and district schools, and gymnasia (secondary instruction); to furnish masters, the pedagogic institutes of Moscow and St. Petersburg. The Universities of Moscow, Wilna, and Dorpat were re-organized; those of Kazan and Kharkof, and, later, that of St. Petersburg, founded. There was a plan of establishing two at Tobolsk and Oustiougue. Fifteen government schools, or corps of cadets, were also founded, where the young nobles could receive a military education. The Lycée Alexander at Tzarskoé-Selo, afterwards transferred to Kamennyi-Ostrof, was built for the same purpose. From this epoch also dates the lycée of commerce, or Gymnasium Richelieu, at Odessa, and the Lazaref Institute, or school for Oriental languages.

SPERANSKI : COUNCIL OF THE EMPIRE ; SCHEME OF THE CIVIL CODE ; IDEAS OF SOCIAL REFORM.

From 1806 to 1812, the preponderating influence over Alexander was that of Speranski. The son of a village priest, educated at a seminary, then mathematical and philosophical professor at the school of Alexander Nevski, preceptor to the children of Alexis Kourakine, thanks to whom he quitted the ecclesiastical career for the civil service, he became secretary to Trochtchinski, at that time chancellor of the imperial council. Later, when director of the department of the Interior under Prince Kotchoubey, Speranski succeeded to the post of Secretary of State, and began to enjoy the absolute confidence of the Emperor. The favorites of the preceding period were all imbued with English ideas; Speranski, on the contrary, loved France, had imbibed the principles of the Revolution, and entertained a deep admiration for Napoleon. These French sympathies, then shared by Alexander I., formed a fresh bond between the prince and the minister—a bond which was severed by the rupture between the Emperor and Napoleon. " Besides," says M. Bogdanovitch, " we know the inclinations of Alexander for representative forms and constitutional governments, which could not fail to seduce the former disciple of Laharpe ; but this taste resembled that of a dilettante who goes into ecstasies over a beautiful picture. Alexander had promptly convinced himself that neither the vast extent of Russia, nor the constitution of civil society, allowed this dream to be realized. He therefore deferred the execution of his utopia from day to day, but delighted to hold conversations with his friends about his projected constitution and the disadvantages of absolutism. Speranski, to please the Emperor, showed himself the ardent defender of the principles of liberty, and thereby was exposed to accusations of entertaining anarchical ideas, and scheming against the institutions consecrated by time and manners." Hard-working, well-educated, both patriotic and humane, he would have been the man to realize all that was practicable in the utopias of Alexander.

Speranski presented a systematic plan of reforms to his sovereign. The Council of the Empire received still more extensive privileges. Composed of the chief dignitaries of the State, it became in some measure the legislative power; it had to examine all the new laws, the extraordinary measures, the relations of the ministers. It was a kind of sketch of a representative government. The Council of the Empire was divided into four departments: war, law, political economy, civil and ecclesiastical affairs. Alexander solemnly opened this parliament of officials on the 1st–13th of January, 1810. Speranski was nominated secretary of the Council of the Empire. All affairs passed through his hands: he became in a manner the Prime Minister. To his mind, the Council of the Empire being at the head of the legislation, and the ministers at the head of the administration, the Senate ought to occupy the same rank in the judicial order. As the legislative power had been re-organized by the reform of the council, and the administrative power by the reform of the ministry, so the judicial power, in its turn, ought to undergo a complete change. The tribunals, in his opinion, ought to be partly composed of judges nominated by the monarch, partly of judges elected by the nobles. It was plain that Speranski had studied the laws of the French assemblies, the system of Siéyès and the Constitution of the year VIII. The judicial was to be followed by a financial reform. Already, by the edict of the 2nd-14th of February, 1810, the *assignats* had been recognized as part of the national debt, and were to be guaranteed by the imposition and new taxes; the budget was to be published, and a fund for the redemption of the bonds to be created. Speranski, in short, had in his mind something like the French Grand Livre and the budget of the Western States. As a minor task he had undertaken to codify the laws. To him the Code Napoléon—that legacy of the French Revolution, which had at that time been adopted by Holland, Italy, the *Bund*, and the Grand Duchy of Warsaw—seemed the very model of all progressive legislation. After the interview at Erfurt, where Napoleon showed him particular attention, Speranski had been exchanging letters with the French legal writers—Locré, Legras, Dupont de Nemours, and had made them correspondents of the legislative commission of the Council of the Empire. The Code Napoléon could only suit a homogeneous nation, free from personal and feudal servitude, where every one enjoyed a certain equality before the law. Thus Speranski looked on the emancipation of the serfs as the corner-stone of his building; he dreamed of forming a middle class, of limiting the numbers of the privileged classes, and of forming an aristocracy of great families like the English peerage. As early as 1809 he had decided that persons holding University degrees should enjoy certain advantages over others, when aspiring to the degrees of the Tchin. Thus a doctor would be on a level with the eighth rank, a master of arts with the ninth, a man of master's standing who had not taken his degree with the tenth, a bachelor of arts with the twelfth.

Speranski, like Turgot, the minister of Louis XVIII., and like Stein, the Prussian reformer, had set everyone in arms against him. The nobles of the court and of the antechamber—the "sweepers of the parquets," as Alexander called them—and the young officials who wished to owe their promotion solely to favor, were exasperated by the edict of 1809. The proprietors were alarmed at Speranski's schemes for the emancipation of the serfs; the senators were irritated by his plan of re-organization, which reduced the first order of the empire to the position of a supreme court of justice; the high aristocracy were indignant at the boldness of a man of low extraction, the son of a village priest. The people themselves murmured at the increase of the taxes. All these injured interests leagued themselves against him. The minister was accused of despising the institutions of Muscovy, of daring to present to the Russians the Code Napoléon as a model; the country being at that time on the eve of a war with France. The ministers Balachef, Armfelt, Gourief, Count Rostopchine, and the Grand Duchess Catherine Pavlovna, the Emperor's sister, influenced Alexander against him. The historian Karamsin addressed to his sovereign his enthusiastic essay on New and Ancient Russia, in which he made himself the champion of serfage, of the old laws, and of autocracy. They went the length of denouncing Speranski as a traitor and accomplice of France. In March 1812 he suddenly vanished from the capital and went as governor to Nijni-Novgorod, but was shortly afterwards deprived of his post and subjected to a close surveillance. In 1819, when passions had calmed down, he was nominated Governor of Siberia, where he was able to render important services. In 1821 he returned to St. Petersburg, but without recovering his former position.

ARAKTCHEEF: POLITICAL AND UNIVERSITY REACTION; MILITARY COLONIES.

Another period, another *season*, had begun. The enemies of Speranski—Armfelt, Schichkof, and Rostopchine—were in places of the highest trust: but the favorite, the *vrémianchtchik ex officio*, was Araktchéef, the rough "corporal of Gatchina," the instrument of Paul's tyranny, the born enemy of all new ideas and all thoughts of reform, the apostle of absolute power and passive obedience. He first gained the confidence of Alexander by his devotion to the memory of Paul; next by his punctuality, his prompt obedience, his disinterestedness and habits of work, and by the naïve admiration which he showed for the "Genius of the Emperor." He was the safest of servants, the most imperious of superiors, and the instrument best fitted for a reaction. His influence was not at first exclusive. After having conquered Napoleon, Alexander liked to think himself the liberator of nations. He had freed Germany; he spared France, and obtained for her a charter; he granted a constitution to Poland, and meant to extend its benefit to Russia If the censorship of the press had become more severe, and forbade the 'Messager des Lettres' (*Viestnik slovesnosti*) to criticise "his Majesty's servants," Alexander had not yet renounced all his utopias. To the French influence succeeded the Protestant and English influence. The French theatres were shut and Bible Societies opened. The British and Foreign Bible Society established itself in the capital, received subscriptions amounting to 300,000 roubles, and published 500,000 volumes in fifty different languages. The Russian Bible Society, with its offshoot, the Cossack Bible Society at Tcherkask, published hundreds of thousands of copies of the holy books. At this time the influence of Madame de Krüdener, and a revival of the terrible memories of March 1801, had made Alexander a dreamy mystic. He received a deputation of Quakers, prayed and wept with them, and kissed the hand of old Allen. Notwithstanding, the first epoch of the ministry of Araktchéef was an epoch of sterility. If at present there were no reaction, everything had at least come to a standstill. The war of 1812 had interrupted the reforms which had been begun, and they were not resumed. There was an end of the Code of Speranski, and the efforts to compile another more suitable to the Russian traditions came to nothing.

The character of Alexander soon sadly changed. He grew gloomy and suspicious. His last illusions had flown, his last liberal ideas were dissipated. After the congresses of Aix-la-Chapelle and Troppau he was no longer the same man. It was at Troppau that Metternich announced to him, with calculated exaggeration, the mutiny of the Semenovski, his favorite regiment of the Guards. From that time he considered himself the dupe of his generous ideas, and the victim of universal ingratitude. He had wished to liberate Germany, and German opinion had turned against him ; his pensioner, Kotzebue, had been assassinated by Maurice Sand. He had sought the sympathy of vanquished France, and at Aix-la-Chapelle a French plot had been discovered against him. He had longed to restore Poland, and Poland only desired to free herself completely, while Russia demanded an explanation from Alexander of the new danger he had created on his frontier, by the reconstruction of the Lechite kingdom. It was at this moment that the Holy Alliance of the sovereigns became an alliance against nations ; at Carlsbad, at Laybach, and at Verona Alexander was already the leader of the European reaction. In the East he disavowed Ypsilanti ; in Russia he owned the influence of Araktchéef and the Obscuranti. The Araktchéevtchina had begun.

Remonstrated with by Archbishop Serafim, Alexander broke with the Bible Societies, and forced his old friend, Prince Galitsyne, the liberal and tolerant Minister of Public Instruction, to resign. Galitsyne was replaced by Schichkof. The censorship became daily more strict. The Jesuits, who had been expelled from St. Petersburg, were banished from the whole empire, as a punishment for their proselytism; and they really were unnecessary in Russia, for the orthodox guardians of the Russian universities could rival them in the art of stifling independent thought. The *popetchitel* of Kazan University was Magnitski, who proposed to organize the teaching in accordance with the "act of the Holy Alliance." He dismissed eleven of the professors; struck out of the list of honorary members Abbé Grégoire, a Frenchman and "a regicide"; and excluded all suspicious books from the library, notably the work of Grotius on International Law. He forbade the geological theories of Buffon and the systems of Copernicus and Newton to be taught, as contrary to the text of Scripture. The professor of history must saturate himself with the ideas of Bossuet in his 'Histoire Universelle.' The science of medicine must be a Christian science; dissection was almost entirely forbidden, as incompatible with the respect due to the dead. The professor of political economy was enjoined to insist principally on the virtues that turned material goods into spiritual possessions, "thus uniting the lower and contingent economy with the true and superior economy, and by this means forming the real science, in a politico-moral sense." Nikolski, professor of geometry, already demonstrated in the triangle the symbol of the Trinity; and in the unity, that is to say, the number *one*, the divine Unity. At Kharkof, the Professors Schad and Ossipovski, and at St. Petersburg the Professors Galitch (philosophy), Hermann and Arsenius (statistics), and Raupach (history), were expelled from the universities. They were summoned by the *popetchitel* Rounitch before a university commission. The first was accused of impiety, because he had taught the philosophy of Schelling, the others of *Maratism* and of *Robespierrism*, for having expounded the theories of Schlœtzer, the *protégé* of Catherine II., or criticised agricultural serfage, and the extent to which the issue of paper money had been carried. It was forbidden in future either to employ professors who had studied in the West, or to send thither Russian students.

The most salient feature of Araktchéef's administration, of which the initiative proceeded from the gentle Alexander, was the creation of military colonies. This system consisted of the settlement of soldiers among the peasants, in a certain number of districts. If these soldiers were married, their wives were also brought to the village; if they were not, they were married to the daughters of the peasants. A village was therefore composed: 1. Of the military settlers, the soldiers; 2. Of colonized peasants, the natives. The soldiers assisted the peasant in his field work; the children of both were destined for military service. The colonized districts were removed from the jurisdiction of the civil authorities, and subjected to military administration and government. The total in these military districts in the governments of Novgorod, Kharkof, Mohilef, Ekaterinoslaf, and Cherson amounted to 138 battalions and 240 squadrons. This system appeared to have certain advantages, which gained over Speranski himself. It secured, people said, regular recruits, lightened the burden on the rest of the population, raised the morals of the soldier by keeping him with his family, guaranteed him an asylum in his old age, restored to agriculture the labor of which the army had formerly deprived it, diminished for the Government the expenses of the army and for the people the cost of lodging the troops and paying requisitions, and finally created a military nation on the frontier of the empire. If the colonization was a heavy weight upon the natives, they were compensated by various advantages. The Government augmented their lots of land, secured them personal liberty like that of the Crown peasant, repaired their houses, and dowered their daughters.

The country people did not understand it thus. Subjected at their hearths to an interference more annoying than that of their former masters and their stewards, forced into a twofold servitude as laborers and as soldiers, their habits and traditions all invaded, they cursed Araktchéef's ingenious idea, which official circles extolled. Revolts broke out, and Araktchéef, blaming the gross ignorance and ingratitude of the mougik, repressed them with implacable severity.

SECRET SOCIETIES : POLAND.

Other elements of trouble fermented in Russia. We are no longer in the time of Catherine II., when the gravest social questions could be discussed with impunity, before an inattentive or indifferent nation. The noble efforts of Alexander's early years now found a decided support in public opinion. Unfortunately the sovereign and his people were at variance. Whilst a party among the nation had become enthusiastic for liberal ideas, Alexander had grown cold about them: formerly his courageous initiative was hardly appreciated; at present it was the backsliding spirit of the Government which irritated the country. A transformation had taken place; it was not in vain that the Russian officers had seen Paris, had dwelt on French soil. Those revolutionary principles of which under Catherine II. men had only a glimpse across the prism of their prejudices, they had found realized in the States of the West, and had been forced to remark the coincidence of their triumph with the rapid development of a new prosperity. "From the time that the Russian armies returned to their country," writes Nicholas Tourguénief, "liberal ideas, as they were then called, began to propagate themselves in Russia. Independently of the regular troops, great masses of militiamen (*opoltchénié*) had also seen foreign places. These militiamen of various ranks recrossed the frontier, went back to their homes, and related all that they had seen in Europe. Facts had spoken louder than any human voice. This was the true propaganda." Pestel, one of the conspirators of 1825, acknowledged that "the restoration of the Bourbons had made an epoch in the history of my ideas and political convictions. I then saw that though the greater number of the institutions necessary to the well-being of a State were brought in by the Revolution, they were continued after the re-establishment of the monarchy as conducive to the public welfare, whilst formerly we all, myself among the earliest, rose against this Revolution. From this I concluded that apparently it was not so bad as we represented to ourselves, and even contained much good. I was confirmed in my idea by observing that the States in which no revolution had taken place continued to be deprived of many rights and privileges."

People not only read Montesquieu, Raynal, Jean-Jacques Rousseau, as under Catherine II., but Bignon, Lacretelle, De Tracy, and Benjamin Constant; and the eloquent voices of the French tribune found an echo in the young Russian nobility and part of the middle class. Politeness, the spirit of justice, and respect for the human person had made great progress. European culture no longer lay only on the surface, but it penetrated deeply into hearts and consciences. Many declared like Wilhelm Küchelbecker: "At the thought of all the brilliant qualities with which God has endowed the Russian people,—that people whose language, so sonorous, so rich and strong, is without a rival in Europe, whose national character is a mixture of *bonhomie*, of tenderness, of lively intelligence, and a generous disposition to pardon offences; at the thought that all this was stifled, and would wither and perhaps perish before having produced any fruit in the moral world, my heart nearly broke." To these noble souls it was absolute suffering to see despotism hold its sway through all the grades of Russian society, in all the relations of the autocrat with the nation, of the officials with those they governed, of the officials with their soldiers, and of the proprietors with the peasants. They were indignant at beholding the Russian people alone in Europe dishonored by the serfage of the soil, and by domestic servitude, that shameful legacy of ancient Slav barbarism and the Tatar yoke, that Asiatic ignominy which continued to defile a Christian people ; at the sight of the Russian soldier, the conqueror of Napoleon, the liberator of Europe, submitting to the degradation of corporal punishment. They did not believe that the inconstant will of the most well-meaning autocrat, that the good intentions of an Alexander—that " happy accident among his family," as he said himself to Madame de Staël—could make up for the want of laws and liberal institutions.

In spite of the watchfulness of suspicious police, freemasonry, forbidden since the time of Catherine II. and Paul, organized itself, and spread over Russia, the kingdom of Poland, and the Baltic provinces. Societies of a more warlike character, and with a definite object, whose existence for a long while remained a secret, were also constituted at certain points. It was in 1818 that the Society of Virtue, an imitation of the Germanic Tugenbund, was formed at Moscow, and reckoned among its members Prince Troubetskoï, Alexander and Nikita Mouravief, Matvei and Sergius Mouravief-Apostol, Nicholas Tourguénief, Feodor Glinka, Michael Orlof, the two brothers Fon-Vizine, Iakouchkine, Lounine, the princes Feodor Schakovskoï and Obolenski, and many others. The members of this association were not agreed as to the form of government they wished to give to Russia, some clinging to the idea of a constitutional monarchy, others to that of a republic, which Novikof had been one of the first to suggest. This society was dissolved in 1822, and gave birth to two others—the Society of the North, or of St. Petersburg, which had constitutional aims, and the Society of the South, which recruited its associates chiefly among the officers of the garrisons of the Ukraine or of Little Russia, where Colonel Pestel preached republicanism. A third and less important society, that of the United Slavs, dreamed of a confederacy of the Slav races, and tried to form ramifications in Bohemia, Servia, and Bulgaria. About 1823, the Russian societies entered into relations with the Patriotic Society of Poland, then preparing for an insurrection, and, in order to secure the help of the Poles, engaged to do all in their power to favor the restoration of the country. The most ardent members of the Russian associations were at that time Colonel Pestel and Ryleef, the one a son of a former director of posts, the other of the head of police under Catherine II. By the warmth of their republican convictions, they seemed to wish to expiate the servility of their fathers. At the period of the meetings at Kief in 1823,

Pestel had read a scheme of a republican constitution and of an equalizing code. As the chief obstacle to the realization of his projects seemed to him to be the existence of the Romanof dynasty, it was decided not to shrink from the murder of the Emperor, and the extermination of the imperial family. In the bosom of the Society of the South, a still closer and more secret association had been formed, with the end of regicide in view. They were to profit by the first opportunity that presented itself, which happened to be a review where Alexander was to inspect, in 1824, the troops of the Ukraine. An active propaganda was set on foot among the soldiers of the garrisons, and common soldiers were gained over by promising them the liberty of the peasants, and the mitigation of the military *régime*.

LITERARY AND SCIENTIFIC MOVEMENT.

The awakening of the Russian mind did not show itself in political schemes alone. In science, in letters, and in arts, the reign of Alexander was an epoch of magnificent blossom. The intellectual, like the liberal, movement had not the exotic and superficial character of the reign of Catherine. It penetrated deeply into the heart of the nation, gained in power and in extent, carried away the middle classes, and propagated itself in the most distant provinces. The impulse given in 1801 had not stopped, although the Government at once tried to quell the spirit it had excited, and Alexander, embittered and *désillusionné*, had become mistrustful of all manifestations of private thought. While the rigor of the censorship had been increased, the number of secret societies was not at all diminished, and reviews and literary journals continued to multiply.

The *Bésiéda* was now formed, the literary club at which Krylof read his fables and Derjavine his odes, and which represented classical tendencies; whilst the *Arzamas* was founded by the romantic school—Joukovski, Dachkof, Ouvarof, Pouchkine, Bloudof, and Prince Viazemski. At St. Petersburg the Society of the Friends of Science, Literature, and Arts; that of the Friends of Russian Literature at Moscow, which published an important collection of its "transactions;" that of the History of Russian Antiquities, and the Society of Patriotic Literature, at Kazan; that of the Friends of Science at Kharkof, and many others of less importance, devoted themselves to letters, archæology, and the mathematical, natural, and physical sciences. At St. Petersburg appeared the *Northern Post*, the

St. Petersburg Messenger, the *Northern Mercury,* the *Messenger of Sion,* organ of the mystic party, *The Beehive,* and *The Democrat,* in which Kropotof declaimed against the influence of French ideas and manners, and in the 'Funeral Oration of Balabas, my dog,' congratulated this worthy animal on having studied at no university, on never having occupied himself with politics, on never having read Voltaire, &c. Literary activity was, as ever, still greater at Moscow. Karamsin there edited a review entitled the *European Messenger,* Makarof the *Moscow Mercury,* Sergius Glinka the *Russian Messenger,* in which he tried to excite a national feeling, now putting the people on their guard against any foreign influence, moral or intellectual, now arming them against Napoleon, "teaching the people to sacrifice themselves to their country," and letting loose the furies of the " patriotic war." " With the victory of Russia over the invader his task ended, aud the *Russian Messenger* disappeared, but his work was taken up by Gretch in his *Son of the Soil,* who continued beyond the frontier the war with Napoleon, whom he taunted as a "murderer" and an "infamous tyrant," and against his companions in arms, whom he called "brigands." "Taste beforehand," he cries to the conqueror, " the immortality which you deserve. Know from this time how posterity will curse your name! You are seated on your throne amidst thunder and flames, like Satan in the midst of hell, encircled with death, with devastation, fury, and fire." The *Invalide Russe* was founded in 1813, for the benefit of wounded or infirm soldiers. Even when the warlike fever calmed down, and men's minds were occupied with other things less hostile to French influence, this great literary movement still continued.

Almost all the writers of this period took their part in the crusade against the Gallomania and the influence of Napoleon. Some had fought in person in the war with France. Joukovski was present at Borodino ; Batiouchkof had marched in the campaigns of 1807 and 1813, and had been wounded at Heilsberg ; Petine was killed at Leipzig ; the Princes Viazemski and Schakovskoï had served among the Cossacks ; Glinka in the *opoltchénie* in which Karamsin, in spite of his age, had wished to enrol himself. Their writings bear the stamp of their patriotic passions. Krylof has written other things besides his fables, which place him not far from La Fontaine, and in his comedies ' The School for Young Ladies ' and the ' Milliner's Shop ' he turned the exaggerated taste for everything French into ridicule. Amongst several classical tragedies (' Œdipus at Athens,' ' Fingal,' ' Polyxena ') Ozérof wrote that of ' Dmitri Donskoi,' which recalled the struggles of Russia against the Tatars, and seemed to predict the approaching contest with another invader. The tragedy of 'Pojarski,' the hero of 1612, by Krioukovski, contains allusions of the same sort. In 1806 the poet Joukovski had sung the exploits of the Russians against Napoleon, in the 'Song of the Bard on the Graves of the Victorious Slavs,' and in 1812 in the 'Bard in the Camp of the Russian Warriors.' Rostopchine, the enemy of the French, did not even await the grand crisis to empty the vials of his wrath against them.

In general the literature of the time of Alexander marks the passage from the imitation of the ancients, or of classic French writers, to the imitation of the German or English masterpieces. The *Besieda* and the *Arzamas* formed, as it were, the head-quarters of the two rival armies, which fought in Russia the same battle as the French romantic and classic schools at Paris. Schiller, Göthe, Bürger, Byron, and Shakespeare were as fashionable as in France, because they were strange, and because they created a kind of literary scandal. If Ozârof, Batiouchkof, and Derjavine kept up the traditions of the old school Joukovski translated Schiller's 'Joan of Arc' and Byron's 'Prisoner of the Chillon,' Pouchkine contributed 'Rousslan and Loudmila,' the 'Prisoner of the Caucasus,' the 'Fountain of Bakhtchi-Seraï,' and the 'Tsiganes' (*i.e.* Gipsies), and began his romance in verse of 'Eugène Onieghine' and the drama of 'Boris Godounof' (1829).

As in France the romantic movement had been accompanied by a brilliant renaissance of historical studies, so in Russia the dramatists and novelists were inspired with a taste for national subjects by Karamsin's 'History of Russia'—a work uncritical in its method, and indiscriminating in its appreciation of historical events, but remarkable for the brilliance and eloquence of its style, as well as the charm of its narrative. Schloetzer had just edited Nestor, the old Kievian annalist, the father of Russian history.

Science enjoyed a certain amount of protection in this reign. In 1803 the Captains Krusenstern and Lisianski, accompanied by the *savants* Tilesius of Leipzig and Horner of Hamburg, accomplished the first Russian voyage round the world, in the *Hope* (Nadéjda) and the *Neva*, and opened relations with the United States and with Japan. In 1815 Captain Kotzebue had explored the Southern Ocean, and next the icy ocean to the North, and sought by Behring's Straits a communication with the Atlantic, that is, the North-west passage; others surveyed the coasts of Siberia, and it was ascertained that Asia was not joined to America, as the Englishman Burney had asserted.

In 1814 the imperial library of St. Petersburg was solemnly

thrown open to the public. It then contained 242,000 volumes and 10,000 manuscripts. The nucleus had been formed by the victories of Souvorof, who had sent to Russia the library of the kings of Poland.

In spite of the expenses of the war, the Russian cities had received some embellishments. At St. Petersburg the better-paved streets and the granite quays gave evidence of the care of the Government. Thomont built the palace of the Bourse, Rosser the new Mikhail Palace, and Montferrand began the vast and splendid cathedral of St. Isaac. St. Peter's at Rome served as a model for our Lady of Kazan, before which the bronze statues of Barclay de Tolly and Koutouzof were afterwards erected. In 1801 a statue was erected to Souvorof. Pultowa had its monument of Peter the Great's victory; Kief that of Vladimir the Baptist; Moscow those of Minine and Pojarski (1818): but the plan of raising on the Hill of Sparrows at Moscow a colossal church dedicated to the Saviour, in memory of the deliverance, failed through the inexperience of the architect. It was only carried out in another place, during the present reign.

In 1825 Alexander quitted his capital to visit the southern provinces, and intended to spend some time at Taganrog, for the benefit of his health. At the moment of his departure he appears to have been shaken by gloomy presentiments, and insisted on a requiem mass being said at the monastery of St. Alexander Nevski. In broad daylight, lighted tapers were left in his room. A frightful flood that had happened at St. Petersburg some time before was looked on by the people as a chastisement from Heaven for Russia's culpable indifference towards the Christians of the East. At Taganrog Alexander received circumstantial accounts as to the conspiracy of the Society of the South and its schemes of regicide. Cruel recollections of 1801 may have mingled with his melancholy. He thought sadly of the terrible embarrassments which he would bequeath to his successor; of his lost illusions; of his liberal sympathies of former days, which in Poland, as in Russia, had ended in a reaction; of his broken purposes and changed life. In the Crimea he was heard to repeat, "They may say what they like of me, but I have lived and will die republican." But what a singular republic is the system preserved in the memory of the people under the name of "Araktchéevtchina"! On the 19th of November (1st December) the Emperor expired in the arms of the Empress Elizabeth. How would Russia celebrate what the Empress-mother Maria Feodorovna already called the "obsequies of Alexander?"

CHAPTER XIV.

NICHOLAS I. (1825–1855).

The December insurrection—Administration and reforms—Public education and literature—War with Persia (1826–1828)—First Turkish war: liberation of Greece (1826–1829)—The Russians and English in Asia—Polish insurrection (1831)—Hostility against France: the Eastern question: Revolution of 1848; intervention in Hungary—Second Turkish war: the allies in the Crimea—Awakening of Russian opinion.

THE DECEMBER INSURRECTION—ADMINISTRATION AND REFORMS —PUBLIC EDUCATION AND LITERATURE.

By the law of primogeniture, Alexander's successor should have been Constantine, the eldest of his brothers, but in order to marry the Countess Groudsinska, afterwards created Princess Lovicz, Constantine had, in 1822, declared to Alexander his intention of renouncing the crown. The Emperor had accepted, and the Empress-mother had approved, his renunciation; and in 1823 Alexander had drawn up a manifesto which sanctioned the resolution taken by Constantine, and summoned Nicholas, Paul's third son, to the throne. This act was deposited at the *Ouspienski Sobor* at Moscow, but was kept secret even from Nicholas himself. When, two years after, Alexander died at Taganrog, Constantine at Warsaw hastened to take the oath of allegiance to Nicholas, but Nicholas at St. Petersburg thought it his duty to swear fealty himself to Constantine, and to make others do so. It was only on the 12th—24th of December, 1825, that he received a letter from Constantine in which he repeatedly and formally declared his intention to renounce the throne. Then Nicholas published a manifesto announcing his own accession, and received the oaths of his subjects.

This contest of generosity between the two brothers, which so strongly contrasted with the ambitious habits and political revolutions of the eighteenth century, was to cost the empire dear. During these few days of interregnum, people's minds were troubled; they did not know whom to obey. The members of the secret societies profited cleverly by this perplexity of opinion, and turned the attachment of the masses to the principle of seniority to the advantage of the revolution. The conspirators of the Society of the North had resolved to act. On the 14th–26th of December they raised some of the troops, the regiments of Moscow, the grenadiers of the navy, and the seamen of the Guard, by persuading them that the news of Constantine's resignation was false, that the Tzarévitch was prisoner in Moscow, and that the oath exacted from them was a sacrilege. The insurgent forces threw themselves on the Place du Sénat, shouting "Long live Constantine!" Some of the conspirators raised the cry of "Long live the Constitution!" but this idea was strange to the masses, and, according to the monarchical historians, the ignorant soldiers believed that Constitution was the name of Constantine's wife. Then the plotters distributed cartridges among them, and gave the signal of revolt by massacring or wounding the officers who attempted to oppose the movement. Nicholas had harangued the crowd who had taken up their position before the Winter Palace, read them the manifesto of Alexander, and had managed to disperse them. The military insurgents thus found themselves deprived of the assistance of the popular element. The other regiments of the Guard and nearly all the garrison remained faithful. The rebels, however, grouped on the Place du Sénat, refused to listen to reason. Miloradovitch, governor of the capital, tried to harangue them; but this hero of fifty-two battles was killed by a pistol-shot. The metropolitan, in his sacerdotal robes, was also shot at, and received four balls in his mitre. The Emperor had placed himself opposite the insurgents; after having exhausted all means of conciliation, he ordered the soldiers to fire on the barricades which had been hastily raised. A few rounds sufficed to scatter the crowd. Five hundred were taken prisoners, and in the night many surrendered at discretion. At seven in the morning Nicholas returned victorious to his palace.

The same night thirteen conspirators of the Society of the South were arrested. This did not check the operations of the society, nor of that of the United Slavs. The two Mouraviefs and Bestoujef-Rioumine had collected some companies, occupied Vassilkof, and marched on Kief; but at the village of Oustimovka they encountered General Geismar, who received them with a discharge of grape-shot: a cavalry charge finally put them to flight: 700 men laid down their arms, and nearly all the leaders were made prisoners.

Nicholas had accorded a disdainful pardon to Prince Troubetskoï, whom the conspirators of the capital had chosen to be head of the Government, and who had ruined everything by his fickle policy. He showed a certain clemency to the mass of the insurgents, but a hundred and twenty-one were brought before a commission. A minute inquiry, and many confessions, enabled him to find the threads of the plot, and the traitors were punished more or less severely. Five of them—Pestel, Ryleef, Sergius Mouravief-Apostol, Bestoujef-Rioumine, and Kakovski, the assassin of Miloradovitch—were condemned to be hanged. They did honor to their cause by their courage in facing a penalty made cruel by the awkwardness of the executioners. Ryleef, the head of the Society of the North, said after his condemnation, "The zeal of my patriotism and my love of my country may have deceived me; but as my actions have been guided by no personal interest, I die without fear. Pestel, the energetic dictator of the South, had devoted all his thoughts to the safety of his Russian Code: "I am certain," said he, "that one day Russia will find in this book a refuge against violent commotions. My greatest error is, that I have wished to gather the harvest before sowing the seed." Many of their ideas were indeed premature, but some were to survive their originators, and be carried into execution by the very power which they defied. They had desired the independence of the peasants, a greater equality of rights, and more stability in the law. In spite of their faults, which they paid for with their lives, they had shown that there existed in Russia men capable of dying for liberty. They gave an impetus to the country that the thirty years' reign of Nicholas could not destroy. This abortive conspiracy was in certain respects the beginning of the regeneration. Many of the old *décembristes* were, in letters, arts, and political economy, the glory of their country, and were able to advance, as far as it was practicable, by other means, the work they had already undertaken. Nicholas, who had inaugurated his reign by conquering one revolution, was to be all his life the enemy of revolution. In Europe as in Russia he was the champion of Conservative principles. If he carried on the work of his brother Alexander, it was the Alexander of later years, without the innovating views of 1801, without his liberal sympathies, and without his humane scruples. Nicholas I., with his colossal stature, his imposing exterior, his mystic pride, his infatuation for the *rôle* of a pontiff-king, his iron will, his power of work, his taste for the details of government, his passion for everything military, always buckled tight in his uniform and playing his part before the people, was a formidable incarnation of autocracy. His reign was a constant protest against the movement of the world. He kept up a perpetual struggle against the living forces of humanity, against the imperceptible and invincible advance of the mind. Nicholas was a drag upon rather than an obstacle to progress. When his power broke, under its ruins was seen a ewn world which had already arrived at maturity.

One of the first cares of Nicholas I. was to take up the work of codification of the Russian laws, so often sketched out by his predecessors: by Peter the Great, with the help of the Germanic laws; by Catherine II., with her great legislative commission; by Alexander, with the almost Napoleonic project of Speranski. Nicholas himself could only collect the materials. The Russian laws could not be definitely codified till society, regenerated by the emancipation, should have found its final constitution. In 1830 appeared the 'Complete Collection of the Laws of the Russian Empire,' which Alexis Mikhaïlovitch had begun in his *oulojénié*; in 1838, the 'Collection of the Existing Laws,' compiled after a systematic scheme, which was provisionally to make legislation more consistent, and the tribunals more active. It was time, for 2,850,000 causes were declared to be pending, and 127,000 persons committed for trial still awaited judgment. In 1849 was published the code of penal and corrective justice. Tribunals of commerce were created, for the more prompt dispatch of commercial affairs.

Peter the Great had established a law of entail. Anne Ivanovna had suppressed it, as being opposed to Russian manners. Nicholas partially re-established it, by granting the father of the family power to make use of it if he pleased. The custom of *pravège* still existed among the Don Cossacks: it was now abolished. Merchants desirous of becoming " noble " thronged the ranks of the public service; Nicholas, to turn their ambition into another channel, while securing them the same advantages, created a new subdivision in the class inhabiting the towns—that of the chief citizens (*bourgeois notables*), who enjoyed the following prerogatives:—Exemption from the poll-tax, conscription, and corporal punishments; right to take part in assessment of the landed property of the town, and the right of being elected to the communal functions of the same rank as those open to the merchants of the first guilds. All might be admitted among the chief citizens (*bourgeoisie notable*) who had a certificate of secondary studies, a student's diploma, or that of a university student eligible for the degree of master of arts, or were freeborn artists and had a certificate from the Academy of Fine Arts. Nicholas I. here took up one of the traditions of Catherine II., who had attempted to constitute a middle class at the same time as a nobility. He tried to regulate the mode of procedure among the assemblies of peasants in the rural communes, and to introduce the ballot by black and white balls. The autocratic Tzar was one of the first to introduce universal suffrage into Russia. As to the vital question of emancipation, it slumbered during this reign. Nicholas contented himself with approval of the great nobles who set free their serfs. The Princess Orlof-Tchesmenski liberated 5518. The class of free cultivators increased very slowly; in 1838 it only counted 72,844 husbandmen. The edict of 1842, which had attempted to fix the conditions of these contracts of emancipation, had disquieted the nobles. The Government hastened to reassure them by affirming that there was no question of the liberation of the peasants, and by ordering the propagators of false news to be arrested, and the recall, by force if necessary, of refractory serfs to their obedience. Nicholas established his aide-de-camp, Protassof, in the court of the Holy Synod; he governed the national church in a military fashion for twenty years, and had no scruples about "dragooning" the dissenters of White Russia.

Nicholas undertook to join the Don and the Volga by means of a canal, and to improve the navigation of the Dnieper. Under this champion of immobility the first railways were created. He traced in a straight line with a ruler the railway between Moscow and St. Petersburg (130 leagues long), without permitting it to go out of its way, so as to pass through any towns of importance. A small branch joined Tzarskoé-Selo to the capital. Russia still only followed at a great distance the new European enterprises; no iron road united her to the West. The annoyances of the police, the censorship, and the custom-house dues all contributed to isolate her in Europe. Her autocrat kept the rest of Europe in a kind of political quarantine. While speaking of public works, we must mention the reconstruction in fifteen months of the Winter Palace, which was destroyed by the fire of 1837.

Nicholas created a "professorial institute"—a sort of normal school for the higher education—to recruit the ranks of public schoolmasters, and a "principal pedagogic institute" for the secondary course of instruction. His object was to remove the Russian youth from the influence of foreign masters. There were restrictions as to the employment of tutors and governesses in private houses. Their capacity and their morality (in which were included their political opinions) were to be certified by one of the universities of the empire, under the penalty of a fine of 250 roubles and of banishment. It was forbidden to send young men to study in Western universities, save in some exceptional cases, for which a special permission was required. In the Government schools, to the prejudice of foreign languages and literature, a greater development was given to the

Russian language, literature, statistics, and history, which were considered less dangerous. Other obstacles were imposed on freedom of foreign travel and residence; the term of absence attested by legal passports was fixed at five years for the nobles, and three for other Russians subjects. The University of St. Vladimir was founded at Kief, to replace that of Wilna, which was suppressed after the Polish insurrection. The scholastic reaction, the mistrust of German philosophy, went so far, that philosophy was finally forbidden to be taught in the universities, and entrusted to the care of ecclesiastics.

Nicholas bestowed his chief attention on the establishments for military education, the *corps* of cadets, and the Military Academy. He created, however, a school of law and a technological institute.

The scientific publications of the Government, and those of the Archæographical Commission, furnished, with the 'complete Collection of Russian Laws,' new materials for the study of national history. The imperial library at St. Petersburg was enriched by Pogodine's cabinet of antiquities; to the liberality of Count Roumantsof Moscow owes the museum and library which bears his name. M. Solovief began his 'History of Russia,' and Nicholas Polévoï wrote his 'History of the Russian People.'

The censorship weighed heavily on the development of the national press. Gretch and Boulgarine founded, however, in 1825, the *Northern Bee;* Biélinski, the prince of critics, wrote successively for the *Observer*, started by Schevyref, for Kraïevski's 'Annals of my Country,' and for the *Contemporary*, founded by Panaïef and Nekrassof, which reckoned Pouchkine among its contributors. Nicholas Polévoï in the *Telegraph*, and Nadéjdine in the *Telescope*, continued the struggle—the one in the name of the romantic, the other in that of the classic school. The Slavophils discussed in the *Muscovite* questions relative to the unity of the Slav races and the nationality of the Russian people.

This period of the nineteenth century was as fertile in Russian as in French literature. To the names of Lamartine, Victor Hugo, and Alfred de Musset correspond those of Pouchkine (the first of Russian poets, and one of the first in Europe); Lermontof, who was inspired in the 'Demon' and others of his masterpieces by the wild and sublime beauty of the Caucasus; Koltsof, who discovered a new source of poetry in the popular songs; Griboïedof, whose comedy 'Goré ot ouma' (Too Clever by Half) has remained one of the stock pieces; and Gogol, who in his play of 'Revisor' and his romance of the 'Dead Souls' has boldly revealed the plague-spots in Russian administration and society. Soukovski translated the Odyssey and some fragments of Indian and Persian poems; Polévoï, in his 'Oath at the Tomb of the Saviour,' 'The Deserted One,' 'Dream and Life,' and 'Hamlet,' continued the romantic movement by imitating Schiller, Hoffmann, Walter Scott, and Shakespeare. It was no barren epoch that witnessed the appearance of Herzen under the name of 'Iskander'; of Ivan Tourguénief, who in his 'Memoirs of a Huntsman' struck the prelude to a European reputation; of the novelists Gontcharof ('A Common Story'), Gregorovitch ('The Emigrants'), Pisemski ('The Liéchi,' 'The Petersburgher'), Dostoevski ('The Poor'); and in which the Russian public could applaud the comedies of Ostrovski, and the operas of the great composer Glinka ('Life for the Tzar,' and 'Rousslan and Loudmila'). The Russian intellect, spite of all obstacles, spread its wings and tried unknown paths, created new openings for itself, and nobly gave the lie to the theories of immobility. Russia, isolated though she was from Europe, still took her place among the great European nations.

PERSIAN WAR (1826-1828)—FIRST TURKISH WAR: LIBERATION OF GREECE (1826-1829)—ENGLISH AND RUSSIANS IN ASIA.

After the Treaty of Gulistan, the Russian and Persian governments were perpetually quarrelling on the subject of the frontiers and the vassal tribes. The Shah continued to receive tribute from the khans of Karabagh and Gandja, but in his turn complained of the encroachments of Russia, and of the arrogance of Ermolof, Governor-General of the Caucasus. Soon the Russians learnt that the Mollahs were preaching on all sides a holy war, that English officers had entered the service of the Shah, and that Abbas-Mirza, Prince Royal of Persia, was ready to cross the Araxes at the head of 35,000 men, and to raise the tributary khanates. Nicholas at once despatched General Paskiévitch to join Ermolof. The Prince Royal was in full march on Tiflis, when he received a check by the heroic resistance, which lasted for six weeks, of the fortress of Choucha. The Russians had thus time to concentrate their forces. Near Elizabethpol they defeated the Persian vanguard, 18,000 strong; on the Djéham, Paskiévitch, with less than 10,000 men, dispersed the whole royal army, 44,000 strong, and obliged the remnant to retreat beyond the Araxes (1826). By the Treaty of Teheran, England promised Persia, in a case of invasion, a body of troops, and a subsidy of five millions. Persia was none the less invaded. Paskiévitch, appointed general-in-chief, forced in 1827 the defiles and the passage of the Araxes; captured 10,000 of the Prince Royal's men; took Erivan, the bulwark of Persia, by assault; entered Tauris, the second city of the kingdom, in triumph, and began his march to Teheran. The king, Fet-Aly-Shah, in alarm, signed the Peace of Tourkmantchaï (10th–22nd February, 1828); he ceded to Russia the provinces of Erivan, and Nakhitchévan, paid an indemnity of 20,000,000 roubles, and promised important commercial advantages to Russian subjects. The Araxes became the frontier of the two empires, and Paskiévitch received the title of Erivanski. The peace was all but broken in 1829 by the massacre of the Russian legation at Teheran, in which the poet Griboïedof, the Russian minister, perished. Asia was always fatal to the Russian poets. Lermontof was to die a tragic death, killed in a duel in the Caucasus. The Court of Teheran disavowed the crime of the people, and, although Russia was then occupied in a war with Turkey, the Prince Royal came to St. Petersburg, to offer the most complete satisfaction. Persia became day by day more subject to Russian influence, to the great disgust of England.

With regard to Turkey, Nicholas had taken up a more decided attitude than Alexander. The enemy of revolutions sympathized with the regeneration of Greece. He made two demands of the Sultan: in concert with the other Powers, he insisted that an end should be put to the extermination of the Greeks, and in his own name he asked for satisfaction for the bloody outrages inflicted on the orthodox Christians since the massacre of Constantinople, and for the insults offered to his ambassador. On one side he, like the rest of Europe, invoked the rights of humanity; on the other, he vindicated his privileges as protector of the members of the orthodox Church, guaranteed by the treaties of Kaïrnadji and Bucharest. Sometimes he acted in unison with Europe, sometimes he stood apart from her, in order to act separately and more energetically.

In March 1826, Nicholas had presented his ultimatum to the Divan. His conditions were—1. The evacuation of the Danubian principalities (occupied by the Turks, under the pretext of the insurrection of 1821) and the re-establishment of affairs on the basis of treaties. 2. The execution of the clauses of the Treaty of Bucharest, relative to the autonomy of Servia, and the liberation of the Servian deputies who were detained in Constantinople. 3. Satisfaction on the debated points, and the despatch of an Ottoman plenipotentiary. The Porte tried to resist, but the European Powers persuaded her to yield. On the 26th of September (8th of October) the Convention of Akkerman was concluded on the following conditions:—1. The confirmation of the Treaty of Bucharest. 2. The autonomy of Moldavia and Wallachia, under a hospodar elected for seven years in an assembly of nobles, and who could only be deposed with the consent of Russia. 3. The final cession to Russia of the disputed territories on the Asiatic frontier. 4. Seven years' delay to enable the Porte to organize Servia in accordance with the Treaty of Bucharest. 5. Fair satisfaction to the Russian subjects who were creditors of the Turkish Government. 6. Free passage for Russian vessels from the Black Sea to the Mediterranean.

The Greek question still remained. The Duke of Wellington and Count Nesselrode had come to an agreement in the St. Petersburg conferences. The Anglo-Russian protocol of the 26th of March, 1826, energetically supported by the French ambassador, was presented to the Porte by the representatives of the three Powers. Greece was to be an autonomous dependency of Turkey, was to pay an annual tribute to the Sultan, to be governed by authorities elected by herself, but over the nomination of whom the Porte was to exercise a certain influence. The Turks settled in Greece were to emigrate, and to receive an equivalent for their fixtures. The Divan rejected these propositions as "violating the passive obedience owed by subjects to their legitimate sovereign." France, England, and Russia then signed the Treaty of London (June 1827), in virtue of which they imposed their mediation on the belligerents, Turkey and Greece. The Porte, when informed of this, replied by disembarking a Turco-Egyptian army in the Morea, under the command of Ibrahim. The three Western squadrons, commanded by Admirals de Rigny, Heiden, and Codrington, received orders to hinder, even by force the prolongation of hostilities in the Peninsula. The Turkish fleet was then annihilated in the battle of Navarino (20th of October, 1827). Nicholas addressed flattering letters to the French and English admirals, with the Order of St. Alexander Nevski for M. de Rigny, and that of St. George for Codrington.

The disaster of Navarino only exasperated Sultan Mahmoud. He sent the three Powers a note in which he demanded that prior to any negotiation he should receive a formal declaration that they would renounce all interference in the affairs of Turkey and Greece, make public and solemn reparation for the insult offered to the Ottoman flag, and pay an indemnity to the Porte for the injuries which it had suffered. In the mosques a holy war was proclaimed, and a general levy. At Constantinople, such a phantom of a national representation as we have again seen recently, was convoked.

England already regretted the destruction of the Turkish fleet, but France, in order to give the force of law to the decisions of the Powers, disembarked a body of troops in the Morea under General Maison, who expelled the Turco-Egyptians from the Peninsula. Nicholas, joining his private grievances to the claims of Europe, declared war on Turkey, and ordered Field-Marshal Wittgenstein to cross the Pruth, while Paskiévitch entered Asia Minor. In Europe the Russians occupied Wallachia and Moldavia, passed the Danube under the eyes of their Emperor, and took Braïlof and Varna. In Asia they carried by assault the ancient fortress of Kars, defeated the Turks under Akhaltsykh, and captured the town after a bloody action.

England began to be uneasy, and Austria made advances to her. Charles X. openly said, "If the Emperor Nicholas attacks Austria, I will hold myself in reserve, and regulate my conduct according to circumstances; but if Austria attacks, I will instantly march against her." The Restoration hoped to find in the struggle in the East a revenge for the treaties of 1815. The "reunion" to France of the left bank of the Rhine or of Belgium was discussed in the king's council in September 1829; and the co-operation of Russia was counted on, in exchange for the aid France was giving her on the Danube. In a word, according to the expression of M. Nettement, the two Powers were then closely united, "France against the European *statu quo*, Russia against the Oriental *statu quo*."

Nicholas was therefore free for the campaign of 1829. In Asia, Paskiévitch defeated two Turkish armies and captured Erzeroum; in Europe, Diébitch, successor to Wittgenstein, defeated the Grand Vizier at Koulevtcha, near Pravady, and threw him back in disorder on the fortified camp of Shumla, after having killed 5000 men and taken forty-three guns. After the capitulation of Silistria, he blockaded Shumla, boldly crossed the Balkans, and entered Adrianople, the second city of the Ottoman empire. At sea the frigate *Mercury* fought two Turkish ships; her crew had sworn either to conquer or to blow themselves up.

At last the Porte yielded. Mahmoud had destroyed the Janissaries, and had not yet constituted a regular army. Persia refused to undertake a new war against Russia. At Adrianople the Porte concluded two treaties—one with the European Powers, and the other with Russia. In the first, she agreed to adhere to the treaty of 1817, and recognized the independence of Greece. By the second she surrendered to Russia the isles of the Danubian delta in Europe, and the fortresses and districts of Anapa, Poti, Akhaltsykh, and Akhalkalaki, in Asia; she paid an indemnity of 119 million francs,* and another of 1,500,000 ducats to the Russian merchants. The immunities formerly granted to Moldavia, Wallachia, and Servia were guaranteed, and the Bosphorus and Dardanelles declared free and opened to all the Powers at peace with the Porte. Russian commerce had access to the Black Sea Thus this first alliance with France had secured the independence of Greece, and prepared for that of the Roumanians and Servians.

From 1840 to 1841 England was occupied with the famous opium war in China The Russians had previously obtained, with less trouble, a much more advantageous footing in the Celestial Empire. By the treaty of 1827 they had acquired the right to establish at Pekin a place of education, where young men might study the language and customs of China. Nicholas had carefully avoided clashing with the Court of Pekin on the subject of opium; and when he heard of the prohibition, he forbade his subjects to introduce this commodity across the Russian frontier. In 1852 a new commercial treaty was made, which opened a market on the Irtych. This Western market, so called in opposition to the Eastern market of Kiakhta, afforded the Russian agents an opportunity of more closely surveying Bokhara. In spite of these cordial relations, the Russian outposts daily and noiselessly encroached on the Chinese territory; and in 1854 European was astonished to find them established on the Amour. Thus, from one end of Asia to the other, Russia and England found themselves face to face. In their attempts to push back their frontiers and to extend their influence, both hastened the inevitable moment when they would be in direct conflict.

By the acquisition of Mingrelia, Imeritia, and Georgia, the Chirvan, and the Persian and Turkish provinces, Russia had possession of the whole southern slope of the Caucasus: by the acquisition of Daghestan she had set her foot on the northern side, and thus completely surrounded the vast mountainous regions which constitute Circassia and Abkhasia. Numerous forts occupied the openings of the valleys. The warlike Tcherkesses and Abkhasians, however, bravely defended their independence. The road from Anapa to Poti was very unsafe, notwithstanding the number of fortified posts. Nicholas was sensible of the necessity of securing communications with Southern Asia by both extremities of the Caucasus and by intermediate

* £4,760,000.

passes, and of making this enormous chain the impregnable citadel from the height of which he was to rule the East. This war with the mountain tribes, fertile in surprises and ambuscades, was a mingled success and failure. It took a more formidable development when Moslem fanaticism, awakened by the sectarian professors of Mirditism, embodied itself in Schamyl, the soldier priest, who gave to these rival races religious unity, and who for twenty-five years held the best Russian generals in check. In 1844, 200,000 men were posted in the Caucasus under the brave and able Voronzof. The English furtively favored the insurrection, and the seizure, in 1837, of the British schooner *Vixen*, as she was unloading arms on the coast of Abkhasia, made some noise Bell, an Englishman, was found at the head of the Georgians in their short revolt.

Persia, where Fet-Aly-Shah, the ally of Napoleon 1., had been succeeded by his grandson Mohammed, was completely under Russian influence. In 1837 and 1838 Mohammed laid seige to Herat, which commanded one of the routes to India. The English obliged him to raise the siege by creating a diversion in the Persian Gulf. They followed up this by another in 1856, and secured the Isle of Karrack and the Port of Bushire. Three years after the siege of Herat the English themselves failed to capture Cabul.

Nicholas, in search of an opening in another direction, declared war against the Khan of Khiva, under the pretext of putting an end to the exactions and robberies practised against the caravans. In 1841 an army led by General Perovski crossed the steppes of Turkestan during a severe winter, but, after gaining some advantages over the nomad tribes, was forced to fall back on the Emba. The Russian army was almost entirely destroyed by fatigue and the severity of the climate. The intimidated Khan, however, offered satisfaction. He decreed the penalty of death against any Khivan who should dare to attempt the life or liberty of a Russian subject, and gave back 415 captives. It was clear that a serious attempt against Khiva would not be practicable till the enormous distance of 200 leagues, which separated this oasis from the Russian frontiers, should be diminished by the establishment of a line of posts, by the more complete subjection of the Turkish hordes, and by the construction of a fleet on the Sea of Aral. The expedition of 1854 was a great success; the Khan then became a kind of vassal of the Tzar, closely watched by the Russian resident.

THE POLISH INSURRECTION (1831).

Towards 1830 Russia found herself in a singular state of uneasiness. The cholera had just made its appearance; fierce revolts had broken out at Sebastopol, Novgorod, and Staraïa-Roussa. The Emperor seemed agitated by gloomy presentiments. He had been shocked by the news of the July revolution, which had expelled his ally, Charles X.; the Belgian and the Italian revolutions followed close on each other. The tricolored flag, the flag of 1799 and 1812, floating over the French Consulate at Warsaw, hastened the explosion of the Polish Revolution.

The time was already far behind when Alexander, while opening the Diet of 1818, boasted of "those liberal institutions which had never ceased to be the object of his solicitude," and which allowed him to show to Russia herself "what he had for so long prepared for her." The time was far away when he congratulated the Polish deputies on having rejected the proposed law of divorce, and proclaimed "that, freely elected, they must freely vote."

No doubt the prosperity of the kingdom was increasing. Commerce and industry had developed, the finances were in a satisfactory state, and from the remnant of the Napoleonic legions the Grand Duke Constantine had formed an excellent army of 60,000 men. Unhappily it was very difficult for Alexander, who had become more and more autocratic in Russia, to accommodate himself in Poland to the liberty of a representative government. The Diet of 1820 had irritated him profoundly by its attack on the ministers, and its rejection of certain projects of law. He looked on these ordinary incidents of parliamentary life as an attempt to undermine his authority. He lent an ear to the counsels of Karamsin and Araktchéef. He put forth an "additional act of the constitution" which suppressed the public sittings of the Diet. After the session of 1822, the convocation of the Estates was adjourned indefinitely. The liberty of the press was restrained, and the police became more vexatious. The soldiers complained of the severity, and sometimes of the brutality, of the Grand Duke Constantine, who was full of good intentions, who loved Poland, and had given proof of it by sacrificing the crown of Russia for a Polish lady, but who could never control his impetuous and eccentric character. The officers who had served under Dombrovski, Poniatovski, and Napoleon could scarcely reconcile themselves to the Muscovite discipline. Ancient jealousies and national hate, revived by the events of

1812, were on the point of breaking out between the two peoples. Besides the Polish malcontents who grumbled at the violations of the Constitution of 1815, and were enraged at the Emperor for not having restored to the kingdom the palatinates of White Russia, there was the party which dreamed of the Constitution of the 3rd of May, 1791, or of a republic, and which desired to re-establish Poland in her ancient independence, and within her ancient limits. The secret associations of the Templars and the Patriotic Society were formed. The trial of the Russian *décembristes* had revealed an understanding between the conspirators of the two nations.

Constantine had made another mistake, that of persuading the Emperor Nicholas that the Polish army should not be employed against the Turks. He loved this army after his own fashion, and his saying has been quoted, "I detest war; it spoils an army." Victories gained in common over the ancient enemy of the two peoples might have created a bond of military fraternity between the Russian and Polish armies, given an opening to the warlike ardor of the Polish youth, and crowned with glory the union of the two crowns. Constantine's unpopularity increased in consequence of this error. Nothing, however, was as yet imperilled. When the Emperor Nicholas came to open the Diet of May 1830 in person, his presence in Warsaw excited some hopes. In spite of the reserve which the deputies had imposed on themselves, they could not refrain from rejecting the unhappy scheme of the law of divorce, from lodging complaints against the ministers, and uttering a wish for the reunion with the Lithuanian provinces. This wish could not, of course, be granted by Nicholas, without deeply wounding the patriotism and the rights of Russia. The "King of Poland" and his subjects separated with discontent on both sides; the secret societies were more active in their conspiracies, and the news from Paris found all the elements of a revolution already prepared.

On the evening of the 17th–29th of November the youths belonging to the School of the Standard-bearers revolted at the command of the Sub-Lieutenant Wysocki. They demanded cartridges: "Cartridges," cried Wysocki, "you will find them in the boxes of the Russians! Forward!" Whilst 130 of them surprised the barracks of the Russian cavalry, a handful rushed to the palace of the Belvedere, where the Tzarévitch resided. Constantine had just time to escape; the director of police and other officials fell beneath the blows of the conspirators. In a few moments all the Polish troops, the infantry, a battalion of sappers, the horse artillery, and a regiment of grenadiers, hastened to the arsenal, seized 40,000 muskets, and distributed arms among the insurgent people. Five Polish generals, accused of treason to the national cause, were put to death. The brave General Noviçki, victim of a mistaken identity, suffered the same fate. The Grand Duke, seeing the insurrection spread, decided to evacuate the town and retire to the village of Wirzba; he even sent back to Warsaw the Polish regiment of mounted sharp-shooters who had alone remained loyal.

Prince Lubeçk hastened to convoke the council of administration, to which was added a certain number of influential citizens. The majority of this council considered the struggle with Russia an act of madness, and entreated the people to " end all their agitations with the night, which had covered them with her mantle." This advice was not listened to: the crowd summoned other men to the head of affairs,—the Princes Czartoryski and Ostrovski, Malakhovski, and the celebrated professor and historian Lélével. The students were organized into a crack regiment; Lélével opened a patriotic club, and published a daily paper; the patriot Chlopiçki, a brave officer who had served with distinction under Napoleon, was appointed generalissimo, but Chlopiçki saw no hope for Poland save in a prompt reconciliation with the Emperor. He despatched envoys to St. Petersburg, to the Grand Duke's head-quarters, and even to London and Paris, to obtain the mediation of the Western Powers. Two parties were concerned in this movement—the moderate party, who wished to mend the link that they had broken with the legal government by soliciting, at the most, a reform of the constitution and the annexation of the Lithuanian palatinates; and the party of the democrats, who insisted on the abdication of the Romanofs, the restoration to the country of its independence, and the recovery by arms of the lost provinces. Nicholas repelled all efforts to treat which were not preceded by an immediate and unconditional submission. His proclamation deprived the insurgents of all hopes " of obtaining concessions as the price of their crimes." From that time the war party at Warsaw triumphed over the peace party. Chlopiçki, disgusted with the conduct of the more advanced spirits, had resigned the post of generalissimo. He finally accepted the dictatorship, and gave himself up, without any hope of success, to organizing the defence, while continuing the negotiations. He and Lélével were particularly uncongenial: the latter was of opinion that the Poles ought to take the offensive, throw themselves into Lithuania and Volhynia, arm the peasants, and raise a levy *en masse*; declaring that when an insurrection did not spread it was certain to fail. " Well, then," exclaimed Chlopiçki impatiently, " make war with your reapers yourself," and he resigned his command a second time for a subordinate post.

NICHOLAS I.

Russia, vol. two.

The Diet now assembled and appointed Prince Radzivill, a weak man, without military talents, generalissimo. His election was hailed by cries of " To Lithuania! to Lithuania ! " In the session of the 13th-25th January, Count Ezerski, one of the two negotiators sent by Chlopiçki to St. Petersburg, gave an account of their interview with the Emperor. The replies of Nicholas did not give more ground for hope than his proclamation of the 17th of December. He refused to parley with rebel subjects. He at once rejected the idea of despoiling Russia of the Lithuanian provinces for the benefit of Poland. He considered it a sacred duty to stifle the insurrection and punish the guilty, adding that if the nation took up arms against him Poland would be crushed by Polish guns. Then the Diet proclaimed the Romanofs to have forfeited the throne. It hoped by this step to engage the sympathy of the Western courts, but in reality it rendered all attempts at pacific mediation impossible; the Poles having abandoned the ground of the treaties of 1815, the only ones to which European diplomacy could appeal. As to an armed intervention in the presence of the hostility of the German Powers, neither England nor France could dream of such a thing. In vain the population of Paris made energetic manifestations of its sympathies, in vain the Chambers resounded with warlike addresses; all these demonstrations had no effect. Six days after its declaration of freedom, the Polish government instituted a provisional government composed of five members: Adam Czartoryski, president; Barzikovski, Niemoievski, Morazski, and Joachim Lélével, who represented democratic tendencies in this supreme council.

The Tzarévitch had completely evacuated the kingdom; Modlin and all the other fortresses were in the hands of the rebels. To protect Warsaw on the east, they had thrown up a formidable work to cover the bridge : the Polish forces with the new levies amounted to 90,000 men, well provided with artillery. In February, 1831, an army of 120,000 Russians, under the command of Diébitch *Zabalkanski,* the hero of the Balkans, entered Poland in a severe frost, driving back the Polish detachments into Warsaw. The insurgent General Dverniéki gained an advantage at the skirmish of Stoczek. A two days' battle at Grochov, glorious for Poland (19th and 20th February), did not hinder the Russians from approaching Warsaw, and the combats of Bialolenska and of the wood of Praga (24th and 25th of February) brought them nearly up to the Praga quarter. Radzivill then resigned his office, and was succeeded by Skrzynecki. The main body of the Russian army had abandoned the bank of the Vistula, with the exception of three small corps—that of **Rosen** at Dembévilkié, that of Geismas at Waver, and a third under Praga. The Polish general attacked them suddenly, and defeated Geismar at Waver and Rosen at Dembévilkié and Iganié, but did not dare to push his advantages further. An expedition directed against Volhynia by Dverniçki failed completely; he was driven back into Gallicia

The Lithuanian expedition ended in a disaster under Wilna; the Poles had to cross the Prussian frontier, and only one division, that of Dembinski, re-entered Warsaw. In the interval, Skrzyneçki having attacked the right wing of the Russians at Ostrolenka on the Narev, was, after a severe fight forced back on the other side of the river (26th of May). Cholera raged in both armies, and carried off successively Diébitch and the Grand Duke Constantine.

Political divisions now as always ruined Poland. After some violent scenes, Skrzyneçki was replaced by Dembinski, and then by Malekhovski. Two days' revolt made the streets run with blood, and the people committed massacres in the prisons. The moderate party took flight, and Czartoryski fled in disguise. The provisional government resigned its power into the hands of the Diet, who invested General Krukoviéçki with the office of dictator. He had some of the mutineers executed, but was not able to re-establish order.

Paskiévitch Erivanski, Diébitch's successor, strengthened by the benevolent help of Prussia, which had thrown open to him her arsenals and magazines of Dantzig and Königsberg, had crossed the Vistula below Warsaw, and transported the theatre of war to the left bank. He intended to attack the capital, not from the side of Praga, as Souvorof had done, but from the side of Vola and the Czysté quarter. Two semicircles of concentric intrenchments corresponded to these two quarters, but the Russians had no longer, as on the side of Praga, to overcome the obstacle of the Vistula. On the 6th of September the Russians attacked Vola, where General Sovinski, who had lost a leg at the Moskowa, and Wysoçki, who began the revolution were killed. The same day Paskiévitch began to cannonade Czysté and the town. The next morning Krukoviéçki asked to capitulate. Paskiévitch exacted the unconditional submission of the army and the people, the immediate surrender of Warsaw, the reconstruction of the bridge of Praga, and the retreat of the troops on Ploçk. The Diet having allowed the time fixed for a reply to pass, Paskiévitch began the attack. Krukoviéçki had accepted his terms, but he had been replaced in the interval by Niemoievski. Czysté was already in flames, and the Russians were scaling the ramparts, when the Poles capitulated. " Sire,

Warsaw is at your feet," wrote Paskiévitch to the Emperor. "Order reigns at Warsaw," such was the funeral oration pronounced by official Europe over the insurrection. Twenty thousand soldiers laid down their arms at Ploçk, 15,000 of whom Ramorino took into Gallicia.

Not only Warsaw, but Poland herself, lay at the feet of Nicholas. Partial insurrections and new plots were later to revive his resentment. At present he was happy at being able to make an example, and intimidate the European revolution. Sequestrations, confiscations, imprisonments, and banishments to Siberia served as commentaries on the amnesty. The constitution granted by Alexander was annulled; the public offices were abolished and replaced by mere commissions emanating from the public offices of Russia; the directors of these commissions formed, under the management of the *namiestnik*, the council of government. No more diets; Poland was administered by the officials of the Tzar. No more Polish army; it was lost in the imperial army. The national orders were only preserved as Russian orders, distributed among the most zealous servants of the government. The Russian systems of taxes, justice, and coinage were successively introduced into the kingdom. The ancient historical palatinates gave way to Russian provinces; the ancient divisions were modified. These governments amounted to five after 1844: Warsaw, Radom, Lublin, Ploçk, and Modlin. Thus were matters ordered in Poland proper.

In Lithuania and White Russia, the Polish element was more narrowly watched: the germs of nationality left by the educational policy of Czartoryski were stifled. In reply to the Lithuanian insurrection, the University of Wilna was suppressed, and the Polish language banished from the schools. In order to attach the south-west provinces more closely to Russia, Nicholas, supported by Bishop Joseph Siemaszko, abolished the *Union*. The Uniate bishops and clergy signed the act of Polotsk, by which they entreated to be admitted into the bosom of the national orthodox Church—a request that the Holy Synod hastened to gratify (1839). Part of the monks and the faithful resisted. Siémaszko, now made Metropolitan as the reward of his services, organized missions in which an amount of violence and zeal was used to destroy the Union, equal to that which the Jesuit party of the 17th century had employed to cement it. The affair of the nuns of Minsk made a special scandal. The orthodox peasants profited, however, by this revolution. In order to protect them against the ill-will of their masters who had remained Catholics or Uniates, the authorities of White Russia and Lithuania were desired to make "inventories" which would exactly determine the amount of their rents and the sum of their dues. The "inventories" put an end to the despotism of the nobles: this was the beginning of emancipation.

ILL-FEELING AGAINST FRANCE: THE EASTERN QUESTION; REVOLUTION OF 1848; INTERVENTION IN HUNGARY.

The Polish insurrection had resulted, as to general policy, in a more intimate union between the three Powers of the North, which bound themselves by a treaty to deliver up each other's rebel subjects; and in a kind of rupture between Russia and the Western Powers, most of which had given evidence of their sympathy for the Polish cause. Nicholas I., the chief representative of European conservatism, looked on France as the hotbed of perpetual revolutions. He wished the world to be immovable; now Paris periodically shook the soil of Europe with her "days." The Revolution of 1830 had overthrown his ally Charles X., caused Belgium and Central Italy to revolt, and the insurrection of Poland was a consequence of it. The sympathies of the French for Poland were strongly manifested; there had been some riots at Paris, and windows were broken at the Russian embassy. Fourteen addresses were successively presented in the Chambers at each new session; the proscribed Poles nowhere received a warmer welcome, and Polish schools were provided for their children. Under the French protection the European revolution and the Polish emigration had become close allies. In Hungary, in Turkey, in the Caucasus, Nicholas was everywhere to find these guests of France, these exiles. He had not waited for these acts of hostility to declare himself against the French. His relations with Louis Philippe, the July king, were a long series of frets, of annoyances, of scarcely disguised insults. In his reply to the notification of the accession of the new sovereign, he had designated the revolution which had given Louis Philippe his crown as an "event for ever to be deplored." He affected a polite impertinence towards the representatives of France, or gave them to understand that the respect he paid them was a tribute merely to their personal merit, and not to their diplomatic quality. MM. de Bourgoing, de Barante, Marshal Maison, and Casimir Périer the younger, were placed one after another in this false position.

The ill-will of Nicholas was shown by acts of a graver kind —by threatening manifestations and displays of military force, by meetings of sovereigns, which seemed ominous of the reconstitution of the Holy Alliance, by attempts at coalition, and even by flagrant violations of treaties. Nicholas was one day to expiate cruelly the dangerous satisfaction to his pride which he derived from these vain provocations to France and the new ideas. This situation of king of kings, of head of the monarchical governments, of arbiter of Europe, which he was allowed to hold by the complaisance of Austria and Prussia, was more apparent than real, and had more *prestige* than force. Once more the so-called policy of principles was to bring misfortune to Russia.

When in December, 1832, the Egyptian army under Ibrahim, victorious at Beïlan and Konieh, seemed to threaten Constantinople, Turkey appealed to the European Powers. Russia was the first to reply by sending her fleet to the Bosphorus, by disembarking 10,000 men on the coast of Asia, and causing 24,000 men to advance to the Pruth. France and England protested through Admiral Ronsin and Lord Ponsonby, and obtained the withdrawal of the Russian forces, the retreat of the Egyptian army, and the treaty of Kutaieh between the Sultan and the Khedive. All seemed to have ended quietly, when a rumor spread that Count Orlof had signed with the Porte the Treaty of Unkiar-Skélessi, which, under the appearance of an offensive and defensive alliance, established the dependence of Turkey on Russia (8th of June, 1833). Each of the two contracting parties engaged to furnish to the other the aid necessary " to secure the tranquillity of its States." This latter article might, in such a distracted country as Turkey, involve a permanent occupation by the Russian forces. By a secret article the Sultan undertook, if the Tzar were attacked, to close the Dardanelles, and to permit no foreign ships to pass through them, on any pretext whatever. England and France protested loudly. This treaty, however, was never executed.

When the war between Egypt and Turkey re-commenced, and Sultan Mahmoud was succeeded by his son Abdul-Medjid (1839), Nicholas took advantage of the lively sympathy shown by France for the Viceroy to isolate her completely from the other Powers. England, always anxious to maintain the integrity of the Ottoman empire, separated herself from France to join the Russians, and associated herself with the conspiracy, whose aim was to exclude the French from the assembly of European Powers. The Tzar saw with satisfaction the affront offered to France by the Treaty of London (15th of July, 1840), concluded between Great Britain, Russia, Austria, and Prussia; the irritation caused at Paris by the intervention of the English, Austrians, and Turks in Syria; the embarrassment into which the French were thrown by the warlike policy of Thiers' cabinet and the imminence of a conflict, where for such a poor stake they would have a general coalition of the great Powers against them. England, which had forsaken France to defend Turkey against Egypt, soon felt the necessity of returning to her, to guarantee Constantinople against the Russian protectorate. On the occasion of the "Convention of the Straits" (13th of July, 1841) France regained her European position. Nicholas had played the singular part of protector of the Ottoman integrity; he had allied himself with the enemy and his natural rival, England; but at the price of these inconsistencies he had given himself the pleasure of humiliating the government of Louis Philippe, and of exposing him to the dangers of a general war.

During all this period he had redoubled his ill offices towards France. In 1833 he had convoked the Congress of Münchengrätz, where the sovereigns of Russia, Austria, and Prussia, and their principal ministers, assembled. In 1835, at the manœuvres of Kalisch, he had reviewed an army of 90,000 men, in the presence of the King of Prussia, the Austrian archdukes, and a multitude of princes. On the death of Charles X. he ordered a court mourning of twenty-four days.

In 1846 troubles broke out in Austrian Gallicia. The upper classes had made great preparations for a rising against Austria, and the peasants in their turn revolted against their lords. The free city of Cracow had given an asylum to the refugees, and had allowed a provisional Polish government to be installed there, which attempted to reconcile the peasants and their masters by promising to the former the abolition of slavery, and the division of all national property. Nicholas, in his character of queller of revolutions, found work here. His troops were the first to enter Cracow, where they were followed by those of Austria and Prussia. The sovereigns declared the republic of Cracow to be suppressed, and the town itself to be annexed to Austria. France and England could only protest against this violation of the treaties of 1815.

The Revolution of 1848 shook Europe with a violence which had been hitherto unfelt. Not only all Italy and Western Germany followed the movement, but the countries which till now had seemed opposed to the new ideas, and which had been the bulwark of monarchic Europe against the revolutionary spirit, caught the infection, and the excitement spread even to the frontiers of Russia. The German constitution was overthrown; the Germans called a parliament at Frankfort; the Slavs called the Congress of Prague. The Emperor Ferdinand was expelled from Vienna; at Berlin, Frederic William IV. saluted the corpses which were displayed by the revolutionists; Hungary rose at the voice of Kossuth ; even the Danubian principalities, influenced by the party of Roumanian unity, dethroned the Hospodar Bibesco in Wallachia, and the Hospodar Stourdza in Moldavia. Where would the movement stop? Plots were discovered in Russia ; Poland, whose flags the Parisian workmen waved in their tumultuous processions, quivered with eagerness.

The Emperor Nicholas planted himself in the face of revolutionary Europe. He first acted in the countries nearest to him; he used his influence with the King of Prussia to prevent him from accepting the imperial crown of Germany ; he protested against the events in Bucharest, and sent an army to the principalities ; he seized the moment when the Hungarian insurrection had received a shock from the counter Croat insurrection, to respond to the appeal of the young Emperor Francis Joseph. In Hungary too, the Russian regiments were to encounter their old enemies of 1799, 1812, and 1831—the irreconcilable Polish legions, re-organized under Ben and Dembinski. Paskiévitch was charged to complete in the plains of Hungary his victory over Poland. He defeated the Polish-Hungarian army at many points, occupied all Transylvania, and obliged the generalissimo Georgey to sign the capitulation of Villagos in the open country (12th of August, 1849). " Hungary is at the feet of your Majesty," writes Paskiévitch. Nicholas put it under the feet of Francis Joseph, who treated it more cruelly than Nicholas had treated Poland.

The Tzar's intervention in the Danish question had more happy results. Nicholas obliged the Prussians to withdraw their troops from the duchies, and their support from the revolted Holsteiners. In 1852 he joined the other Powers to cause the integrity of the Danish monarch to be recognized at the Treaty of London (8th May).

At the other extremity of Europe arose a man who seemed to work with Nicholas to put an end to the European revolution. By the expedition to Rome, he extinguished the Italian republic ; by the December *coup d'état*, the French republic. Nicholas, almost reconciled to the hated name of Bonaparte, and to the imminent restoration of a Napoleonic empire, remarked: " France has set an evil example ; she will now set a good one. I have faith in the conduct of Louis Napoleon." The Second Empire was to force him to expiate his hostile and mpolitic conduct towards the July monarchy and the republic of 1848. His desire for the *coup d'état* was realized to his own hurt. His power blazed for the last time when, on the 15th of May, 1852, he reviewed the Austrian army on the slopes of Vienna, and pressed to his heart that Austrian sovereign " whose ingratitude was to astonish Europe."

SECOND TURKISH WAR ; THE ALLIES IN THE CRIMEA—AWAKENING OF RUSSIAN OPINION.

Nicholas was irritated to see his influence in the East held in check by France and Austria. In the question of the " holy places," France had just obtained a solution favorable to the pretensions of the Catholic Powers. " The Porte authorized the Latins to build an ambry in the cave of Bethlehem." After Omar Pacha's invasion of Montenegro, it was the Austrian ambassador who, without the aid of Russia, had procured the retreat of the Ottoman troops. Nicholas affected to see in these two decisions of the Porte an attempt to annul the right of protectorate over the Eastern Christians, conferred on the Russian sovereign by the treaties of Kaïrnadji, Bucharest, and Adrianople. Prince Menchikof was sent to Constantinople with orders to obtain a new recognition of his right, and guarantees for the future. The Porte, feeling herself supported by France—on the 20th of March a French fleet had appeared in the Greek waters—refused ; and Menchikof, after having uselessly presented his ultimatum, abruptly broke off the negotiations, and quitted Constantinople. England hesitated to take part in a quarrel in which she saw little but the question of the " holy places " and the pretensions of France : but on the 9th and 14th of January, 1853, two private interviews between Nicholas and the English ambassador, Sir Hamilton Seymour, revealed to the British minister the ultimate aim of all the Emperor's schemes. Their aim was nothing less than to wind up the bankrupt estate of the " sick man." Servia, the Principalities, and Bulgaria were to form independent States under the protection of Nicholas. As to Constantinople, if circumstances obliged him to occupy it, he would establish himself there as trustee and not as proprietor. England should in her turn be free to appropriate territories at her convenience, provided she did not stretch out her hand for Constantinople. " Now," he said, " it is as a friend and a gentleman that I speak to you : if England and myself can come to an understanding about this affair, the rest matters little to me, and I shall care very little as to what *the others* may think or do." He insisted on this latter point. " If we are only agreed, I am completely at ease about the West of Europe ; what *the others* may think at the bottom of their heart is of small importance." These " others " were first France and then Austria. Nicholas flattered himself that he could persuade and carry away the English; but it did not enter into his calculations that Napoleonic France could ever form an alliance with the England of Waterloo, of St. Helena, and of Hudson Lowe. The imprudent confidence to Seymour rendered the strange alliance possible. England took fright, and it was now her turn to urge France to energetic measures. The invasion of the Principalities appeared to her to be the first step towards the execution of the schemes of dismemberment.

On the 3rd of July, 1853, the Russian troops crossed the Pruth, under the command of General Gortchakof. Nicholas published a proclamation, in which he announced that he did not intend to begin the war, but that he wished to have some securities on which he could rely for the Divan's strict execution of the treaties. The English and French fleets now approached the threatened points, and took up a position in Besika Bay, without crossing the Straits, which the conditions of the treaties still kept closed to ships of war. Russia, however, declared in a circular that this transaction was a threat, which was sure to cause new complications.

Austria proposed that a conference should assemble at Vienna, and delegates from the five Powers met and took part in it. Prussia had made advances to Austria. At this moment peace might have been secured. The Tzar was disposed to make certain concessions, provided his right to the protectorate was recognized; but Turkey took the initiative in war by summoning Russia to evacuate the Principalities. The Turks displayed more energy in this war on the Danube than the Russians expected. On November 30, 1853, the destruction of the Turkish fleet at Sinope by Admiral Nakhimof destroyed all hopes of localizing the war. The French and English fleets, which at the beginning of hostilities had entered the Bosphorus, now sailed into the Black Sea, and obliged the Russian fleet to withdraw into ports.

On the 26th of January, 1853, Napoleon III. had addressed an autograph letter to Nicholas as a last attempt at peace. Things, however, had now gone too far, and the Tzar's reply left no alternative but to make war. Meanwhile, England had published Seymour's despatches about his interview with Nicholas, and this violation of the secrecy asked by the Emperor, "speaking as a friend and a gentleman," profoundly irritated Russia. The consequences of these revelations were very serious. France, Austria, and Prussia, saw how completely Nicholas intended to sacrifice them, and were stung by his contempt for all that " the others " might think or do. On the 12th of March, 1854, France and England assured Turkey of their support. On the 10th of April an offensive and defensive treaty of alliance was concluded. On the 20th, Austria, which was making a threatening concentration of troops on the Danube, signed with Prussia a treaty of guarantee and a treaty of alliance in case the Tzar attacked Austria or crossed the Balkans. Nicholas had found means to unite the whole of Europe against him.

The immense superiority of the navy of the allies allowed them to attack Russia in all her seas. In the Black Sea they bombarded the military port of Odessa (22nd of April, 1854), while respecting the town and the commercial port. The Russian settlements on the coast of the Caucasus—Anapa, Redout-Kale, and Soukoum-Kale—had been burned by the Russians themselves. In the Baltic the allies blockaded Cronstadt, disembarked on the isles of Aland, took the fortress of Bomarsund (16th of August 1854), and in 1855 bombarded Sveaborg. In the White Sea they attacked the fortified monastery of Solovetski. In the Sea of Okhotsk they blockaded the Siberian ports, destroyed the arsenal of Petropavlovsk, and threatened the position of the Russians on the river Amour.

The Russians, menaced by the Austrian concentration on the Danube, by the disembarkation of the French and English (first at Gallipoli and then at Varna), made a last effort to take Silistria, the siege of which (April to July) had already cost them many men. They failed. In the Dobrudscha, an expedition directed by the French had no military results, but the army was decimated by the cholera and fevers from the marshes. The Russians decided to evacuate the Principalities, which were then occupied by the Austrians, according to an agreement with Europe and the Sultan. The war on the Danube was ended; the Crimean war had begun!*

It had been finally resolved on in a council held at Varna on the 21st of July between the generals of the French, English, and Turkish armies. On the 14th of September, 500 ships landed the expeditionary troops near Eupatoria; on the 20th, the battle of the Alma opened them the way to Sebastopol. This was a thunderbolt to Russia. Since 1812 no enemy had landed on her soil; the Crimea, protected by a formidable fleet, impregnable fortresses, and a numerous army, seemed secure from all attacks. Now the army was beaten, and the Black Sea fleet, which had retreated to the harbor of Sebastopol, only served to obstruct the channel. Sebastopol itself was so badly protected

* See Camille Rousset, ' Histoire de la Guerre de Crimée,' 2 vols. with an atlas : and M. Rambaud's ' Français et Russes, Moscou et Sevastopol.'

and armed—at least, on the land side—that many officers still think that a bold march of the allies on Sebastopol would have made them masters of the town.

When, however, the first moment's surprise had passed, the Russians set to work. In a few days they repaired years of carelessness or official peculation. Townsfolk, soldiers, and sailors labored at the earthworks. In a very short time, thanks to their marvellous activity, the stony soil of the Chersonesus was raised in redoubts, and in ramparts crowned with fascines. The bastions of the Centre, of the Mast, of the two Redans, and of the Malakof, all afterwards so celebrated, bristled with guns taken from the navy. Fourteen or fifteen thousand sailors, all eager to avenge the ruin of the fleet, came to reinforce the garrison. Admirals Kornilof, Istomine, and Nakhimof, who were all three to die on the bastion of the Malakof, directed the defence. The allies had marched on the port of Balaclava, which they had captured. They then took up a position on the south of Sebastopol, investing at the same time both the town and the Karabelnaïa, and getting supplies by the ports of Kamiesch and Balaclava. On the northern side, the beleaguered place communicated freely, by the bridges over the great harbor, with the Russian field-army, and could continually receive reinforcements and supplies. It was less a city besieged by an army than two armies intrenched opposite each other and keeping all their communications. Many times the allies were interrupted in their labors by the field-army ; and they had to give battle at Balaclava (25th October), at Inkermann (5th November), and at Eupatoria (17th February). Whilst the allies dug trenches, bored mines, and multiplied their batteries, the Russian engineers, directed by Todleben, strengthened the town fortifications, and built new ones—Transbalkan, Selinghinsk, Volhyne, and Kamschatka (White Works, Green Mamelon)—under the enemy's fire. The allies, in spite of the hardships of a severe winter, established themselves more and more firmly, braving in a corner of the Crimea all the forces of the empire of the Tzars.

On the day of the 26th of December, 1825, Nicholas had been consecrated, in the blood of conspirators, the armed apostle of the principle of authority, the exterminating angel of the counter-revolution. This position he had held for thirty years, not without glory. He had subdued the Polish, Hungarian, and Roumanian revolutions, and prevented Prussia from yielding to the seductions of the German revolution and to the appeals of disaffection in Holstein. He had, if not humiliated, at least troubled the French revolution in all its legal phases—

July royalty, republic, and empire. He had saved the Austrian empire, and hindered the creation of a democratic German empire. He stationed himself wherever the contrary principle made its appearance. People surnamed him the Don Quixote of autocracy: like Cervantes' hero, he possessed a chivalrous, generous, and disinterested spirit; but, like him too, he represented a superannuated principle in a new world. His part of chief of a chimerical Holy Alliance became more visibly an anachronism day by day. Since 1848 particularly, the "aspirations" of the people were in direct contradiction with his theories of patriarchal despotism. This opposition was apparent all through Europe. The Tzar's *prestige* began to suffer. In Russia he still contrived to sustain it: his successes in Turkey, Persia, the Caucasus, Poland, and Hungary, and the apparent deference of the European princes, permitted him to play his part of Agamemnon among kings. Russia hoped to indemnify herself for her internal submission by her external greatness. People forgot to exclaim at the interference of the police, at the fetters imposed on the press, at the intellectual isolation of Russia, and they renounced the control of government, diplomacy, war, and administration. The hard-working monarch, they thought, would foresee all, watch over all, and bring all to a happy conclusion. The men with liberal "aspirations," the discontented and critical spirits, were not listened to. In reply to the objections timidly expressed by a few, was urged the monarch's success. It seemed to justify absolute confidence and relinquishment of themselves to the Government.

The disasters in the East caused a terrible awakening. The invincible fleets of Russia were forced to take refuge in the ports, or to retreat into the harbor of Sebastopol. The army was vanquished at the Alma by the allies, at Silistria by the much-despised Turks. Fifty thousand Westerns installed under Sebastopol insulted the majesty of the empire; the allies of old had failed: Prussia was passive, Austria a traitor. The silence of the press had during thirty years favored the thefts of the *employés*: the fortresses and the armies had been ruined beforehand by administrative corruption. The nation had expected everything of the Government, and the Crimean war appeared as an immense bankruptcy of autocracy: the absolute and patriarchal monarchy handed in its schedule in face of the Anglo-French invasion. The greater men's hopes had been—the more people expected the conquest of Constantinople, the upheaval of the East, the extension of the Slav empire, the deliverance of Jerusalem—the harder and more cruel was the awakening. Then a vast movement was felt in Russia. Tongues were unloosed, and in default of the press an immense manuscript literature was secretly distributed. The Government was pelted with unexpected charges, accusing the Emperor, the ministers, the administration, the diplomatists, the generals, every one at once. "Arise, O Russia!" said one of these anonymous pamphlets. "Devoured by enemies, ruined by slavery, shamefully oppressed by the stupidity of *tchinovniks* and spies, awaken from thy long sleep of ignorance and apathy! We have been kept long enough in serfage by the successors of the Tatar khans. Arise, and stand erect and calm, before the throne of the despot; demand of him a reckoning of the national misfortunes. Tell him boldly that his throne is not the Altar of God, and that God has not condemned us forever to be slaves. Russia, O Tzar, had confided to thee the supreme power, and thou wert to her as a god upon earth. And what hast thou done? Blinded by passion and ignorance, thou hast sought nothing but power; thou hast forgotten Russia. Thou hast consumed thy life in reviewing troops, in altering uniforms, in signing the legislative projects of ignorant charlatans. Thou hast created a despicable race of censors of the press, that thou mightst sleep in peace, and never know the wants, never hear the murmurs of thy people, never listen to the voice of truth. Truth! thou hast buried her; thou hast rolled a great stone before the door of her sepulchre, thou hast placed a strong guard round her tomb, and in the exultation of thine heart thou hast said, 'For her, no resurrection!' Now, on the third day, Truth has arisen; she has quickened herself amongst the dead. Advance, O Tzar! appear at the bar of God and of history! Thou hast mercilessly trodden Truth under thy feet, thou hast refused liberty, at the same time that thou wast enslaved by thine own passions. By thy pride and obstinacy thou hast exhausted Russia; thou hast armed the world against her. Humiliate thyself before thy brothers. Bow thy haughty forehead in the dust, implore pardon, ask counsel; throw thyself into the arms of thy people. There is no other way of salvation for thee."

More than once, towards the end of his life, the Tzar was seized with doubts, but this advocate of absolute power could not make atonement. "My successor," he said, "may do what he will: I cannot change." He could not change, he could only disappear. He was a man of another age, an anachronism in the new Europe. When, from his ..... at Peterhof, he could follow the manœuvres of the enemy's fleet; when he heard raised against him the voice of the hitherto silent nation, then this proud heart bled,—the "iron Emperor" was broken. He longed to die. One day in February 1855, having already bad influenza, he went out without his great-coat, in a cold of 23° Centig. His doctor, Karrel, tried to restrain him. "You have fulfilled your duty," replied the Emperor, " let me do mine." Other imprudences aggravated his illness. He gave his last instructions to his heir, and himself dictated the despatch which he sent to all the great towns of Russia—"The Emperor is dying." On February 19th–March 3rd he died.

CHAPTER XV.

ALEXANDER II. (1855-1877).

End of the Crimean war: Treaty of Paris—The Act of the 19th of February, 1861 : judicial reforms : local self-government—The Polish insurrection— Intellectual movement ; Industrial progress ; military law—Conquests in Asia--European policy.

END OF THE CRIMEAN WAR: TREATY OF PARIS.

ALEXANDER II., born in 1819, succeeded to the throne at the age of thirty-seven, in circumstances which were as complicated within as without. "You will find the burden heavy," said his father on his death-bed. His first care was to terminate on honorable conditions the war which was exhausting Russia. At the news of the death of Nicholas, the Funds had risen on all the exchanges of Europe. This peaceful hope did not allow itself to be discouraged by the proclamation by which the new Emperor proposed to himself "to accomplish the schemes and desires of our illustrious predecessors—Peter, Catherine, Alexander the well-beloved, and our father of imperishable memory." The new sovereign knew better than anyone how little the ambitious projects of Peter and Catherine were appropriate to the circumstances in which he found himself. A conference was again opened at Vienna, between the representatives of Austria, Russia, and the two Western Powers. They could not agree as to the guarantees to be exacted from Russia. France demanded the neutralization of the Black Sea, or the limitation of the number of vessels which the Tzar might keep in it. "Before you limit our forces," Gortchakof and Titof, the representatives of Russia, might reply, "at least take Sebastopol."

The siege continued. Sardinia in her turn now sent 20,000 men to the East. Austria had engaged (2nd December, 1854) to defend the Principalities against Russia, and Prussia to defend Austria. Napoleon III. and Queen Victoria exchanged visits. Pélissier had succeeded General Canrobert (16th of May). In the night of the 22nd of May, two sorties of the Russians were repulsed. The allies encamped with a strong force on the left bank of the Tchernaïa, an expedition destroyed the military establishments of Kertch and Ienikale, occupied the Sea of Azof, and bombarded Taganrog, thus leaving to the Russians no base of supplies except Perekop. The Turks were in Anapa, and summoned the Circassians to revolt.

Pélissier had announced that he would take Sebastopol. On the 7th of June he took the Green Mamélon and the White Works by assault. On the 18th the French assailed the Malakof, and the English the Redan, but they were repulsed with a loss of 3000 men. On the 16th of August the Italian contingent distinguished itself at the battle of Traktir on the Tchernaïa. The last day of Sebastopol had come : 874 guns thundered against the bastions, and against the town. The Russians displayed a stoical bravery and a reckless intrepidity. In the last twenty-eight days of the siege they lost 18,000 men by the bombardment alone ; a million and a half of bullets, bombs, shells, and grenades had been thrown into the town. The French had dug fifty miles of trenches during the 336 days of the siege, and 4100 feet of mines before one bastion alone. They had pushed their lines within 100 feet of the Malakof, under " a hell fire," the noise of which was heard for more than sixty-two miles round. The Russian bastions crumbled, bomb-proof roofs were driven in, the gunners fell by hundreds, the soldiers of the reserve by thousands. Kornilof, Istomine, and Nakhimof had fallen. The besieged had no longer time to repair the breaches made by the batteries, to charge the useless pieces, hardly to carry away the dead. In one single day 70,000 projectiles were fired into the town. It was the beginning of the end. On the 8th of September, 1855, at twelve o'clock, the allied batteries suddenly ceased to fire. The French threw themselves on the Malakof, and maintained their position against all efforts to dislodge them, and, in spite of the check of the English at the Great Redan, Sebastopol was taken. The Russians evacuated the city and the Karabelnaïa, burning and blowing up everything in their rear, and retreated to the northern side. Meanwhile the navy had continued to threaten the coasts ; it destroyed the fort of Kinburn, and the Russians blew up that of Otchakof.

Russia, however, did not yet seem ready to submit. Gortchakof announced to the army assembled at the north of the harbor of Sebastopol that " he would not voluntarily abandon this country where St. Vladimir had received baptism." Alexander too encouraged the brave troops with his presence, and wept over the ruins of the great fortress. The *Bee* newspaper officially announced to Europe " that the war was now becoming serious, and that Sebastopol being destroyed, a stronger fortress would be built," but the fact could no longer be disguised that the country wished for peace. This war had cost 250,000 men; the banks only paid in paper, and the public refused that of the Government. England, on her side, manifested the most warlike disposition. Palmerston and the greater part of the British newspapers did not consider Russia sufficiently humiliated, but it was obvious that the war was drawing to a close. The Treaty of November 1855, between France and Sweden, only contained a simple guarantee, and no mention was made of the offensive alliance proclaimed by the Gazettes. The fall of Kars, by consoling the military vanity of Russia, made her more inclined to treat. Alexander II. declared his intention of adhering in principle to the "ultimatum of the four guarantees" presented by Count Esterhazy, and a congress met at Paris on the 25th of February, 1856. France, England, Austria, Prussia, Sardinia, and Turkey appeared at it, and Russia was represented by Baron de Brünnow and Alexis Orlof. Peace was signed on the 30th of March on the following bases:—1. Russia renounced her exclusive right of protection over the Danubian principalities, and all interference with their internal affairs. 2. The free navigation of the Danube was to be effectually secured by the establishment of a commission, in which the contracting parties should be represented. Each of them should have the right to station two sloops of war at the mouth of the river. Russia consented to a rectification of frontiers which should leave Turkey and the Roumanian principalities all the Danubian delta. 3. The Black Sea was made neutral ground: her waters, open to merchant ships of all nations, were forbidden to men-of-war, whether of the Powers on the coasts or of any others. No military or maritime arsenals were to be created there. Turkey and Russia could only maintain ten light ships to watch the coasts. 4. The *hattischerif* by which the Sultan Abdul-Medjid renewed the privileges of his non-Mussulman subjects was inserted in the treaty, but with the clause that the Powers could not quote this insertion as authorizing them to interfere between the Sultan and his subjects.

By the Treaty of Paris Russia lost both the domination of the Black Sea and the protectorate of the Eastern Christians, thus annihilating the fruits of the policy of Peter I., Anne, Catherine II., and Alexander I. Thus were condemned to ruin the fleets and naval arsenals created by Potemkine, the Duc de Richelieu, the Marquis de Traversay, and Admiral Lazaréf; thus the fortresses of Sebastopol, Kinburn, and Ienikale were deserted. The treaties of Kaïrnadji, Bucharest, and Adrianople were deprived of all the hopes of conquest and dominion to which they had given rise. The imprudent policy of Nicholas had compromised the work of two centuries of successful efforts.

Russia also took part in the Convention of 1858, which organized the principalities of Wallachia and Moldavia, and in that of 1859, which allowed them to become one State, namely Roumania, a precious relic of the great Roman colony founded by the Emperor Trajan on the Lower Danube.

THE ACT OF THE 19TH OF FEBRUARY, 1861: JUDICIAL REFORMS; LOCAL SELF-GOVERNMENT.

In the manifesto which announced to his people the termination of the Eastern war, Alexander expressed his conviction that "by the combined efforts of the Government and the nation," government, law, and police would undergo important reforms. He understood that the disasters of the Danube and the Crimea must in a great measure be imputed to the administration, protected as it was by the silence of public opinion, the slavery of the press, and the rigor of the police and of the censorship. The events of 1855 taught the important lesson that a people in which the majority of the agricultural classes was subjected to serfage could not rival the European nations in intellectual, scientific, or industrial progress. Now, in modern warfare, success is the result of all the moral and material forces of a State. The system of governing Russia without giving the people a voice in the management of their own affairs, of conducting all public business in the routine and silence of the bureaux, was condemned. The officials, so haughty under Nicholas, bowed their heads under the public execration. The name of *tchinovnik*, once so formidable, became a term of derision and contempt; public opinion naturally associated it with everything superannuated, ridiculous, or odious. The servants of the autocracy, stooping beneath the weight of a crushing responsibility, displayed a kind of shame by hiding their pompous titles and the decorations which they had formerly flaunted with pride. It seemed as if the Conservative Russia of Nicholas I. had sunk into the earth; every one called himself a Liberal. A breath of audacious hope, of courageous enterprise, passed through the country. The movement, which in 1801 only affected the immediate surrounding of Alexander, now spread through all Russia. A thousand voices were raised in the papers, in the reviews, and in the books, all suddenly emancipated; in the drawing-rooms and in the streets, where the bewildered police forgot to spy. What had been murmured in the manuscript literature of the last months of Nicholas was now printed freely. "The heart beats with joy," said one of the leading organs of the press, " in expectation of the social reforms which are on the point of being carried out—reforms which will give satisfaction to the minds, wishes, and hopes of the public. The ancient harmony and community of sentiment which, in all but short and exceptional periods, have always existed between the Government and the people, are completely re-established. The absence of all sentiment of caste, the feeling of a common origin, and of a fraternity which binds all classes of Russia into a single homogeneous people, will permit the easy and peaceful fulfilment, not only of those great reforms which have cost Europe centuries of bitter struggles, but of other reforms that the nations of the West, enchained by their feudal traditions and their caste prejudices, are even now in no state to accomplish." And again: "We have to fight in the name of the highest truth with egotism and the pitiful interests of the moment. We must prepare our children from their tenderest years to take part in the struggle that awaits every brave man. We must thank the war which has opened our eyes to the dark sides of our political and social organization, and it is our duty to profit by the lesson. But we ought not to suppose that the Government can of itself cure us of our faults. Russia is like a stranded ship, which the captain and the crew alone could never rescue; she can only be floated by the all-powerful reflux of the national life." Men of letters, suspected and spied upon during the preceding reign, now led public opinion. Literature took a militant and practical character; the old quarrel of the romantic and classical schools was left far behind. " It did not seem strange," says Mr. Mackenzie Wallace, "that a drama should be written to defend free trade or a poem to extol a certain form of impost, nor that political ideas should be expressed in a story, whilst the adversary replied in a comedy." The delicate questions that the Russian press feared to bring forward, and the great personages that it did not dare to attack, were left to the exiled Hertzen in London, with his terrible *Bell* (*Kolokol*), the dread of dishonest officials. The proscribed numbers of the *Kolokol* made their way by thousands into Russia, were laid on the table of the Emperor, and revealed to him the most secret iniquities.

In their eagerness for reform the people wished everything to be undertaken at once, but it was soon seen that all questions remained in abeyance till that of the emancipation of the peasants was settled. Whether it was a question of self-government, of education, of industrial liberty, of military service, or legal equality, it was sure to come back to social reform, where therefore they must begin.

The unfree population of Russia amounted at that time to 47,100,000 individuals, divided into 20,000,000 Crown peasants, 4,700,000 peasants of appanages, mines, factories, etc., 21,000,000 belonging to proprietors, and 1,400,000 *dvorovié*, or domestic servants. The peasants of the Crown and of the appanages might be considered as freemen, subject to the payment of a rent, or of other well-defined dues, settled by the State, which was represented either by the administration of the domain or by the department of the appanages. The Crown peasants even enjoyed a sort of local self-government. They regulated their affairs in their communes or *mirs* through an elder and an elected council. They were judged by elected tribunals—the tribunal of the village and the tribunal of the *volost* or district, which applied the peasant customs. Nothing more was needed than to give the name of freemen to men substantially free. This was done when their right to personal liberty was proclaimed, and when certain restrictions on their right to come and go, to acquire new lands, or to dispose of their goods were abolished. This was accomplished by a series of edicts, the first dating July 1858.

The case of peasants belonging to private owners, and the position of the *dvorovié*, were different. The emancipation of these 22,500,000 men was to bring about the most prodigious social change which has taken place in Europe since the French Revolution. The liberation of the peasants properly so called, which would make them owners of part of the soil which they cultivated, was an enterprise surrounded with difficulties on all sides. As to the question of personal liberty, every one was agreed, but there were dissensions as to the question of property. To elucidate this it was necessary to go back to the historic origin of Russian property, to choose between the systems and theories formulated by different schools of historians. The most authoritative of these proved that serfage was not introduced into Russia by the conquest of one race by another, for it was exactly in those provinces conquered by the Russians—in the Finnish or Tatar countries—that serfage did not exist, while its greatest development was to be found in the midst of the conquering people. Serfage had been sanctioned by a series of acts emanating from the throne; and the nearer a province was to the Muscovite centre, the more ancient and the more firmly established was serfage found to be. The northern regions, the governments of Archangel and Vologda, were exempt from it. The *krépostnoé pravo* was therefore a Muscovite institution, a creation of the Tzarian power. It took its rise in the period when, under the pressure of the Mongol yoke, Russian society formed itself into a rigorous hierarchy, in which the sovereign of Moscow arrogated to himself absolute authority over the nobles, as the nobles did over the peasants—their subjects. The *krépostnoé pravo* sprang from the new wants of the infant State. The grant of lands to the military class, to the nobles, was the recompense for the service exacted from them; the revenues of the soil constituted their pay, and were to defray the expenses of their outfit and equipment. They were besides charged to govern and administer the lands of their domain, and to pay in the amount of the poll-tax to the prince, whose tax-gatherers they were. But the land had no value without the hands that cultivated it, the revenues of an estate diminished with the number of peasants; the noble who was deserted by his peasants was ruined, and in no condition to serve the prince. In order that military service might be secured, and that the produce of the tax might suffer no diminution, it was necessary to hinder the emigration of the peasants. The interest of the noble, as well as the interest of the State, demanded that the liberty of coming and going should be restrained, that the noble should be armed with a formidable authority over the peasant, and that the laborer should be fixed to the soil. Almost everywhere, without any intervention on the part of the legislature, the husbandman gradually became a serf. Legally free, the peasant had become a slave; legally a simple tenant for life, the noble had become in fact the owner of the land, the proprietor of the peasants. The state of things created by arbitrary power was afterwards legalized by a series of legislative acts, which one after the other restrained the liberty of the mougik and augmented the authority of the lord. Such were the *oukazes* of Feodor Ivanovitch in 1592 and 1597, of Boris Godounof in 1601, of Vassili Chouïski in 1607, of Peter the Great in 1723, and of Catherine II. for Little Russia in 1783.

The peasant, while resigning himself to this condition of affairs, had not entirely lost all sense of his rights. His ancient right to the ownership of the land he expressed after his own fashion in the proverb, " Our backs are the lord's, but the soil is our own." He forgot less easily than the Government the fact that the peasant's obligation to serve the lord was co-relative to the lord's obligation to serve the Tzar. When Peter III. in his short reign freed the nobles from the obligation of serving the State, the peasant expected that the corollary of this first edict would be a second edict, setting free the peasant from his bondage to the soil and from paying dues to the lord. Hence the troubles of 1762, the insurrection of 1773, when a false Peter III. appeared to finish the work of the deceased Emperor.

During the campaign of 1812, the peasants for a moment believed that Napoleon was bringing them liberty, and the agitation was revived during the Crimean war. Serfage was decidedly the weak point of Russia. An invader could raise against her at once a servile and a foreign war.

We have seen the efforts at emancipation under Alexander I., and the edict of Nicholas in 1842. The latter, by the *oukazes* of 1845, 1847, and 1848, had recognized the right of individuals and communes to acquire landed property. One of Nicholas's enemies has not been able to refuse him this testimony: "However hostile may have been his views of liberty, we must do him the justice to say that he never ceased through the whole of his life to cherish the idea of emancipating the serfs" ('Truth about Russia'). He had to bequeath this task to his son. A few days after the Treaty of Paris was signed, in March 1856, Alexander II., in an address to the marshal of the Moscow nobility, while guarding himself against the notion that he aimed at the instant emancipation of the serfs, invites "his faithful nobles" to seek the proper means to prepare for the execution of this measure. The Muscovite proprietors showed, however, but little enthusiasm. The Emperor had to content himself with appointing (2nd–14th January, 1857) "a chief committee for the amelioration of the condition of the peasants." He understood that such a measure could only be carried out by an energetic exercise of the imperial power. This same year the nobles of the governments of Kief, Volhynia, and Podolia, disturbed by the measures taken by Nicholas I. after the institution of the "inventories," "took," says Schnitzler, "a desperate resolution." They declared themselves ready to emancipate the peasants. Whether they thought that the bare idea of so radical a measure would alarm the Government, or whether they hoped that the emancipation would necessarily be based on the idea of a proportionate pecuniary indemnity, they furnished the Emperor with the occasion he sought to give the question a final impulse. He authorized by an edict the nobility of the three Lithuanian governments to proceed with the work of emancipation. He sent this edict and the ministerial instructions which formed its commentary to all the governors and all the marshals of the nobility throughout the provinces of the empire, "for their information," and also, adds the circular, "for your direction, in case that the nobles confided to your care should express the same intention as the three Lithuanian governments. The nobles of St. Petersburg, Nijni-Novgorod, and Orel made a reply which encouraged the Emperor.

Another encouragement came to him from the press, almost

the whole of which hailed with enthusiasm a measure " which was to open a new and glorious epoch in the national history." " All sections of the literary world," says Mr. Mackenzie Wallace (vol. ii. p. 277), " had arguments to offer in support of the foregone conclusion. The moralists declared that all prevailing vices were the product of serfage, and that moral progress was impossible in an atmosphere of slavery; the lawyers asserted that the arbitrary authority of the proprietors over the peasants had no firm legal basis; the economists explained that free labor was an indispensable condition of industrial and commercial prosperity; the philosophical historians showed that the normal historical development of the country demanded the abolition of barbarism; and the writers of the sentimental, gushing type poured forth endless effusions about brotherly love to the weak and oppressed."

Already the question was not one of giving the peasant his liberty alone. In order to prevent the peasant, now free, but detached from the soil, from falling into the hands of his ancient master, and into a state of dependence more insupportable than that of the past; to hinder the formation of an immense proletariat, more hungry and more dangerous than that which, it was said, menaced the kingdoms of the West, it was necessary to give the newly liberated men some property, to reconstitute and strengthen the Russian commune, whose strong unity and indestructible life formed the best rampart against pauperism. Many proprietors associated themselves with this movement; they trusted that the abolition of the serfage of the peasants would have as its consequence the limitation of the autocratic authority of the Tzars, and that by enfranchising their serfs they would themselves gain political liberty. The re-establishment of the ancient *douma* of the *sobor* was more than once spoken of, the kind of national parliament which under more modern forms would associate the country with the exercise of the supreme authority.

The Government, supported by the addresses of many bodies of nobility, ordered the creation of committees of landowners, charged to examine the question. Forty-six committees, composed of 1336 landowners, assembled to discuss the rights of 23,000,000 of serfs, and of 120 proprietors. The forty-six committees unanimously pronounced for the abolition of serfage without any recompense, but opinions were divided as to the distribution of lands and the conditions of indemnity. The Emperor had again to interfere. He called a chief committee, composed of twelve persons, over which he presided. This committee more than once opposed, in conjunction with some of the provincial committees, passive resistance to the beneficent schemes of the sovereign. The Emperor went through the provinces, appealing to the conciliatory spirit and devotion of his nobility, reprimanding those who hung back, and reminding them that "reforms came better from above than from below." To subdue the resistance of the superior committee he created another, to which the old one was subordinated, and which he packed with men devoted to the new idea.

The new "imperial commission" did not content itself with elaborating the materials furnished by the provincial committees. Directly inspired by the Emperor, who sent them his paper on "the progress and issue of the peasant question," they legislated on all sides, at the risk of throwing into opposition proprietors who were well disposed, but who complained that they had never been consulted, and that the commission seemed desirous of depriving them of the merit of their sacrifices. The commission gradually gave to the reform a more and more radical character. It admitted the principle that the emancipation should not take place gradually, but that the law should insure the immediate abolition of serfdom; that the most effectual measures should be taken to prevent the re-establishment of the seignorial authority under other forms, by the liberal organization of the rural communes; and that the peasant should become a proprietor on the payment of an indemnity. From these deliberations resulted the new law, announced by the manifesto of the 19th of February–3rd of March, 1861.

The fundamental principles of the new legislation may be summed up thus :—1. The peasants up to that time attached to the soil were to be invested with all the rights of free cultivators. 2. The peasants should obtain, *minus* the dues fixed by law, the full enjoyment of their enclosure (*dvor*), and also a certain quantity of arable land, sufficient to guarantee the accomplishment of their obligations towards the State. This "permanent enjoyment" might be exchanged for an "absolute ownership" of the enclosure and the lands, subject to a right to buy them back. 3. The lords were to concede to the peasants or to the rural communes the land actually occupied by the latter; in each district, however, a maximum and a minimum were to be fixed. On the whole there was an average of three *dessiatines* and a half for each male peasant; but it varied from one to twelve *dessiatines*, that is to say, the peasants in general received less in the Black Land, and more in the less productive zones. 4. The Government was to organize a system of loans, which would permit the peasants immediately to liberate themselves from their lords, while remaining debtors to the State. 5. The *dvorovié*, who were not attached to the soil, were only to receive their personal liberty, on condition of serving their masters for two years. 6. To bring the great work of partition into seignorial lands and peasant lands, to a happy conclusion; to regulate the amount of the dues, the conditions of repurchase, and all the questions which might arise from the execution of the law, the temporary magistracy of the *mirovyé possrédniki*, or mediators of peace, was instituted, who showed themselves for the most part honest, patient, impartial, equitable, and who deserve a great part of the honor of this pacific settlement.

The peasants, freed from the seignorial authority, were organized into communes; or rather the *commune*, the *mir*, which is the primordial and antique element of Slavo-Russian society, acquired a new force. It inherited the right of police and of surveillance, held by the lord over his subjects; it administered and judged with more liberty the suits of the peasants. In accordance with the ancient Slav law, the land bought from the lord remained the common property of all the members of the *mir*: each peasant only held as his private property his enclosure and the land thereto pertaining. Arable lands are subject to periodical partition, more or less frequent, among the heads of families, and only possessed by them by way of usufruct. The law, which does not permit a final partition of the common land, except when two-thirds of those interested consent, will for long maintain against the destructive action of new manners and new wants this old European institution, which in our Western countries has disappeared for centuries, in France especially, and has left no trace, except so-called communal properties. The communes, freed from the lords, were grouped, as in the case of the imperial domains, into *volosts*: a *volost* tribunal received the appeal from the communal justices, and a *volost* municipality was charged to watch over the common interests of all the villages under its jurisdiction. The mayor of the commune was called *starost*; the *volost* mayor, *starchina*. The Russian peasants were thus given a complete system of local self-government, of an absolutely rural character, for the former lord was kept absolutely apart from it. Since his ancient domain had been divided into seignorial lands and peasant lands, he ceased legally to be an inhabitant of the village. His interests being absolutely distinct from those of the peasants, he was forbidden to meddle either with them, their elections, their administration, or their justice.

The great measure of emancipation was, in fact, a settlement of accounts as to the ancient community existing between masters and peasants. It imposed sacrifice on both the interested parties. If the proprietors were forced to renounce their seignorial rights, the *obrok*, the *corvée*, and part of their lands in exchange for an indemnity, the peasant found it hard to be obliged to buy the very ground whereon his cottage stood; the soil which his ancestors had cultivated in the sweat of their brows, even the land reserved for the lord, they regarded in many places as their own property, because it had been cultivated by them from time immemorial. The partition imposed by the law seemed spoliation to them. The discontent often showed itself in an obstinate resistance to the advice of the "mediators of peace," by the refusal to acquit themselves of their legal obligations, and to enter into negotiation with the lord for the repurchase of the land. They persuaded themselves that the nobles and officials had falsified the edict of the Tzar, or that a fresh act of emancipation, the true one, was to be proclaimed. A strange ferment arose in many provinces; it was necessary to call out the soldiery, and three times the troops had to fire on the people. In the government of Kazan, 10,000 men rose at the call of the peasant Pétrof, who announced to them "the true liberty." A hundred perished, and the chief himself was taken and shot. The emancipation was none the less a beneficent and essential reform, of which the present generation will have to pay the price, while its good results will develop in future generations. The Russian peasants owe their liberty above all to the firm will of the Emperor; to the generous efforts of the Grand Duke Constantine, and of the Grand Duchess Helena, who in 1859 gave an example by emancipating her own peasants; to the enlightened patriotism of Rostovtsof, of Panine, Minister of Justice, of Nicholas Milioutine, of Prince Tcherkasski, of Iouri Samarine, members of the Imperial Commission, of Kochelef, Solovief, Ioukovski, Domotouvitch, etc.; and to a great part of the proprietors, many of whom granted their peasants more than the maximum of land fixed by law.

As a reward for their sacrifices the upper classes in Russia demanded reforms, and more political liberty. If they were refused the re-establishment of the *douma*, that is to say constitutional government, great reforms were at last accomplished in justice and in provincial administration.

In judicial affairs, the edicts from 1862 to 1865 introduced innovations sanctioned by the experience of Western States. Public accusation and defence succeeded to the written and inquisitorial procedure of former times. Criminal justice was placed in the hands of a jury; the police were deprived of the judicial *instruction*, which was given to special magistrates, the *juges d'instruction;* and district courts (*okroujnyé soudi*) were established in each group of *ouiezdi*, or districts. Appeals were carried up to "palaces of justice" (*soudebnya palaty*) similar to the French courts of appeal, but which only reversed the sentences of the first judges in cases where the law was misinterpreted and misapplied. The senate, made into a court of revision or of annulment, crowns all this organization, in which we find certain wholly French ideas. The justices of the peace constitute a separate hierarchy: the judge of peace (*mirovoi soudia*), elected by the landed proprietors of the district, sits also in a tribunal of arbitration and of ordinary police; his jurisdiction, much more extensive than in France, includes the civil cases not exceeding 500 roubles, and criminal cases where the penalty does not exceed 300 roubles, or more than a year's imprisonment. The sentence can only be appealed from when the the sum involved exceeds thirty roubles in civil, and fifteen roubles or three days' imprisonment in criminal cases. In this case the appeal is taken, not as in France before the district tribunal, but before the assembly of justices of the peace for the district (*arrondissement*), or *mirovoi siezd*, whose verdict can only be annulled by the senate.

The Russian provinces or governments (*gouvernii*) are divided into *ouiezdi* or districts. In each district the law of 1864 institutes a district council, formed by deputies elected every three years, in certain fixed proportions, by the three orders of the State,—the landed proprietors, or gentlemen; the rural communes, or *mirs;* and the towns. The council assembles once a year, and is replaced in the interval between its sessions by a permanent executive committee. The functions of the district council, which occupies in the administrative hierarchy the rank immediately superior to the municipal council of the towns and to the councils of the rural *volosts*, consist in being obliged to keep the roads and bridges in repair, to watch over education and sanitary affairs, to inspect the state of the harvest, and to take measures for the prevention of famine. Above the district council (*ouiezdnoé zemstvo*) was instituted the general council (*goubernkoé zemstvo*), elected, not by the primary electors, but by the district councils of the provinces, and in which there was practically a large proportion of noble deputies, in consequence of the tendency of the peasants to avoid all public charges, more considerable in this than in the other assembly. The general council occupies itself with affairs concerning several districts, and votes the provincial budget. Such is a summary of the system of self-government with which the present reign has endowed Russia.

Corporal punishments, that blot on ancient Russia, have

been abolished in the army and the imperial tribunals. They only remain in vigor in the tribunals of the peasants, who, from their attachment to the ancient patriarchal customs, still apply some blows with a cord to delinquents. The censorship has been mitigated; the newspapers of both capitals have received the right to choose between censorship or the liberty of appearing at their own risk and peril. In this case an arrangement borrowed from the second French empire is applied: after three warnings, the paper may be suspended or suppressed. The periodical press of St. Petersburg and Moscow has developed in a surprising manner in an atmosphere of comparative liberty; on the other hand, the provincial press, even in the largest towns, such as Kief and Kazan, scarcely exists. That of Warsaw is in an exceptional situation; that of the Baltic provinces enjoys a greater freedom.

Since 1859 the table of receipts (559 million roubles), and that of State expenses (553 millions), have been given a kind of publicity. In 1860 foreigners acquired all the civil rights accorded to natives, and which are held by Russians in foreign countries. The barriers raised by Nicholas between his empire and Europe have been partially overthrown. The Jews, those at least exercising a trade, were authorized to remove from Poland and the western governments into the interior of the empire. The universities have been freed from the shackles imposed by Nicholas, the limitation of the number of students abolished, the charges of study lowered, and numerous scholarships created.

THE POLISH INSURRECTION.

Great hopes awakened in Poland at the accession of the new sovereign; they went as far as the re-establishment of the constitution, and even to the reunion of the Lithuanian provinces with the kingdom. The awaking of Italy had made that of Poland appear possible; the concessions of the Emperor of Austria to Hungary led men to expect the same from Alexander II. The interview of the three Northern sovereigns at Warsaw, in October 1860, caused a certain irritation among the people. It is necessary also to take into consideration the intrigues set on foot by the Polish committees abroad. If many Poles counted on the support of Alexander II. to help them to raise their country, others wished to emancipate her entirely from Russia. There existed, therefore, two parties in Warsaw and in the foreign committees; the one wished to take Italy as an example, the other would be content with the new lot of Hungary.

The emancipation of the peasants was in Poland, as in Russia, the question of the day, but the conditions of the question were different in Warsaw from what they were in Moscow: the personal liberty of the rustics had been decreed by Napoleon I., at the time that the Grand Duchy was created; but as they had received no property, they continued to farm the lands of the nobles, and paid their rent either in money or by *corvées*. The substitution of a fixed money payment instead of a *corvée* was the first step in the path of reform, which might be carried further by allowing the husbandman to become a proprietor, by paying annually a fixed sum towards the repurchase of the land, and putting means of credit at his disposal. The Agricultural Society, presided over by Count Andrew Zamoiski, found that it was the interest of the Polish nation to anticipate the Russian Government, and to secure to the native nobility the honor of emancipation: the Government, on the contrary, represented by M. Moukhanof, director of the Interior, decided that it was to its advantage to fetter the activity of the society, to forbid the discussion of the question of repurchase, and to confine its functions to the mutation of the *corvée* into fixed dues.

The contest between the Agricultural Society and the Government increased the agitation which already existed at Warsaw. On the 29th of November, 1860, on the occasion of the thirtieth anniversary of the revolution of 1830, demonstrations at once national and religious took place in the streets of the capital, and portraits of Kosciuszko and Kilinski were distributed. On the 25th of February, 1861, the day of the anniversary of the battle of Grochov, the Agricultural Society held a meeting to deliberate on an address, in which the Emperor should be asked for a constitution. Tumultuous crowds gathered in the streets, singing national songs. On the 27th, on the occasion of a funeral service for the victims of the preceding insurrections, there was a new demonstration, which had to be suppressed, with the loss of five killed and ten wounded. Prince Gortchakof, Viceroy of Poland, touched by these strange manifestations, in which the disarmed people confined themselves stoically to facing the musketry without interrupting their songs, labored with Count Zamoiski for the restoration of order. The address to the Emperor circulated in Warsaw, and was covered with signatures; 100,000 persons quietly followed the obsequies of the victims of the 27th of February.

Without desiring to grant a constitution, the Emperor Alexander II. made, however, many important concessions. He decreed (edict of March 26) a council of state for the kingdom, a department of public education and of worship, elective councils in each government and each district, and municipal councils at Warsaw and the principal cities of the kingdom. The Marquis Viélépolski, a Pole belonging to the party which hoped for the re-establishment of Poland by Russia, was named director of public worship and education.

These concessions were likely to reconcile at least the constitutional party; unhappily their effect was destroyed by the sudden dissolution of the Agricultural Society, in which the mass of the people had placed its hopes, and the demonstrations continued. On the 7th of April a crowd assembled in the square of the *Zamok* (castle of the Viceroy) to demand that the edict of dissolution should be withdrawn, but it dispersed without any result before the hostile attitude of the troops. On the 8th of April the multitude reappeared, more numerous and more violent, shouting that they wanted a *country;* a postilion, who was driving a postchaise, played on his cornet the favorite air of Dombrovski's legions, "No, Poland shall not perish." The crowd, composed in great part of women and children, presented a passive resistance and invincible *vis inertiæ*, on which the charges of cavalry had no effect. The troops then had recourse to their arms, and fifteen rounds of shot laid 200 dead and a large number of wounded at the feet of the statue of the Virgin. On the following days the people appeared only in mourning, in spite of the prohibition of the police. This uneasy state of things was prolonged for many months. On the 10th of October a Polish and a Lithuanian procession celebrated at Hodlevo, on the Polo-Lithuanian frontier, the four hundreth anniversary of the union of the two countries. The humanity of the Russian commandant allowed the fête to be held without the effusion of blood.

The Government still made one attempt at conciliation when the Emperor appointed Count Lambert as Viceroy, with orders to apply the reforms decreed in March 1761, but the effect of his nomination was weakened by the presence at his side of men devoted to the policy of repression. The anti-Russian party, besides, had not disarmed. On the 15th of October, on the anniversary of Kosciuszko, the people flocked to the churches of Warsaw; the military authorities caused the churches to be surrounded by detachments, without seeing that the inoffensive inhabitants, alarmed at this display, would refuse to leave the churches, and that it would be necessary to drag them out by force. In fact, after a useless blockade that lasted a day and a night, up to four in the morning, the soldiers had to force the cathedral, and carry 2000 people to the fortress. Count Lambert loudly complained to General Gerstenszweig, the military governor. After a fierce altercation the latter blew out his brains, and Lambert was recalled.

He was succeeded by Count Lüders, who began a period of reaction, and a certain number of influential Warsovians were transported. The Grand Duke Constantine, made Viceroy on the 8th of June, 1862, again tried a policy of reconciliation. Viélépolski, one of the promoters of the address to the Emperor, was nominated chief of the civil power. Enthusiasts attempted the lives of Lüders, of Viélépolski, even of the Grand Duke, and violent men profited by all the errors of the Government to push things to extremity, and to turn its good intentions against it. The Poles of Warsaw committed the error of disquieting Russia about the provinces which she regarded as Russian, and an integral part of the empire; the proprietors did not content themselves with demanding, in an address to Constantine, that the government of Poland should be Polish, which was reasonable and just, but insisted that the Lithuanian palatinates should be reunited to the kingdom. The upper classes of Podolia expressed the same wish with regard to that province, to Volhynia and the Ukraine. These imprudences caused the exile of Zamoiski and the arrest of the Podolian agitators. All understanding became impossible; an exercise of authority precipitated the explosion: in the night of the 15th of January, 1863, the military government laid violent hands on the recruits.

The conscripts who had escaped from the police formed the nucleus of the rebel bands which promptly appeared at Blonié and at Siérock. The war could no longer assume the great character of those of 1794 or of 1831; there was now no Polish army to struggle seriously with that of Russia: it was a little war of guerillas and sharpshooters, who could nowhere hold their own against the Russians, but who plunged into the thick forests of Poland, and concealed themselves there only to appear further on and harass the columns. There were no battles, only skirmishes, the most serious of which was that of Vengrov, on the 6th of February, 1863. A few chiefs made themselves names: among these were Leo Frankovski, Sigismond Padlevski, Casimir Bogdanovitch, Miélençki, the energetic Bossak-Hauke (who was one day to fall under the French flag in the fields of Burgundy), the French Rochebrune and Blankenheim, Mademoiselle Poustovoijov, Siérakovski (ex-colonel in the Russian army, who was hanged after his check in Lithuania), the priest-soldier Maçkiévicz, Narbutt (son of the historian), Lélével (a pseudonym adopted by a Warsaw workman), and Marian Langiévicz, soon appointed dictator, but who, after the skirmishes of the 17th, 18th, and 19th of March, was driven back into Gallicia, and detained there by the Austrians. The secret committee of insurrection, or anonymous government of Poland, had summoned the peasants to liberty and the enjoyment of property.

The exasperated Russians treated the towns and villages concerned in the affair with great cruelty. The village of Ibiany was destroyed, and the Polish chiefs taken with arms in their hands were shot or hanged. General Mouravief in Lithuania declared that it was "useless to make prisoners." Berg in Poland, Dlotovskoï in Livonia, and Annenkof in the Ukraine, were the agents of rigorous repression. Felinski, Archbishop of Warsaw, was transported into the interior of Russia, as a punishment for having written a letter to the Emperor.

Europe was touched. On the 5th of January, 1863, the French minister Billault, in the tribune of the Corps Législatif, had blamed the "baseless hopes excited in the minds of patriots, whose powerless efforts could only bring about new evils"; he recommended the insurgents to the clemency of Alexander. Then France, England, and Austria decided to have recourse to diplomatic intervention, invited the other Powers who had signed the Treaty of Vienna to join in their efforts, and laid before the Russian government the notes of April 1863, which invited her to put an end to the periodical agitations of Poland by a policy of conciliation. On June 17 the three Powers proposed a programme with the following conditions:—1. An amnesty; 2. The establishment of a national representation; 3. The nomination of Poles to public offices; 4. The abolition of restrictions placed on Catholic worship; 5. The exclusive use of the Polish language, as the official language of the administration, of justice, and of education; 6. A regular and legal system of recruiting. This intervention of the Western Powers, which was supported by no military demonstration, was rejected by the famous note of Prince Gortchakof, Chancellor of the empire, and the idea of a European conference was likewise rejected. Europe found herself powerless, and Napoleon III. had to content himself in his speech from the throne with the declaration that the treaties of 1815 were "trampled under foot at Warsaw." The conduct of Prussia had been quite different; she had concluded with Russia the convention of the 8th of February, 1863, for the suppression of the Polish manifestations, and thus laid the foundation of that Prusso-Russian alliance which was to prove so useful to her.

This insurrection was to cost Poland dear. The last remains of her autonomy were extinguished. To-day the "kingdom" is nothing but a name, and the country has been divided into ten provinces (1866). The Russian language has replaced the

Polish in all public acts; the University of Warsaw is a Russian university; the primary, secondary, and superior education all lend their aid to the work of denationalization. Poland lost her institutions without obtaining the benefit of those of Russia—the *zemstva*, the jury, and the new tribunals. As the Government held the nobles responsible for the insurrection, it therefore markedly favored the peasants, authorizing them to " enter into full and entire possession of the lands which they held." An oukaze of the 10th of December, 1865, rendered the sale of confiscated and sequestrated property imperative, and Russians alone might be purchasers.

Finland, on the contrary, had all her privileges confirmed. In 1863, Alexander convoked the diet of the grand duchy, the second that had been held since the annexation to the empire. The German nobility of the Baltic provinces, more docile and more politic than that of Poland, were not disturbed. The University of Dorpat remained a German university; the Government only took measures to protect the language and religion of the empire against the propagation of the German tongue and of the Protestant religion. The bold demands of the Slavophil Iouri Samarine, in his 'Russian Frontiers,' and the lively polemic sustained against him by the Baltic writers Schirren, Wilhelm von Bock, Julius Eckart, and Sternberg, did not lead to any important changes in the three governments of Livonia, Courland, and Esthonia.

INTELLECTUAL MOVEMENT ; MATERIAL PROGRESS ; MILITARY LAW.

The Russian agitation began simultaneously with the Polish troubles. At the beginning it seemed associated with the Polish movement. The students of St. Petersburg openly sympathized with the Warsaw anniversaries ; and the students of Kazan attended the funeral of Andrew Petrof, an insurgent peasant. The augmentation of the cost of study in the provincial universities, the prohibition of meetings, promenades, deputations, libraries, and students' conferences, brought about troubles which ended in the universities of the two capitals being closed and numerous arrests being made. Then came addresses from the assemblies of nobles : that of Tver had in 1862 requested the abolition of privileges, and the convocation of a national assembly ; in that of Toula a meeting of the States-general was discussed. Events in Poland soon gave the current of ideas a new direction. The *Moscow Gazette*, under M. Katkof, seized the leadership of opinion. It awakened the national Russian sentiment against the demands of Poland, and signified to her that nothing now remained to her "but to unite her aspirations with those of Russia, and to inoculate herself with the principles which have been elaborated, and elaborate themselves in the political development of the Russian people." It provoked demonstrations in honor of Mouravief, glorified his energetic and pacific measures in Lithuania, and actually ascribed the numerous fires of 1862 to Polish emissaries. By making itself the advocate of Russian nationality, the press gained unexpected freedom, which was also exacted by M. Katkof, even from the ministers. He was the man of the new state of things, as Hertzen had been that of the liberal movement at the beginning of the reign. The attempt of Karakozof upon the life of the Emperor in the Summer Garden in 1866, made in the name of the Russian revolutionaries, and that of Berezovski at Paris in 1867, in the name of the Polish revolutionaries, show how deeply men's minds were troubled. It would be idle to insist on the changes of ministers, sometimes progressionists, sometimes reactionaries, who reflected the impressions produced by events on the mind of the Emperor. Under a government which on the whole was liberal, Russia still continued to transform herself. It will be sufficient to enumerate a few of the results.

The preceding Government had only bequeathed to Russia 218 miles of railway; to-day the Russian lines, fifty-three in number, are composed of 10,384 miles already being worked, and 1145 miles in process of construction. The railways unite nearly all the large towns of Russia in Europe: in the north they end at Helsingfors and at Vologda; in the east at Nijni-Novgorod, Saratof, Samara, with a line projected as far Orenburg; in the south at Kichenef, Odessa, Cherson, Sebastopol, and Taganrog, with a line projected as far as Vladikavkaze. Russia is placed in communication with the West by means of the lines of St. Petersburg and Berlin, Warsaw and Berlin, Warsaw and Vienna, and Kichenef and Iassy. The Caucasian line already unites Poti on the Black Sea to Tiflis; it will be prolonged as far as Bakou on the Caspian. The Siberian railway is at present under consideration. The four seas, the great lakes, the rivers and canals of Russia, are furrowed by numerous steamboats. The telegraph and the post, of which the cost has been lowered, put the empire in rapid and regular communication with the whole world.

Trade has also greatly developed. "The people are beginning to move," writes Mr. Herbert Barry, "and many manufactories are in course of construction. The Russians are clever at all handicrafts. An Englishman, the director of a paper factory which I was astonished to find in the middle of the Oural Mountains, told me that in England many years of apprenticeship were needed to make a good paper-worker, but that a Russian learnt as much in three months as an Englishman in three years." The branches of commerce which have prospered the most are the manufactures of cotton and silk, metallurgy, steel, &c. Numerous banks have been started, even in some of the most remote towns of the empire.

Primary education leaves more to be desired than that of any other country in Europe. Russia, with her 9 or 10 per cent. of people who can read, is below even Austria, which only reckons 29 per cent. In France the average is 77 per cent. Thanks to the efforts of the Minister of Public Instruction, and the Minister of War in his regimental schools, the average is slowly but surely rising. Primary education is more advanced in Poland because of the efforts of the Government; in the Baltic provinces and in Finland, because of the Protestant culture; in Central Russia, because of the industrial influences. In 1871 the minister Tolstoï, in his report to the Emperor, enumerates 24.000 schools attended by 875,000 scholars, and 424 superior primary schools, attended by 27,830 scholars.

On the 1st of January, 1872, there existed 126 *gymnasia* and 32 *progymnasia*, including 42,791 pupils. At this same date M. Tolstoï had issued an order to introduce or confirm the study of Greek and Latin in these establishments. On the other hand, the regulation of the 12th of May, 1873, instituted practical schools for the teaching of professions.

In 1876 the eight universities of the empire (St. Petersburg, Moscow, Kharkof, Kazan, Kief, Dorpat, New Russia or Odessa, founded in 1864, and Warsaw, founded in 1869) reckoned 5466 students and 457 free pupils. Amongst the students 1325 were scholars.

To the educational institutions for the daughters of the nobility, established by Catherine II. and developed by Maria Feodorovna, wife of Paul, were added seminaries of a kind more appropriate to the new needs, and where young girls of all classes are received. There are the female *gymnasia* and *progymnasia*,—a kind of lyceums for girls, where boarders are not admitted. The earliest of these schools were founded under the auspices of the present Empress, on the basis of the 4th section of the imperial chancery. They are 26 in number—6 at St. Petersburg, 5 at Moscow, 15 in the provinces. The Minister of Public Instruction had in his turn created, in 1871, 56 *gymnasia* and 130 *progymnasia* on the same model, attended by 23,404 pupils. Nowhere in Europe has such a vast development been given to the scientific education of young girls, and nowhere have they been given such easy access to liberal careers, and to Government employments, posts, telegraphs, &c. In 1875, 169 lady students followed the courses of surgery and medicine in the University of St. Petersburg.

Periodical publications have enormously increased since the Crimean war. There exist at present about 472 newspapers, of which 377 are in the Russian language. At St. Petersburg are published the *Golos*, which has the largest circulation; the *Gazette de St. Petersbourg;* the *Gazette de la Bourse*, which sympathized with France in the war of 1870; the *Monde Russe*, which has had some military discussion with the *Invalide;* and the *New Era*, devoted to Slav interests: at Moscow the *Gazette de Moscou*, which has not ceased to belong to the university, has passed into the editorship of M. Katkof. Amongst the reviews which are of general interest, we may enumerate the *Messager d'Europe* of M. Stasioulévitch, the *Messager Russe* of M. Katkof, the *Citoyen*, the *Annales de la Patrie*, and the *Diélo* (Action), an advanced organ. Others have a specially historic character; such are the *Archive Russe* of M. Barténief, the *Antiquité Russe*, the *Russe Ancienne et Nouvelle*, and the *Recueil de la Société Imperiale d'Histoire Russe*, started in 1867.

The present time is remarkable for its literary activity. We can only quote names: in the novels of manners, MM. Tourguénief, Pisemski, Dostoiévski, Gontcharof, Melnikof, Stebnitski, Boborikine, Madame Krestovski, and the Little Russian Marko-Vovtchok; in historical novels, MM. Alexis Tolstoï (' Le Prince Sérébrannyi, ou Ivan le Terrible'), Leo Tolstoï (' La Guerre et la Paix,' a study of the Napoleonic wars), and Sahlias (' Les Compagnons de Pougatchef'); in satirical novels, the dreaded Chtchedrine; in play writing, MM. Ostrovski, Potiékhine, and Solohoup; and for historical dramas, Meï, A. Tolstoï (' La Mort d'Ivan le Terrible'), and Averkief (' Vassili l'Aveugle').

Among the historians must be cited Pogodine (' Russia up to the Invasion of the Tatars '), Kostomarof (' Historical Monographs and Researches,' ' History of the Fall of Poland,' ' History of Russia in Biographies '), Solovief (' History of Russia from the most ancient Times,' twenty-six volumes, as far as Catherine II.), Ilovaïski (' The Origins of Russian History,' ' The Diet of Grodno '), Oustriélof (' History of Peter the Great'), Zabiéline (' Private Life of the Tzars, the Tzarinas, and the Russian People'), Bogdanovitch (' History of Alexander I.,' and the ' History of the War in the East '), Milioutine (' Campaign of 1799'), Galitsyne ('Universal Military History '),

Pékarski ('Science and Literature under Peter the Great'), Pypine ('Progress of Ideas under Alexander I.'), Kovalevski, Korff, and Popof ('Epoch of Alexander I.'). MM. Sreznevski, Afanasief, Rybnikof, Kiriéevski, Bezsonof, Hilferding, Oreste Miller, and Bouslaief have collected or illustrated precious monuments of popular literature.

The artistic movement likewise took more breadth and variety. The composers Tchaïkovski, Siérof, Dorgomyjski, and Rubistein; the landscape-painter Aïvazovski; the portrait-painters Tropinine, Kharlamof, and Zarenko; the painters of history, Makhovski, Semigradski, Gay, and Flavitski; the painters of *genre*, or of battles, Sterenberg, Verechtchaghine, Repine, &c.; and the sculptors Antakolski, Kamenski, and Piménef, have acquired a European reputation. In 1862 M. Mikiéchine unveiled the monument of Novgorod, and in 1874 the statue of Catherine II., at St. Petersburg, surrounded by the great men of her time. At Moscow the magnificent Church of the Saviour, projected by Alexander I., is being finished after the plan of M. Tonn.

The tradition of the great scientific voyages has been continued by Baer, Middendorff, Maximovitch, Lütke, Helmersen, Schrenk, and Schmidt. Ethnography and philology can count some illustrious names: Castren, Sjœgren, Schiefner, Bethlinjk, Dorn, Kunik, Lerch, Wiedmann, Radlow, Kanikof, Brosset, Storch, and Kœppen. In natural science we must mention Brandt, Gappert, Borchtchof, Ovsiannikof, Kokcharof, &c.; in physics, Jacobi, Kuppfer, Kœmtz, and Lenz; in chemistry, Engelhardt, Fritzsche, and Chichkof; in astronomy, Savitch and Strube; in mathematics, Ostrogradski, Bouniakovski, Somof, Tchebychef, Forsch, and Maievski. The Geographical Society has rendered immense services; MM. Sossnovski, Kostenko, Fedchenzo, and Prjévalski have explored Central Asia.

At last Russia has been able to invite learned Europe to her international gatherings—to the Ethnographical Congress of Moscow in 1867, the Statistical Congress of St. Petersburg in 1872, the archæological meetings of St. Petersburg, Moscow, Kief, and Kazan (1869–1877), and the Congress of Orientalists of St. Petersburg in 1876.

The novel situation in which Europe has been placed by the development of the Prussian military power has obliged the empire of the Tzars to reform its military system also. This has been provided for by the law of 1873, which orders that all Russian subjects, without distinction of condition or nationality, shall be forced to submit to the conscription. Now it is impossible to call out every year 676,000 men, reckoning from the class of 1874; hardly a third of this number march under the standards. The educated conscript can, if the lot falls on him, obtain in four ways a reduction of his six years' term of service. If he has received the superior education, he only serves six months; if he has received the secondary course of instruction at the gymnasia, eighteen months; if he has passed through the primary superior schools, three years; if through the primary school, four years. This law has, therefore, the character of a law of social equality, and offers, besides, a premium on education. The time can be abridged still further by voluntarily forestalling the conscription. The Russian army is divided into the regular army, the reserve troops, and the irregular corps. It comprises 1,200,000 men, a number which Peter the Great had never dreamed of. In 1867 Russia adhered to the Convention of Geneva for the relief of the wounded.

CONQUEST IN ASIA—EUROPEAN POLICY.

The power of Russia continues to extend in Asia. The Crimean war had lent new strength to the Circassian insurrection; but the seizure of Vedeni, the fortified residence of Schamyl, in 1858, was a mortal blow to his rule. In 1859, he was besieged in his castle of Gounib, and was forced to surrender to Prince Bariatinski, the pacifier of the Caucasus. The emigration of the mountaineers, encouraged by England from hostile feelings to Russia, rendered the latter on the contrary the service of relieving the country of the most turbulent elements, and of making room for colonization. The conquest was secured by numerous fortresses and strategic routes, like that from Vladikavkaze to Tiflis. The Russian element, especially in the north of the Caucasus and in the towns, has struck deeper roots.

Turkestan is a sandy region traversed by the Syr Daria and the Amou-Daria (the Jaxartes and Oxus of the ancients) on their way to empty themselves into the Sea of Aral. These two rivers take their rise in the chain of the Bolor Mountains, on the other slope of which flow the Kashgar and the Jarkent, tributaries of the Tarim, which runs in its turn into Lake Lob.

To the north of the Jaxartes are the encampments of the Kirghiz; on the banks of the Caspian wander tribes of Turkomans. On the Upper Jaxartes the khanate of Khokand is situated, with its capital Khokand, and the principal towns of Turkestan, containing the tomb of Achmet-Yasavi, the Mussulman Apostle of Turkestan, Tashkent, Tchemkent, Khodjend, *Alexandria Heskata*, or the *last Alexandria* founded by Alexander the Great; on the Upper Oxus, the khanate of Balkh, capital

Balkh (the ancient Bactria, the cradle of our race), the khanate of Samarcand (residence of the famous Tamerlane), and the khanate of Bokhara; on the Lower Oxus, the khanate of Khiva, situated in a fertile oasis, in the midst of sandy deserts; on the Kashgar, the khanate of Kashgar, including also Yarkand (40,000 souls), a powerful State founded in 1864 by the bold and able Yakoub Khan. All these States lie on the commercial route to India and China; and the English have always looked uneasily on the progress of the Russians in these regions.

The Russian rule in Turkestan was founded by the submission of the Kirghiz under Nicholas I., and the fall of their Khan Khazimof in 1844. To protect these new subjects, it has been necessary since 1853 to enter upon a war with the khanate of Khokand, a war signalized by the capture of Ak-Masjid by Colonel Perovski, who gave it his name. In 1860 Colonel Kolpakovski, with 800 men, defeated a Khokandian army of 15,000 men in the defile of Urzun-Agatch; in 1864, Colonel Verevkine left Orenburg and seized Turkestan, whilst Colonel Tchernaïef left Siberia and subdued Aulié-Ata. The two columns took Tchemkent by assault, and the year following Tashkent, a town with a population of 100,000 souls, surrendered to 2000 Russians.

The Bokharians on their side intervened in the civil wars of Khokand. and ended by entering into conflict with the Russians. Their Emir, whose *prestige* throughout Central Asia was great, was vanquished in spite of the frantic attempts of the Mollahs to raise a holy war, in two battles—that of Irdjar in 1866, which brought about the conquest of Samarcand, and that of Zera-Buleh in 1868, which led to the treaty of the 5th of July. By this treaty, the Emir of Bokhara ceded to the Russians the khanate of Samarcand, and paid an indemnity of two millions. Bokhara itself would have been annexed, if the Russian generals had not feared to weaken their conquests by extending them. Khokand, on whose throne the Russians established their *protégé* Khudayar, became a vassal State.

In the interval (1867) Alexander II. had created the government of Turkestan, at whose head he placed a governor-general, a sort of vice-emperor, whose pomp and magnificence are likely to give to the natives a high idea of his sovereign the White Tzar.

The Khan of Khiva, in the midst of the deserts which girdled his States, braved the power of the Russians, who had been repulsed by the climate in 1839. He reduced their merchants to slavery, and in 1870 and in 1871 sent help to the Kirghiz. In 1872 Colonel Markozof quitted the Caucasus to chastise the Khan, but thirst and privations decimated his little troop, and obliged them to retreat. In 1873, three columns advanced on Khiva, from three different sides: Markozof from the shores of the Caspian, General Verevkine from Orenburg, and Kaufmann, general-in-chief, from Tashkent. The first was obliged to retreat; the third suffered greatly, but ended by entering Khiva, which Verevkine, however, had already reached. The vanquished Khan acknowledged himself vassal of the White Tzar; the portion of his States on the right bank of the Oxus was annexed; the navigation of the river was reserved exclusively to the Russians; extensive commercial privileges were secured to their merchants; their quarrels with the natives were to be judged by the nearest Russian authority; a council of government, composed of Khivian dignitaries and Russian officers, was to assist the Khan. A contribution of 2,200,000 roubles exhausted his remaining resources: it was a disguised annexation. Only the fear of a conflict with England, a consequence which was averted by the mission of Count Schouvalof to London, prevented the reduction of Khiva to the condition of a Russian province.

The Russian policy, like that of the English in Hindostan, avoided public annexations, and allowed the situations created by its victories to ripen. Khudayar, Khan of Khokand, had been forced in 1873 and 1874 to fight his revolted subjects, who were exasperated by his submission to the "infidels." In 1875 another and more general revolt took place; and abandoned even by his two sons, who joined the insurgents, he quitted his capital with his harem and his treasures, and established himself at Orenburg. Khokand was annexed. It is a State sixty leagues long by thirty broad, and wonderfully fertile. The difficulties of the Khan of Khiva with his subjects, who despised him for his submissiveness, were not less. Deprived of part of the tribute that he collected from the Turkomans (declared Russian subjects in 1875), he entreated the following year to be allowed to exchange his domains for a pension; the reply was not given immediately, but it is only a question of time.

The Kirghiz and the Turkomans being subdued, Khokand and Samarcand annexed, Khiva and Bokhara reduced to the condition of vassals, only one prince of these nations made head against the Russians, and this was Yakoub Khan of Kasbgar, the *protégé* of the English, who had persuaded the Sultan of Constantinople to grant him the title of Emir. With his army of 40,000 men, disciplined by Polish or Anglo-Indian officers, with his arsenals and his foundries, he prepared to defend the passes of the mountains. In 1870 the Russians had anticipated him by occupying the Chinese province of Khuldja, whence the rebellious Mussulmans had expelled the troops of the Celestial Empire, and which Yakoub coveted. Russia offered to hand it over to China, which did not care about it, and meanwhile it was administered by the Russians. Their policy created last year (1876) an unexpected difficulty for Yakoub; an invasion of Kashgar by the Chinese troops is imminent (1877,) if it is not already accomplished. Yakoub Khan died this year (1877), leaving to his successor a situation which is gravely compromised.

In these countries, for centuries devastated and dishonored by Mussulman fanaticism, by wars between the khans, and by traffic in slaves, the Russians appear as the soldiers of civilization, and bring with them a more humane and equitable rule.* Following on the banks of the Ovus and Jaxartes the traces of Alexander the Great, they complete the revenge of the Iranian race against the Touranian peoples who invaded, with Genghis Khan, semi-Greek Bactria, and ruined the ancient Macedonian colonies. They do not conquer; they only colonize. "All these enterprises," says M. Cucheval-Clarigny, "will profit civilization at the same time that they consolidate the Russian power; but the chief strength of the latter lies in the qualities which make the Russian soldier the most admirable instrument of conquest and colonization. Docile as well as brave, easily contented, supporting without complaint all fatigues and privations, and ready for everything, the Russian soldier constructs roads, clears canals, and re-establishes the ancient aqueducts. He makes the bricks with which he builds the forts, and the barracks which he inhabits; he fabricates his own cartridges and projectiles; he is a mason, a metal-founder, or carpenter, according to the need of the hour, and the day after he is dismissed he contentedly follows the plough. With such instruments at her disposal, the Russian power will never give way: a few years will suffice to render final the conquest of any land on which she has set her foot.

At the other extremity of Asia, General Mouravief signed in 1858 with the Court of Pekin the Treaty of Aïgoun, which secured to Russia all the right bank of the river Amour, a territory of 1278 square miles, which now forms the province of the Amour and the maritime province. Japan had already ceded the southern part of the island of Saghalian. The steamboats of the Amour Company already plough the waters of the river, and place Russia in direct communication with San Francisco and the Pacific Isles.

By the treaty of 1867 Russia sold to the United States her American possessions, thus drawing closer the bonds which unite her to the great republic.

---

* The kindly character of Russian colonization " in the Circassian manner" has been described by Mr. Schuyler.—TRANSLATOR.

The European policy of Russia during this period offers results which are more debatable than her Asiatic policy. In 1856 Prince Alexander Gortchakof succeeded old Count Nesselrode as Chancellor of the Empire. In one of his earliest circulars he thus characterized the attitude imposed on Russia by the consequences of the Eastern war: "Russia does not sulk, she collects her forces." At the Conferences of Paris there had been a visible *rapprochement* between this country and France, which had already grown cold to her old ally, Austria. Russia allowed Italy to emancipate herself, while drawing her own conclusions about the emancipation of the Christians in the East. After having protested against the dispossession of the Italian princes, she ended by recognizing the new kingdom. She applauded the French occupation of Syria, which she would have even wished to be more important and more prolonged. France in her turn favored the demands of the Roumanians, Servians, and Montenegrins against Turkey, and received graciously the observations of Prince Gortchakof on the "wretched and precarious situation" of the Christians of Bosnia, the Herzegovina and Bulgaria.

The diplomatic demonstrations of France in 1863, *à-propos* of Polish affairs, destroyed the growing intimacy of the two States, and threw Russia into the Prussian alliance. To maintain this the Russian Chancellor made irreparable sacrifices to Bismark. In 1864 Russia allowed Denmark to be crushed, when she lost the duchies of the Elbe. In 1866 she permitted Prussia not only to expel Austria from the Germanic Confederation, but to dethrone the reigning houses of Hanover, Nassau, and Cassel, more or less related to the imperial house of Russia. Those of Darmstadt, Baden, and Wurtemberg, which had given empresses to Russia, were subordinated, so as to constitute Germany, formerly inoffensive, into a formidable military Power, which holds on the Baltic, the Vistula, and the Danube interests diametrically opposed to those of Russia.

It will be remembered that Bestoujef-Rioumine, the Chancellor of Elizabeth, finding the Prussia of Frederick II. too powerful, and the annexation of Silesia disquieting for Russia, fought the Seven Years' War to "diminish the forces" of the ambitious neighbor. Did not Alexander I. dare all the power of Napoleon for the sake of Oldenburg and the Hanseatic towns? Already in 1867, in the new Germany, an agitation was begun about the so-called German provinces of Russia. The demands of the Baltic writers found an echo in the public meetings and in the Berlin press, and M. Kattner dedicated to the German army his book on the 'Mission of Prussia in the East.' Russia had hoped for the support of new Germany in its Eastern policy, "but," wrote M. Benedetti, "any conflict in the East would put the German Chancellor in the power of Russia, and he will try to prevent it. This was proved in the Græco-Turkish difference last year. Russia is a card in his game for events that may take place on the Rhine, and he holds it to be necessary not to invert the *rôles*, not to become himself a card in the game of St. Petersburg."

In June 1870 the sovereigns of Prussia and Russia had an interview at Ems; on the 9th of July Prince Gortchakof said to the English ambassador "that Russia did not feel at all alarmed at the power of Prussia." This confidence was to be put to a new proof. In July 1870 the Franco-German war broke out, which was to end by overthrowing the European equilibrium, for the benefit of Prussia. The menacing attitude of Russia forced Austria to maintain her neutrality, and this neutrality carried with it that of Italy. Russian diplomacy weighed in the same manner upon Denmark, whose royal house had given in 1866 a princess in marriage to the Tzarévitch. France found herself isolated in Europe. Russia not only prevented the formation of "the league of neutrals," but by diplomatic means discouraged the collective intervention of Europe. On the 3rd of September the Emperor, on hearing of his uncle's victory at Sedan, drank his health, and broke the glass to give his toast more solemnity. No doubt he counselled his uncle to be moderate, "but," says M. Sorel, "this intimate and sympathetic exchange of private letters did not for one moment alter the friendship of the two sovereigns. The King of Prussia received the observations of his nephew without impatience; and the Tzar, although his observations never had any effect, was never affronted by the refusals of his uncle."

The nation did not contemplate the fall of France and the overthrow of Europe with the same eyes as the Government. "The public sentiment towards France," writes the representative of the United States, "is perhaps still more friendly since the recent successes of Prussia. The officers of the army are, it is said, almost unanimous in the desire for a war against Prussia. I know many occasions on which toasts have been drunk to the ruin of the Germans and of *Fritz*. The journals daily publish articles showing the danger which will result to Europe from the growth and consolidation of a military Power like that of Northern Germany. The last victories of Prussia have called attention to the vulnerable points of Russia, in case of a complete victory of Prussia; these are two—Poland, and the Baltic provinces." Subscriptions were everywhere made for the benefit of the wounded French, and the news of the smallest successes of France excited **public joy.**

The mission of M. Thiers at St. Petersburg, in **September** 1870, had no results; and this check caused his efforts in Austria, Italy, and England to remain fruitless. He had only received soft words in Russia, amongst others the remark that " the former enemy of France would do more for her than her former ally, England." In reality, the Russian policy, while serving Prussia, intended to cajole France, so as to attain with more certainty the end of its efforts, the revision of the Treaty of 1856. On the 29th of October Prince Gortchakof, in a circular addressed to the Powers signing the treaty, declared that events had " placed the imperial cabinet under the necessity of examining the consequences which might follow for the political position of Russia." He demanded the revision of article 2, which imposed a limitation on her maritime forces in the Black Sea. A conference was held in London, and Russia insisted that the French Government should be represented there. This was an indirect opportunity offered to the new republic to submit her quarrel with Prussia to the examination of the Powers. On the 13th of March, 1871, the French ambassadors in London set the signature of France to the revision of the Treaty of 1856, but in the interval his country had been forced to submit to the harsh terms of the Peace of Frankfort. The restoration of the German empire had been recognized by Russia on the 24th of January, 1871, and the Tzar had granted to the generals of the victorious army the highest marks of distinction. The princes Frederick William and Frederick Charles already bore the title of Russian field-marshals.

After the fall of France, the Emperors of Russia and Germany, dragging with them the Emperor of Austria, undertook to constitute what is called the alliance of the three emperors for the regulation of the affairs of the East and West. The Congress of Berlin in 1872, the journey of the Emperor William to St. Petersburg in 1873, and frequent interviews between the heads of the State, made the good understanding between them obvious to the eyes of Europe.

The Russians were well aware of all that Prussia had gained by this alliance of ten years with Russia. The profits secured to the latter were less visible. Prussia had acquired provinces and kingdoms, fortified harbors, a formidable army, and was mistress of the situation; Russia had obtained the erasure of the article which limited her forces on the Black Sea.

The new war in the East is not yet a matter of history. **We have yet to wait for the** *dénoûment*.* **A few years will allow**

* 1877.

many great events to be related with certainty : the rising in the Herzegovina, the massacres of Bulgaria, the taking up arms and defeat of Servia, the rapid dethronement of two Sultans, the first attempt at an Ottoman constitution, the weakness of European diplomacy in the Conference of Constantinople, the entrance of the Russians into the ancient Principalities and their alliance with Roumania and Montenegro, the passage of the Danube by the Grand Duke Nicholas, the brilliant surprise of the defiles of the Balkan by General Gourko, the bloody battles round Plevna, the vicissitudes of the war in Asia, and, lastly, the victory of Shipka, the occupation of Adrianople, and the march of the Russians, with Skobélef at their head, on Gallipoli and Constantinople.

Russia, sketched out by Rurik, dispersed after Iaroslaf the Great, re-united by the dynasty of the Ivans, Europeanized by Peter the Great and Catherine II., delivered from serfage by Alexander II., now enters into a new phase of her history. The wars of to-day have their consequences, not only upon the external relations of peoples, but also upon their internal development. The foreign policy of Russia, in spite of all changes, has never allowed itself to be turned from the three aims which she has followed since Ivan the Great—the conclusion of the duel with the Polo-Lithuanian State for the hegemony of the Slav world ; the struggle with her Western neighbors to secure the freedom of the Baltic and the Black Sea ; and the revenge for the Tatar yoke, whether taken on the Turanians of Central Asia or those of Constantinople. In the interior a new path has been opened to her by the civilizing reforms of the eighteenth century, and by the emancipating reforms of the present reign. After having conquered her place among the European States, she has to secure her rank among free nations. Here is a tradition which deserves following. May Russia in her liberal schemes display even more logic, resolution, and prudence than in her diplomacy ! We have related the history of the Russian State ; the history of the Russian people is now beginning. With the Russian State France has been often at strife ; her sympathies with Russia are growing since she has found in her a nation.

CHAPTER XVI.

ALEXANDER II., ALEXANDER III. AND NICHOLAS II. (1877-1898).

The Russo-Turkish War—The Treaty of San Stefano, and the Congress of Berlin—Nihilism and the Czar—Russia in the East—What the Czar Wills.

IN preceding chapters Russia's defense of Christians suffering under Turkish misrule has been related. The war of 1827-28 was the result of aid accorded to Greece in the latter's struggle for independence, while the Crimean ostensibly originated in Turkey's attitude toward Christian people and Christian sites. These conflicts were followed by that of 1877-78, the primal cause of which has been credited to barbarities in the Danubian provinces, where the Moslems were strong and the Christians weak. As a matter of fact, Turkey, rendered insolent by reason of anterior successes, grossly ill-treated there her Christian subjects. Throughout the rural districts of Servia, Montenegro and Herzegovina, taxes were increased to such an extent and were extorted with such rapacity that the peasantry, already intolerably oppressed, found it impossible to satisfy the demands exacted of them.

In the summer of 1875 matters culminated. Herzegovina rebelled. The insurrection which then ensued, and in which, a few months later, Servia and Montenegro joined, was punished in May of the following year by the massacres perpetrated by the Bashi-Bazouks—the Turkish irregular cavalry—on unarmed men, women, and children, and which became known as the "Bulgarian atrocities."

The report of these massacres occasioned great excitement throughout Europe. The details were so ghastly and revealed such inhumanity that energetic representations were addressed to the Porte by all the great powers, and a Conference was convoked at Constantinople in which England, France, Germany, Austria, Italy and Russia joined.

After several sittings the Conference finally embodied a series of reforms and concessions, which were then submitted to the Sultan, who promptly and unceremoniously rejected the proposals therein contained. A protocol, subsequently signed by all the powers on March 31, 1877, was treated in a similar manner.

Three weeks later Russia declared war with the Porte, and hostilities at once ensued, Russia immediately occupying Roumania and eventually crossing the Danube, where the army was joined by the Czar. The Turks neither resisted the occupation of Roumania, nor did they effectually oppose the passage of the Danube, and by the end of July a small Russian force had actually crossed the Balkans. But the aspect of the campaign was presently changed by the energy of Osman Pasha, who, after inflicting a repulse on General Krudener, threw himself into Plevna, an open town, which he rapidly intrenched and held against the invading armies. The Russian advance was stopped and the force beyond the Balkans receded, intrenching itself in the Shipka Pass, where it was besieged by the Turks. For nearly five months the struggle continued on these lines, the Russians and Roumanians hurling continued attacks on Plevna, which not even the heroism of Skobeleff could render successful against the gallant resistance of Osman. Finally, the place was completely invested, Osman's provisions were exhausted, and, on December 10, he attempted to break his way through the lines of the enemy, but was overwhelmed and forced to capitulate with his 30,000 men, he himself being wounded in the action. A force of 80,000 Russians and Roumanians were then disengaged, the Balkans broken through, and the road to Constantinople open. Meanwhile the war in Asia had also been successful. Mukthar Pasha had been defeated, Ardohan and Kars had fallen, and the investment of Erzeroum had occurred.

A little later an armistice was signed which resulted in the Treaty of San Stefano. Subsequently modified in the Congress of Berlin, through the provisions then arranged Roumania, Servia and Montenegro gained their independence. Bulgaria was divided; the old province of that name between the Balkans and the Danube being erected into a tributary principality, while the new province of Eastern Roumelia was left to the Porte, but with powers of self-government and certain securities against oppression. In Asia, Russia gained more of Armenia, together with the long-coveted port of Batoum ; but as a guarantee against further aggression England in exchange for Cyprus agreed to support Turkey in the defense of her other Asiatic possessions. In the campaign of which these arrangements were the result, Russia lost nearly 100,000 men and the expense incurred was not less than $600,000,000.

During the period immediately succeeding the termination of this war, conditions, if peaceful abroad, were threatening at home. The spread of Nihilism was a cause of great internal commotion, and attempts on the life of the Czar ensued which, unfortunately, were at last successful. In cities through which despots had walked unattended, Alexander II. lived in daily peril. On April 14, 1879, Solovieff, a schoolmaster, shot at him. In the same year an effort was made to blow up the Winter Palace in which he resided; and later an effort was made to wreck a train in which he was journeying from Moscow to St. Petersburg. Ultimately, on March 13, 1881, struck by a bomb—the explosion of which killed the assassin—the emperor perished.

Alexander II. was succeeded by Alexander III., whose reign, marked by further Nihilistic attempts, by famine, by pestilence, terminated very quietly at Lividia, November 1, 1894. The sceptre was then taken by his son, Nicholas II., whose marriage to Princess Alix of Hesse, superb coronation, peace circular, together with the alliance formed by his government with that of France, constitute events sufficiently recent to dispense with further notice. It is the Empire itself, its progress and policy, which remain to be considered.

RUSSIA IN THE EAST.

The growth of the Russian Empire supplies one of the most remarkable features in modern history. Consisting, less than four centuries ago, of the Tsardom of Muscovy, with an area of 37,000 square miles, it includes to-day no less than 8,660,282 square miles—one-seventh of the land surface of the globe—and of this enormous territory 6,564,778 square miles are in Asia. This vast empire, stretching from the Baltic to the Pacific, and from the Polar regions to Afghanistan, is but sparsely inhabited, the density of population in the Asiatic dominions being only 3 per mile, while that of the whole empire is only 13 per mile, the population in England being 370. In connection with this disparity the question naturally occurs—How does it come about that an empire which is so thinly populated should constantly try to add to its territories? The explanation is not difficult to discover. The Russians are an agricultural people, and have a natural tendency to wander in search of fresh fields as the fertility of their own lands becomes impoverished. And thus it came about that, early in the history of Russia, the people went further and further abroad, the gradual enlargement of the empire meeting, up to a certain point, with no dispute. But the extensions which took place gradually brought the people into contact with new races, and when they confronted Turkomans, Mongolians, and the fierce Asiatic tribes, conquest of a less peaceful nature than mere progression had to be resorted to, if only to prevent border warfare and constant raids. And so, while the people spread further afield in search of land, and the merchants followed in search of trade, Russia was forced to determine in what manner she should deal with hostile nations. Her option narrowed into a choice between two alternatives. She might maintain a strong force along her boundaries, or she might conquer and absorb. Invariably she chose the latter course, and so by degrees moved across Northern Asia and into the heart of the Continent. As a result, during the past forty years the territories of the Czar have become doubled in extent.

The recent growth of Russian dominion may be said to date from 1848, when Peroffsky marched on Kazala and subjugated the tribes on the northern shores of the Caspian. Then an expedition found its way across the Steppes and seized Lower Amoor, an acquisition immediately followed by the taking of Ak Musjid, and the establishment of Fort Peroffsky. The Amoor province, comprising the whole of Northern Manchuria, was absorbed in 1859. The Khanate of Turkistan was added to the Russian Empire in 1859. Samarkand was seized in 1868. Kuldja was occupied in 1870. Khiva and Bokhara were taken in 1873; Khokand, in 1875; Merv, in 1884, and what remained of Turkomania in 1885. Since then have occurred the Penjdeh incident, the Pamirs wrangle, and the aggression on Eastern Turkistan. In short, barring Persia, Asiatic Turkey and Afghanistan, the whole of western Asia Russia has absorbed. From the Urals to the Pacific, the entire northern half of the continent is hers. In addition, she gave a suggestion of her arms by taking Saghalien from Japan, by the annexation of Manchuria, and by the founding of Vladivostock as a future naval base.

These successes have one and all been brought about by a single policy—that of expansion. But while this policy is steadily kept in view, the necessary steps are cautiously taken. Except where territory lies without the possibility of international complications it is occupied by slow degrees.

The successes that have resulted from this policy are due to an obvious—yet generally unconsidered—factor. There is in Russia no government to come in or go out at the will of the people. There are no ministers to reverse what their predecessors have accomplished. There is but one supreme head, one Autocrat of all the Russias. Public opinion there is none. Individual thought allied to individual action is as impossible as newspaper criticism. The Czar wills: such is the formula by the aid of which ideas become accepted throughout the land. What the Czar wills, all classes will; the result being that no year passes that does not bring some gain to the great empire, great in extent, great in ambitions, and greatly served. Every addition goes to its enlargement, to the increase of its strength; and one does not need to probe the philosophy of history to understand the advantages belonging to a people who fight with the north wind at their back.

OBSERVATIONS.

In spelling the Russian names I have adhered to the rational orthography, of which the first example was given by Schnitzler. Thus the Russian к (the Greek *kappa*) has been rendered by *k*, the letter х (aspirated *k*, the Greek *khi*) by *kh*, and the letter ш by *ch*. The *bi* or dumb *i* has been rendered by the French *y*, and the other Russian *i* by I. The letters *tch* and *chtch* have been kept to express the *tchèrve* and the *chtcha*. The Russian vowel *y*, pronounced *ou*, is translated by the French diphthong *ou*, not by the German *u*.

I have sought to relieve the Russian names of their redundant *s* (the Germans employ seven letters, *s c h t s c h*, to express the single Russian *chtcha*), and of the *ff* and the double *w*, which give them such a repulsive appearance. Only in a few names, sanctioned by usage, I have conformed to the usual orthography; instead of *Chouvalof* and *Chakovskoï*, diplomacy and literature have familiarized *Schouvalof* and *Schakovskoï*.

In the same way I write *Moscow* and *Moskowa*, instead of Moskva, which designates both the river and the town.

I have tried to reproduce the orthography of the Russian names, though not their pronunciation, which is still more fantastic than in English. We print *Orel*, *Potemkine*, but they must be pronounced *Ariol*, *Patiomkine*.

The terminations in *vitch* and *vna* indicate filiation: *Peter Alexiévitch*, Peter son of Alexis; *Elizabeth Pétrovna*, Elizabeth daughter of Peter.

The Russian calendar has not adopted the Gregorian reform; it is, therefore, behind it, and for every date it is necessary to indicate whether it is after the old or new style. For important dates, both styles are generally given. In the eighteenth century the Russian style is eleven days behind ours: in the nineteenth century it is twelve days. Thus the date of the death of Catherine II. has been given as 6th–17th of November, a difference of eleven days, since the event happened in the eighteenth century. But we say the revolution of the 14th–26th of December, 1825, as we are speaking of the nineteenth century.

*   *   *   *

The Translator has retained the orthography of M. Rambaud where it appeared to her to convey to English ears the correct pronunciation. A list of variations in the spelling of ethnographic names will be found in the Preface.

BIBLIOGRAPHICAL NOTES.

I.

AMONG the Russian books not translated into French which I have consulted for this history, I will cite the most important.

General Histories.—' History of Russia from the most ancient Times,' by M. Serge Solovief (26 vols. have already appeared, up to Catherine II.), Moscow, 1851-1878. 'Russian History,' by M. Bestoujef-Rioumine (only 1 vol., up to Ivan III.), St. Petersburg, 1872. 'History of the Russian Nation,' by Polévoï. 'Russian History contained in the Biographies of the principal Actors,' by M. Kostomarof, 4 vols., St. Petersburg, 1873-1877 ; by the same, 'Historical Monographs and Researches,' 11 vols., St. Petersburg, 1868. The little school histories of M. Solovief and M. Ilovaïski I have found most useful.

First Period.—'Chronicle' (of Nestor and his continuators), edited by Miklosich, Vienna, (1860, in the 'Monumenta historica Poloniæ' of Biälovski, Lemberg, 1869, and by the Archæological Commission, St. Petersburg, 1872, after the Laurentian MSS. M. Samokvassof. 'Ancient Towns and *Gorodichtche* of Russia.' Moscow. 1874. Dorn, 'The Caspian,' St. Petersburg, 1875. M. Gedeonof, 'Varangians and Russians,' 2 vols., St. Petersburg, 1876. M. Ilovaîski, 'Researches on the Origin of Russia,' and the 'History of Russia,' Kievian period, Moscow, 1872 ; both contrary to the Varangian-Norman theory. Pogodine, 'Ancient Russian History to the time of the Mongol Yoke,' Moscow, 1871, 2 vols., with a valuable atlas of prints, ancient maps, and miniatures. M. Biélaef, 'Accounts of Russian History (Novgorod),' Moscow, 1866. M. Zabiéline, 'History of Russian Life from the earliest Times,' Moscow. 1876.

Period of Ivan the Terrible.—' Narrative of Prince Kourbski,' published by Oustriélof, 3rd edition, St. Petersburg. 1868. 'Life and Historic Rôle of Prince Kourbski,' by Serge Gorski, Kazan, 1858. 'Russia and England' (1553-1593), by M. Iouri Tolstoï, St. Petersburg, 1875. 'Private Life of the Tzarinas,' and 'Private Life of the Russian Tzars,' by M. Zabiéline, Moscow, 1869 and 1872. The 'Domostroï' edited by M. Iakovlef, St. Petersburg, 1867. 'Essays and Historico-Literary Researches on the Domostroï,' by M. Nékrassof, Moscow, 1878. The 'Stoglaf,' edit. Kojantchikof, St. Petersburg, 1868. 'Laws of the Grand Prince Ivan III., Vassiliévitch, and of the Tzar Ivan IV., Vassiliévitch,' edited by Kalaïdovitch and Stroéf, Moscow, 1819. 'Songs' collected by Kiriéevski, Ivan the Terrible.

Seventeenth Century.—Bantych-Kamenski, 'History of Little Russia,' M. Kostomarof, 'Bogdan, Khmelnitski.' M. Koulich 'History of the Reunion of the Rouss,' 3 vols., St. Petersburg and Moscow, 1874, 1877 ; by the same, 'Memoirs on Southern Russia,' St. Petersburg, 1856-57. M. Zabiéline 'Studies of Russian Antiquaries,' 2 vols., Moscow, 1872-73. 'The Russian

Empire in the middle of the Seventeenth Century,' by Krijanitch, edited by M. Bezsonof, Moscow, 1860. M. Aristof, 'Troubles in Moscow under the Regency of Sophia Alexiévna,' Warsaw, 1871. M. Lechkof, 'The People and the Russian State ; History of Russian Public Law up to the Eighteenth Century,' Moscow, 1858. M. Tchitchérine, 'Provincial Institutions of Russia up to the Eighteenth Century,' Moscow, 1856. M. Zagoskine, History of Law in the Russian State,' Kazan, 1877.

Peter the Great.—Oustriélof, 'History of the Reign of Peter the Great,' 6 vols., St. Petersburg, 1858-63. M. Grote, 'Peter the Great, Civilizer of Russia,' St. Petersburg, 1872. M. Solovief, 'Public Lectures on Peter the Great,' Moscow, 1872. M. Guerrier, 'The Last of the Varangians' in 'Old and New Russia.' Bytchkof, 'Letters of Peter the Great,' St. Petersburg, 1872. Pékarski, 'Science and Literature under Peter the Great.'

Successors of Peter the Great.—M. Andréef, 'Representatives of the Sovereign Power in Russia after Peter I.,' St. Petersburg, 1871. Pékarski, 'The Marquis de la Chétardie in Russia' (1740-42), St. Petersburg, 1862. Weidemayer, 'Review of the Principal Events,' &c., and the 'Reign of Elizabeth Pétrovna,' 1835 and 1849. Chtchébalski, 'Political System of Peter III.' Moscow, 1870. Bolotof, 'Memoirs,' edited by the Rousskaïa Starina, 4 vols., St. Petersburg, 1871-75; and 'Recollections of Past Times,' Moscow, 1875. M. Choubinski, 'Historical Sketches and Narratives,' St. Petersburg, 1869. M. Bestoujef-Rioumine on Tatichtchef, and M. Korsakof on Biren, in 'Old and New Russia.'

Catherine II.—M. Tratchevski, 'The Fürstenbund and the German Policy of Catherine II.' St. Petersburg, 1877. M. Solovief, 'History of the Fall of Poland,' Moscow, 1863. M. Kostomarof, 'Last Years of the Polish Pospolite,' St. Petersburg, 1870. 'Journal of Khrapovitski,' edited by M. Barsoukof, St. Petersburg, 1874. 'Memoirs of G. R. Derjavine,' edited by the Rousskaïa Bésiéda, Moscow, 1860. 'Memoir of the Life and Services of Alexander Bibikof,' edited by his son, Moscow, 1865. M. Melnikof, 'Princess Tarakanof,' St. Petersburg, 1868. Papers relative to the great legislative commission, published, with a preface, by M. Poliénof, in the Coll. of the Imp. Soc. of Russian History, 3 vols., St. Petersburg, 1869, and following.

Paul I.—General Milioutine, 'History of the Russian War with France in 1799,' 5 vols., St. Petersburg, 1852-53. Polévoï, 'History of Souvorof-Rymniski, Prince of Italy,' Moscow, 1811. Accounts of Souvorof, by an Old Soldier,' published by the *Muscovite*, Moscow, 1847. 'Memoirs of L. N. Engelhardt,' published by the *Archive Russe*, Moscow, 1868.

Alexander I.—M. Bogdanovitch, 'History of the War of Patriotism,' 3 vols., and 'History of the Reign of Alexander I.,' 6 vols., St. Petersburg, 1869-71. Pypine, 'Progress of Ideas under Alexander I.' Korff, 'Life of Count Speranski,' Kief, 1873. M. Ikonikof, 'Count Mordvinof,' St. Petersburg, 1873. Mikhaïlovski Danilevski, 'Description of the first War with Napoleon,' St. Petersburg, 1844, and all the wars of Alexander I. M. Alex. Popof, 'Moscow in 1812; the French at Moscow,' Moscow, 1875-76. 'Relations of Russia with the European Governments before the War of 1812,' St. Petersburg, 1876. Madame Tolytchéva, 'Account by Eye-witnesses of the year 1872,' Moscow, 1872-73.

Nicholas and Alexander II.—M. Bogdanovitch, 'History of the Eastern War,' 5 vols., 1876-77. 'Collection of MSS. about the Defence of Sebastopol,' published under the auspices of the Tzarévitch, 3 vols., St. Petersburg, 1872-73. Kovalevski, 'War with Turkey and Rupture with the European Governments in 1853-54,' St. Petersburg, 1871.

Berg, 'Essays on the Polish Insurrections and Conspiracies,' Moscow, 1873. M. Kropotof, 'Life of Count M. N. Mourovief,' St. Petersburg, 1874. Likhoutine, 'Memorials of the Hungarian Campaign in 1849,' Moscow, 1875. M. Nil Popof, 'Russia and Servia,' 2 vols., Moscow, 1869.

M. Golovatchef, 'Ten Years of Reforms, 1861-1871,' St. Petersburg, 1872. M. Mordovtsof, 'Ten Years of the Russian Zemstvo,' St. Petersburg, 1877. To these works we must add the 'Archives of Prince Voronzof,' published by M. Barténief, 12 vols., Moscow, 1870-78. The Coll of the Imp. Soc. of Russian History, 20 vols., St. Petersburg, 1867-78. Numerous articles in the 'Russian Archives' of M. Barténief (Moscow, 1862-77, 22 vols.) 'The Eighteenth Century' (14 vols.) and 'The Nineteenth Century' (2 vols.), by the same. 'Russian Antiquity,' St. Petersburg, 1870-77, 20 vols. 'Ancient and Modern Russia,' St. Petersburg, 1875-77, 9 vols. The immense collection of the 'Tchénia,' or 'Lectures,' &c. The Transactions of archæological societies and archæological meetings.

Bantych-Kamenski has left a bibliographical dictionary of Russian personages.

The archæology, ethnography, geography, and separate history of the Baltic provinces, of Little Russia, and of the ancient kingdom of Kazan, popular literature, and cultivated literature, would require a far more extensive bibliography. Polévoï has given us a 'History of Russian Literature;' likewise M. Porphyrief, 2 vols., Kazan, 1876.

For geography consult the Geographical-Statistical Dictionary of the Russian Empire, by M. Semenof, St. Petersburg, 1863-72; the 'Tentative Statistical Atlas of Russia,' by Colonel Iline; the small school atlas of Russian history, by M. Dobriakof.

II.

It will, no doubt, be more useful to indicate to the reader the French books, or books translated into French, that help to complete the former list.

General History.—The following may always be consulted with profit:—Karamsin, 'Histoire de l'Empire de Russie' (to the 17th century), translated by Saint Thomas and Jauffret, 11 vols., Paris, 1819-26. Lévêque, 'Histoire de Russie et des principales nations de l'Empire Russe,' continued. by Malte-Brun and Depping, 8 vols., Paris, 1812. Esneaux and Chennechot, 'Histoire philosophique et politique de Russie,' 5 vols., Paris, 1830. Choppin, 'Russie,' in 'L'Univers Pittoresque,' 2 vols., Paris, 1838-46. M. Geffroy, 'Histoire des états scandinaves,' Collection Duruy, Paris, 1851. Lélével, 'Histoire de Pologne,' 2 vols., Paris, 1844.

In German: 'Geschichte des Russischen Staates,' by Strahl and M. Hermann. 7 vols., Hamburg and Gotha, 1832-66; and 'Geschichte Russlands,' by M. Bernhardi, 4 vols., Leipzig.

General Studies.—Baron de Haxthausen, 'Etudes sur la situation intérieure, la vie nationale et les institutions nationales de la Russie,' 3 vols., Hanover, 1847-53. Schnitzler, 'L'Empire des Tsars,' 4 vols. Paris and Strasburg, 1862-69. The excellent articles of M. Anatole Leroy Beaulieu in the *Revue des Deux Mondes*, since 1873. Mackenzie Wallace, 'Russia,' translated into French by M. Henri Bellenger, 2 vols., Paris, 1877. Herbert Barry, 'Contemporary Russia,' translated into French, Paris, 1873. Dixon, 'Free Russia,' translated into French, Paris, 1872. M. Léouzon le Duc, 'Etudes sur la Russie et le Nord de l'Europe, la Baltique, la Russie contemporaine.' M. X. Marmier, 'Lettres sur la Russie, la Finlande et la Pologne.' Madame Hommaire de Hell, 'Les Steppes de la Mer Caspienne'. M. Anatole Demidof, 'La Crimée.' Prince Galitsyne, 'La Finlande.' M. Louis Léger, 'Le Monde Slave,' and 'Etudes slaves,' Paris, 1873 and 1875. M. Legrelle, 'LeVolga,' Paris, 1877.

Ancient Period.—M. Bergmann, 'Les Scythes, les ancêtres des peuples germaniques et slaves,' Halle, 1860. M. Georges Perrot, 'Le Commerce des céréales en Attique au 4e siècle avant notre ère' (*Revue Historique*, May 1877). 'La Chronique de Nestor,' translated into French by Louis Paris, 2 vols., Paris, 1834. M. L. Leger, 'De Nestore rerum russicarum scriptore,' Paris, 1868; by the same, ' Cyrille et Méthode,' historical study of the conversion of the Slavs to Christianity, Paris, 1868. M. A. Rambaud, ' L'Empire Grec au 10e siècle,' Paris, 1870.

In English: Mr. Ralston, ' Early Russian History,' London, 1874.

From the 16*th to the* 18*th century.*—In the Russo-Polish library of Franck: Meyerberg, ' Voyage en Moscovie.' Giles Fletcher, ' Russia in the Sixteenth Century.' Korb, ' Récit de la Révolte des Strélitz; ' Journal du boyard Chérémétief, une ambassade Russe à la cour de Louis XIV.;' 'Mémoires' of Manstein, Princess Dachkof and Tchitchagof.

Prince Emmanuel Galitsyne, ' La Russie au 17e siècle, récit du voyage du prince Potemkine,' Paris, 1855. Augustin Galitsyne, ' La Russie au 18e siècle ; mémoires inédits sur la règne de Pierre I.' Paris, 1865. Prosper Mérimée, ' Episodes de l'Histoire de Russie. 'Histoires des Guerres de Moscovie (1601-11).' by Isaac Massa of Haarlem, Brussels, 1876. Serge Galitsyne, ' La Régence de la Tzarine Sophie,' translated from the Russian of Chtchebalski, Carlsruhe, 1857. ' Mémoires du prince Pierre Dolgoroukof,' 2 vols, Geneva, 1867-71.

Voltaire, 'L'Histoire de Charles XII.,' and ' L'Histoire de Russie sous Pierre le Grand.' Johann Gotthilf Vockerodt and Otto Pleyer, 'Russland unter Peter dem Grossen,' published by M. Hermann, Leipzig, 1872. M. Mintzlof, ' Pierre le Grand dans la littérature étrangère,' St. Petersburg, 1872. Posselt ' Der General und Admiral Franz Lefort,' 2 vols., Frankfort, 1866. Bachoutski, ' Panorama de Saint-Pétersbourg,' translated from the Russian, St. Petersburg, 1831-34. M. Saint-René Taillandier, 'Maurice de Saxe.' Paris, 1870. M. Boutaric, 'Correspondance secrète de Louis XV.' 2 vols., Paris, 1866. ' Mémoires of Lady Rondeau, the Chevalier d'Eon, &c. Rathery, ' Le Comte de Pléio,' Paris, 1876. Salvandy, ' Histoire de Jean Sobieski et du royaume de Pologne,' 2 vols., Paris, 1855.

Catherine II. and Paul I.—Rulhière, ' Histoire et anecdotes sur la révolution de Russie en 1762,' Paris, 1797. Tooke, ' History of the Empire of Russia under the Reign of Catherine II.,' translated from the English, 6 vols., Paris, 1801. Jauffret, 'Catherine II. et son règne,' 2 vols., Paris. 1860. Augustin Galitsyne, ' Le faux Pierre III.' translated from Pouchkine, Paris, 1858. 'Mémoires,' by the Comte de Ségur. 'Memoires secrets,' by Major Masson. ' Histoire de Catherine II.' Castéra, &c. ' Mémoires de l'impératrice Catherine II,' published by Herzen, London, 1857. Sabatbier de Cabres, ' Catherine II., sa Cour et la Russie,' Berlin, 1869. ' La Cour de Russie, il y a cent ans, extraits des dépêches des ambassadeurs anglais et français,' Leipzig and Paris, 1860. M. A. Rambaud, ' Catherine II. dans sa Famille;' ' Catherine II. et ses Correspondants français,' in the *Revue des Deux Mondes* of the 1st of February, 1874, and the 1st of February and 1st of March, 1877. M. A. Geffroy, ' Gustave III. et la Cour de France.' 2 vols, Paris, 1867., 'Mémoires ' or ' Récits ' of Smith, Fuchs, Laverne, Anthing, and Gillaumanches, on Souvorof.

Epoch of Alexander I.—Besides the ' Histoire du Consulat et de l'Empire,' by Thiers, ' L'Histoire de France depuis le 18 Brumaire,' by Bignon, there exist numerous ' Mémoires ' of the campaigns, and especially that of 1812, the most important of which I have indicated in vol. ii. p. 275. Consult particularly the ' Mémoires ' of Savary, Duke of Rovigo: 'Mémoires et Histoire du général Philippe de Ségur,' 6 vols., Paris, 1873 ; ' Souvenirs militaires de 1804 à 1814,' by M. le Duc de Fezensac, Paris, 1870; Schnitzler, ' La Russie en 1812,' Rostopchine et Koutouzof, Paris, 1863 ; A. de Ségur, ' Vie du Comte Rostopchine,' Paris, 1872; M. Albert Sorel, ' Histre du Traité de Paris.' Paris, 1873.

Nicholas and Alexander II.—' Documents servant a eclaircir l'histoire des provinces occidentales de la Russie (in French and Russian), St. Petersburg, 1865. Schnitzler, ' Histoire intime de la Russie,' 2 vols., Paris, 1847. Nicholas Tourguénief, ' La Russie et les Russes,' 3 vols., Paris 1847, Baron Korff ' Avènement au trône de l'empereur Nicholas, translated from the Russian, Paris, 1857. Balleydier, ' Histoire de l'empereur Nicolas,' 2 vols., Paris, 1857; a somewhat second-rate though useful book. Peter Dolgoroukof, ' La Vérité sur la Russie,' Paris, 1860. M. Lacroix (Bibliophile Jacob), ' Histoire de la vie et du règne de Nicolas I., Paris, 1864 and following years. Admiral Jarien de la Gravière, ' Les missions extérieures de la marine,' *Revue des Deux Mondes* of 1873.

There is no definite history of these two reigns.

To the writings of the historiographer M. de Bazancourt, to the works of Niel and Todleben, and to the accounts of eye-witnesses or tourists, we must now add 'L'Histoire de la Guerre de Crimée,' by M. Camille Rousset, 2 vols., Paris, 1877. M. J. de la Gravière, ' La Marine d'aujourd'hui,' Paris, 1872. See also ' Français et Russes, Moscou et Sévastopol,' by M. Alfred Rambaud, Paris, 1877.

On the Russian policy in the Franco-German war, consult the excellent work of M. Albert Sorel, ' Histoire diplomatique de la guerre France-Allemande,' 2 vols., Paris, 1875, and the ' Deux Chanceliers,' by M. Klaczko. On the progress of the Russians in Asia, M. M. Weil, 'L'Expédition de Khiva;' ' Khiva, rapports de Hugo Stumm,' translated from the German, Paris, 1874; some articles in the *Revue des Deux Mondes*, especially that of M. Cucheval-Clarigny (15th May, 1877); the ' Annuaires' of the same review, &c.

For Literature.—M. Courrière, ' Hist. de la litt. contemporaine en Russie,' Paris, 1875: M. Rambaud, ' La Russie épique,' 1876; Mr. Ralston's ' Tales of the Russian People,' translated into French, Paris, 1876; tolerably numerous translations of Pouchkine, and of M. Ivan Tourguénief, by M. Louis Viardot; of Gogol, by M. Ernest Charrière; of Gontcharof (*oblomof*) by M. Charles Deulin; and of Alexis Tolstoï (' Le prince Sérébrannyi, ou Ivan le Terrible '), by Prince Augustin Galitsyne.

For the Fine Arts.—M. Viollet-le-Duc, ' L'Art Russe,' Paris, 1877.

TABLE OF MEASURES, WEIGHTS, &c.

(Abridged from Mr. Murray's 'Handbook of Russia.')

Length.

1 dium	= 1 inch.
12 dium	= 1 foot.
1 vershok	= 1.75 inch.
16 vershoks	= 1 arshin, or 28 inches **English**.
3 arshins	= 1 sajen, or fathom.
500 sajens	= 1 verst = 2-3 of a mile.
2400 sajens **square**	= 2.86 acres.

Money.

1 grivna	= 10 kopeks.
100 kopeks	= 1 rouble.
1 rouble	= 32 pence, or from 25*d.* to 38*d.*

One English sovereign is worth about 7.50 roubles.

Capacity.

8 shtofs = 1 vedro = 3.25 gallons wine **measure.**

Dry Measure.

1 garnets	= 0.34 peck.
8 garnets	= 1 chetverik = 0.68 bushel.
8 chetveriks	= 1 chetvert = 5.46 bushels

Weight.

96 zolotniks	= 1 funt = 14.43 oz.
40 pounds	= 1 pùd = 36.08 lbs.
10 pùds	= 1 berkovets = 360.80 **lbs.**

INDEX.

Abo, treaty of, ii. 72.
Academy of Sciences, ii. 37, 78.
Adachef Alexis, favorite of Ivan IV., i. 187, 192.
    Treachery and banishment, i. 193.
Agriculture of Slavs, i. 43.
    National, ii. 34.
Aix-la-Chapelle, Treaty, 1818, ii. 206.
Akhmet, Khan of Kazan, i. 167.
Akkerman, fall of, ii. 116.
Alexander Nevski, son of Iaroslaf, i. 119.
    Origin of surname, i. 120.
    Counsels tribute to Tatars, i. 122.
    Death, i. 123.
Alexander son of Casimir IV., i. 169.
    Marries daughter of Ivan III., i. 170.
Alexander I., ii. 142.
    Treaty with France, ii. 143.
    Interview with Prussian Sovereigns, ii. 147.
    Czartoryski counsels peace, ii. 151.
    Hatred of the English, ii. 157.
    Interview with Napoleon at Tilsit, ii. 157.
    Empowers Bennigsen to treat, ii. 157.
    Changes his Cabinet, ii. 159.
    His foreign policy unpopular, ii. 160.
    Differences with Napoleon, causes, ii. 170.
    Rupture with Napoleon, ii. 175.
    Military resources, ii. 177.
    Negotiates with Frederick William III. ii. 190.
    The soul of the Coalition, ii. 193.
    Scorns intrigues of Bourbons, ii. 200.
    Influence in European affairs, ii. 206.
    Radical change of character, ii. 207.
    Review of his reign, ii. 210.
    Favorites of, ii. 210, 219.
    Later bigotry, ii. 217.
    Death, 1825, ii. 225. *See also* Russia.
Alexander II. succeeds Nicholas I., ii. 255.
    Emancipation of the serfs, ii. 260, 265.
    Judicial reforms, ii. 266.
    Polish insurrection, ii. 269.
    European policy ii. 282. *See also* Russia.
Alexis Mikhailovitch, son of Michael Romanof, i. 272.
    Takes Little Russia under protection, i. 276.
    Abandons Livonia, 278.
    Turns his arms against Sweden, i. 278.
    Resents execution of Charles I., i. 289.
Alexis, son of Peter the Great, ii. 47.
    Marries Charlotte of Brunswick, ii. 48.
    Compelled to renounce the crown, ii. 48.
    Seeks refuge in Vienna, ii. 48.
    Centre of conspiracy against Peter, ii. 49.
    Punishment and death, ii. 49.

Ambassadors, foreign, i. 216.
Ambrose, Archbishop, insurrection against, i. 97.
American War, ii. 111.
Amiens, Peace of, ii. 145.
Ancient peoples, customs and costumes, i. 30.
Ancona, siege of. ii. 137.
Andrew Bogolioubski (of Souzdal), i. 83.
    Takes Kief by assault, 1169, i. 83.
    Founds Vladimir on the Kliazma, i. 86.
    Creates autocracy, i. 87.
    Superiority and despotism, i. 87.
    Triumphs over the Bulgarians, i. 87.
    Assassinated by his boyards, 1174, i. 88.
Anglo-Russian Protocol, 1826, ii. 234.
Anne Ivanovna crowned Empress, ii. 60.
    Severity of her reign, ii. 61.
Anne Leopoldovna, regency of, ii. 68.
Anne Petrovna, ii. 58, 71.
Appanaged princes, 15th and 16th cent., i. 184
Apraxine, Russian Generalissimo, ii. 74, 75.
Araktchéef, ii. 216.
Archæologists, Russian, discoveries, i. 24.
Architecture, i. 226.
Aristotele Fioraveuti, Italian architect, work, i. 172 228.
Arkhangel, i. 203; ii. 33.
Army. *See* Russia.
Art, development, i. 226, ii. 277.
    Græco-Scythian, i. 24.
Aryan family, i. 28.
Asia, Russian conquests, ii. 278.
Asiatic character of Russian society, i. 219.
Astrakhan conquered by Ivan IV., i. 190.
    Tzarate of, i. 166.
Augustus of Poland accepts humiliating terms from Charles XII., ii. 15.
Ansterlitz, battle of, ii. 150.
Austria and Russia, relations, i. 232.
    Fears success of Russia, ii. 66.
    Submits to Napoleon terms of allies, ii. 192.
    Joins the coalition, ii. 193.
    Seeks only weakening of Napoleon's power, ii. 195.
Austrian succession, war of, ii. 72.
Anstro-Russian alliance, ii. 64.
Azof capitulates to Peter the Great, i. 300.
    Surprised by Cossacks, i. 261.

Bachkirs, the, i. 30.
Bagration, Prince, ii. 147, 153, 155, 179.
Balaclava, battle of, ii. 251.
Baltic, navigation of, i. 14.
    A Swedish Mediterranean, ii. 9.
Banks founded, ii. 77.
Barbaric invasions of 4th cent., i. 26.
Barclay de Tolly, i. 157, 179, 199, 202.
Bartenstein, convention of, ii. 155.

Bati, khan of Mongols, i. 93, 115.
    Reception of Daniel, i. 93.
    Court on the Volga, i. 124.
    Death, 1255, i. 119.
Batory, Stephen, king of Poland, i. 201.
    Repels Russians at Polotsk, i. 201.
    Death, 1586, i. 233.
Battle of the Ice, 1242, i. 121.
Bela, King of Hungary, i. 91.
    Enters Galitch, i. 91.
Belskis, leaders of faction, i. 185.
Bells, i. 146, 238.
Bennigsen, Generalissimo of allies, ii. 152.
    Claims victory of Eylau, ii. 154.
    At Leipzig, ii. 194.
Berendians. *See Black Caps.*
Berezina, passage of, ii. 189.
Berlin occupied by the French, ii. 151.
Bernadotte, French General, ii. 153.
    Elected King of Sweden, ii. 165.
    Treasonable scheme, ii. 195.
Bestoujef, Russian Chancellor, ii. 73.
    Fall of, ii. 75.
Betski, scheme of national education, ii. 106.
Biarmaland, country of Permians, i. 30.
Bibikof, Alexander, ii. 98.
Bibliographical notes, ii. 288.
Biren, favorite of Anne Ivanovna, ii. 67.
    Named Regent by Anne Ivanovna, ii. 68.
    Arrest and banishment, ii. 68.
Black Caps, Russian barbarians, i. 82.
    Land, The, i. 21.
    Russia, i. 34.
Black Sea. *See Russia.*
Blucher, military energy, ii. 197.
Bog, Slavonic name for God, i. 38.
Bogdan Khanelnitski, Cossack leader, i. 274.
    Offensive operations against Russians, i. 274, 279.
Bogolioubski, Andrew, son of George Dolgorouki, i. 83. *See Andrew of Souzdal.*
Bokhara open to communication, i. 206. *See also* ii. 236.
Bolgary destroyed by Tatars, i. 115.
Bolotnikof. *See Second false Dmitri.*
Bonaparte in German affairs, ii. 144.
Bonaparte. *See Napoleon.*
Boris Godounof, i. 231. *See also Godounof.*
Borodino, battle of, ii. 181.
Boulgakof, Russian envoy to Turkey, ii. 114.
Bowes, Jerome, English envoy to Russia, i. 205.
Boyards of Galitch, i. 91.
    Surrenders of the Prince, i. 210.
Brest, council of, i. 267.
"Brigand of Touchino." *See Touchino.*
Brigandage, prevalence, ii. 30.
Bucharest, congress at, 1812, ii. 169.
Bulgaria, i., 53; ii. 248.
Bulgarian war, i. 53.
Bulgars, ancient, mix with Mongols, i. 166.
Building-stone in Russia, i. 17.
Byzantine forces defeat Igor, i. 50.
    Literature, i. 71.
    Monarchism, influence, i. 221.
Byzantium fears extension of Russian power, i. 54, 63. *See Tzargrad.*

Campo Formio, treaty of, ii. 130.
Cannon in Russian army, 1389, i. 153.
Cardis, peace of, i. 278.

Carlsbad, congress of, 1819, ii. 206.
Casimir, John, King of Poland, i. 275.
Casimir IV., King of Lithuania and Poland i. 169.
Castes, i. 67.
Catherine I. in Russian camp, ii. 42.
    Declared Empress, ii. 51, 54.
    Marriage to Peter, ii. 50.
    Humble origin and character, ii. 50.
Catherine II.
    Usurpation, ii. 85.
    Foreign policy, ii. 87.
    Successes over the Turks, ii. 94.
    Difficulties in her empire, ii. 97.
    Extinguishes the Zaporogue republic ii. 99.
    Influence of the Orlofs, ii. 100.
    The new code, ii. 101.
    Extends serfage, ii. 102.
    Administration and justice, ii. 103.
    Colonization, ii. 104.
    Secularization of church property, ii. 105.
    Interest in education, ii. 106.
    Introduces inoculation, ii. 106.
    Influence of French genius, ii. 107.
    Place in literature, ii. 108.
    Armed neutrality, 1780, ii. 111.
    Enemies on all sides, ii. 115.
    Signs peace of Iassy, ii. 117.
    Receives Polish malcontents, ii. 118.
    Treasonable conduct towards France, ii. 126.
    Outlines her position, ii. 127. [ii. 127.
    Excites jealousy of Prussia and Austria
    Death, 1796, ii. 127.
Caulaincourt, French ambassador, ii. 196, 198.
Chancellor, English navigator, i. 203, 204.
Charles I. of England, mission of Russian envoy, i. 287.
Charles II. of England, i. 289.
Charles X. of Sweden aids Poland, i. 278.
Charles X. of France, ii. 235.
    Expelled from France, ii. 238.
Charles XI. orders restoration of crown lands, ii. 9.
Charles XII. of Sweden, ii. 12.
    Success at Narva, ii. 12.
    Receives Marlborough in his camp, ii. 14.
    Knight rather than soldier, ii. 15.
    Invades Russia, ii. 17.
    Breaks Patkul upon wheel, ii. 17.
    Sufferings of army, 1709, ii. 18.
    Defeated and wounded at Pultowa, ii. 19.
    A fugitive with Mazeppa, ii. 20.
    Killed, 1718, ii. 46.
Charlotte of Brunswick marries Alexis, ii. 48.
Chatillon-sur-Seine, congress of, ii. 198.
Chemiaka, treachery and death, i. 158, 159.
Cheremetief, Russian cavalry commander, ii. 11, 24.
China, Russian treaty, ii. 57, 236.
    "Opium war" with England, ii. 236.
Chinese description of the Ta-tzis, i. 113.
Choiseul, minister of Louis XV., ii. 92.
Cholera, outbreak, ii. 238.
Chouiskis, leaders of faction, i. 185.
Chouiski, Skopine, popularity and death, i. 245.

INDEX.

Chouiski, Vassili heads revolt against Dmitri, i. 243.
    Becomes Tzar, i. 244.
    Assailed by Tzar of Touchino, i. 246.
    Alliance with Sweden, i. 246.
    Dragged prisoner through Warsaw, i. 250.
Christianity, progress and results, i. 52, 67.
Church, combat with paganism, i. 39.
Church of Vassili the Blessed, i. 230.
Churches of Kief, i. 64.
Civil wars, i. 76, 78.
Civilization of the Slavs, i. 43.
Class distinctions in Novgorod, i. 101.
Clergy, Black, i., 213.
    White, i. 213.
Coalition against France, strength, ii. 193.
    Demands regarding France, ii. 203.
Coast-line of Western Europe, i. 13.
Coins, first appearance, i. 153
Commerce in 10th cent., i. 102. See also i. 218.
Commune an expansion of family, i. 42.
Congress of Princes at Loubetch, i. 78.
Conscription, ii. 31.
Constantine, brother of Alexander I, ii. 204.
    Renounces the crown, ii. 226
    Mistakes in Poland, ii. 238.
Constantinople besieged by Varangians, i. 49.
    Gives Christianity to Russia, i. 67.
    Taken by Mahomet II., i. 160.
    First Russian ambassador, i. 173.
    Terrified at Russian success, ii. 94.
    Treaty of 1783, ii. 113.
    Mussulman riot, ii. 208.
Contarini, Venetian ambassador, i. 173
Convents as prisons, i. 213.
Copenhagen, bombardment, 1807, ii. 162.
Cossack life, development, i. 36.
    Take Azof, i. 261.
    Part in Russian conflicts, i. 261, 269, 275, 279.
    Revolt, 1706, i. 306.
    Make war upon French, ii. 187.
    Black Sea, ii. 99.
    Dnieper, i, 178, 191.
    Don declare for Moscow, i. 191. See also i. 241.
Cracow expels Russian garrison, ii. 122.
    Taken by Prussians, ii. 123
Crimea, becomes deadly enemy of Russia, i. 179.
    Composite character of population, i. 161.
    Khanate of, i. 166.
    Ceded to Russia, ii. 113.
    Turkish rule ended, ii. 94.
Crimean war, ii. 250.
Croi, Duc de, general of Peter the Great, ii. 10.
Cronstadt founded, ii. 13
Czartoryski, Russian minister, ii. 147, 151, 210.

Daniel, Prince of Galitch seeks alliance with Rome, i. 93.
Daniel, son of Roman, i. 94.
Daniel, son of Alexander Nevski, i. 140.
Danish fleet, seizure by English, ii. 141.
    Question, Nicholas I., intervention, ii. 247.
Dardanelles, treaty concerning, ii. 236.
David disputes Volhynia with his nephews, i. 78.

Deity of Russian Slavs, i. 38.
Debtors, law regarding, i. 213.
D'Enghien, Duc, execution, ii. 145.
Denmark forced to adhere to the Coalition, ii. 195.
Diderot, ii. 108.
Diplomacy. *See* Russia.
Directorate, armies of, ii. 131.
Dmitri, son of Michael of Tver, i. 142.
Dmitri Donskoi, i. 147, 152.
    Breaks the Tatar power, i. 151.
Dmitri, son of Ivan IV., slain, i. 235.
Dmitri, the false, i. 238.
    Heads a rebellion, i. 239, 240.
    Proclaimed Tzar, i. 241.
    Character and death, i. 243.
Dmitri, the second, false, i. 245.
Dmitri, third false, i. 244.
Dnieper, importance to Russia, i. 19.
Doktourof, Gerasimus, in England, i. 287.
Dolgorouki, George, son of Vladimir Monomachus, i. 81.
Dolgoroukis profit by the revolution, ii. 55.
Dolgorouki, Prince, interview with Napoleon ii. 148.
Domestic manners of pagan Russia, i. 41.
"Domostroi," i. 221, 222, 223.
Don, the commercial importance, i. 19, 20.
Dorastol (Silistria), battle, i. 55.
D'Oubril, sent to Paris, ii. 146, 151.
Drabans, guards of Charles XII., ii. 16.
Dreviians, subjection by Olga, i. 51.
Droujina, the warriors surrounding the prince, i. 65, 97, 211.
Drunkenness, prevalence in Russia, i. 221; ii. 22.
Dualism among the ancient tribes, i. 31.
Duckworth, Admiral, burns Turkish vessels, ii. 168.

Education under Peter the Great, ii. 35. *See also*, ii. 101, 213, 230.
Education, primary, ii. 275.
Edward VI., of England, expedition, i. 203.
Egypt revolts against Turkey, ii. 94.
Elizabeth Petrovna, daughter of Peter the Great, ii. 55.
    Plans for French marriage, ii. 46.
    Declared empress, ii. 70.
    Names her nephew heir, ii. 71.
    Hatred of King Frederic, ii. 73.
    Lessens power of Prussia, ii. 75.
    Death, ii. 75.
    Review of her reign, ii. 76.
    Elizabeth, Queen, signs treaty with Ivan IV., i. 205.
England opens White Sea to Russia, i. 203.
    Sends envoys to Russia, i. 205.
    Asks free passage to Persia, i. 256, 259.
    Services to Russia, i. 258.
    Compromise with Russia, ii. 142.
    Refuses to guarantee Russian loan, ii. 155.
    Supports Russian policy toward France ii. 203.
    Opium war in China, ii. 236.
English fleet repulsed by Turks, ii. 155.
    In the Dardanelles, ii. 168.
Entail abolished by Anne Ivanovna, ii. 63.
Erfurt, terms of convention, 1808, ii. 163.
Esthonia frightfully devastated, ii. 13.
Ethnography of Russia, i. 24.

INDEX.

Eupatoria, battle of, ii. 251.
Europe, unequal division, i. 13.
    Terror-stricken by Tatar conquests, i. 118.
    In 15th and 16th cents., i. 161, 208.
    Watches Sweden, ii. 14.
    Equilibrium of, ii. 203.
Eylau, battle of, ii. 153.

Feodor Ivanovitch, son of Ivan IV., i. 231.
    Two important actions of his reign, i. 233.
    Death, 1598, i. 235.
    Feodor succeeds Alexis, i. 290.
Finland, population, i. 29.
    Conquest by Peter the Great, ii. 43.
    See also, ii. 273.
Finns, the, i. 28, 30.
France opens relations with Russia, i. 206.
    Asks trade privileges of Russia, i. 256.
    Fails to make alliance with Russia, ii. 69.
    Diplomatic success in Sweden, ii. 96.
    Internal affairs, 1791, ii. 126.
    Coalitions against, ii. 146, 151.
    Military resources, ii. 176.
    Return of Bourbon princes, ii. 199.
    Revolution of 1830, ii. 244.
    And England support Turkey, 1854, ii. 250.
Francis II., interview with Napoleon, ii. 150.
Franco-German war, ii. 283.
Franco-Russian Treaty, first, i. 259.
Frankfort, Conditions of, ii. 195.
Frederic II. of Prussia defeated by Russians, ii. 75.
    Saved by death of Elizabeth, ii. 75.
    Influence with Peter III., ii. 83.
    Responsible for dismemberment of Poland, ii. 94.
Frederic William III., vacillating policy, ii. 147.
    Negotiations, ii. 190.
Freemasonry, spread of, ii. 221.
French influence in Russia, see France.
Frontier defence, i. 67.

Galitch, i. 91.
    Great Mongol invasion, i. 93.
Galitsyne, ii. 93.
Gallicia or Red Russia, i. 75.
    Introduction of Jewish element, i. 93.
    Austrian uprising, 1846, ii. 246.
Gallicians under Hungarian yoke, i. 91.
    Throw off the Hungarian yoke, i. 91.
Gedimin, Lithuanian ruler, 1315-1340, i. 131.
Genghis-Khan, tribes, i. 113, 114.
George Dolgorouki founds Moscow, i. 139.
George II. founds Nijni-Novgorod, i. 90.
George Danielovitch, i. 140.
    Struggle with the house of Tver, i. 140.
    Takes a Tatar wife, i. 141.
    Slain by Dmitri, 1325, i. 142.
Grand Prince of Kief, i. 82.
George the Black, ii. 168.
Georgian princes ask Russian protection, i. 205.
German invasions and settlements, i. 107, 111.
    Rule in Livonia, i. 108. [64.
Germans effect upon Russian civilization, ii.
    Fear growing strength of Russia, i. 101.
    In Novgorod, i. 102.

Germany, Russian armies enter, ii. 43.
    Constitution overthrown, ii. 246.
Glinskis, maternal relatives of Ivan IV., i. 186.
Godounof, Boris, regency, i. 231.
    Events of his reign, ii. 236, 238.
    Death, 1605, i. 241.
Golden Horde, the, i. 118.
"Good Companions," Novgorod adventurers, i. 152, 158, 206.
Gortchakof, Russian general, ii. 155, 249, 256, 282.
Grand Prince, ruler of Kief, i. 77.
    In 12th cent., i. 81.
Great Britain, maritime tyranny, ii. 137.
Great Mongol Companies, i. 159.
Great Russia, i. 34.
Greece, independence recognized by Turkey, ii. 235.
Greek art and barbaric taste, i. 25.
    Colonies, i. 24.
Greek Church, entrance of Russians, i. 68.
Greeks check advance of Russia, i. 55.
Grimm, ii. 107.
Gustavus Adolphus, i. 257.
    Seeks friendship of Russia, i. 258.
Gustavus III. re-establishes royal power in Sweden, ii. 96.
    Takes up arms against Russia, ii. 115.
Gustavus IV. of Sweden, ii. 164.
    Arrest and confinement, ii. 165.

Hamilton, Seymour, Sir, ii. 248.
Hanseatic League, i. 102.
Hastings, Lady Mary, cousin of Queen Elizabeth, i. 206.
    Sought in marriage by Ivan IV., i. 206.
Helena Glinski, i. 184, 185.
Herat besieged by Mohammed, 1837-38, ii. 237.
Herodotus, account of ancient peoples, i. 26.
High Council, aims to govern Russia, ii. 58.
Holland united to French empire, ii. 173.
Holy Alliance, act of, ii. 218
Horde, the Empire dissolved, i. 166.
Horodlo, congress of, 1413, i. 136.
Hospitality of primitive peoples, i. 69.
Human sacrifices, i. 31.
Hungarians in Gallicia, i. 91.
Hydrographic centre of Russia, i. 18.

Iaroslaf the Great, son of Vladimir, i. 61.
    Sole master of Russia, i. 62.
    Position among contemporary princes, i. 63.
    Successors of, i. 77.
Igelstrom, Gen., Russian officer, ii. 122.
Igor, son of Rurik, i. 49.
    Attacks Kief, 50.
    Expedition against Tzargrad, i. 50.
    Assassinated by the Drevlians, i. 51.
India, English rule in, ii. 138.
Inkerman, battle of, ii. 251.
Innocent III. seeks conversion of Roman, i. 92.
Inoculation introduced, ii. 106.
Ionian Isles, ii. 130, 151.
Irmak Timofeevitch, conquistador of Siberia, i. 206.
Isiaslaf, grandson of Monomachus, i. 77, 81.
    Called to throne of Kief, i. 81.
    Defeated at Pereiaslavl, i. 82.
    Operations in Kief, i. 82.

INDEX. 303

Italians in Russia, i. 172.
Italy furnishes artists and artizans, i. 230.
Ivan Kalita, brother of George Danielovitch, i. 142.
 Establishes supremacy of Moscow, i. 145.
Ivan II., "the Debonnaire," i. 146.
Ivan III. the Great, character, i. 162.
 Accomplishes submission of Novgorod, i. 162, 164.
 Undertakes conquest of Northern Russia, i. 165.
 Friendship for Mengli-Ghirei, i. 167.
 Promotes Tatar rivalries, i. 167.
 Refuses tribute to the Horde. i. 167.
 As Prince of Bulgaria, i. 168.
 Reconquers portion of Western Russia, i. 171.
 Marries a Byzantine princess. i. 172.
 Compared to Louis XI., i. 173.
 Exchanges embassies with Eastern Europe, i. 173.
 Review of his career, i. 173.
Ivan IV., (the Terrible), i. 182.
 Takes title of Tzar, i. 182, 186.
 Childhood and youth, i. 185.
 Marries into family of Romanof, i. 187.
 Besieges and conquers Kazan, i. 189.
 Conquers Astrakhan, i. 190.
 Seeks direct relations with Europe, i. 191.
 Treachery revealed during illness, i. 193.
 Banishes Silvester and Adachef, i. 193.
 Intrigues of the boyards, i. 193.
 Quits Moscow, i. 196.
 Resumes the crown on his own conditions, i. 196.
 His reign of terror, i. 197.
 Synodical letter, i. 198.
 Correspondence with Queen Elizabeth, i. 198
 Curious memorial of his vengeance, i. 198.
 Captures Polotsk, 1563, i. 199.
 Submits Poland's proposition to a States-general, i. 199.
 Makes Magnus King of Livonia, i. 199.
 Establishes towns on Dnieper, i. 200.
 Covets the crown of Poland, i. 201.
 Cedes Livonia to Poland, i. 202.
 Implores mediation of Pope Gregory III., i. 202.
 Authorizes trade with England, i. 203.
 Treaty with Queen Elizabeth, i. 205.
 Desires to make an English marriage, i. 206.
 Conquest of Siberia, i. 206.
 Review of his work in Russia, i. 207.
 Slays his son Ivan, i. 208.
 Killed by his warders, ii. 86.

Jagellon, son of Olgerd, i. 133.
 Receives crown of Poland, i. 134.
Janissaries, Servian, ii. 167.
Japan cedes Saghalien, ii. 281.
Jenkinson, English sailor and diplomat, i. 204, 205.
 Distrusted by Persia, i. 205.
Jesuits, intrigues in Poland, i. 265.
 Banished by Peter the Great, ii. 33.

Jews pillaged at Kief, i. 79.
 Expulsion during reign of Elizabeth, i. 76.
Job, favorite of Godounof, i. 236, 240.
Joseph II., Alliance with Russia, ii. 113.
 Death of, ii. 116
Joubert, French general, ii. 133.
Judiciary the, i, 212.

Kalevy-poeg. the, i. 110.
Kalisch, Treaty of, ii. 191.
Kalka, the battle of, i. 114.
Kalmucks. i. 33 ; ii. 38.
Kalmuck-Torgaouts retire to China, ii. 98.
Kavgadi, Mongol general, i. 141.
Kars, ii. 257.
Kashgar, ii. 280.
Kaufman, General, ii. 280.
Kazan, Tzarate of, i. 166.
 Conquered by Ivan IV., i. 188.
 Political consequences of surrender, i. 190.
Keremet, divinity between good and evil, i. 31.
Kestout, son of Gedimin, i. 132.
Khazars, ancient Finnish people, i. 31.
 Empire and commerce, i. 32.
 Religious toleration, i. 32.
 Civilization of, i. 79.
Khiva, ii. 237.
Khylnof, City of, i. 106.
Kief, city of Russia, i. 19.
 Its water communications, i. 19.
 After death of Iaroslaf, i. 64.
 Principality of, i. 73.
 Strife for throne, 1146-1154, i. 81.
 Sacked by the Polovtsi, 1203, i. 83.
 Sacked by Tatars, i. 117.
 Under the Lithuanians, i. 131.
Kievans, respect for Monomachus, i. 82.
Kiptchak, gradual decay, i. 149.
Knout, punishment by, ii. 77.
Kolomna, battle of, i. 116.
Korosthenes, city of the Drevlians, i. 51.
Kosciuszko wounded, and a prisoner, ii. 124.
 Thaddeus, ii. 119. 121.
 Liberated by Paul I., ii. 130.
Kossuth, Hungarians under, ii. 247.
Kotzebue, Captain, explorations, 1815, ii. 224.
Koulikovo, battle of, i. 151.
Kourakine, Russian envoy at Paris, ii. 173.
Kourbski, Andrew, defection to Ivan IV., i. 194.
 Permits defeat of Russians, i. 194.
 Takes refuge in Poland, i. 195.
 Writings in exile, i. 225.
Kourgans. See *tumuli.*
Koutchouk-Kaïrnadji, Peace of 1774, ii. 95.
Koutouzof, Russian, Gen., ii. 147, 181, 183, 188.
Kremlin, the, of Moscow, i. 228.
 Destroyed by French. ii. 187.
Krijanitch, Iouri, learned Slav, i. 285.
Krudener, Madame de, ii. 203
Kunersdorff, defeat of Frederic by Russians, ii. 75.
Kutaïeh, treaty of, ii. 245.

Ladoga founded by Rurik, i. 49.
Ladoga, Canal of the, ii. 33.
Landon, Austrian general, ii. 116.

INDEX.

Language, dialectical differences, i. 34.
Lapoukhine, Eudoxia, first wife of Peter the Great, ii. 47.
    Banished and divorced, ii. 47.
    Whipped and confined in New Ladoga, ii. 49.
Laps or Laplanders, i. 29.
Latin missionaries on the Baltic, i. 107.
Leipzig, battle of, ii. 194.
Leopold II. of Austria, ii. 116.
    Abandons war against Turkey, ii. 116.
Lestocq, Prussian general, ii. 152.
Lewenhaupt, Swedish general, ii. 17.
Letts, ii. 107.
L'Hôpital, French Ambassador in Russia, ii. 74.
Library of St. Petersburg, ii. 224.
Literature, Byzantine in Russia, i. 71.
    Of Novgorod, i. 103.
    Development under Catherine II., ii. 109.
    Under Alexander I., ii. 222.
    Of modern Russia, ii. 276.
Lithuania under Olgerd and Kestout, i. 132.
    Ceases to be formidable, i. 137.
    Becomes Polish, i. 137.
    Defections, i. 170.
Lithuanian tribes, i. 107, 130.
    Wars, effect on Europe, i. 178.
Lithuanians, the, i, 28.
    Religion, i. 130.
    Summary conversion, i. 134.
Little Russia, i. 34.
Little Russia. *See also* Russia.
Livonia, frightful devastation, ii. 13.
    Ceded to Poland, i. 202.
    Devastation, ii. 13.
Livonian Knights, i. 108.
Livonian order, i. 161, 191.
    War with Ivan IV., i. 192.
    Dissolved, i. 199.
Livonians, the, i, 29.
    Converted to Christianity, i. 107.
    Revolt against missionaries, i. 108.
Lomonossof, ii. 78.
London, treaty of, 1827, ii. 234.
    Treaty of, 1852, ii. 247.
Loubetch, town on the Dnieper, i. 78.
Louis XIV. postpones visit of Peter the Great, i. 302.
Louis XV., private correspondence with Elizabeth of Russia, ii. 74.
    Projected marriage with Elizabeth of Russia, ii. 46, 56.
Louis XVIII. enters the Louvre, ii. 200.
Louis Philippe, ii. 244.
Lublin, union of, i. 200, 264.
Lutzen, battle of, ii. 191.

Macdonald, French general, ii. 133.
Magistrates of Novgorod, i. 100.
Magnus, Danish prince, i. 199.
Magyars, founders of Hungary, i. 30.
Mahmoud, Sultan, ii. 234.
Malta, knights of, ii. 131.
    Reduction by Bonaparte, ii. 131.
Mamai, Tatar ruler, i. 119.
Manufactures, ii. 34, 274.
Marfa, widow of possadnik Boretski, i. 163.
    Heads anti-Muscovite party, i. 163.

Marina, wife of false Dmitri, i. 239, 254, 255.
Markof, Russian representative at Paris, ii. 145.
Marriage, i. 31.
Massena, French general, ii. 134.
Maurice de Saxe, son of Augustus, ii. 56.
    Fruitless defence of Duchy of Courland, ii. 56.
Maximus the Greek, i. 180.
Mazeppa, i. 306.
    Goes over to the Swedes, i. 308.
    Intrigues with King of Poland, i. 308.
    Opinion of Charles XII., ii. 16.
Menchikof, Russian leader, ii. 17, 24, 54.
    Arrested and banished, ii. 55.
Mengli-Ghirei, Tatar leader, i. 167.
    Declares against Vassili, i. 178.
Merrick, John, ambassador of James I., i. 256.
    Seeks commercial concessions from Russia, i. 256, 259.
Metternich, negotiations with Napoleon, ii. 196. *See also* ii. 198, 207, 217.
Michael of Tver, i. 140.
    Assassinated, 1319, i. 142.
Michael Romanof assembles the Estates, i. 257.
Migrations of the husbandmen, i. 36.
Mikouline, Gregory, i. 237.
Military organization of Slavs, i. 44.
    System of Russia, ii. 277.
Militia of Novgorod, i. 99.
Miloradovitch, ii. 147, 227.
Minine, i. 251, 253.
Mirovitch, conspiracy, ii. 86.
Missionaries, Byzantine, i. 58.
Moldavia, ii. 234, 247.
Mongol invasion of Galitch, i. 93.
    Influence upon Russian development, i. 127. *See also* Tatars.
Monomachus leaves paper of instructions, i. 80. *See also* Vladimir.
Monomachivitches descendants of Vladimir Monomachus, i. 81.
Monuments of ancient tribes, i. 29, 42.
Mordvians, the, i. 30.
Morea. French in the, ii. 256.
Morozof, counsellor of Alexis, i. 272.
Moscow, origin, i. 139.
    Besieged by Tatars, i. 152.
    First coronation of Grand Prince, i. 156.
    Becomes capital of Russia, i. 156.
    Evacuated and burned by the French, ii. 187.
    Entry of French army, ii. 186.
    Terrible fire, 1547, i. 187.
    Burned by the Tatars, i. 200.
    During the Renaissance, i. 227.
    Foreign ambassadors, i. 216.
    December insurrection, ii. 227.
    Revolts against Sigismond, i. 249.
    Burned by the Poles, i. 250.
    Terrible revolt, 1648, i. 273.
    An academy established, i. 262.
    Return of the court, ii. 56.
    Insurrection, ii. 97.
    Plague of, 1771, ii. 97.
Moskowa, battle of. *See* Borodino, ii. 181.
Mountain systems of Europe, i. 14.
Mstislaf the Brave, prince of Smolensk, i. 86, 98.

INDEX.

Mstislaf the Brave defeats Andrew of Sourdal at Vychegorod, i. 86.
Mstislaf the Bold, i. 98.
Munich, Austrian marshal, ii. 65, 68.
Murat, French general, ii. 148.
Muscovite Empire, the, i. 34.
Muscovites, i. 34. *See also* Russians.
Muscovy, how formed, i. 34.
    Extent in 1472, i. 165.
    Extends her frontier, i. 170.
    Lower classes, i. 217.
Muscovy. *See also* Russia.
Mythology of Russia, i. 38.

Naples, French expelled from, ii. 133.
Napoleon crowned Emperor, ii. 146.
    Diplomatic activity, ii. 155.
    And Alexander I. at Tilsit, 1807, ii. 157.
    War with Austria, ii. 166.
    Creates parliamentary Poland, ii. 171.
    Question of Russian marriage, ii. 172.
    Consummates the Austrian marriage, ii. 172.
    Invasion of Russia, ii. 178.
    Enters Moscow, ii. 186.
    Evacuates Moscow, ii. 187.
    Crosses the Berezina, ii. 189.
    Reorganizes his army, ii. 191.
    Destruction of the rear guard, ii. 194.
    Battle of Leipzig, ii. 194.
    Defection of German allies, ii. 195.
    Defeats army of Silesia, ii. 197.
    Dethronement proclaimed, ii. 200.
    Abdication at Fontainebleau, ii. 200.
    Exile to Elba, ii. 200.
    Return to Paris, ii. 202.
Narva, siege of, ii. 10.
Navarino, battle, 1827, ii. 234.
Navy, Russian. *See* Russia.
Nepei, Osip, first Russian ambassador to England, i. 204.
Nesselrode, Count, ii. 234.
Nestor's list of Russian Slavs, i. 27.
Neva, importance as a river, i. 21.
    The, battle of, i. 120.
Newspaper, first, ii. 36. *See also* ii. 276.
Ney, French marshal, ii. 153, 187.
    Covers retreat of the French, ii. 189.
Nicholas I., accession, ii. 226.
    Character, ii. 228.
    Codification of the laws, ii. 229.
    Builds the first Russian railways, ii. 230.
    Schools established, ii. 230.
    Advance of literature, ii. 232.
    Ultimatum to the Divan, ii. 233.
    Declares war on Turkey, ii. 235.
    Declares war against Khiva, ii. 236.
    Relations with Louis Philippe, ii. 244.
    Intervention in European affairs, 1848, ii. 247.
    Schemes regarding Turkey, ii. 248.
    Death, ii. 251.
Nicon, ecclesiastical reforms, i. 283.
Nijni-Novgorod founded, 1220 i. 90.
Nobility, Russian, ii. 25.
Nogais, Horde of, i. 166.
Nomad races in Russia, i. 74, 83.
Normans of Russia, i. 47.

Novgorod, city of Russia, i. 18.
    Geographical position, i. 18.
    Siege, 1170, i. 85.
    Reduced to starvation by Iaroslaf, 89.
    Description, i. 95.
    A political centre, i. 95.
    Commercial interests, i. 98.
    Institutions, i. 99.
    Frequent change of rulers, i. 99.
    Reduced by famine and fire, i. 99.
    Magistrates, i. 100.
    Letter of Justice, 1471, i. 101.
    Constitution considered socially, i. 101
    Commerce of, i. 101.
    Religion and literature, i. 102.
    Pays tribute to Dmitri Donskoi, i. 152.
    The Republic dies, 1478, i. 164.
Nystad, peace of, 1721, ii. 46.

Odessa, bombardment of, ii. 250.
Office under the Tzar, i. 211.
Oldenburg, ii. 157.
Oleg succeeds Rurik, i. 49.
    Invasion of Tzargrad, 907, i. 50.
Oleg Sviatoslavitch, prince of 11th cent., i. 78.
Oleg of Riazan, i. 149.
Olga, widow of Igor, i. 51.
    Assumes the regency, i. 51.
    Converted to Christianity, i. 51.
    Besieges Korosthenes, i. 51.
Olgerd, son of Gedimin, i. 132.
Olgovitches, decendants of Oleg of Tchernigof, i. 81.
Oktai, second Emperor of Tatars, i. 118.
Orenburg, ii. 138.
Oreof, Alexis, annihilates Turkish fleet at Tchesme, ii. 94.
Orlof, Gregory, favorite of Catherine II., ii. 100.
Orthography, ii. 286.
Ostermann, ii. 154, 183.
Otrepief, Gregory. *See* Dmitri, false, i. 238.
Oural, Tatar signification, i. 14.

Pagan districts of the Volga, i. 31.
    Ceremonies, i. 60.
Painting, i. 226.
Palmerston, Lord, ii. 257.
Paper replaces parchment, i. 146.
Paris, entrance of the allies, ii. 199.
    Treaty of, ii. 200.
    Senate proclaims dethronement of Napoleon, ii. 200.
    Treaty of, 1856, ii. 257.
Patkul, John Reinhold, ii. 9.
    Plans attack upon Sweden, ii. 10.
    Death upon the wheel, ii. 17.
Patriarchal principle among Slavs, i. 41.
    Organization of family, i. 220.
Patriarchate established, i. 235.
Patzinaks, a barbarian people, i. 53. *See also* Black.
Paul, Grand Duke, tour of, 1784, ii. 113.
    See also Paul I.
Paul I. peace policy, ii. 128.
    Craze for Prussian methods, ii. 129.
    Peculiar foreign policy, ii. 130.
    Difficulties with France, ii. 130.
    Offers asylum to Louis XVIII., ii. 130.
    Alliance with Turkey, ii. 131.

Alliance with Bonaparte, ii. 138.
Expedition against English India, ii. 138.
Orders Louis XVIII. to quit Mittau, ii. 138.
Death, 1801, ii. 141.
Peasant population, i. 217, 233. *See also* Serfs.
Penal legislation, i. 213.
Pereiaslaf, Bulgarian Capital, i. 54.
Pernia, i. 30.
Permian branch of Finnish nation, i. 30.
Permians, civilization of, i. 30.
Persia, mistress of the Caspian, ii. 47.
    Seeks to regain Georgia and the Caucasus, ii. 169.
    Under Russian influence, ii. 237.
Peter the Great, i. 293.
    Youth and education, i. 296.
    Intrigues of his sister Sophia, i. 292.
    Democratic conduct, i. 298.
    Goes to Arkhangel, i. 299.
    Creates a navy, i. 300.
    Departs for Western Europe, i. 301.
    At the German courts, i. 301.
    As a ship carpenter, i. 302.
    Goes to London, i. 302.
    Tastes offend the Russians, i. 303.
    Revolt and destruction of the Streltsi, i. 303.
    Revolt of the Cossacks, i. 306.
    Confidence in Mazeppa, i. 307.
    Convinced of Mazeppa's treason, i. 308.
    Declares war against Sweden, ii. 10.
    Profits by the lesson of Narva, ii. 12.
    Seeks possession of Neva, ii. 13.
    Internal factions, ii. 13, 17.
    Victory over Swedes, ii. 13.
    Tries to negotiate with Charles XII., ii. 17.
    Reception of Swedish Generals, ii. 20.
    Reforms of, ii. 22.
    Chosen companions of, ii. 24.
    War against seclusion of women. ii. 26.
    Provincial governments, ii. 28.
    Creates State inquisition, ii. 30.
    Creates the Russian alphabet, ii. 36.
    Education of the people, ii. 35.
    Founds St. Petersburg, ii. 37.
    War with Turks, ii. 41.
    Completes conquest of Livonia and Esthonia, ii. 41.
    Goes to Versailles, ii. 43.
    His allies fear his ambition, ii. 43.
    Expels Swedes from Pomerania, ii. 43.
    Compels Sweden to treat, ii. 46.
    Domestic tragedies, ii. 47.
    Desires a port on the Caspian, ii. 47.
    Marries a Lutheran slave, ii. 50.
    Children by second marriage, ii. 51.
    Will of, ii. 51.
    Claims right to name successor, ii. 51.
    Death, ii. 51.
Peter II., grandson of Peter the Great, ii. 54.
    Treaty of commerce with Chinese Empire, ii. 57.
    Dies of small-pox, ii. 56.
Peter III., first measures, ii. 81.
    Private life. ii. 85.
    Foreign policy, ii. 85.
    Deposition and death, ii. 85.
    The false, ii. 98.

Philarete, father of Michael Romanof, i. 253, 258, 262.
Piracy, ii. 77.
Plateaus of Russia, i. 15.
Pleswitz, armistice of, ii. 192.
Poetry. *See Literature.*
Poland, formation of, i. 27.
    Absorbs Galitch, i. 94.
    Unites with Lithuania, i. 133.
    Alliance with Livonian Order, i. 192.
    Contest for the throne, i. 200.
    Henry de Valois proclaimed king, i. 201.
    Under Batory, i. 202.
    Cession of Livonia, 1582, i. 202.
    National and religious prejudices, i. 232.
    Rupture with Sweden, i. 233.
    Perfidious policy, i. 246.
    Renders assistance to false Tzars, i. 244, 247.
    Truce with Russia, i. 257.
    Influence of the Jesuits, i. 265.
    Reduced by Russian conquests, i. 278.
    Dismemberment considered, ii. 57.
    Question of succession, 1733, ii. 64.
    Thrice dismembered, ii. 88.
    Causes of her ruin, ii. 88, 89.
    System of agriculture, ii. 90.
    Religious dissensions, ii. 90.
    The Confederation, ii. 91.
    Dismemberment, ii. 94.
    Needful reforms, 1773-1791, ii. 117.
    Constitution abolished, ii. 119.
    Deserted by her allies, ii. 119.
    Second partition, ii. 117.
    Compelled to legalize partition, ii. 120.
    Tribunal punishes the traitors, ii. 123.
    Third partition, ii. 124.
    Under King of Saxony, ii. 170.
    Constitution of, 1807, ii. 170.
    Kingdom re-established, ii. 177.
    Fourth partition, ii. 201.
    Restoration, 1815, ii. 205.
    Insurrection of, 1831, ii. 239.
    Intervention of the western powers, ii. 272.
Poles, the, of Slav origin, i. 28.
Police, ii. 29.
Poliessa or Russian forest, i. 21.
Polish succession, war of, ii. 65.
    Renaissance, ii. 117.
    Slavs, i. 28.
Political effect of battle of Eylau, ii. 154.
Polotsk taken by Ivan IV., i. 199.
    Recapture by Batory, i. 201.
Polovtsi invasions, i. 72.
Polovtsi, a barbarian tribe, i. 78.
Polygamy, i. 41.
Pope Eugenius IV., i. 160.
    Vainly seeks union of the two churches, i. 160.
Pope Gregory III. as mediator, i. 202.
Possevino, Antonio, account of Ivan IV., i. 202.
Potemkine, favorite of Catherine II., 99, 100, 114, 116.
Potsdam, treaty of, ii. 147.
Pougatchef, Emilian, Cossack, revolt, ii. 97, 98.
Praga, taken by assault, ii. 124
Pratzen, battle of, ii. 149.

Preobrajenskoe, treaty of, ii. 10.
Presburg, treaty of, ii. 150.
Press, censorship of, ii. 231.
Printing protected by Ivan IV., i. 225.
Printing, ii. 36.
Property, division of, ii. 26.
Prussia neutral on the Polish succession, ii. 64.
    Dangerous to Russia, ii. 73.
    Alliance with Russia, ii. 83.
    Insatiable greed, ii. 89.
    Position on Polish question, ii. 94.
    Fall consummated at Tilsit, ii. 157.
    Value of the Russian alliance, ii. 284.
Prussians take Cracow, ii. 123.
    Defeated by French, 1806, ii. 151
Pruth, treaty of, 1711, ii. 42.
Pskof, the old town of, i. 104.
Pultowa, siege of, ii. 18.
    Political result of Russian victory, ii. 20.
Puritans, Russian, i. 35.

Railways, ii. 230, 274.
Rainfall in Russia, i. 17.
Raskolniks, the, ii. 212.
Red Russia, i. 34.
Reforms of Peter the Great, ii. 22.
Religion of ancient tribes, i. 31.
Revenues of the State, i. 211.
Revolution of 1848, ii. 246.
Rinzan, battle of, i. 115.
Richelieu, Duc de, succeeds Talleyrand, ii. 203, 204.
Riga, foundation laid, 1200, i. 108.
Roman, prince of Volhynia, conquers Galitch, i. 91.
Romanof, Michael, elected Tzar, i. 253.
Romanof, Anastasia, wife of Ivan IV., i. 187.
Romanofs, opposition of the boyards, i. 193.
Rome, relations with Russia, i. 68, 108, 132, 160, 202.
Rostopchine, Count, Governor of Moscow, ii. 258.
Roumania, ii. 258.
Rousskaia Pravda, or Code of legislation, i. 63.
Rurik, reign of, i. 49.
Russia, geographical extent, i. 13.
    Coast waters, i. 13.
    Inequalities of soil, i. 15.
    Climate, i. 16.
    Rivers, i. 18.
    Its four zones, i. 21.
    Barbarism of inland tribes, i. 25.
    Primitive peoples, i. 30.
    Still pagan in parts, i. 31.
    Its real aborigines, i. 32.
    How it was colonized, i. 33.
    Beginning of true history, i. 48.
    Byzantine influence, i. 58.
    Receives Christianity from Constantinople, i. 67.
    Has no alliance with Rome, i. 68.
    Divided into principalities, i. 72.
    Natural elements of cohesion, i. 76.
    Civil wars, i. 76.
    Ecclesiastical constitution, i. 103.
    Subjugated by Mongols, 13th cent., i. 112.
    Under the Mongol yoke, i. 117, 123, 129.

Relations with Rome, i. 132.
Establishes relations with the West, i. 153.
End of the Tatar yoke, i. 166.
New armorial bearings, i. 172.
Relations with Western Europe, i. 173, 178.
Growing importance as a political power, i. 180
Unity accomplished, i. 183.
Commercial treaty with Sweden, i. 191.
Excites jealousy of Germany, i. 191.
Aims at control of the Baltic, i. 191.
Frontier war with Sweden, 1554, i. 191.
Commercial relations with England, i. 204.
Sends ambassador to England, i. 204.
Receives envoys from Holland, Spain, and Italy, i. 206.
The power of family, i. 207
In 16th and 17th centuries, i. 209.
Civilization retarded by her neighbors, i. 209.
State revenues, i. 211.
Courts of civil justice, i. 212.
Penal legislation, i. 213.
Legislation in matter of debts, i. 213.
The national army, i. 214.
Seeks regular relations with foreign Powers, i. 215.
Ambassadors to European Courts, i. 216.
Treatment of foreign Ambassadors, i. 216.
Rural classes, i. 217.
Commerce, i. 218.
Towns, i. 218.
Domestic Slavery, i. 219.
Seclusion of women, i. 219.
Superstitions, i. 222.
Literature, i. 223.
Literature of oral tradition, i. 225.
General prevalence of drunkenness, i. 221.
Renaissance 15th to 17th cent, i. 226.
Resumes war with Sweden, i. 233.
Famine, 1601-1604, i, 238.
And Austria, i. 232.
Elements of disorder, i. 239.
Torn by civil war, i. 250.
National uprising against Poland, i. 251.
At accession of the Romanofs, i. 254.
Concentrates forces against Poland, i. 257.
Asks help from Holland and England, i. 255.
Concludes peace with Sweden, 1617, i. 257.
Relations with Europe, i. 258.
Asks aid of Louis XIII. 1615, i. 259.
Renews war against Poland, i. 260.
Parliamentary history, i. 261.
Privilege granted to foreigners, i. 261.
Desires control of Black Sea, i. 261.
Forbids use of tobacco, i. 262.
The bishops struggle with Catholicism, i. 266.
Makes successful war on Poland. i. 277.
Revolution under Stenko Razine, i. 282.
Writers of the 17th cent., i. 284.
Accession of Peter the Great, i. 293.

INDEX.

Declares herself a European Power, ii. 20.
Rural population, ii. 24.
Rights of foreigners, ii. 25.
Obligations of nobility, ii. 25.
Seeks Alliance with France, ii. 46.
Under Catherine. ii. 54.
War of quadruple alliance, ii. 56.
Aristocratic constitution attempted, ii. 59.
War with Turks, ii. 66.
Significance of revolution of 1741, ii. 71.
On the Austrian succession, ii. 72.
Army crosses Prussian frontier, ii. 74.
Direct relations with France, ii. 79.
Diplomatic complications, ii. 74.
Restoration of religious tolerance, ii. 105.
Annexes the Crimea, ii. 112.
During American war, 1780, ii. 111.
Plans dismemberment of Turkey, ii. 113.
Quadruple alliance, ii. 126.
Rupture with France, ii. 126.
Joins coalition, ii. 131.
First war with Napoleon, ii. 142.
Popular feeling against Napoleon, ii. 160.
War against Austria a comedy, ii. 166.
Invasion of Moldavia, ii. 168.
Suffers from continental blockade, ii. 174.
Propagation of liberal ideas, ii. 220.
Establishment of secret societies, ii. 221.
Voyage around the world, 1803, ii. 224.
Secures commercial access to the Black Sea, ii. 236
Relations with China, ii. 236.
Possessions in Asia, ii. 236.
Polish insurrection, 1831, ii. 238.
Influence checked by France and Austria, ii. 248.
Attacked in all her seas, ii. 250.
Progress during reign of Alexander II. ii. 274.
Military system, ii. 277.
Conquest in Asia, ii. 278.
Foreign policy, ii. 285.
Russian race, extent of, i. 33.
Instinct of emigration, i. 35.
Faculty of absorption, i. 36.
And Anglo-Saxon compared, i. 35.
Academy, ii. 109.
Army, foreign mercenaries, i. 215.
Calendar, ii. 286.
Russian Church, i. 213.
Russians of Slav origin, i. 28.
Patriarchal principle. i. 41.
Tribute and subjection to Tatars, i. 124.
Intermarry with Tatars, i. 126.
Averse to innovation, ii. 22.
Enter Berlin, ii. 75.
Dislike to Polish allies, ii. 166.
Russification, stages of, i. 37.

St. Petersburg. relative location, i. 17.
Foundation, 1703, ii. 37.
Imperial library. ii. 224.
Saltydof, Daria, trial of, ii. 102.

Samoyedes, the, i. 29.
Savary, French ambassador to Russia, ii. 160.
Saxo-Polish conflict, ii. 201.
Saxony, Augustus of, ii. 10.
Scandinavian armies, decline of, ii. 72.
Schamyl, soldier priest of Moslems, ii. 237.
Schonbrunn, treaty of, ii. 151.
Schouvalof, Count Ivan, ii. 77.
Science, ii. 277.
Scythia of Herodotus, the, i. 24.
Scythian worship and customs, i. 25.
Idiom identified, i. 25.
Scythians, the, i. 25.
Sebastopol, siege of, ii. 250, 256.
Secret societies, ii. 221.
Segur, Comte de, ii. 113.
Selim III., ii. 167.
Senate established, ii. 27.
Serfs, ii. 23, 260.
Servia, revolt of Janissaries, ii. 167.
Severia, defection to Godounof, i. 240.
Severians, country of, i. 43.
Siberia added to Russia, i. 206.
Begins to be peopled, ii. 77.
Russian survey of the coast, ii. 224.
Sigismond I. reunites crowns of Wilna and Poland, i. 177.
Asks truce of Ivan IV., i. 199.
Sigismond Augustus II., King of Poland, death, 1572, i. 200.
Sigismond of Sweden elected King of Poland, i. 233.
Designs upon throne of Russia, i. 247, 250.
Demands Russia for Vladislas, i. 254.
Dies, 1632, i. 260.
Silvester, favorite of Ivan IV., i. 187, 192.
Treachery and banishment, i. 193.
Simeon the Proud, son of Kalita, i. 146.
Sit, the battle of, i. 116.
Slavery, domestic, i. 219.
Slaves, sale of, ii. 25.
Slavs, appearance in history, i. 27.
Towns and tribes, i. 27.
Geographical distribution, i. 27.
Russian and Polish, i. 28.
Religion, i. 38.
Civilization, i. 43.
Race extent, i. 54.
Tribes, distribution, i. 54.
Tribes, disappearance of ancient names, i. 72.
Law of succession, i. 77.
Smolensk, principality of, i. 73.
Political importance, i. 73.
Taken by Poles, i. 250.
Social conditions from 9th to 10th cent., i. 67.
Society in time of Iaroslaf, i. 65.
Society of Virtue, ii. 221.
Sophia Palaeologus marries Ivan III., i. 172.
Sophia, sister of Peter the Great, i. 291.
Regency of, i. 291.
Foreign policy, i. 295.
Plots against Peter, i. 298.
Conspiracy for her deliverance, i. 304.
Confined in a monastery, i. 305.
Sophia of Anhalt. *See* Catherine II.
Souvorof, Russian general, ii. 116.
Before Praga, ii. 123.
Exiled, ii. 129.
Recalled from exile, ii. 131.
Heroic retreat, ii. 136.

INDEX.

Souzdal, principalities of, i. 74.
    Becomes centre of Russia, i. 83.
    Resists Tatar impost, i. 122.
Souzdalian army defeated by Tatars, i. 116.
Sovereignty of Russian princes, i. 69.
Spanish succession, war of, 1712-1713, ii. 42.
Speranski, ii. 213.
Stanislas Leszczinski declared King of Poland, ii. 64, 65.
Stanislas Poniatovski, King of Poland, ii. 117.
    King, captivity, ii. 130.
States-General convoked by Ivan IV., i. 199.
Statues, ii. 225.
Stenko Razine, a Cossack leader, i. 281.
Steppes, arable, zone of, i. 21.
    Barren, zone of, i. 22.
Stolbovo, peace of, 1617, i. 257.
Streitsi founded by Ivan IV., i. 208.
    Mutiny in reign of Peter the Great. i. 303.
Strogonofs explore mineral wealth of the Ourals, i. 206.
Sublime Porte. *See* Turkey.
Superstition, i. 222.
Suomen-maa. *See* Finland.
Suomi, the three tribes of, i. 29.
Sviatopolk, nephew of Vladimir, i. 61.
    Usurps throne of Kief, i. 62.
Sviatoslaf, son of Igor, i. 51.
    Assumes the government, i. 52.
    Defeats the Khazars, i. 53.
    Death of, i. 56.
Sweden, frontier war with Russia, i. 191.
    Rupture with Poland, i. 233.
    Renewed war with Russia, i. 233.
    Terms of peace with Russia, 1617, i. 257.
    Struggle between aristocracy and crown, ii. 9.
    Relations to France, ii. 14.
    Becomes Power of third rank, ii. 20.
    Deserted by her allies, ii. 43.
Swedes invade Russia, i. 202.
Swedish army destroyed, ii. 20.
Synod, Holy, ii. 31.

Talleyrand, ii. 199, 201.
Tamerlane, head of Mongols, i. 151.
    Invades Russia, i. 154.
    Pillages the Golden Horde, i. 154.
Targovitsa, Confederates of, ii. 119.
Ta-ta. *See* Tatar.
Tatars, the, i. 35.
    First appearance, 1224, i. 72.
    Invasion, i. 93.
    A Mongol tribe, i. 112.
    Second invasion, i. 115.
    Success, cause of, i. 117.
    Embrace the Islam faith, i. 119.
    Religious toleration, i. 129.
    Allies under Mamaï, i. 149.
    Of Crimea, i. 167.
    Allies of Sigismond and Vassili, i. 178.
    Dissensions, i. 179.
    Crimea, i. 179.
    Of Crimea, raids, i. 199.
    Burn Moscow, i. 200.
    Message to Ivan IV., i. 200.
Taurian invasion of Russia, i. 179.

Taxes, ii. 30.
Tcheremisses, the, i. 30.
Tcherinchef, mission to Napoleon, ii. 174.
Tchoud or Lett tribes of Baltic, i. 107.
Tchouvaches, the, i. 30.
Telegraphs, ii. 274.
Teheran, ii. 254.
Teutonic Knights, power crushed, i. 136.
Theatres, ii. 63, 79.
Thugut, ii. 132.
Tilsel, Conference between Napoleon and Alexander I., ii. 157.
    Treaty of, 1807, ii. 158.
Tobacco, use forbidden, i. 262.
Torques. See *Black Caps*.
Touchino, Tzar of, i. 246.
Towns, i. 43.
Trees of Northern Russia, i. 21.
Tribes, i. 24.
Tributes in time of Iaroslof, i. 66.
Troppan, Congress of, ii. 217.
Tumuli, See monuments.
Turkestan, Russian rule, ii. 279.
Turkey declares war on Russia, ii. 93.
    Ultimatum rejected declares war against Russia, ii. 114.
    Serious internal troubles, ii. 208.
    Demands European non-interference, ii. 234.
    Concludes two treaties, ii. 235.
    Russian protectorate, ii. 245.
Turkish races in Russia, i. 33.
    Fleet, destruction at Navarino, ii. 235.
Turks and Tatars besiege Astrakhan, i. 200.
Tzar, relations with his people, i. 209.
Tzar, mode of selecting wives, i. 211.
Tzargrad (Byzantium), expedition against, i. 49.
Tzars, the empire of, i. 15.

Ukraine, rebels, i. 241, 270.
    Undermined by factions, i. 307.
Ulm, Capitulation of, ii. 147.
Uniate Church, i. 270.
United States, Russia opens relations, ii. 224.
Unity of Russian States, i. 76.

Valdaï, the plateau of, i. 18.
Valleys of Russia, i. 15.
Varangians, origin of, i. 45.
    As soldiers and sailors, i. 46.
    Princes, administration of, i. 66.
Vassili Dmitrievitch, i. 153.
    Accession to throne, i. 154.
Vassili the Blind, i. 156.
Vassili the Squinting, i. 157.
Vassili Ivanovitch son of Ivan III., i. 175.
    Wars with Lithuania, i. 177.
    Acquires Smolensk, i. 177.
Varojevski succeeds Kosciuszko, ii. 124.
    Accept convention at Radochitse, ii. 125.
Verona, Congress of, ii. 208.
Vetche, assembly of the citizens, i. 96.
    Extensive powers, i. 100.
Victoria, Queen, visits Louis Napoleon, ii. 256.
Vienna, Congress of, ii. 200.
    Conference of the five powers, ii. 240.

Villeneuve, French ambassador, ii. 66.
Vistula, legions of, ii. 171.
Vititchevo, town on the Dnieper, i. 79.
Vitovt, career of, i. 124, 137.
    Crusade of the Vorskla, 1399, i. 155.
Vladimir, son of Sviatoslaf, i. 58.
    The Russian Clovis, i. 38.
    Religious aspirations, i. 39.
    Is baptized, i. 60.
    Destroys the idols, i. 60.
    Builds churches, i. 60.
    Marries sister of Greek Emperors, i. 60.
    Dies, 1015, i. 61.
    Successors of, i. 62.
Vladimir Monomachus, son of Vsevolod, i. 78.
    Becomes Grand Prince, i. 79.
    Successes against the nomads, i. 79.
Vladislas, son of Sigismond, i. 248, 257.
    Becomes King of Poland, i. 260.
    Death, i. 275.
Volga, principal river of Russia, i. 20.
    Basin and tributaries, i. 20.
Volhynia, division of South-east Russia, i. 74.

Volost. See Commune, i. 42.
Voltaire, relations with Schouvalof, ii. 80.
    Correspondence with Catherine II., ii. 108.
Vsevolod, brother of Isiaslaf, i. 78.
Wallachia, ii. 234, 247.
Warsaw, plan to make Ivan IV. King of Poland, i. 200.
    Diet of, ii. 117.
    Expels Russians, ii. 122.
Water-system of Russia, i. 19.
Waterloo, battle of, ii. 202.
Wellington, Duke of, ii. 234.
White Russia, i. 33.
White Sea. English expedition, i. 203.
    Natural obstructions to commerce, ii. 33.
Wife capture, custom of, i. 31.
Willoughby, Sir Hugh, expedition, i. 203.
Wilna revolts against Russian authority, ii. 123.
    Recaptured by Russians, ii. 124.
Zaporogues, i. 269, 300.

www.ingramcontent.com/pod-product-compliance
Lightning Source LLC
Chambersburg PA
CBHW022022240426
43667CB00042B/1059